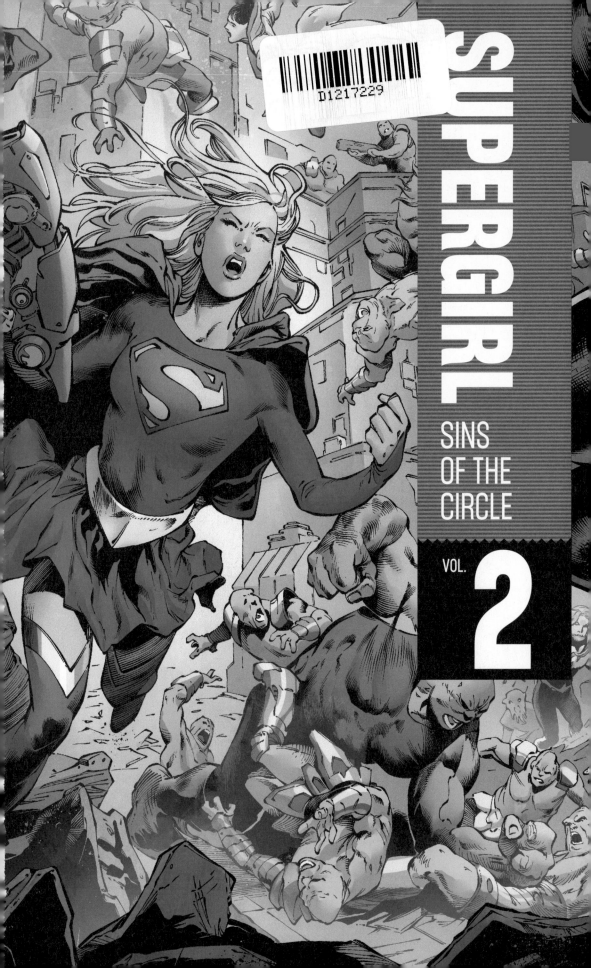

SUPERGIRL

SINS OF THE CIRCLE

VOL. 2

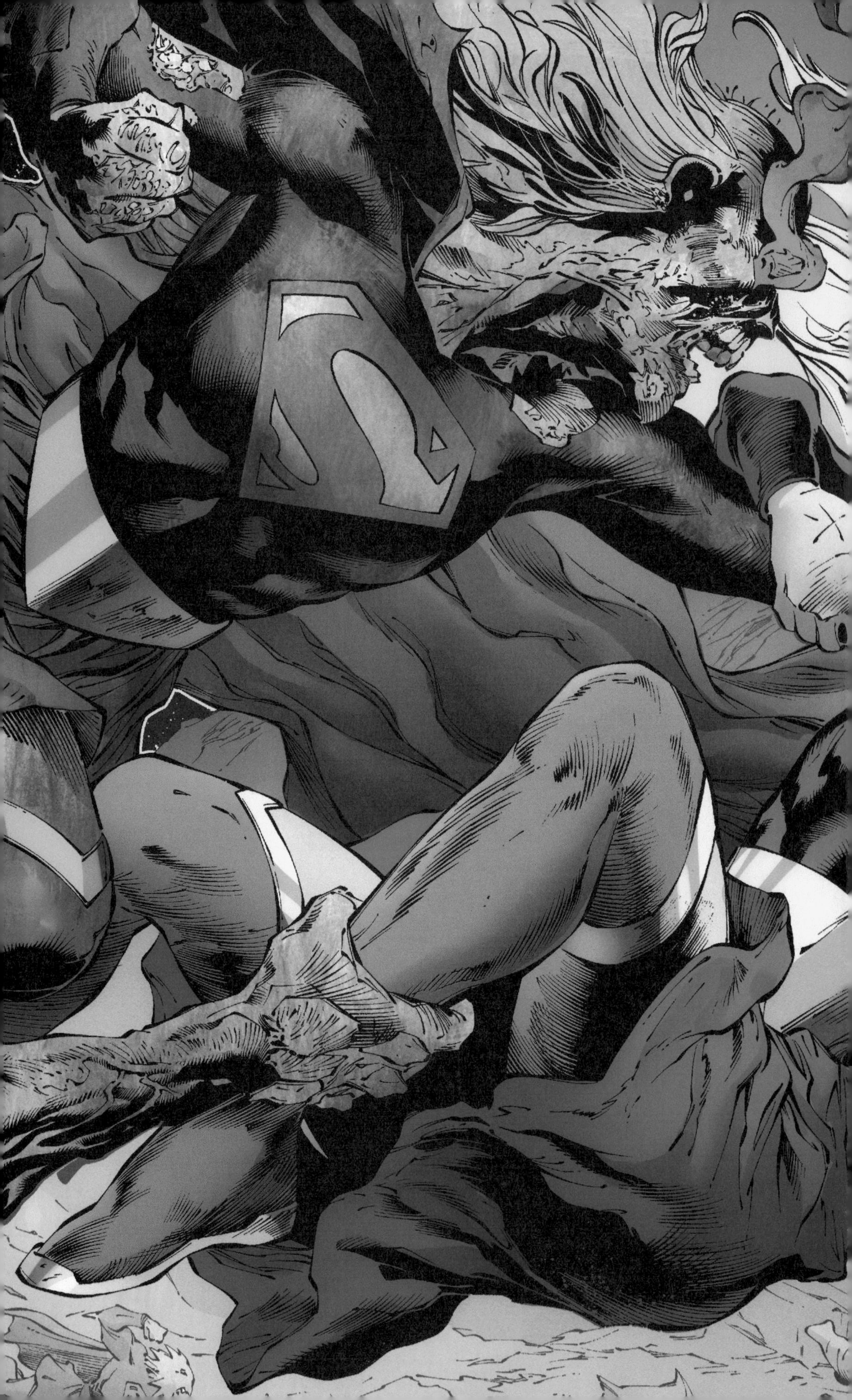

SUPERGIRL
SINS OF THE CIRCLE

writer
MARC ANDREYKO

artists
KEVIN MAGUIRE
EDUARDO PANSICA
JULIO FERREIRA
SEAN PARSONS
EBER FERREIRA
SCOTT HANNA

colorists
FCO PLASCENCIA
CHRIS SOTOMAYOR

letterer
TOM NAPOLITANO

collection cover artists
YANICK PAQUETTE and
NATHAN FAIRBAIRN

VOL.
2

JESSICA CHEN Editor – Original Series
JEB WOODARD Group Editor – Collected Editions
ERIKA ROTHBERG Editor – Collected Edition
STEVE COOK Design Director – Books
JOHN J. HILL Publication Design
ERIN VANOVER Publication Production

BOB HARRAS Senior VP – Editor-in-Chief, DC Comics
PAT McCALLUM Executive Editor, DC Comics

DAN DiDIO Publisher
JIM LEE Publisher & Chief Creative Officer
BOBBIE CHASE VP – New Publishing Initiatives & Talent Development
DON FALLETTI VP – Manufacturing Operations & Workflow Management
LAWRENCE GANEM VP – Talent Services
ALISON GILL Senior VP – Manufacturing & Operations
HANK KANALZ Senior VP – Publishing Strategy & Support Services
DAN MIRON VP – Publishing Operations
NICK J. NAPOLITANO VP – Manufacturing Administration & Design
NANCY SPEARS VP – Sales
MICHELE R. WELLS VP & Executive Editor, Young Reader

SUPERGIRL VOL. 2: SINS OF THE CIRCLE

DC Comics, 2900 West Alameda Ave., Burbank, CA 91505
Printed by LSC Communications, Owensville, MO, USA. 11/22/19. First Printing.
ISBN: 978-1-4012-9454-0

Library of Congress Cataloging-in-Publication Data is available.

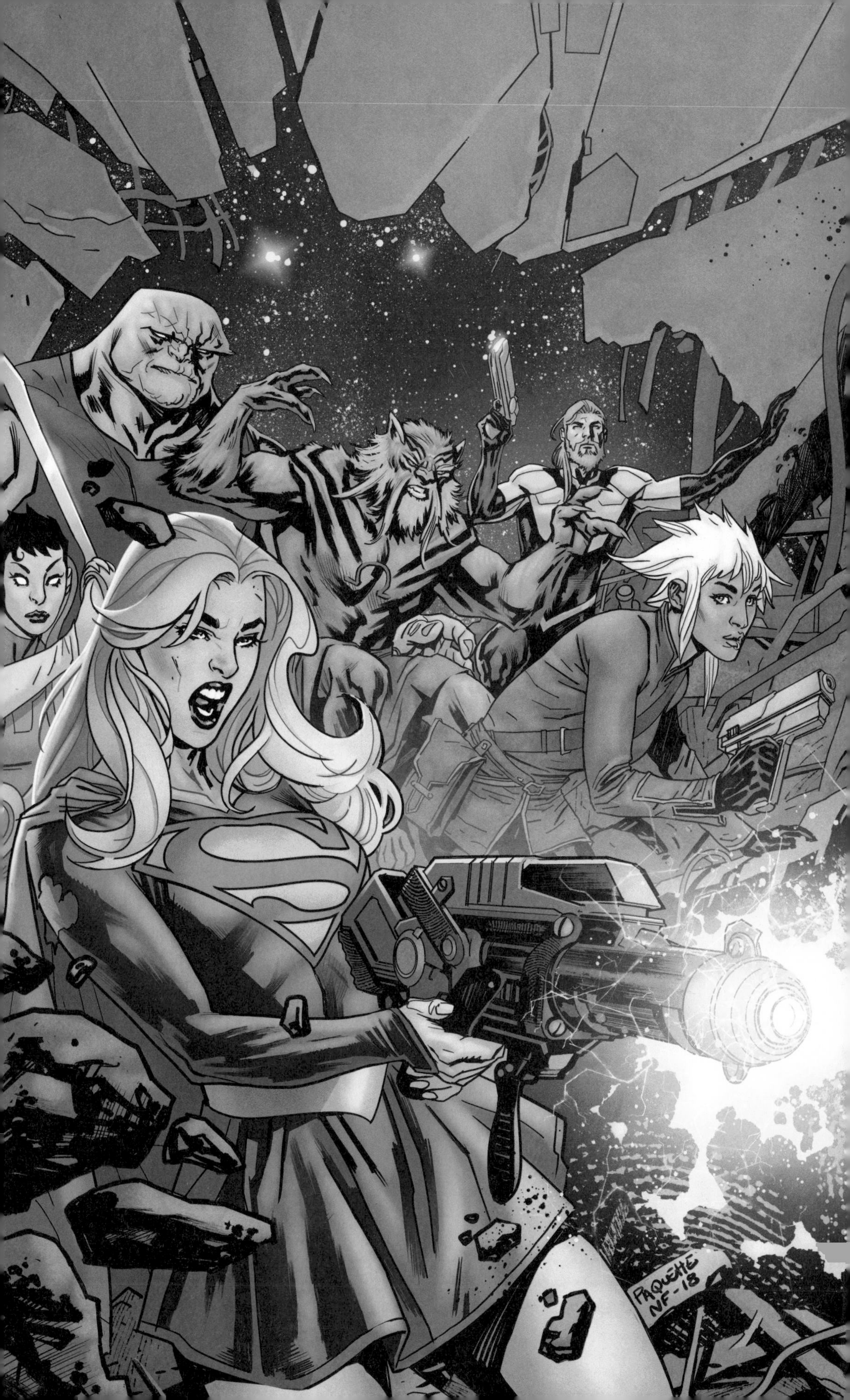
PAQUETTE
NF-18

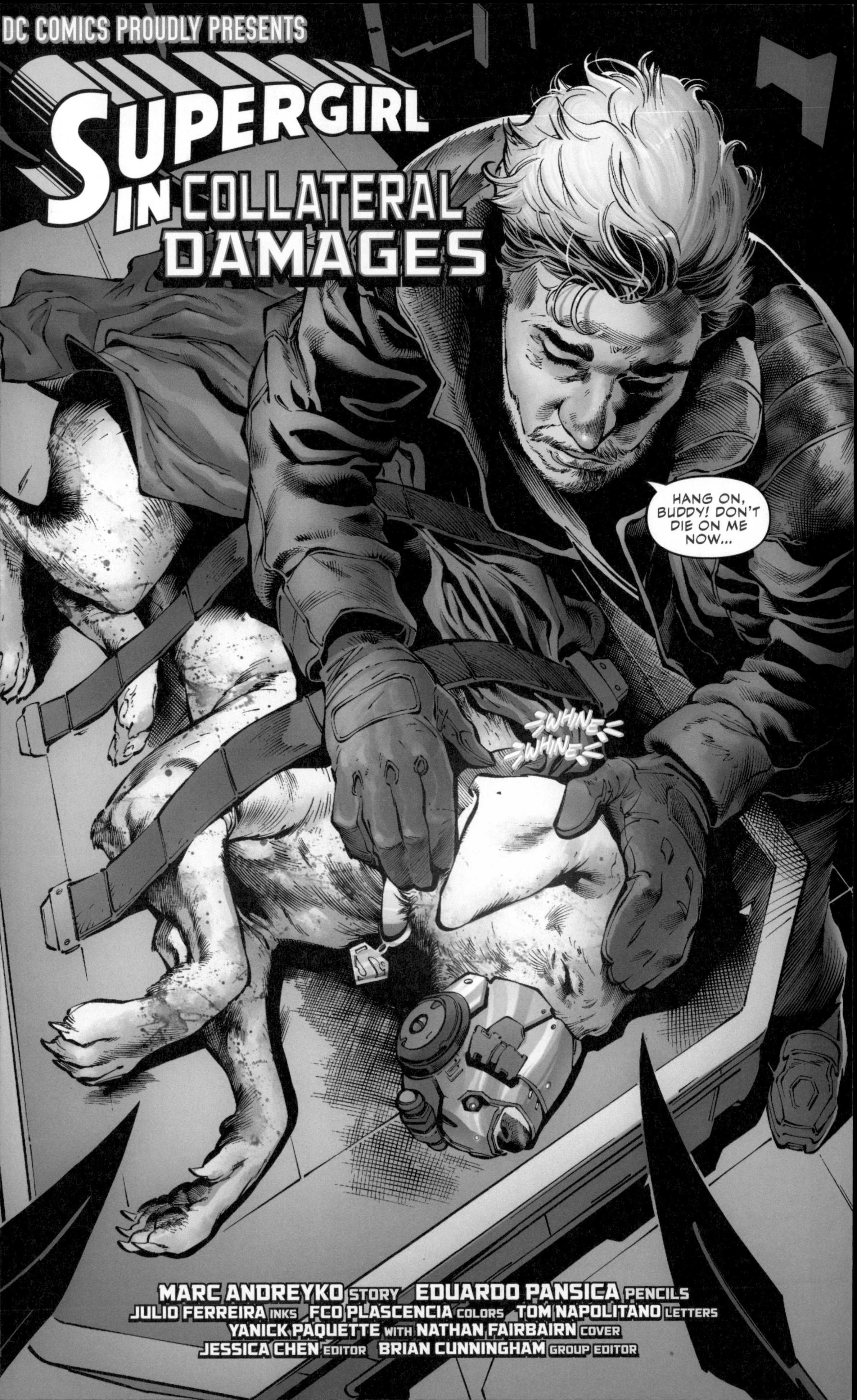
DC COMICS PROUDLY PRESENTS
SUPERGIRL
IN COLLATERAL DAMAGES
HANG ON, BUDDY! DON'T DIE ON ME NOW...
WHINE
WHINE
MARC ANDREYKO STORY EDUARDO PANSICA PENCILS
JULIO FERREIRA INKS FCO PLASCENCIA COLORS TOM NAPOLITANO LETTERS
YANICK PAQUETTE WITH NATHAN FAIRBAIRN COVER
JESSICA CHEN EDITOR BRIAN CUNNINGHAM GROUP EDITOR

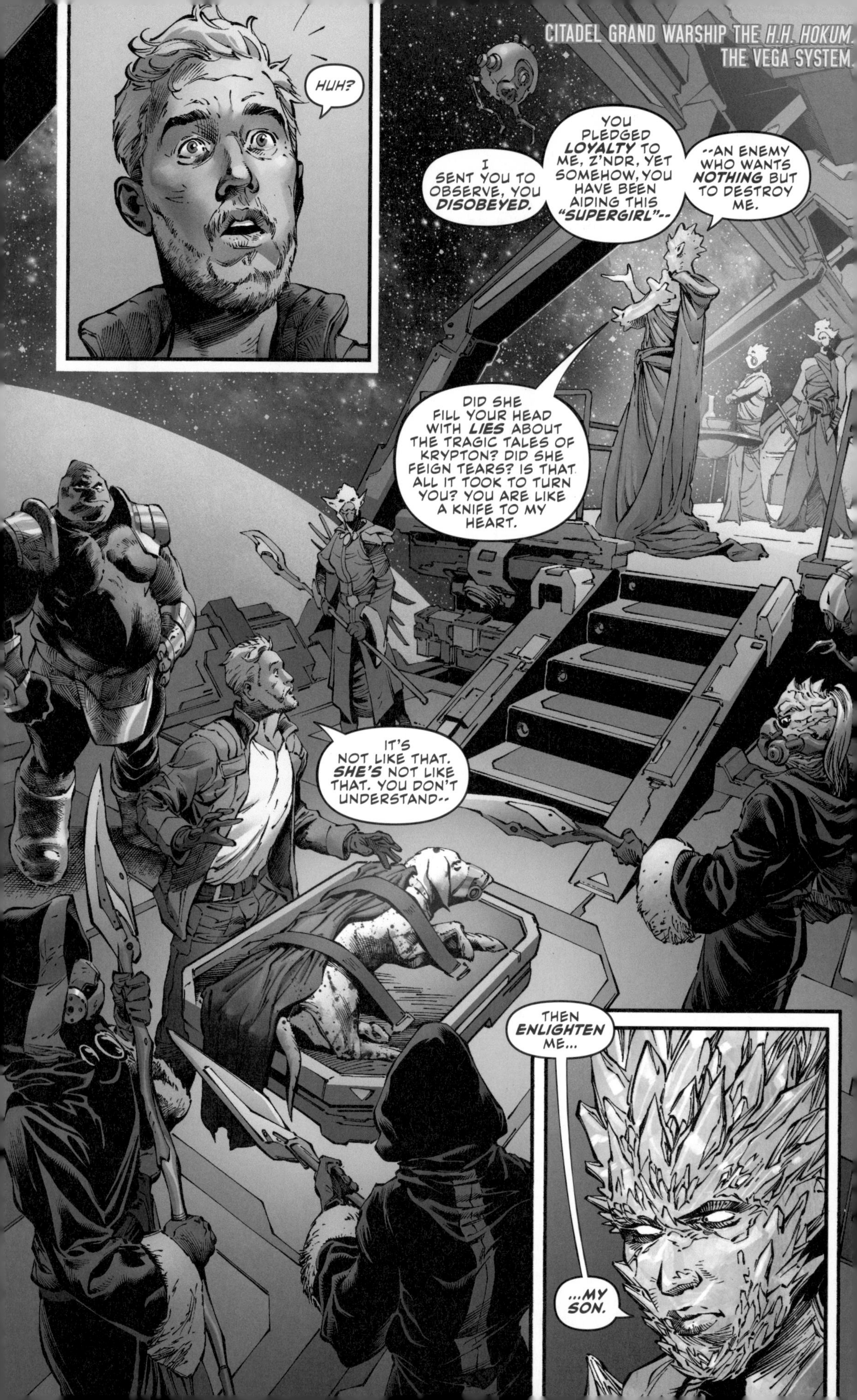
HUH?
CITADEL GRAND WARSHIP THE H.H. HOKUM. THE VEGA SYSTEM.
I SENT YOU TO OBSERVE, YOU DISOBEYED.
YOU PLEDGED LOYALTY TO ME, Z'NDR, YET SOMEHOW, YOU HAVE BEEN AIDING THIS "SUPERGIRL"--
--AN ENEMY WHO WANTS NOTHING BUT TO DESTROY ME.
DID SHE FILL YOUR HEAD WITH LIES ABOUT THE TRAGIC TALES OF KRYPTON? DID SHE FEIGN TEARS? IS THAT ALL IT TOOK TO TURN YOU? YOU ARE LIKE A KNIFE TO MY HEART.
IT'S NOT LIKE THAT. SHE'S NOT LIKE THAT. YOU DON'T UNDERSTAND--
THEN ENLIGHTEN ME...
...MY SON.

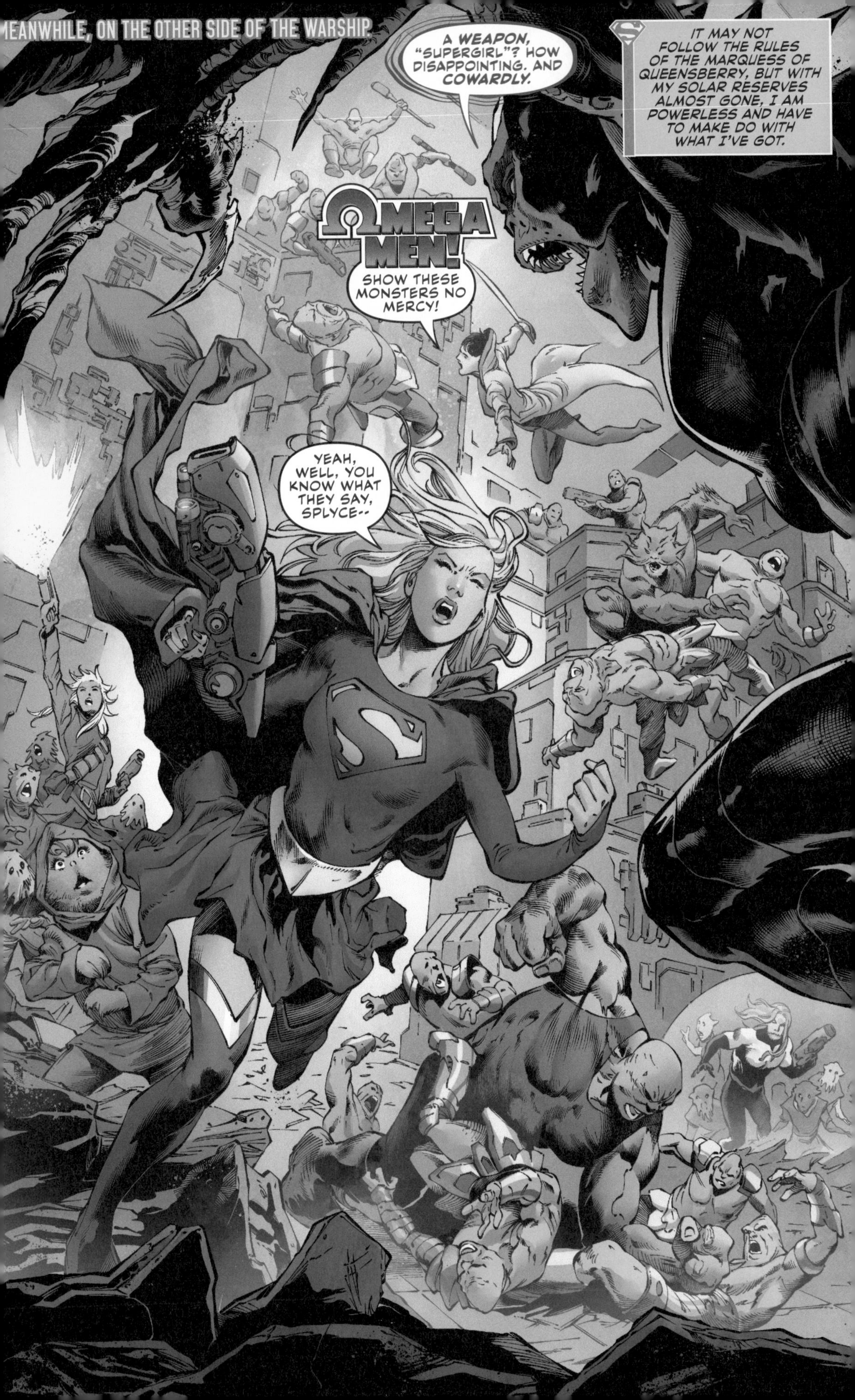
MEANWHILE, ON THE OTHER SIDE OF THE WARSHIP.
A WEAPON, "SUPERGIRL"? HOW DISAPPOINTING. AND COWARDLY.
IT MAY NOT FOLLOW THE RULES OF THE MARQUESS OF QUEENSBERRY, BUT WITH MY SOLAR RESERVES ALMOST GONE, I AM POWERLESS AND HAVE TO MAKE DO WITH WHAT I'VE GOT.
ΩMEGA MEN!
SHOW THESE MONSTERS NO MERCY!
YEAH, WELL, YOU KNOW WHAT THEY SAY, SPLYCE--

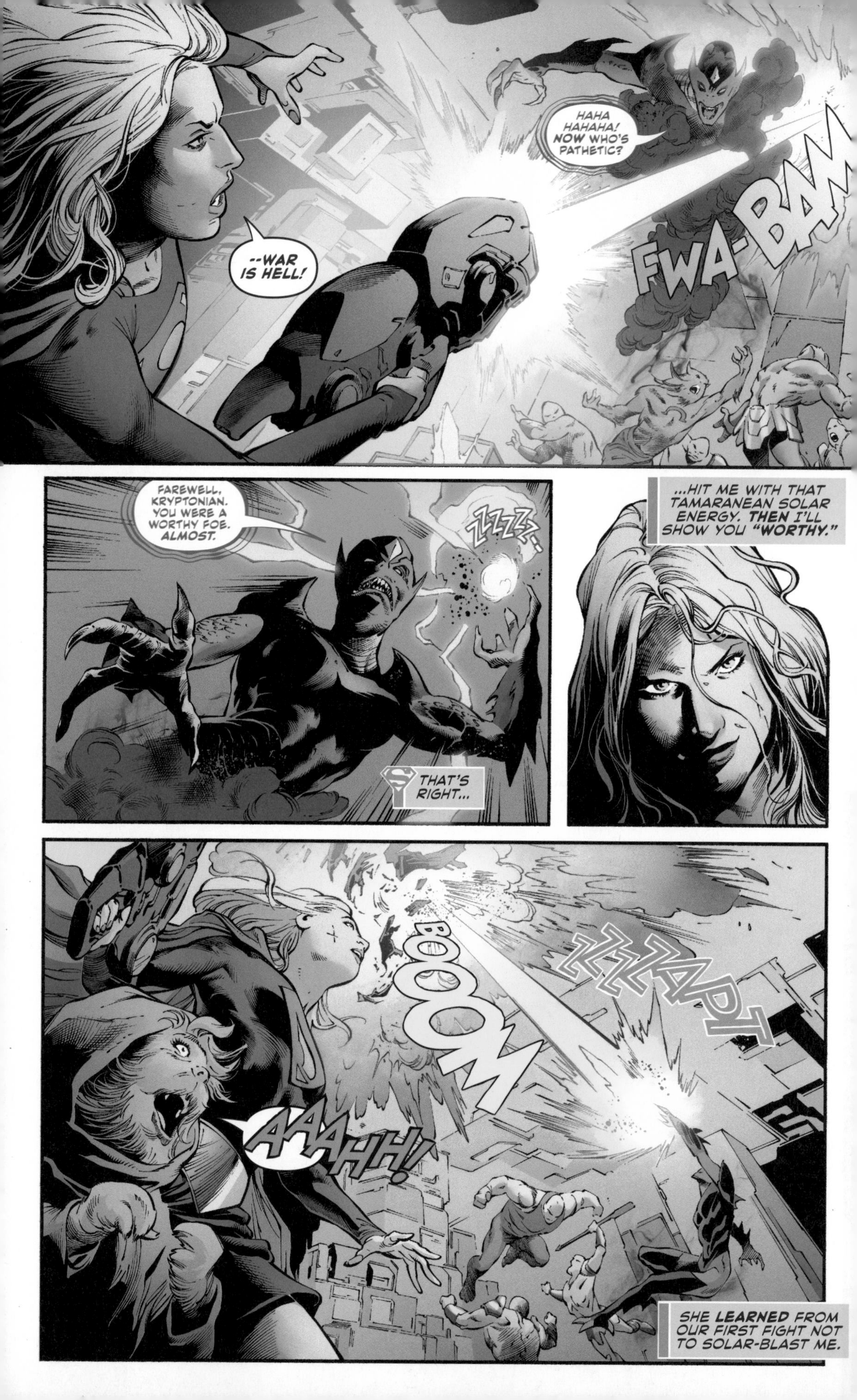

HAHA HAHAHA! NOW WHO'S PATHETIC?
--WAR IS HELL!
FWA-BAM
FAREWELL, KRYPTONIAN. YOU WERE A WORTHY FOE. ALMOST.
ZZZZZ
THAT'S RIGHT...
...HIT ME WITH THAT TAMARANEAN SOLAR ENERGY. THEN I'LL SHOW YOU "WORTHY."
BOOOM
ZZZAPT
AAAHH!
SHE LEARNED FROM OUR FIRST FIGHT NOT TO SOLAR-BLAST ME.

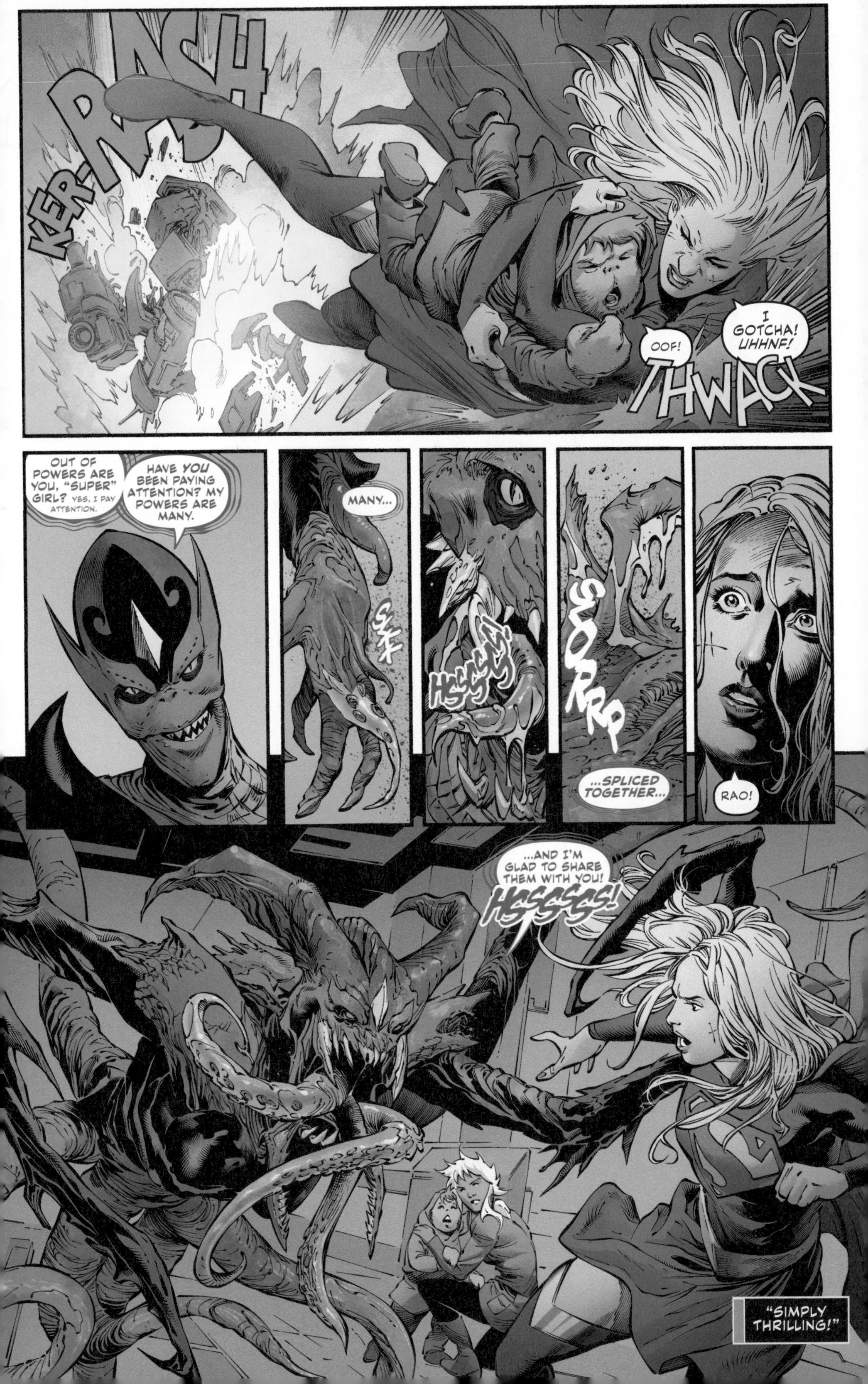
KER-RASH
I GOTCHA! UHHNF!
OOF!
THWACK
OUT OF POWERS ARE YOU, "SUPER" GIRL? YES, I PAY ATTENTION.
HAVE YOU BEEN PAYING ATTENTION? MY POWERS ARE MANY.
MANY...
...SPLICED TOGETHER...
RAO!
...AND I'M GLAD TO SHARE THEM WITH YOU!
HSSSSS!
"SIMPLY THRILLING!"

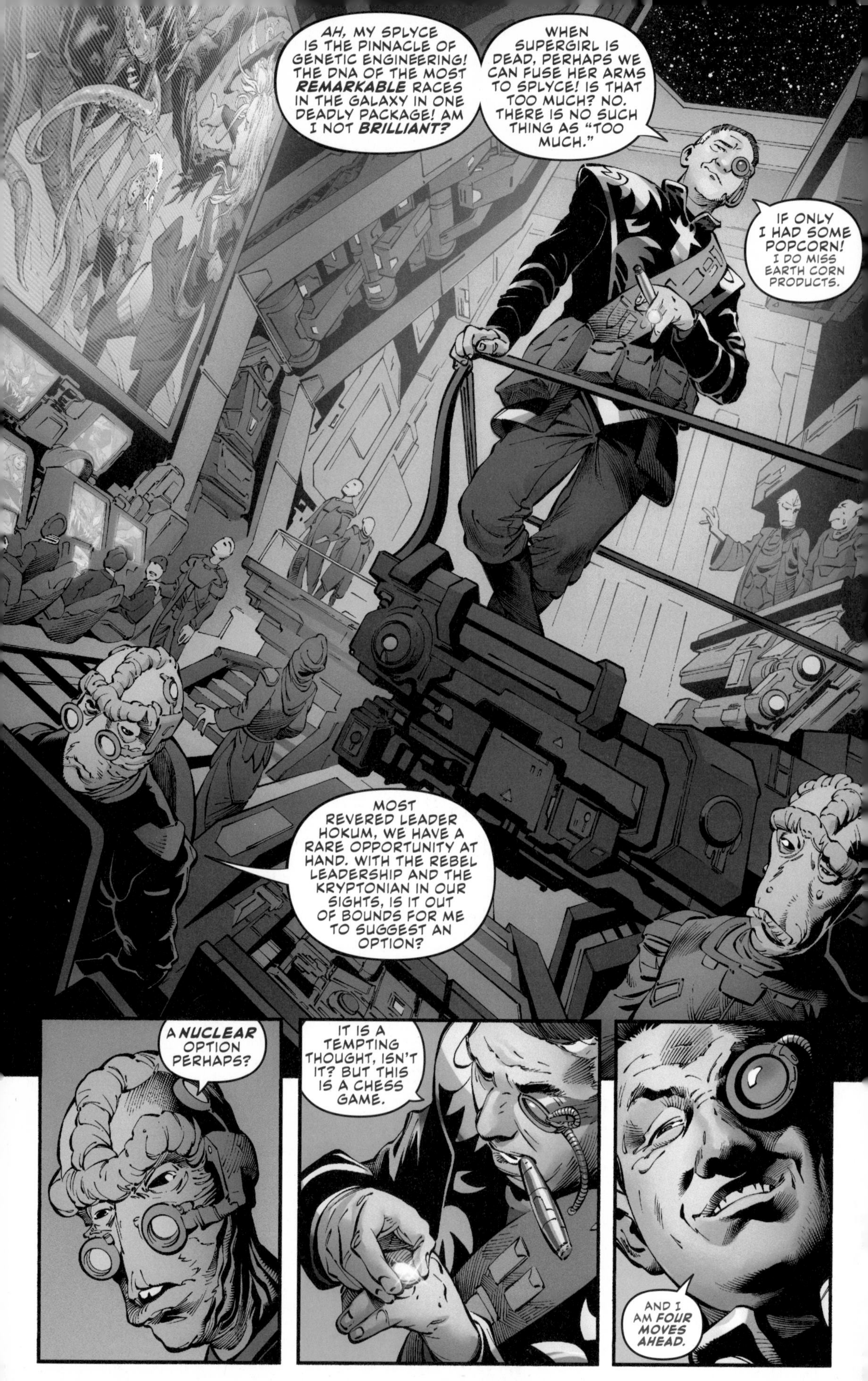
AH, MY SPLYCE IS THE PINNACLE OF GENETIC ENGINEERING! THE DNA OF THE MOST *REMARKABLE* RACES IN THE GALAXY IN ONE DEADLY PACKAGE! AM I NOT *BRILLIANT?*
WHEN SUPERGIRL IS DEAD, PERHAPS WE CAN FUSE HER ARMS TO SPLYCE! IS THAT TOO MUCH? NO. THERE IS NO SUCH THING AS "TOO MUCH."
IF ONLY I HAD SOME POPCORN! I DO MISS EARTH CORN PRODUCTS.
MOST REVERED LEADER HOKUM, WE HAVE A RARE OPPORTUNITY AT HAND. WITH THE REBEL LEADERSHIP AND THE KRYPTONIAN IN OUR SIGHTS, IS IT OUT OF BOUNDS FOR ME TO SUGGEST AN OPTION?
A *NUCLEAR* OPTION PERHAPS?
IT IS A TEMPTING THOUGHT, ISN'T IT? BUT THIS IS A CHESS GAME.
AND I AM *FOUR MOVES AHEAD.*

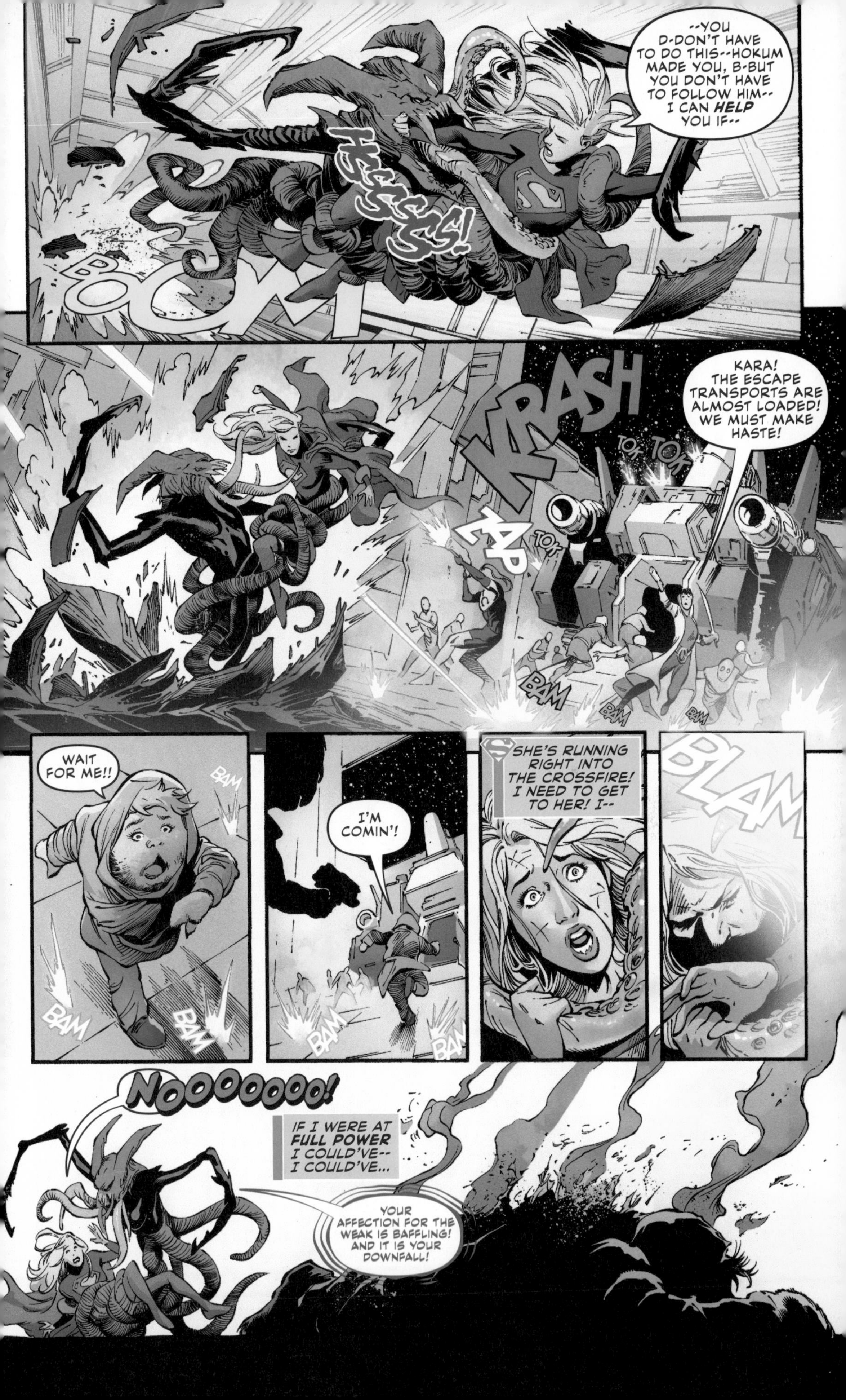
--YOU D-DON'T HAVE TO DO THIS--HOKUM MADE YOU, B-BUT YOU DON'T HAVE TO FOLLOW HIM--I CAN HELP YOU IF--
HISSSSS!
BOOM
KRASH
KARA! THE ESCAPE TRANSPORTS ARE ALMOST LOADED! WE MUST MAKE HASTE!
TOK TOK
ZAP
TOK
BAM
BAM
BAM
WAIT FOR ME!!
BAM
BAM
BAM
I'M COMIN'!
BAM
BAM
SHE'S RUNNING RIGHT INTO THE CROSSFIRE! I NEED TO GET TO HER! I--
BLAM
NOOOOOOO!
IF I WERE AT FULL POWER I COULD'VE-- I COULD'VE...
YOUR AFFECTION FOR THE WEAK IS BAFFLING! AND IT IS YOUR DOWNFALL!

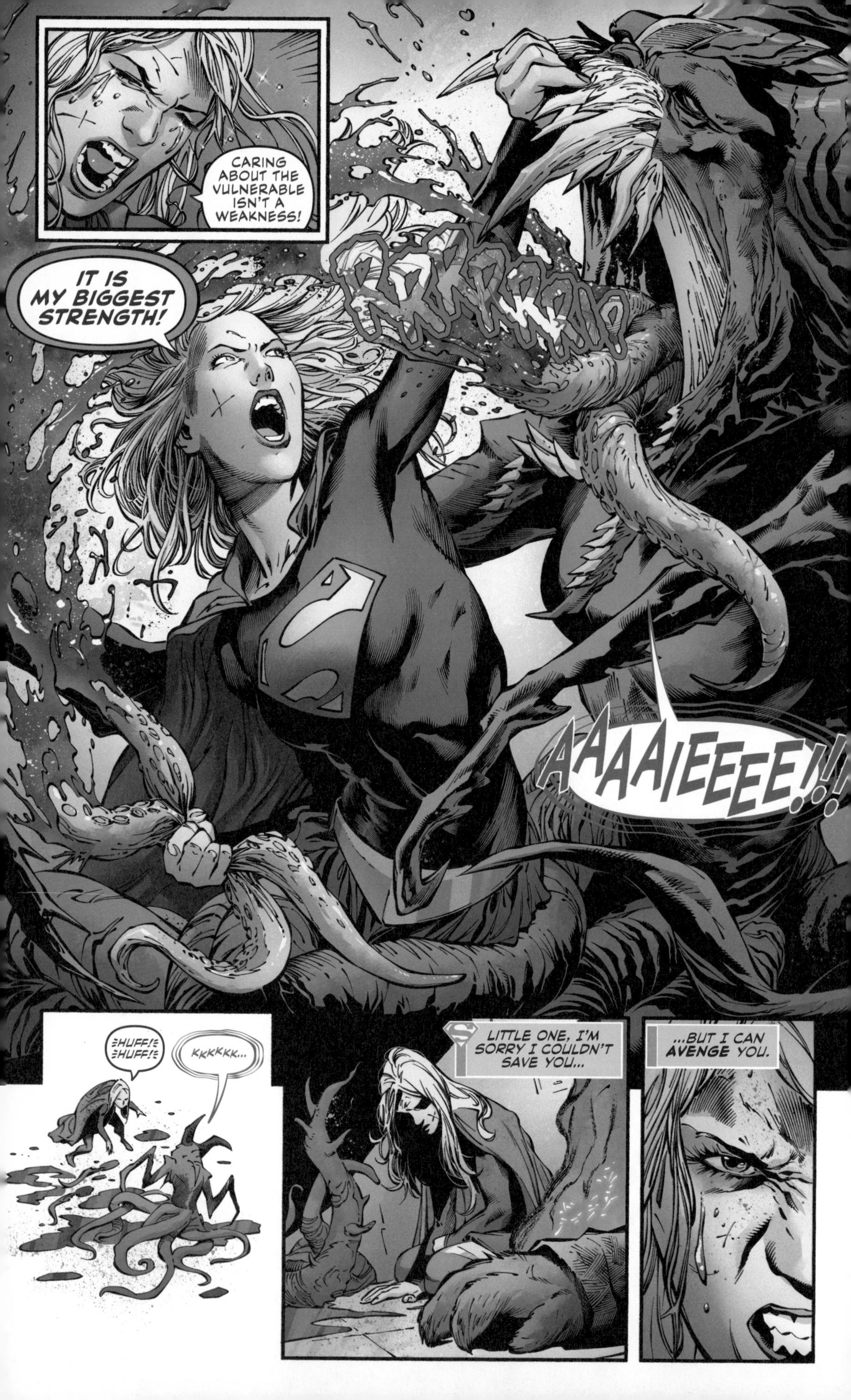
CARING ABOUT THE VULNERABLE ISN'T A WEAKNESS!
IT IS MY BIGGEST STRENGTH!
AAAAIEEEEE!!!
HUFF! HUFF!
KKKKKK...
LITTLE ONE, I'M SORRY I COULDN'T SAVE YOU...
...BUT I CAN AVENGE YOU.

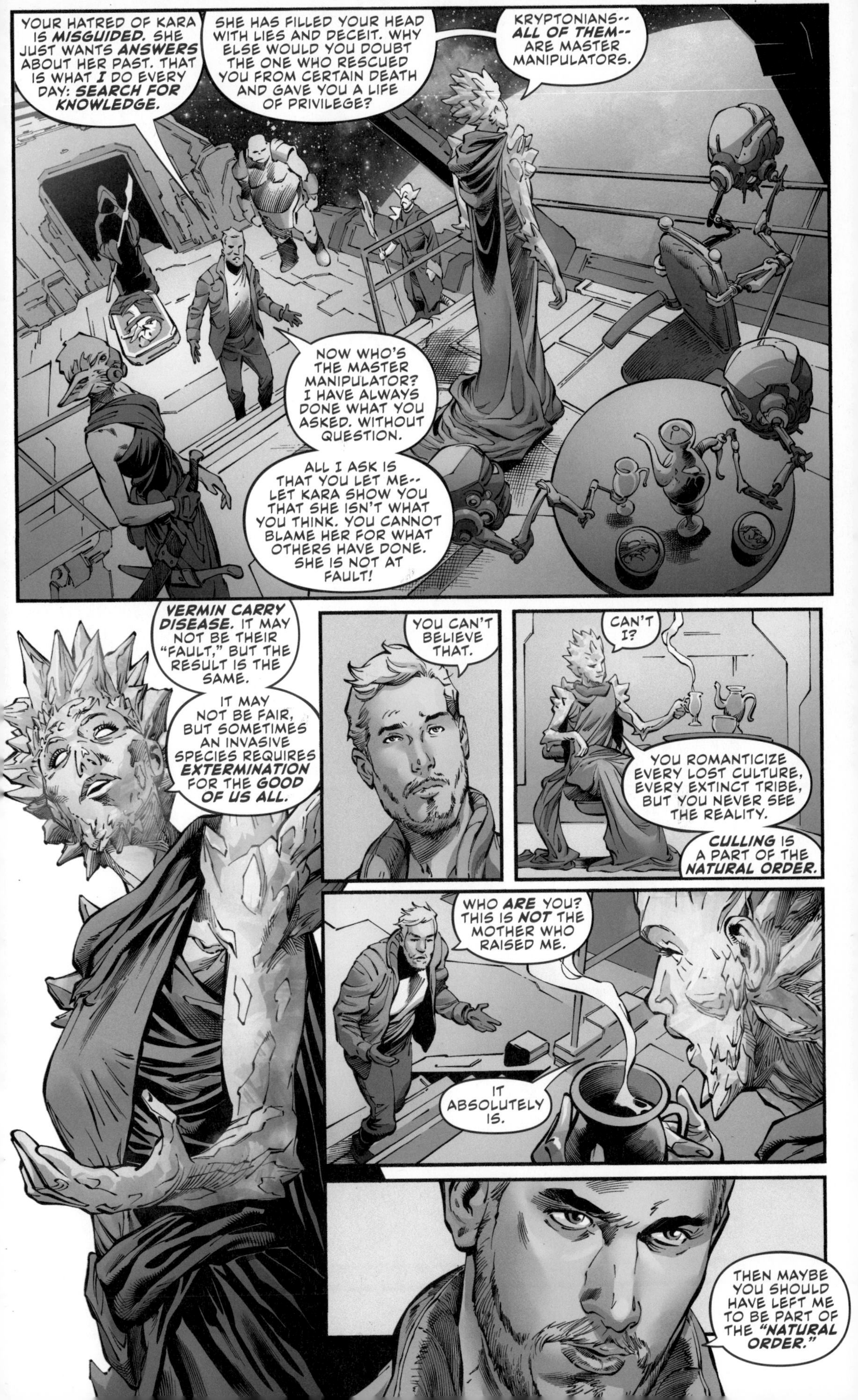
YOUR HATRED OF KARA IS MISGUIDED. SHE JUST WANTS ANSWERS ABOUT HER PAST. THAT IS WHAT I DO EVERY DAY: SEARCH FOR KNOWLEDGE.
SHE HAS FILLED YOUR HEAD WITH LIES AND DECEIT. WHY ELSE WOULD YOU DOUBT THE ONE WHO RESCUED YOU FROM CERTAIN DEATH AND GAVE YOU A LIFE OF PRIVILEGE?
KRYPTONIANS-- ALL OF THEM-- ARE MASTER MANIPULATORS.
NOW WHO'S THE MASTER MANIPULATOR? I HAVE ALWAYS DONE WHAT YOU ASKED. WITHOUT QUESTION.
ALL I ASK IS THAT YOU LET ME-- LET KARA SHOW YOU THAT SHE ISN'T WHAT YOU THINK. YOU CANNOT BLAME HER FOR WHAT OTHERS HAVE DONE. SHE IS NOT AT FAULT!
VERMIN CARRY DISEASE. IT MAY NOT BE THEIR "FAULT," BUT THE RESULT IS THE SAME.
IT MAY NOT BE FAIR, BUT SOMETIMES AN INVASIVE SPECIES REQUIRES EXTERMINATION FOR THE GOOD OF US ALL.
YOU CAN'T BELIEVE THAT.
CAN'T I?
YOU ROMANTICIZE EVERY LOST CULTURE, EVERY EXTINCT TRIBE, BUT YOU NEVER SEE THE REALITY.
CULLING IS A PART OF THE NATURAL ORDER.
WHO ARE YOU? THIS IS NOT THE MOTHER WHO RAISED ME.
IT ABSOLUTELY IS.
THEN MAYBE YOU SHOULD HAVE LEFT ME TO BE PART OF THE "NATURAL ORDER."

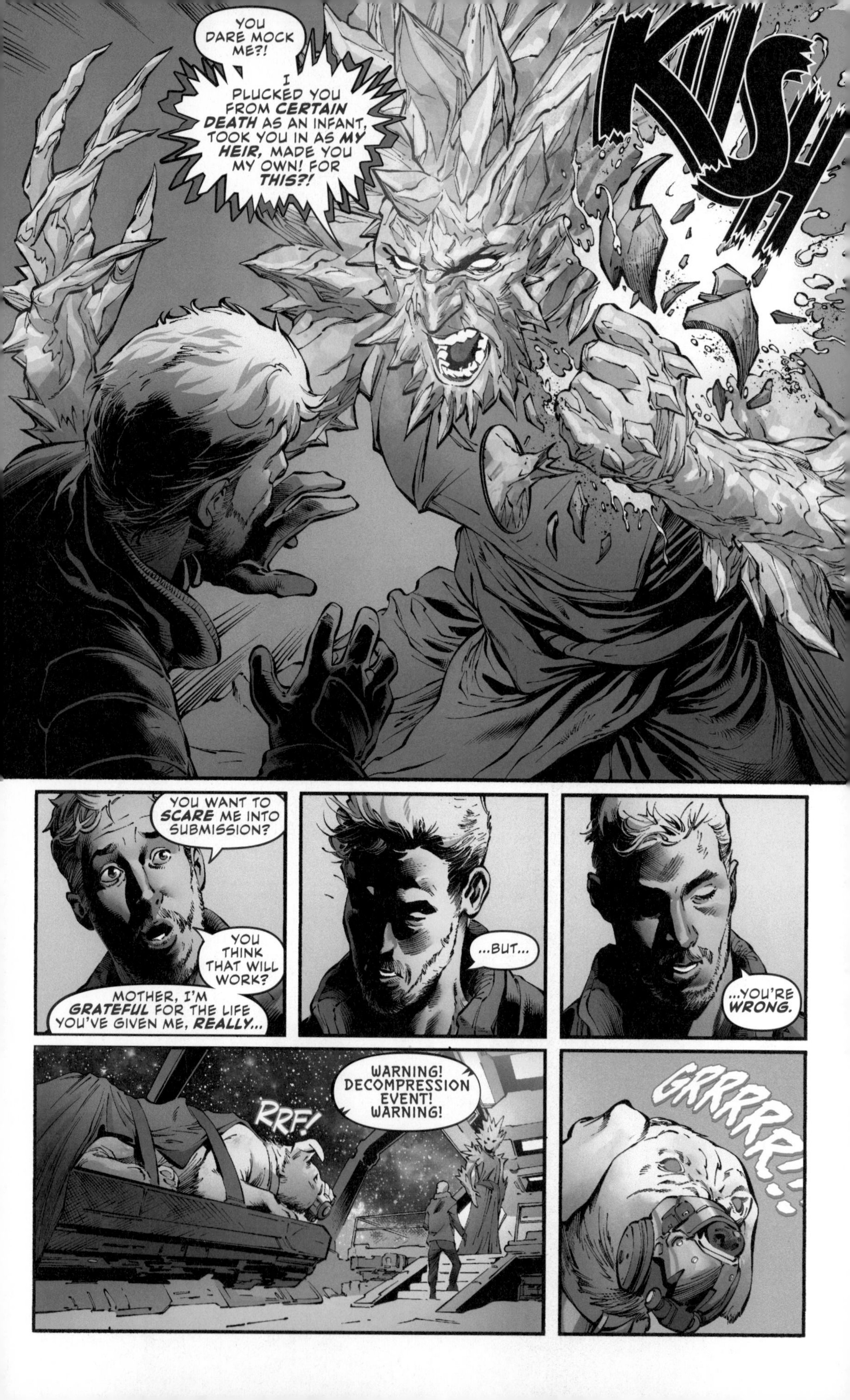
YOU DARE MOCK ME?!
I PLUCKED YOU FROM CERTAIN DEATH AS AN INFANT, TOOK YOU IN AS MY HEIR, MADE YOU MY OWN! FOR THIS?!
KRSH
YOU WANT TO SCARE ME INTO SUBMISSION?
YOU THINK THAT WILL WORK?
MOTHER, I'M GRATEFUL FOR THE LIFE YOU'VE GIVEN ME, REALLY...
...BUT...
...YOU'RE WRONG.
RRF!
WARNING! DECOMPRESSION EVENT! WARNING!
GRRRRR!!

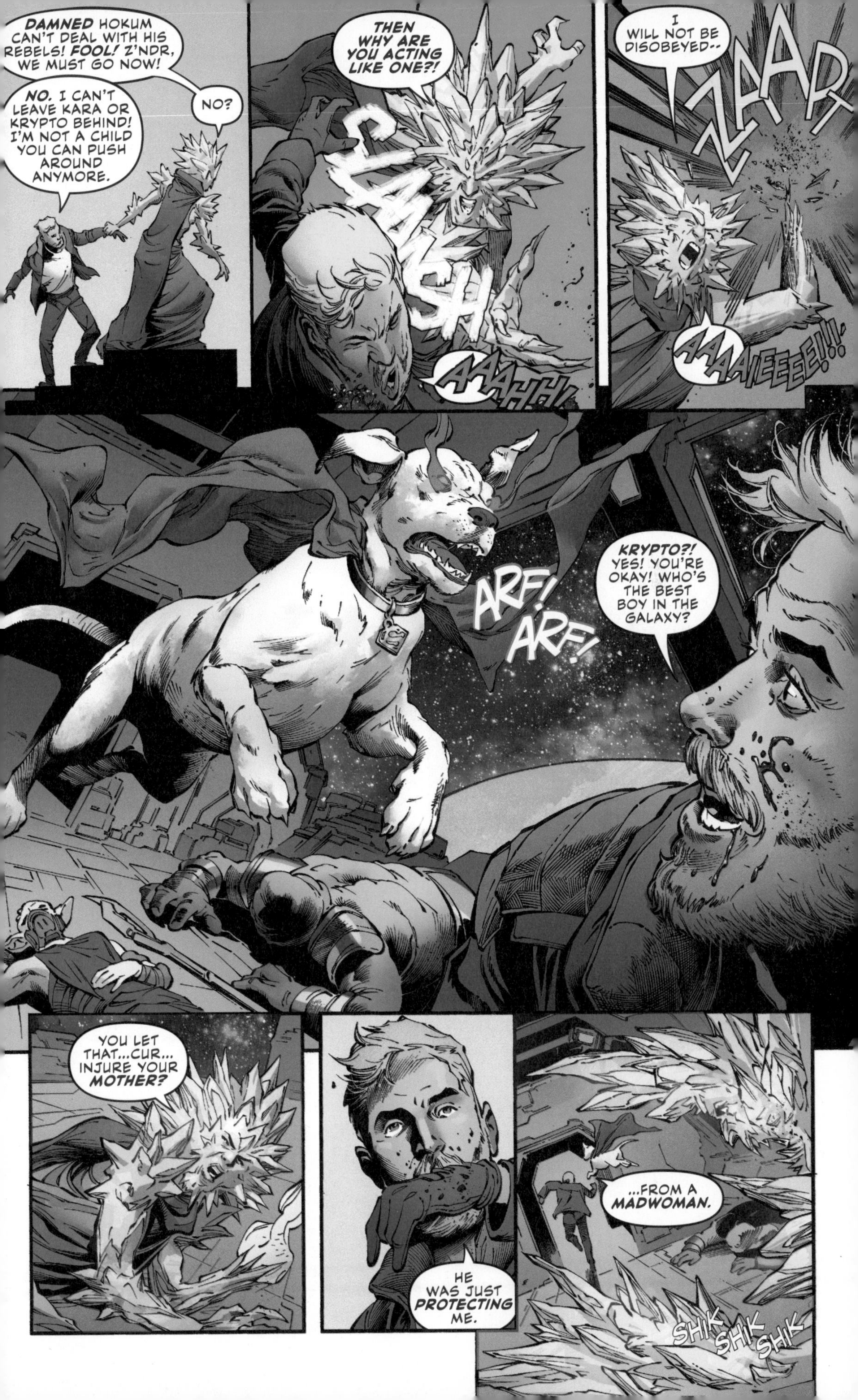

DAMNED HOKUM CAN'T DEAL WITH HIS REBELS! FOOL! Z'NDR, WE MUST GO NOW!
NO. I CAN'T LEAVE KARA OR KRYPTO BEHIND! I'M NOT A CHILD YOU CAN PUSH AROUND ANYMORE.
NO?
THEN WHY ARE YOU ACTING LIKE ONE?!
SLASH
AAAHH!
I WILL NOT BE DISOBEYED--
ZAAAP!
AAAAIEEEEE!!!
ARF! ARF!
KRYPTO?! YES! YOU'RE OKAY! WHO'S THE BEST BOY IN THE GALAXY?
YOU LET THAT...CUR... INJURE YOUR MOTHER?
HE WAS JUST PROTECTING ME.
...FROM A MADWOMAN.
SHIK SHIK SHIK

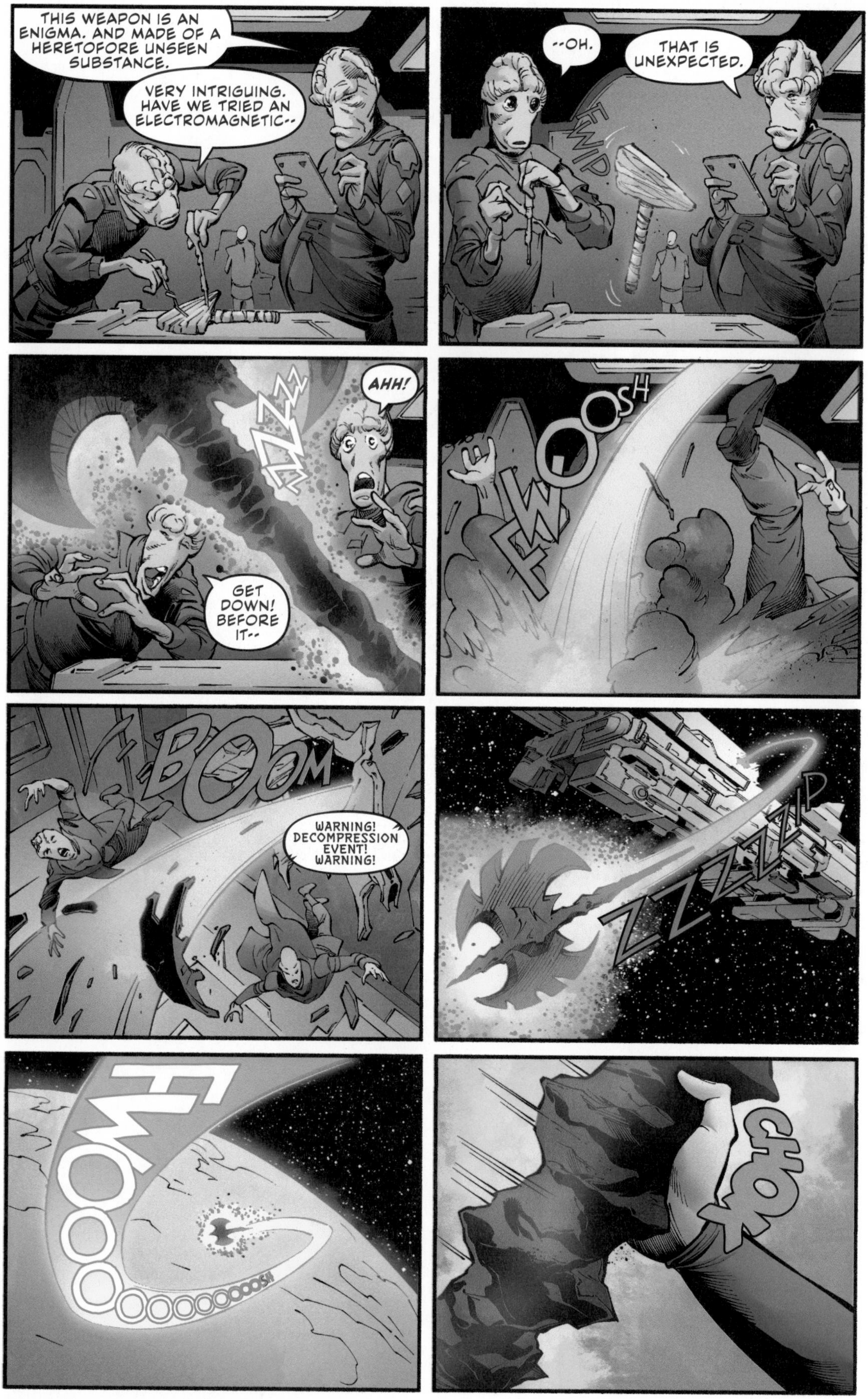
THIS WEAPON IS AN ENIGMA. AND MADE OF A HERETOFORE UNSEEN SUBSTANCE.
VERY INTRIGUING. HAVE WE TRIED AN ELECTROMAGNETIC--
--OH.
THAT IS UNEXPECTED.
FWIP
AHH!
GET DOWN! BEFORE IT--
FWOOSH
BOOM
WARNING! DECOMPRESSION EVENT! WARNING!
CHOK

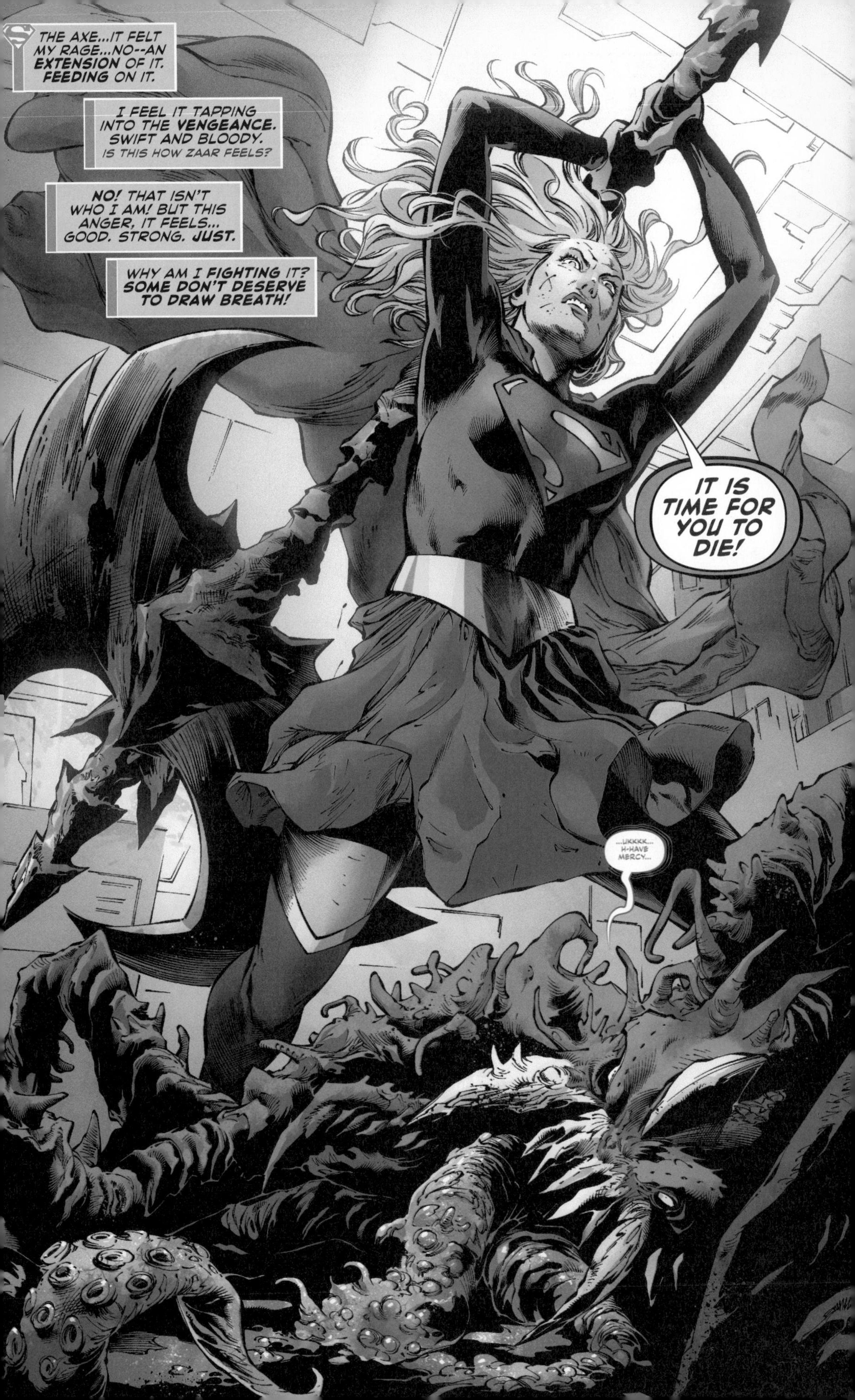
THE AXE...IT FELT MY RAGE...NO--AN EXTENSION OF IT. FEEDING ON IT.
I FEEL IT TAPPING INTO THE VENGEANCE. SWIFT AND BLOODY. IS THIS HOW ZAAR FEELS?
NO! THAT ISN'T WHO I AM! BUT THIS ANGER, IT FEELS... GOOD. STRONG. JUST.
WHY AM I FIGHTING IT? SOME DON'T DESERVE TO DRAW BREATH!
IT IS TIME FOR YOU TO DIE!
...UKKKK... H-HAVE MERCY...

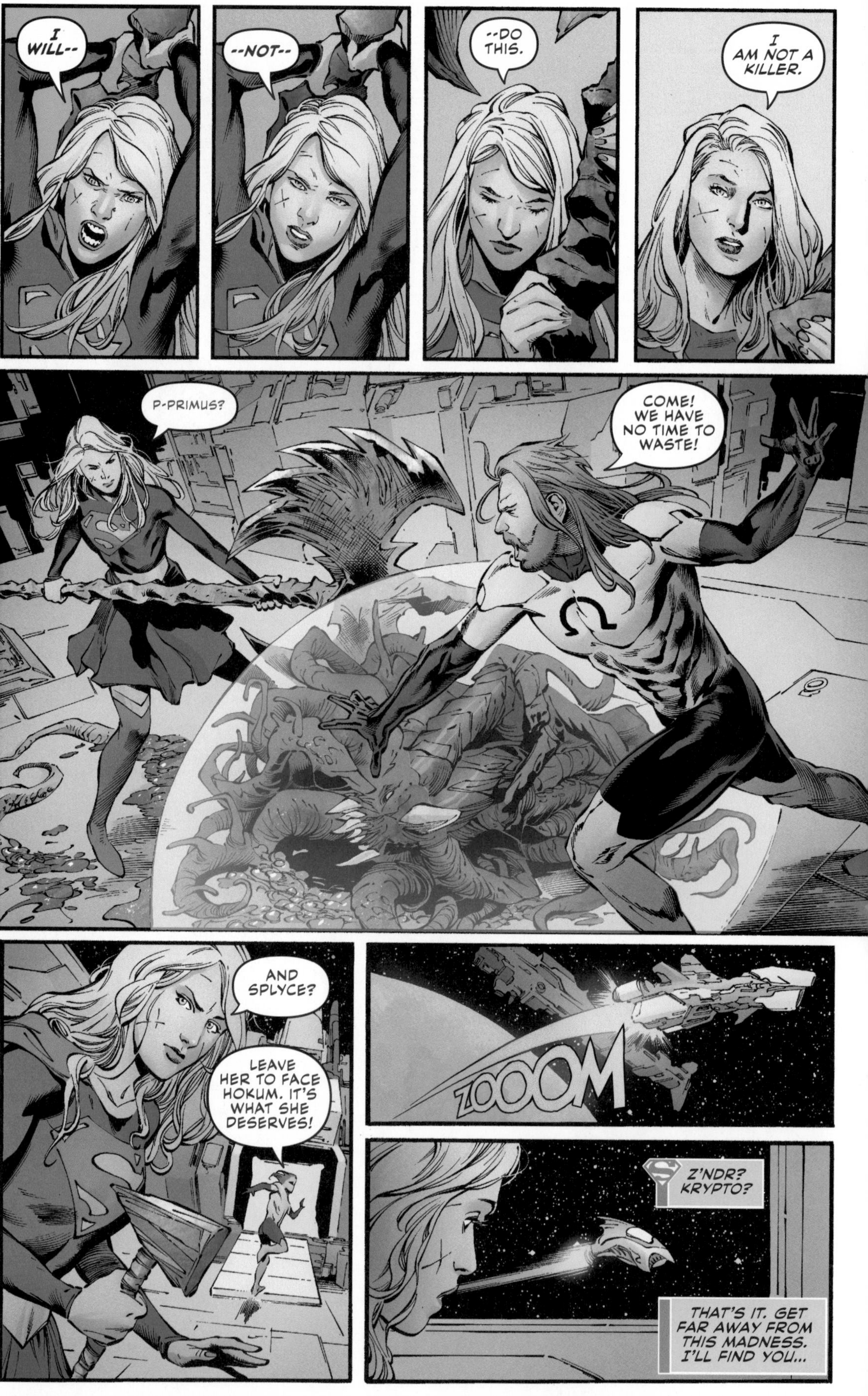
I WILL--
--NOT--
--DO THIS.
I AM NOT A KILLER.
P-PRIMUS?
COME! WE HAVE NO TIME TO WASTE!
AND SPLYCE?
LEAVE HER TO FACE HOKUM. IT'S WHAT SHE DESERVES!
ZOOOM
Z'NDR? KRYPTO?
THAT'S IT. GET FAR AWAY FROM THIS MADNESS. I'LL FIND YOU...

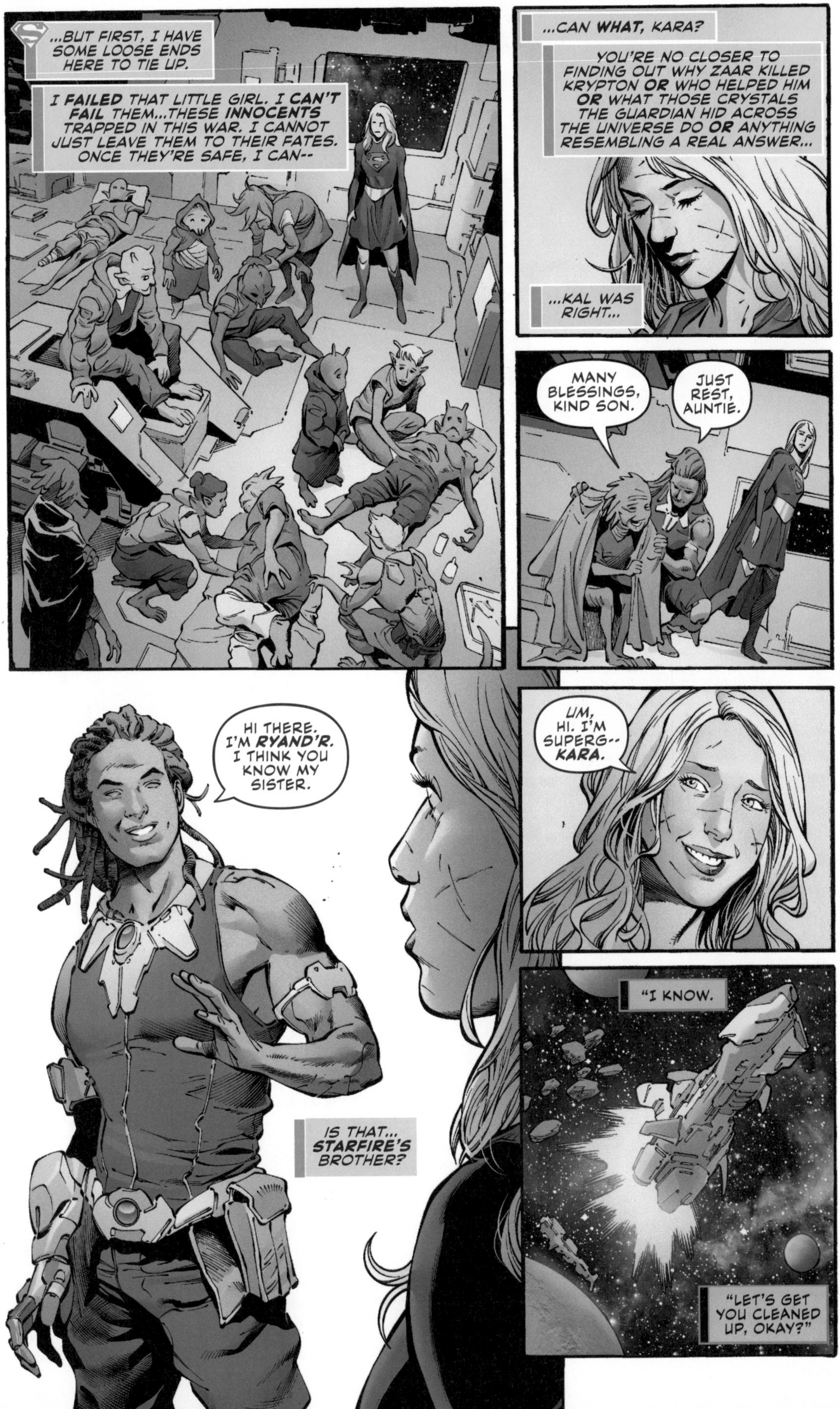
...BUT FIRST, I HAVE SOME LOOSE ENDS HERE TO TIE UP.
I FAILED THAT LITTLE GIRL. I CAN'T FAIL THEM...THESE INNOCENTS TRAPPED IN THIS WAR. I CANNOT JUST LEAVE THEM TO THEIR FATES. ONCE THEY'RE SAFE, I CAN--
...CAN WHAT, KARA?
YOU'RE NO CLOSER TO FINDING OUT WHY ZAAR KILLED KRYPTON OR WHO HELPED HIM OR WHAT THOSE CRYSTALS THE GUARDIAN HID ACROSS THE UNIVERSE DO OR ANYTHING RESEMBLING A REAL ANSWER...
...KAL WAS RIGHT...
MANY BLESSINGS, KIND SON.
JUST REST, AUNTIE.
HI THERE. I'M RYAND'R. I THINK YOU KNOW MY SISTER.
IS THAT... STARFIRE'S BROTHER?
UM, HI. I'M SUPERG-- KARA.
"I KNOW.
"LET'S GET YOU CLEANED UP, OKAY?"

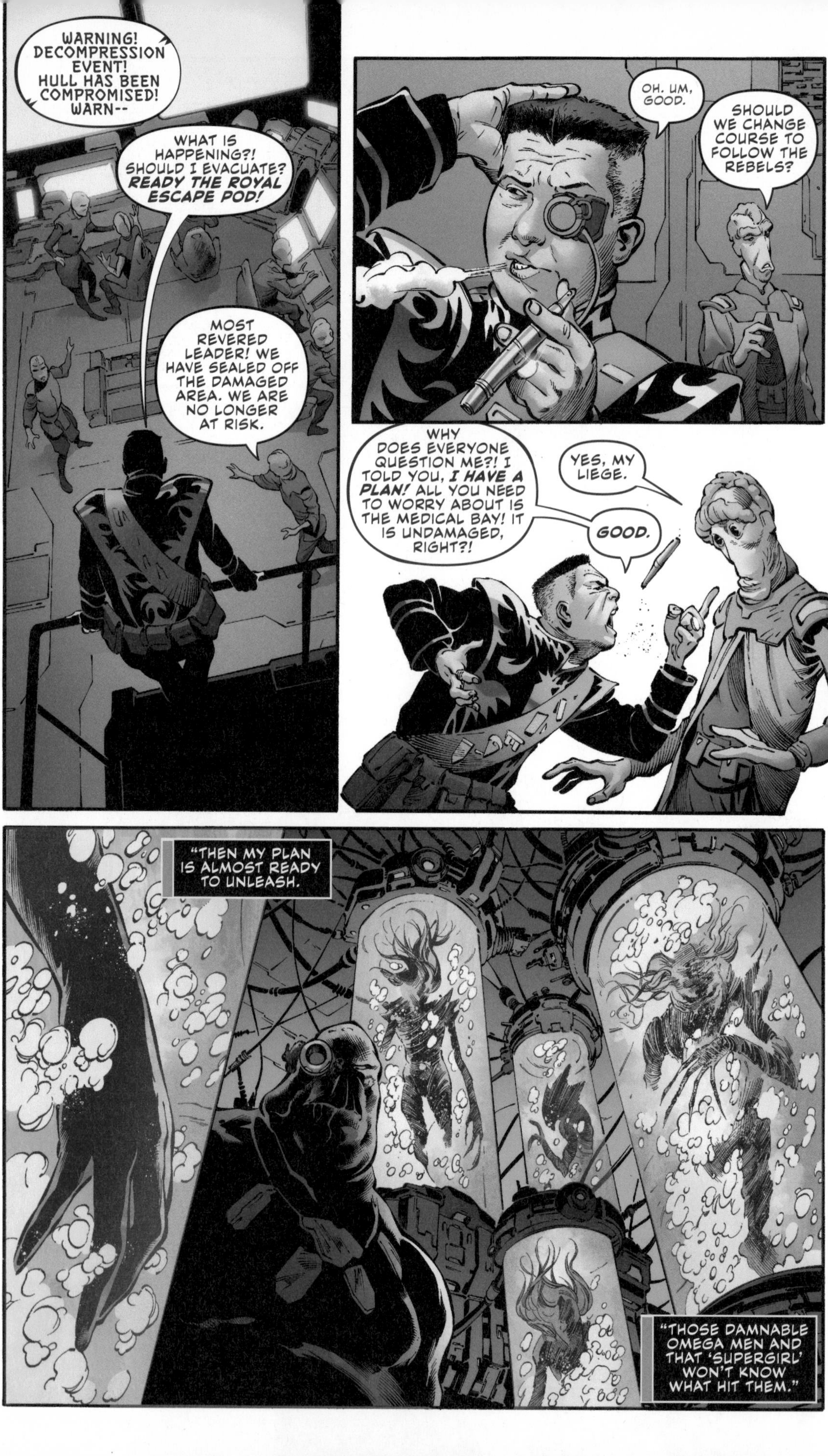
WARNING! DECOMPRESSION EVENT! HULL HAS BEEN COMPROMISED! WARN--
WHAT IS HAPPENING?! SHOULD I EVACUATE? READY THE ROYAL ESCAPE POD!
MOST REVERED LEADER! WE HAVE SEALED OFF THE DAMAGED AREA. WE ARE NO LONGER AT RISK.
OH. UM, GOOD.
SHOULD WE CHANGE COURSE TO FOLLOW THE REBELS?
WHY DOES EVERYONE QUESTION ME?! I TOLD YOU, I HAVE A PLAN! ALL YOU NEED TO WORRY ABOUT IS THE MEDICAL BAY! IT IS UNDAMAGED, RIGHT?!
YES, MY LIEGE.
GOOD.
"THEN MY PLAN IS ALMOST READY TO UNLEASH.
"THOSE DAMNABLE OMEGA MEN AND THAT 'SUPERGIRL' WON'T KNOW WHAT HIT THEM."

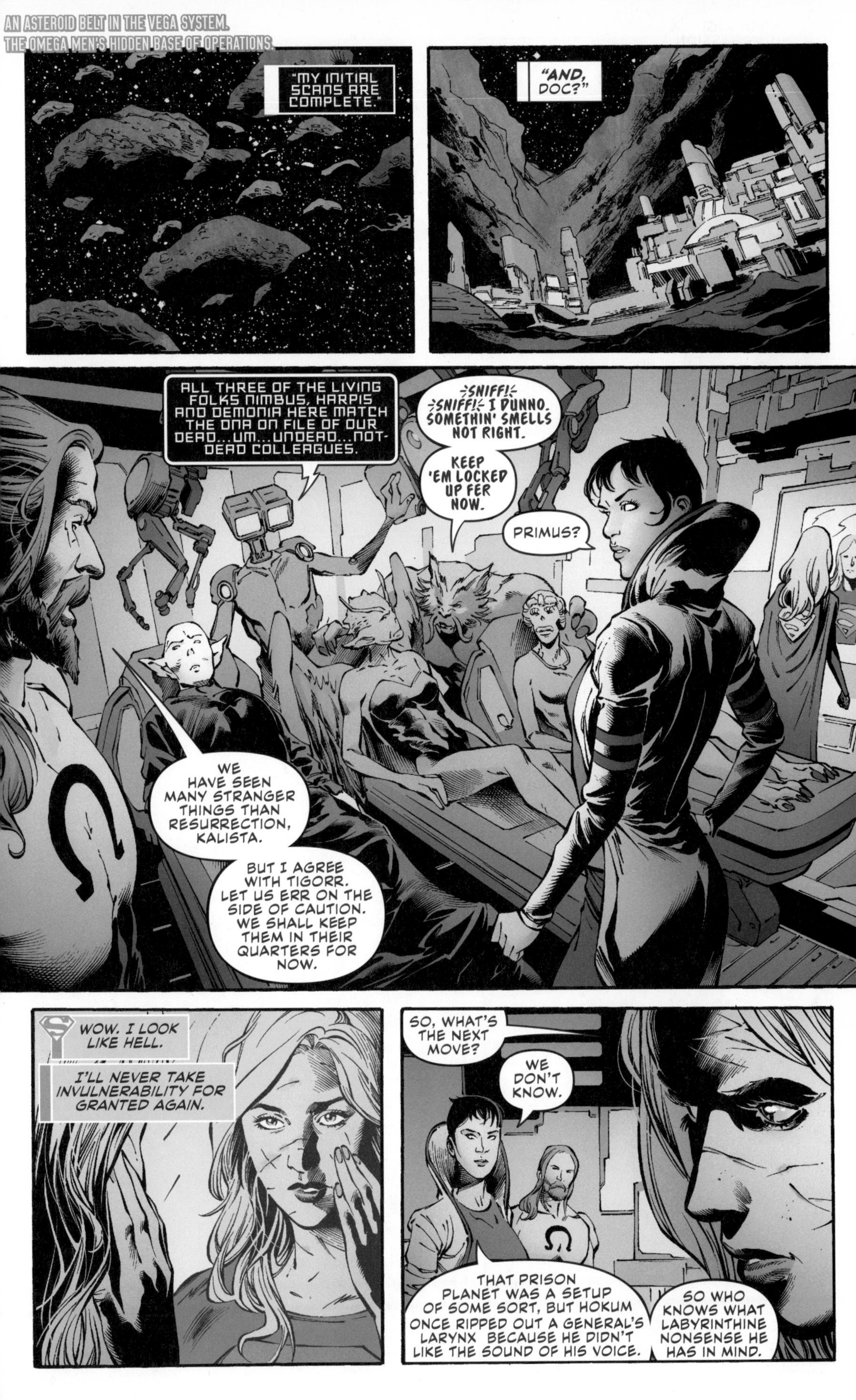
AN ASTEROID BELT IN THE VEGA SYSTEM.
THE OMEGA MEN'S HIDDEN BASE OF OPERATIONS.
"MY INITIAL SCANS ARE COMPLETE."
"AND, DOC?"
ALL THREE OF THE LIVING FOLKS NIMBUS, HARPIS AND DEMONIA HERE MATCH THE DNA ON FILE OF OUR DEAD...UM...UNDEAD...NOT-DEAD COLLEAGUES.
SNIFF! SNIFF! I DUNNO. SOMETHIN' SMELLS NOT RIGHT.
KEEP 'EM LOCKED UP FER NOW.
PRIMUS?
WE HAVE SEEN MANY STRANGER THINGS THAN RESURRECTION, KALISTA.
BUT I AGREE WITH TIGORR. LET US ERR ON THE SIDE OF CAUTION. WE SHALL KEEP THEM IN THEIR QUARTERS FOR NOW.
WOW. I LOOK LIKE HELL.
I'LL NEVER TAKE INVULNERABILITY FOR GRANTED AGAIN.
SO, WHAT'S THE NEXT MOVE?
WE DON'T KNOW.
THAT PRISON PLANET WAS A SETUP OF SOME SORT, BUT HOKUM ONCE RIPPED OUT A GENERAL'S LARYNX BECAUSE HE DIDN'T LIKE THE SOUND OF HIS VOICE.
SO WHO KNOWS WHAT LABYRINTHINE NONSENSE HE HAS IN MIND.

NIMBUS, HARPIS, DEMONIA--WHAT IS THE LAST THING ANY OF YOU REMEMBER?

YESSSSS, WHAT HARPISSS SSSSSAID-- ASSSSS IF THERE ISSSS A WALL INSIDE MY MIND.

I REMEMBER BEING IN BATTLE...THEN ALL IS BLACK. UNTIL YOU FOUND US, PRIMUS.

I CAN HELP WITH THAT. A SIMPLE PSI-SCAN WILL--

NO! PLEASE!

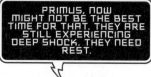

PRIMUS, NOW MIGHT NOT BE THE BEST TIME FOR THAT. THEY ARE STILL EXPERIENCING DEEP SHOCK. THEY NEED REST.

THAT SCAR ON HER NECK. I KNOW THAT. BUT FROM WHERE?

REST IS A GOOD PRESCRIPTION FOR US ALL.

LET US TAKE ADVANTAGE OF THIS RESPITE.

KARA?

WHERE DID SHE GO?

THAT MEMORY OF MY DAD WHEN I WAS FIGHTING SPLYCE... WHAT IF IT'S *TRUE*?

DID HE *CREATE* THE MACHINE THAT *KILLED* KRYPTON? WAS HE PART OF *"THE CIRCLE"*?

IT DOESN'T MAKE ANY SENSE AT ALL, BUT...BUT...

...WILL I EVER GET ANSWERS?

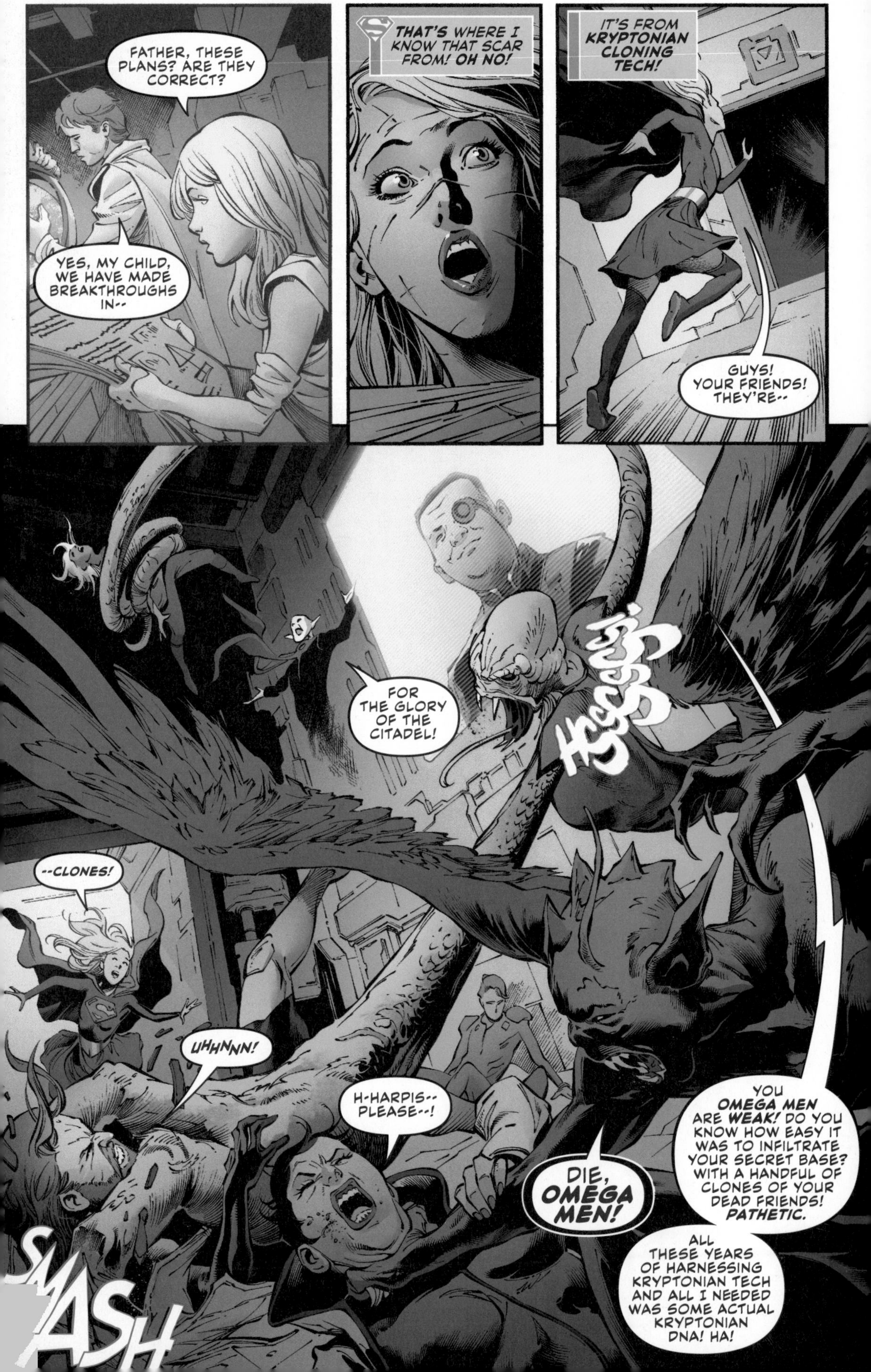

FATHER, THESE PLANS? ARE THEY CORRECT?
YES, MY CHILD, WE HAVE MADE BREAKTHROUGHS IN--
THAT'S WHERE I KNOW THAT SCAR FROM! OH NO!
IT'S FROM KRYPTONIAN CLONING TECH!
GUYS! YOUR FRIENDS! THEY'RE--
--CLONES!
FOR THE GLORY OF THE CITADEL!
UHHNNN!
H-HARPIS-- PLEASE--!
DIE, OMEGA MEN!
YOU OMEGA MEN ARE WEAK! DO YOU KNOW HOW EASY IT WAS TO INFILTRATE YOUR SECRET BASE? WITH A HANDFUL OF CLONES OF YOUR DEAD FRIENDS! PATHETIC.
ALL THESE YEARS OF HARNESSING KRYPTONIAN TECH AND ALL I NEEDED WAS SOME ACTUAL KRYPTONIAN DNA! HA!
SMASH

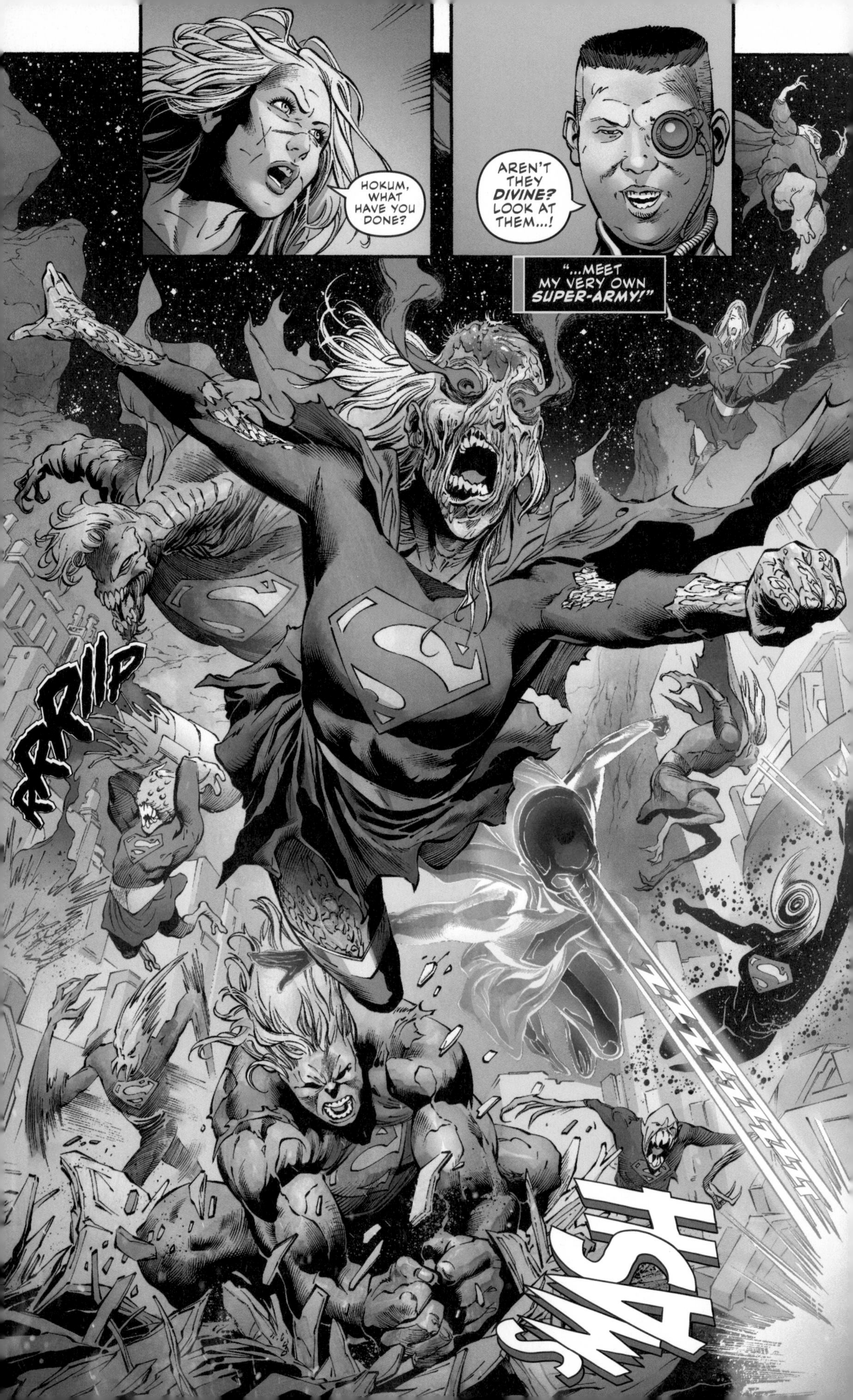
HOKUM, WHAT HAVE YOU DONE?
AREN'T THEY DIVINE? LOOK AT THEM...!
"...MEET MY VERY OWN SUPER-ARMY!"
RRRIIP
SMASH

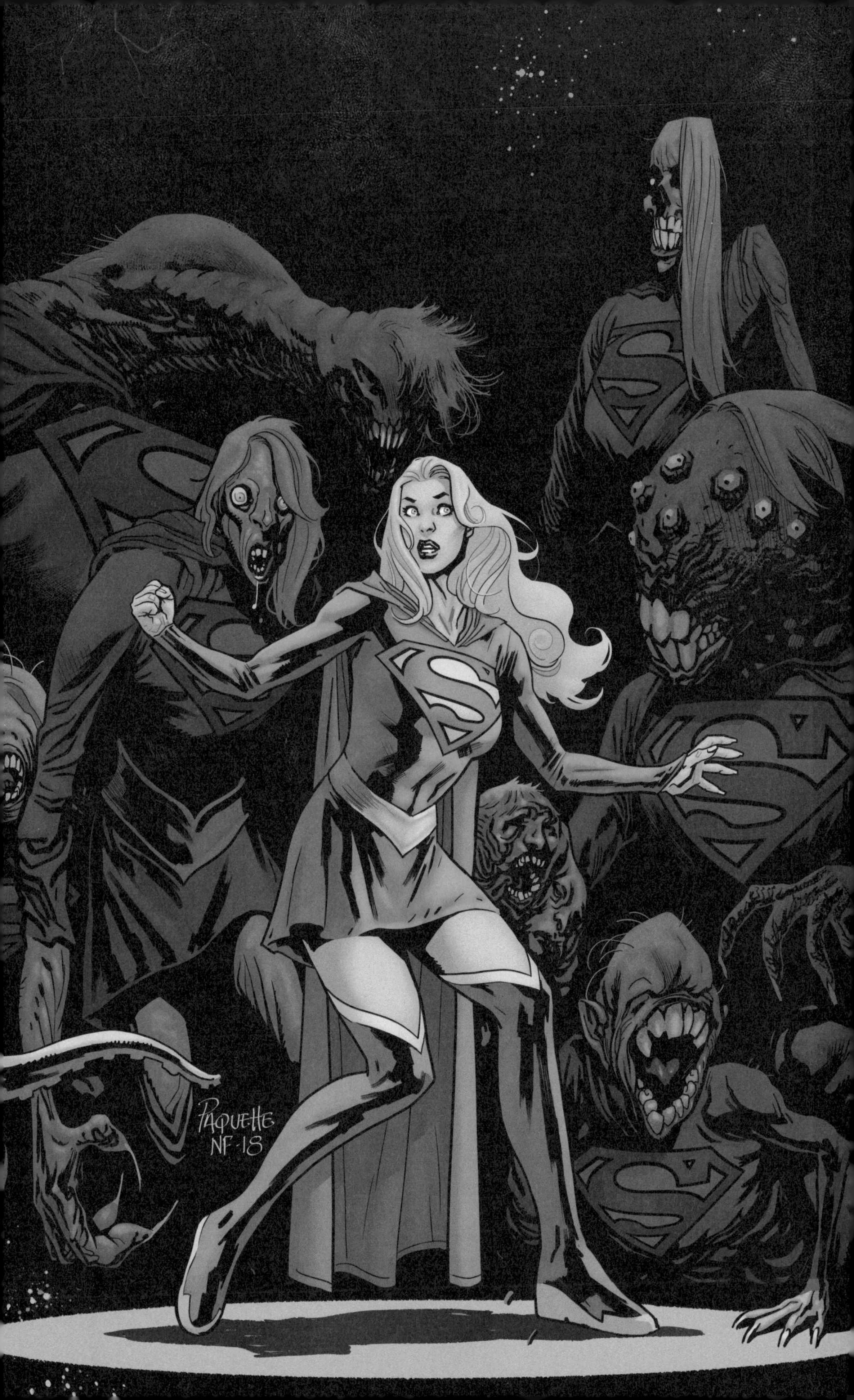
PAQUETTE
NF·18

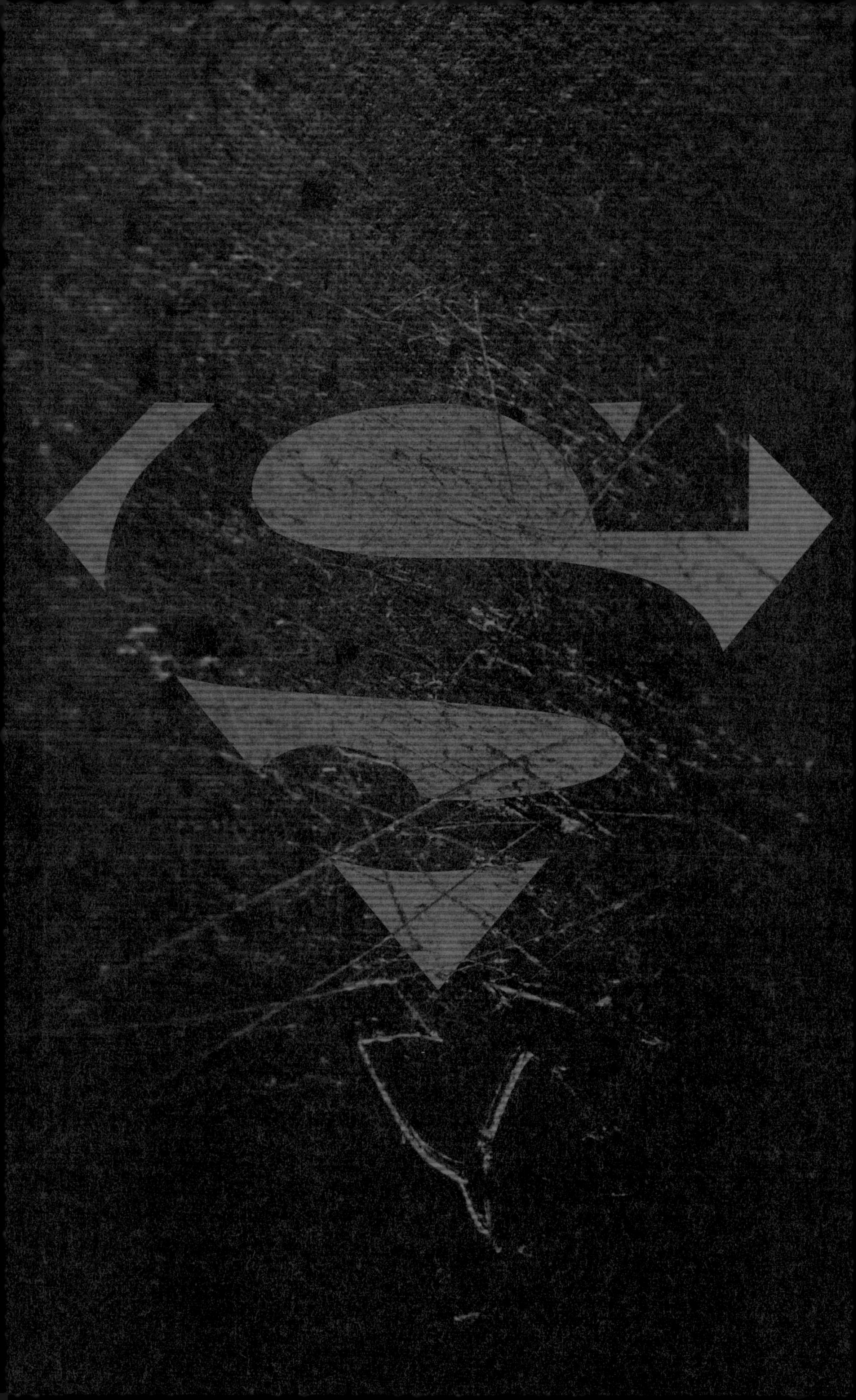

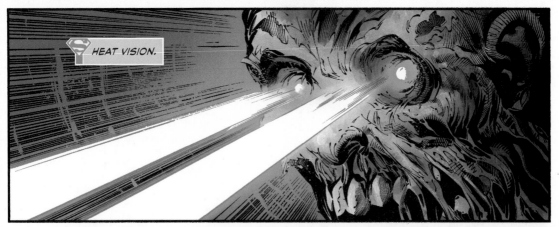

HEAT VISION.

SUPER-STRENGTH.

X-RAY VISION.

I USED TO TAKE THEM FOR GRANTED.

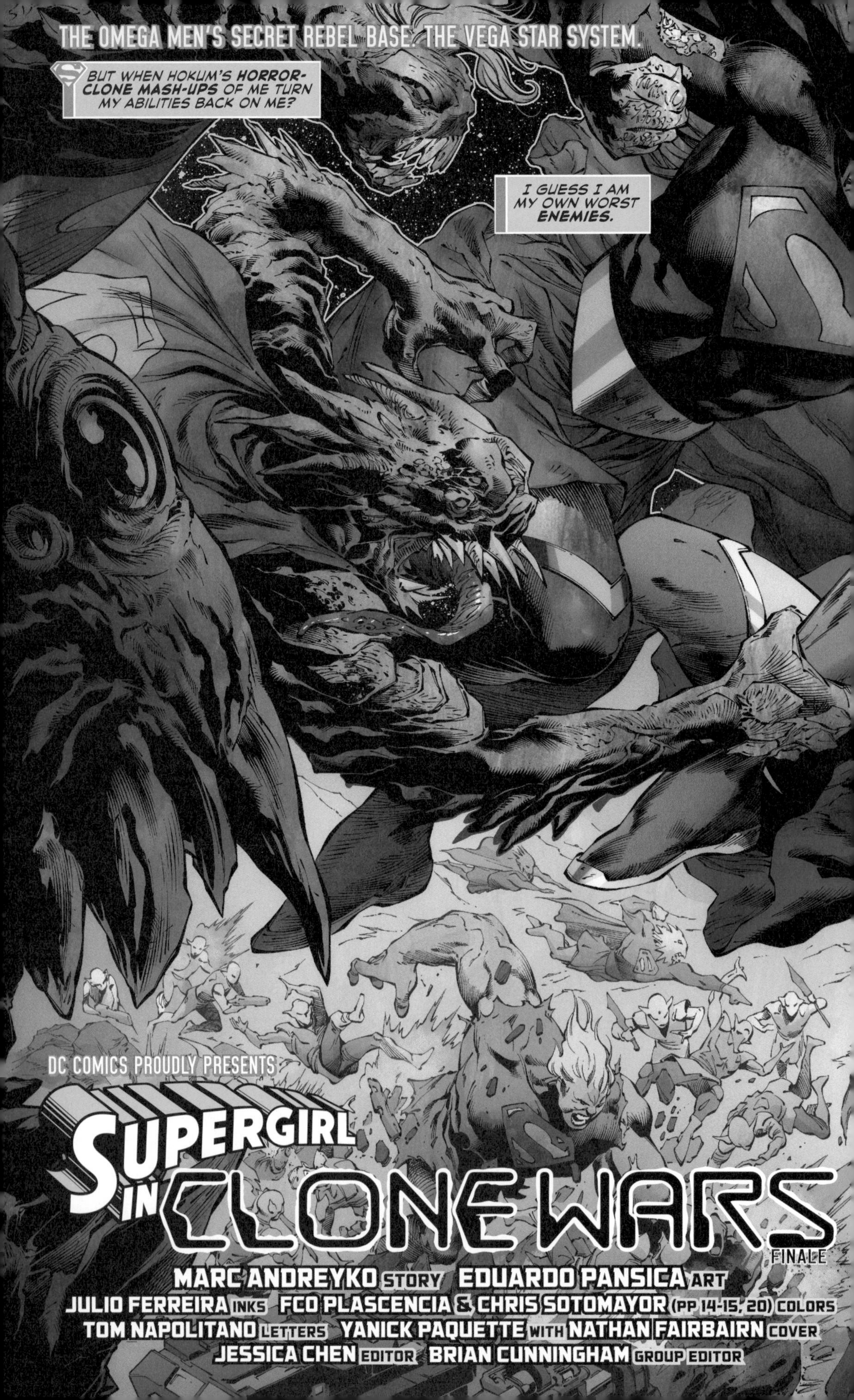
THE OMEGA MEN'S SECRET REBEL BASE: THE VEGA STAR SYSTEM.
BUT WHEN HOKUM'S HORROR-CLONE MASH-UPS OF ME TURN MY ABILITIES BACK ON ME?
I GUESS I AM MY OWN WORST ENEMIES.
DC COMICS PROUDLY PRESENTS
SUPERGIRL IN CLONE WARS FINALE
MARC ANDREYKO STORY EDUARDO PANSICA ART
JULIO FERREIRA INKS FCO PLASCENCIA & CHRIS SOTOMAYOR (PP 14-15, 20) COLORS
TOM NAPOLITANO LETTERS YANICK PAQUETTE WITH NATHAN FAIRBAIRN COVER
JESSICA CHEN EDITOR BRIAN CUNNINGHAM GROUP EDITOR

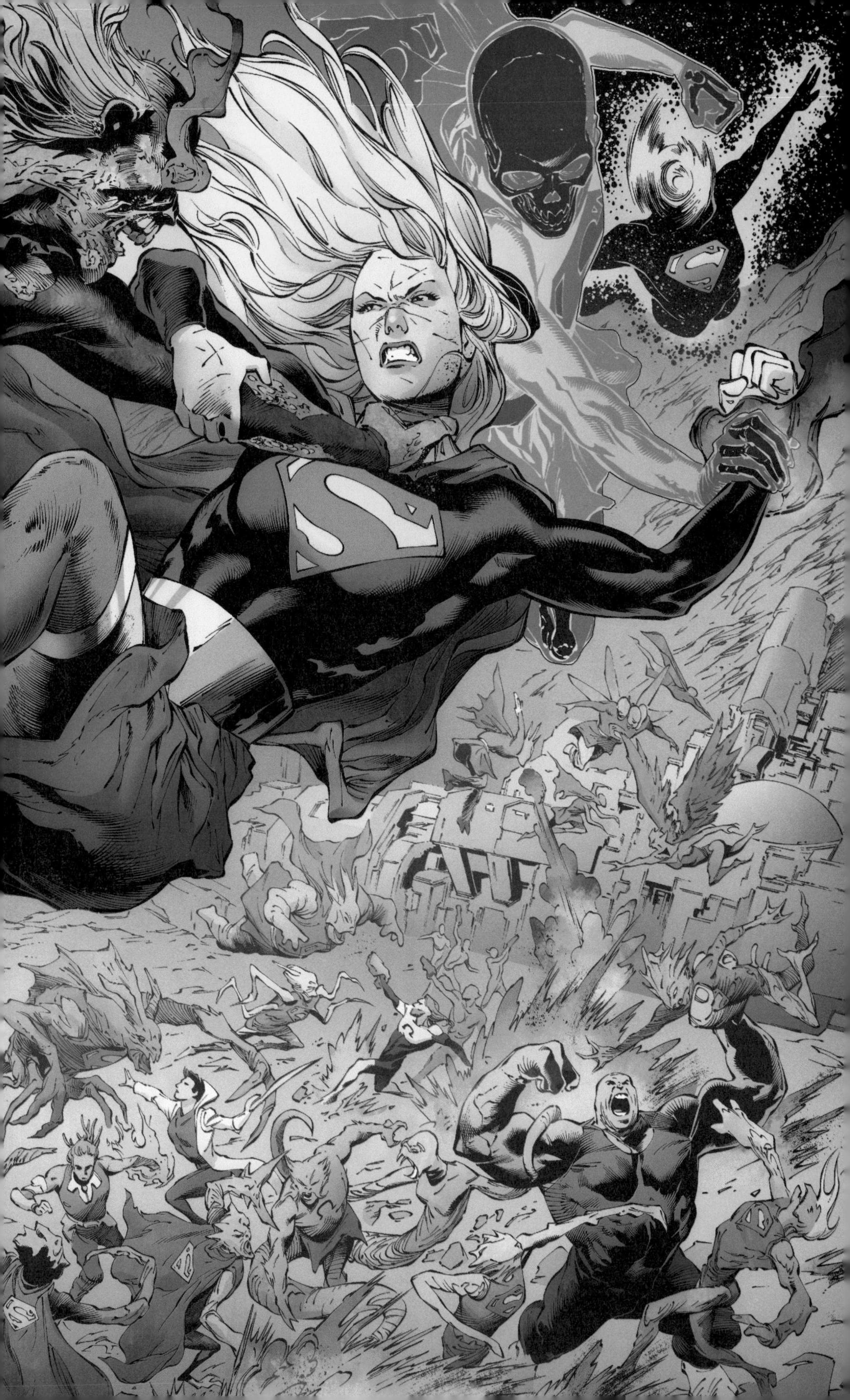

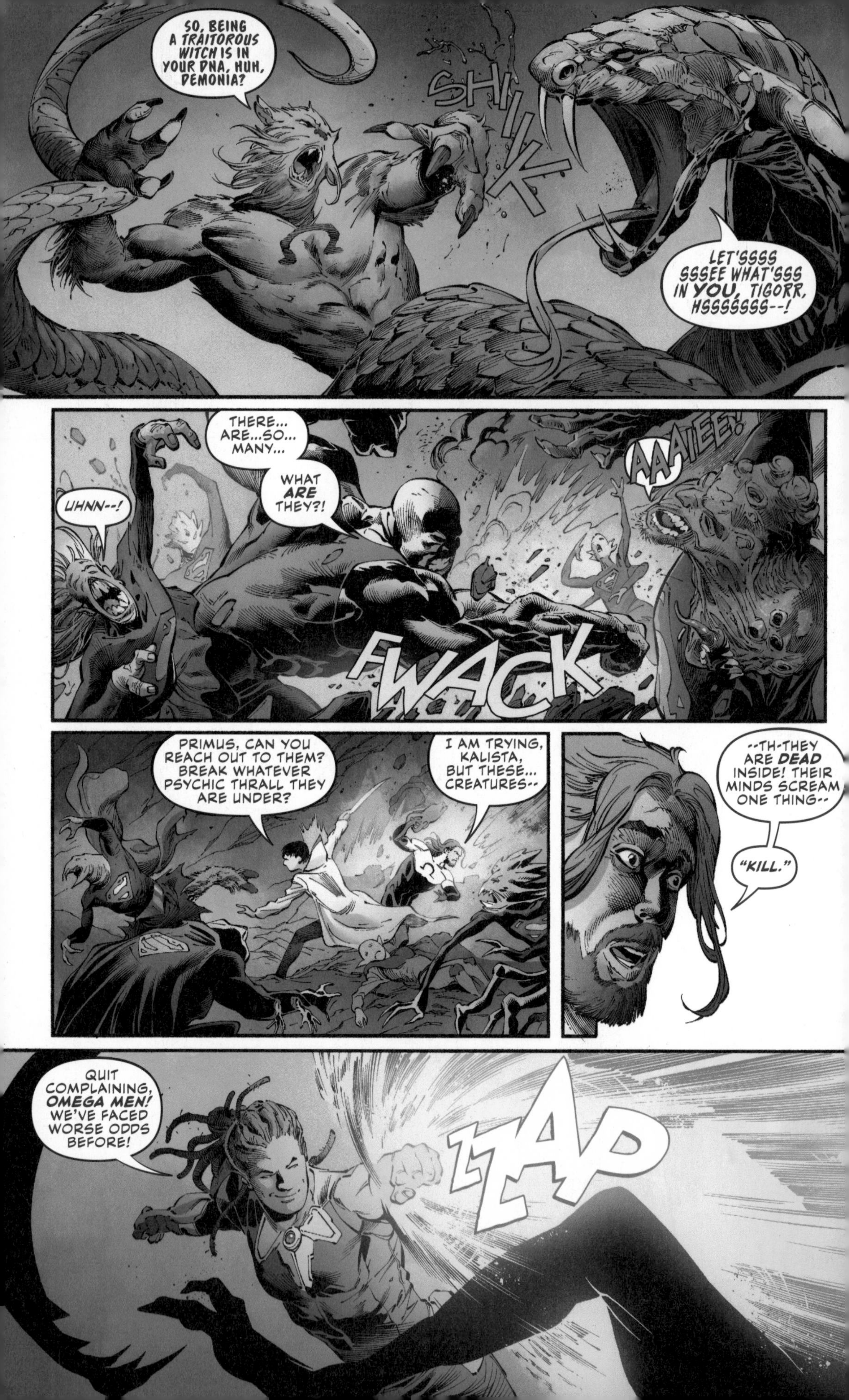
SO, BEING A TRAITOROUS WITCH IS IN YOUR DNA, HUH, DEMONIA?
SHIIIK
LET'SSSS SSSEE WHAT'SSS IN YOU, TIGORR, HSSSSSSS--!
THERE... ARE...SO... MANY...
WHAT ARE THEY?!
UHNN--!
AAAIEE!
FWACK
PRIMUS, CAN YOU REACH OUT TO THEM? BREAK WHATEVER PSYCHIC THRALL THEY ARE UNDER?
I AM TRYING, KALISTA, BUT THESE... CREATURES--
--TH-THEY ARE DEAD INSIDE! THEIR MINDS SCREAM ONE THING--
"KILL."
QUIT COMPLAINING, OMEGA MEN! WE'VE FACED WORSE ODDS BEFORE!
ZZAP

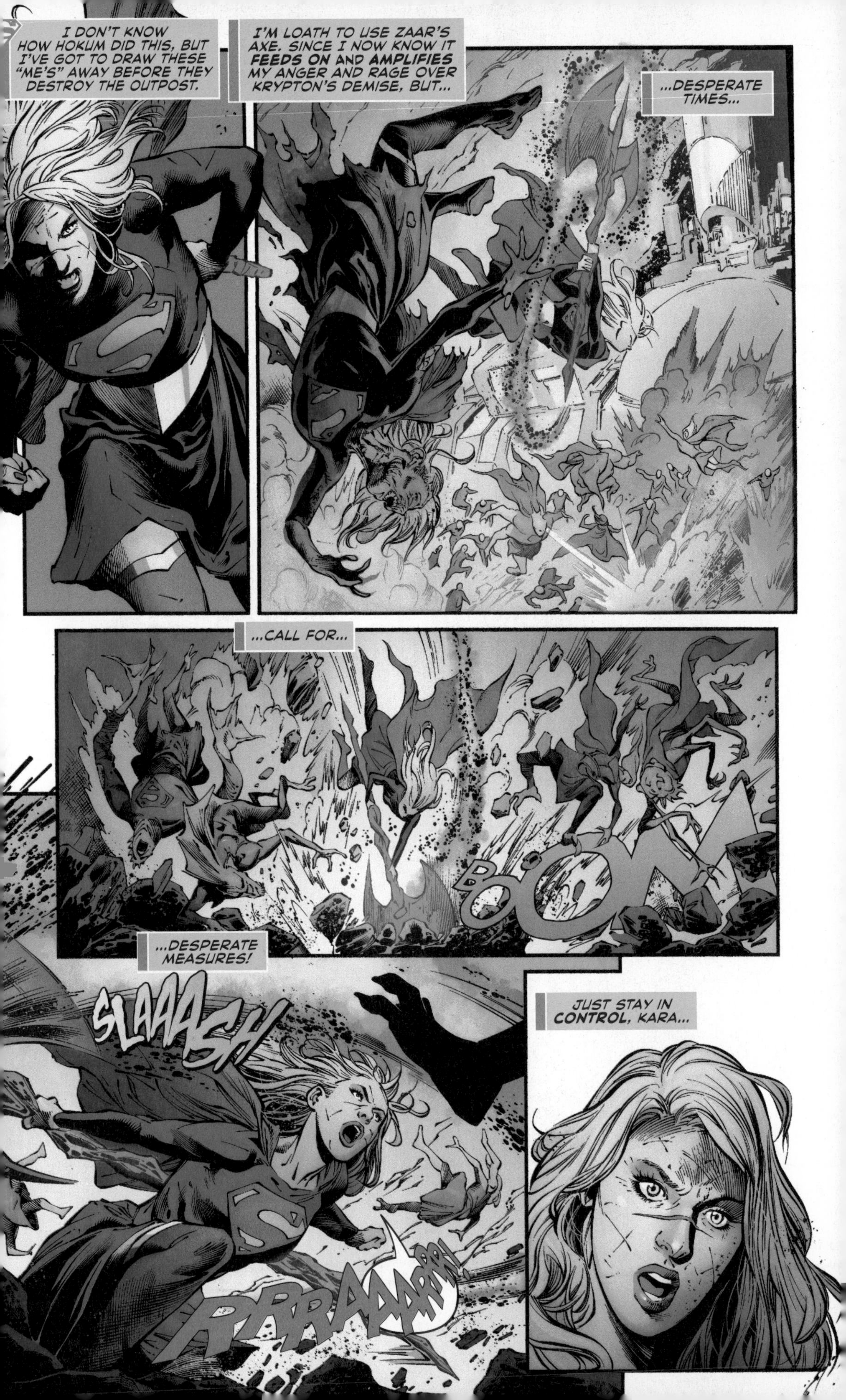
I DON'T KNOW HOW HOKUM DID THIS, BUT I'VE GOT TO DRAW THESE "ME'S" AWAY BEFORE THEY DESTROY THE OUTPOST.
I'M LOATH TO USE ZAAR'S AXE. SINCE I NOW KNOW IT **FEEDS ON** AND **AMPLIFIES** MY ANGER AND RAGE OVER KRYPTON'S DEMISE, BUT...
...DESPERATE TIMES...
...CALL FOR...
BOOM
...DESPERATE MEASURES!
SLAAASH
RRRAAAARRR!
JUST STAY IN **CONTROL**, KARA...

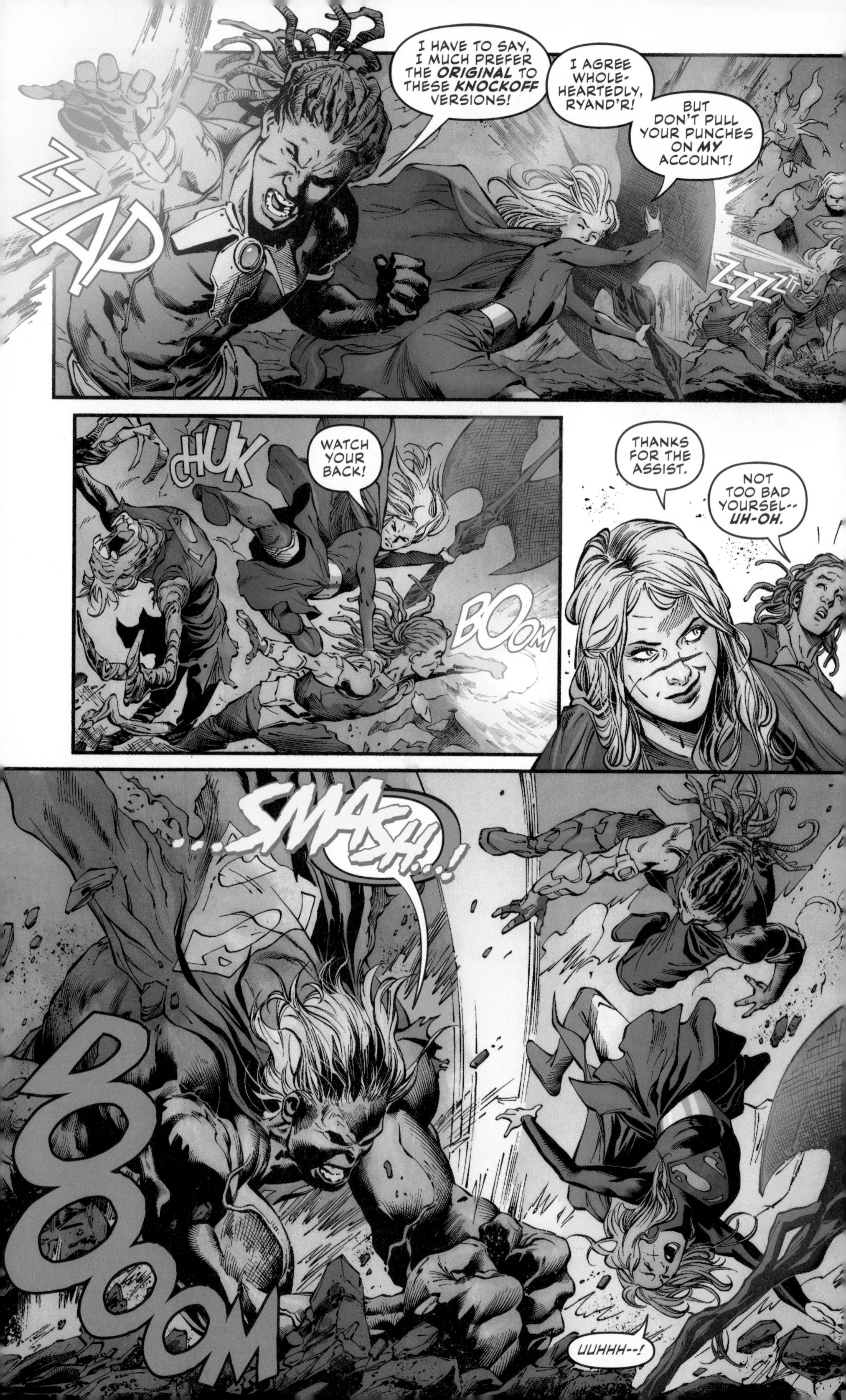
ZZAP
I HAVE TO SAY, I MUCH PREFER THE ORIGINAL TO THESE KNOCKOFF VERSIONS!
I AGREE WHOLE-HEARTEDLY, RYAND'R!
BUT DON'T PULL YOUR PUNCHES ON MY ACCOUNT!
ZZZZZT
CHUK
WATCH YOUR BACK!
BOOM
THANKS FOR THE ASSIST.
NOT TOO BAD YOURSEL-- UH-OH.
...SMASH...!
BOOOOM
UUHHH--!

MANY LIGHT-YEARS AWAY.

"RRRF?"

"I'M *TRYING,* KRYPTO--

--BUT TRACKING KARA ACROSS THE *VASTNESS OF SPACE* IS EASIER SAID THAN DONE.

AND IT'S TOO DANGEROUS TO GO BACK THERE. TRUST ME, YOU *DON'T KNOW* WHAT MY MOTHER IS CAPABLE OF.

RUFF!!!

YEAH, I KNOW. I MISS KARA, TOO.

BUT *EVEN* IF WE GO BACK TO FIND HER, HOW DO I EXPLAIN THAT MY MOTHER WANTS HER *DEAD*? OR THAT I WAS SENT AS A *SPY* ON HER? WILL SHE BELIEVE *ANYTHING* I HAVE TO SAY AFTER THAT?

BUT DON'T YOU TELL HER THAT, DEAL?

ARF!

YOU'RE A GOOD WINGMAN, PUP. BUT WE STILL CAN'T GO BACK.

EH?

ARRROOO!

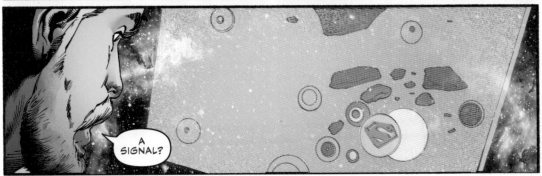

A SIGNAL?

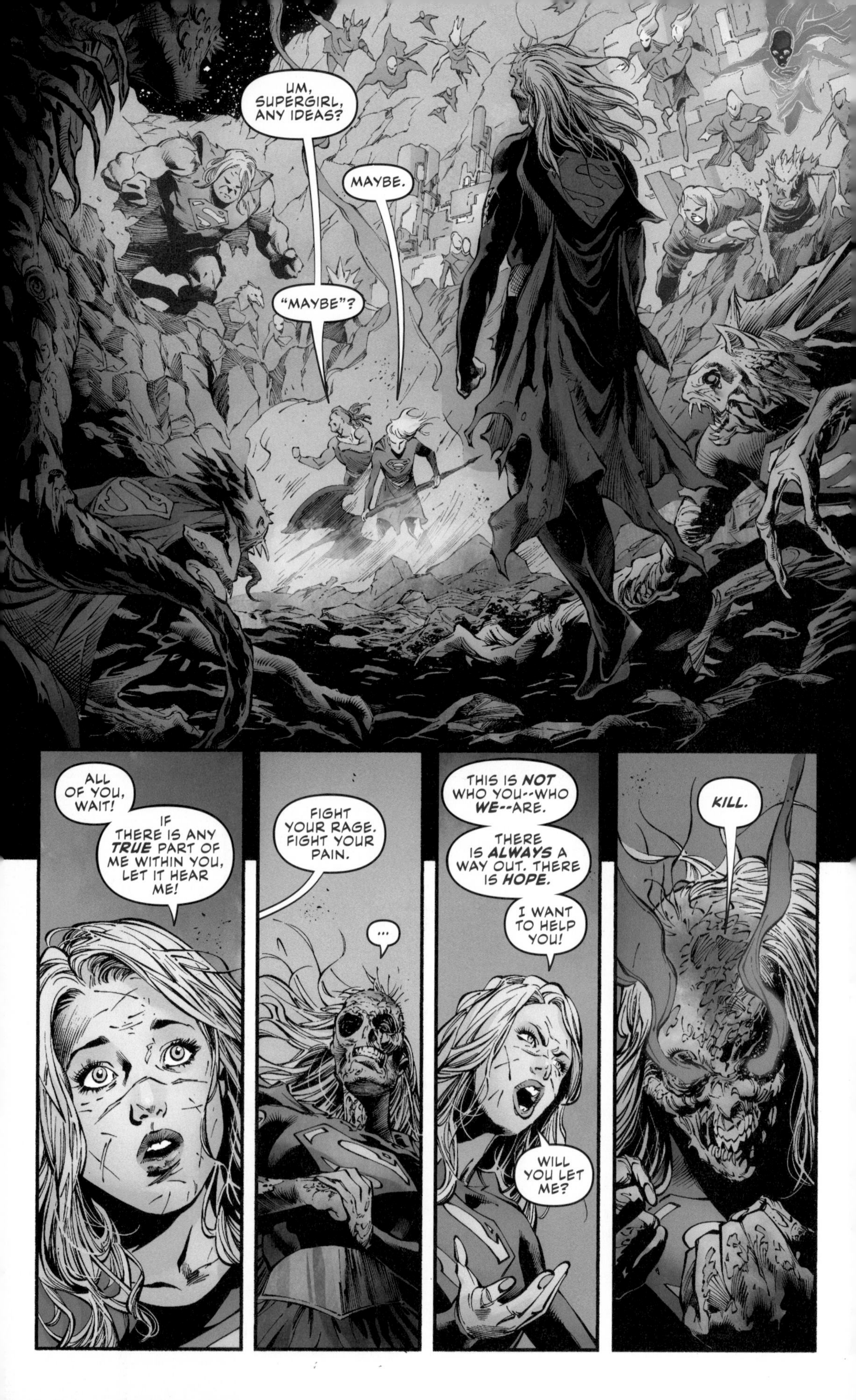

UM, SUPERGIRL, ANY IDEAS?
MAYBE.
"MAYBE"?
ALL OF YOU, WAIT!
IF THERE IS ANY TRUE PART OF ME WITHIN YOU, LET IT HEAR ME!
FIGHT YOUR RAGE. FIGHT YOUR PAIN.
...
THIS IS NOT WHO YOU--WHO WE--ARE.
THERE IS ALWAYS A WAY OUT. THERE IS HOPE.
I WANT TO HELP YOU!
WILL YOU LET ME?
KILL.

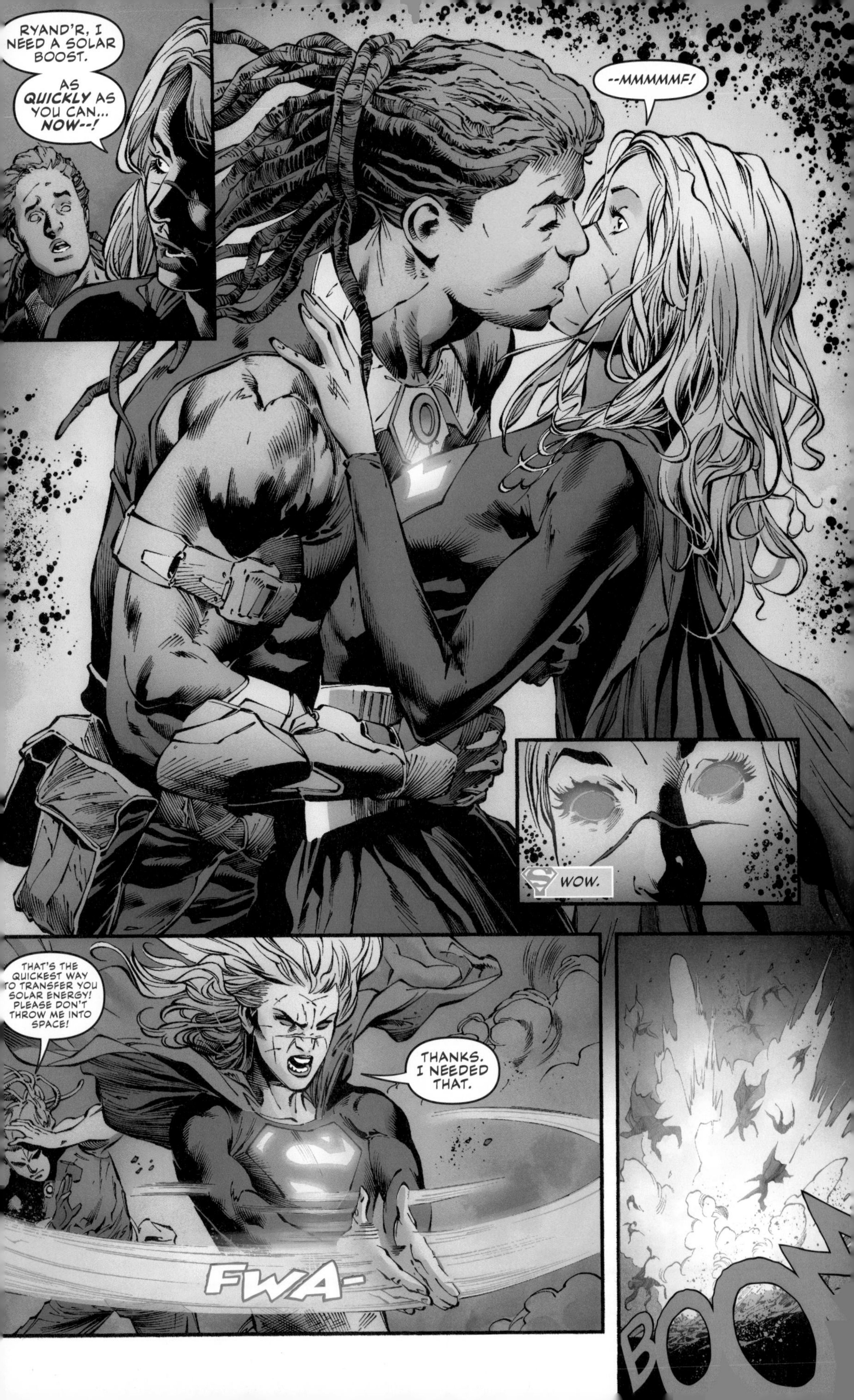

RYAND'R, I NEED A SOLAR BOOST.
AS QUICKLY AS YOU CAN... NOW--!
--MMMMMF!
WOW.
THAT'S THE QUICKEST WAY TO TRANSFER YOU SOLAR ENERGY! PLEASE DON'T THROW ME INTO SPACE!
THANKS. I NEEDED THAT.
FWA-
BOOM

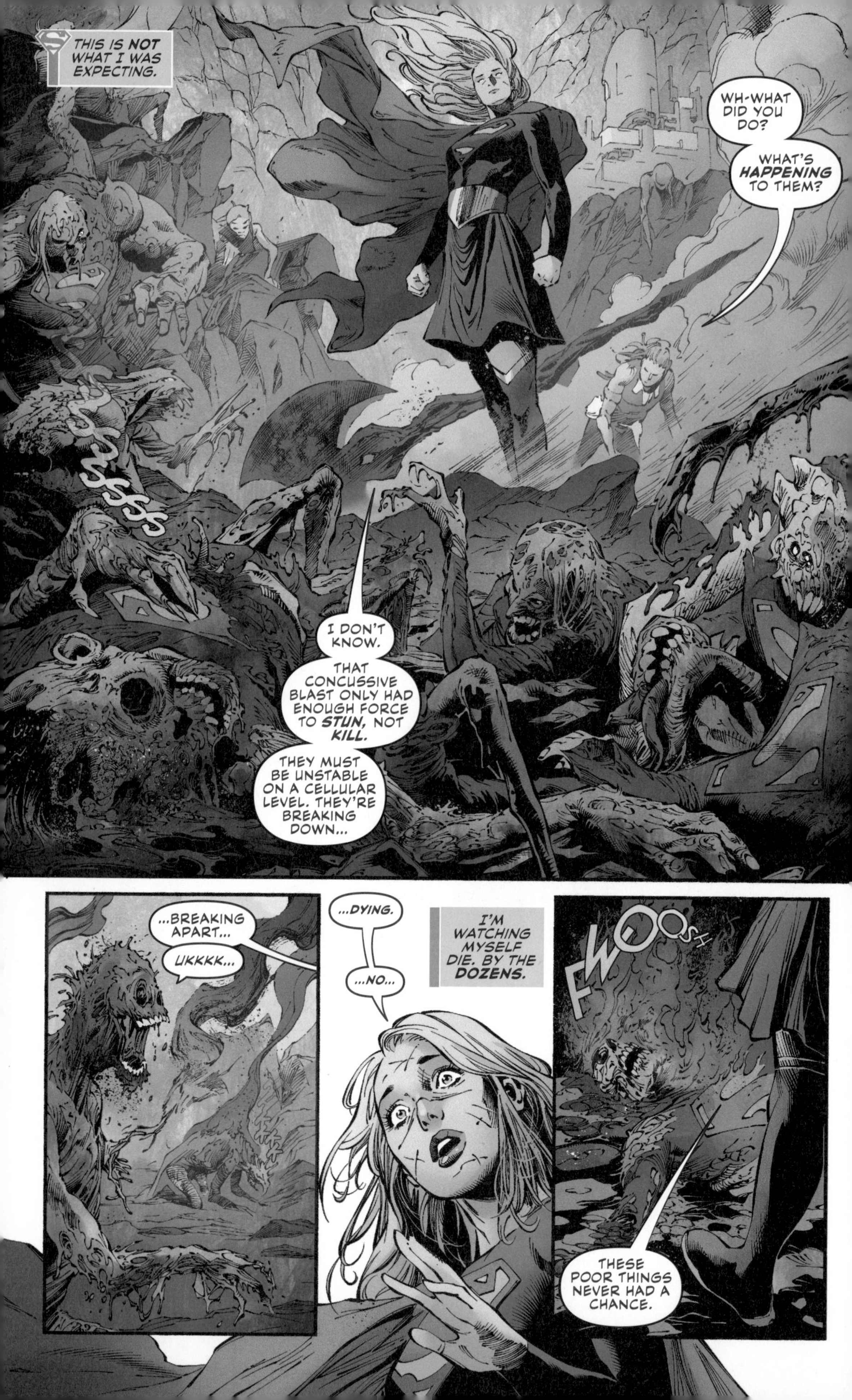
THIS IS NOT WHAT I WAS EXPECTING.
WH-WHAT DID YOU DO?
WHAT'S HAPPENING TO THEM?
SSSSSSS
I DON'T KNOW.
THAT CONCUSSIVE BLAST ONLY HAD ENOUGH FORCE TO STUN, NOT KILL.
THEY MUST BE UNSTABLE ON A CELLULAR LEVEL. THEY'RE BREAKING DOWN...
...BREAKING APART...
UKKKK...
...DYING.
...NO...
I'M WATCHING MYSELF DIE. BY THE DOZENS.
FWOOSH
THESE POOR THINGS NEVER HAD A CHANCE.

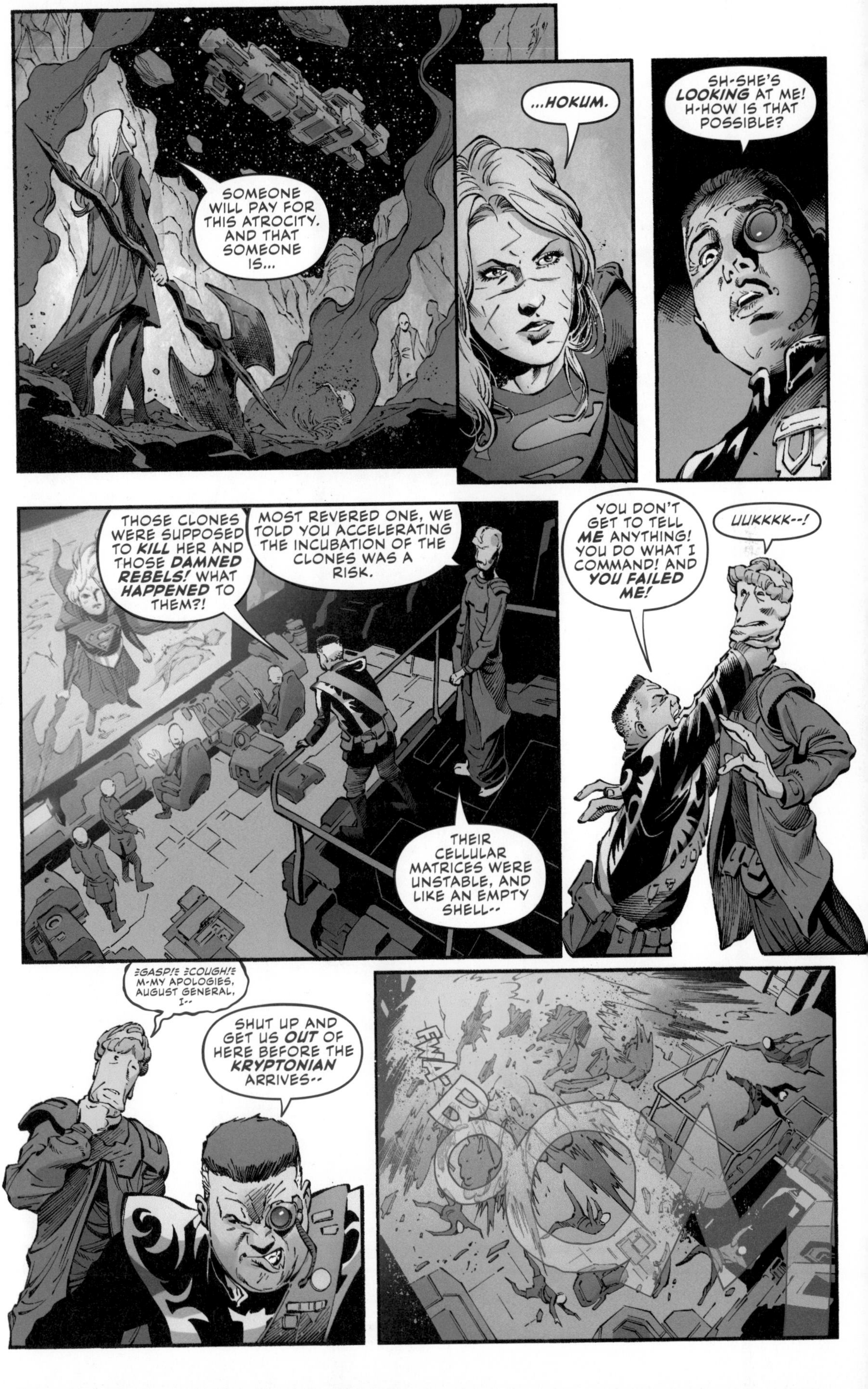
SOMEONE WILL PAY FOR THIS ATROCITY. AND THAT SOMEONE IS...
...HOKUM.
SH-SHE'S LOOKING AT ME! H-HOW IS THAT POSSIBLE?
THOSE CLONES WERE SUPPOSED TO KILL HER AND THOSE DAMNED REBELS! WHAT HAPPENED TO THEM?!
MOST REVERED ONE, WE TOLD YOU ACCELERATING THE INCUBATION OF THE CLONES WAS A RISK.
THEIR CELLULAR MATRICES WERE UNSTABLE, AND LIKE AN EMPTY SHELL--
YOU DON'T GET TO TELL ME ANYTHING! YOU DO WHAT I COMMAND! AND YOU FAILED ME!
UUKKKK--!
GASP! COUGH! M-MY APOLOGIES, AUGUST GENERAL, I--
SHUT UP AND GET US OUT OF HERE BEFORE THE KRYPTONIAN ARRIVES--

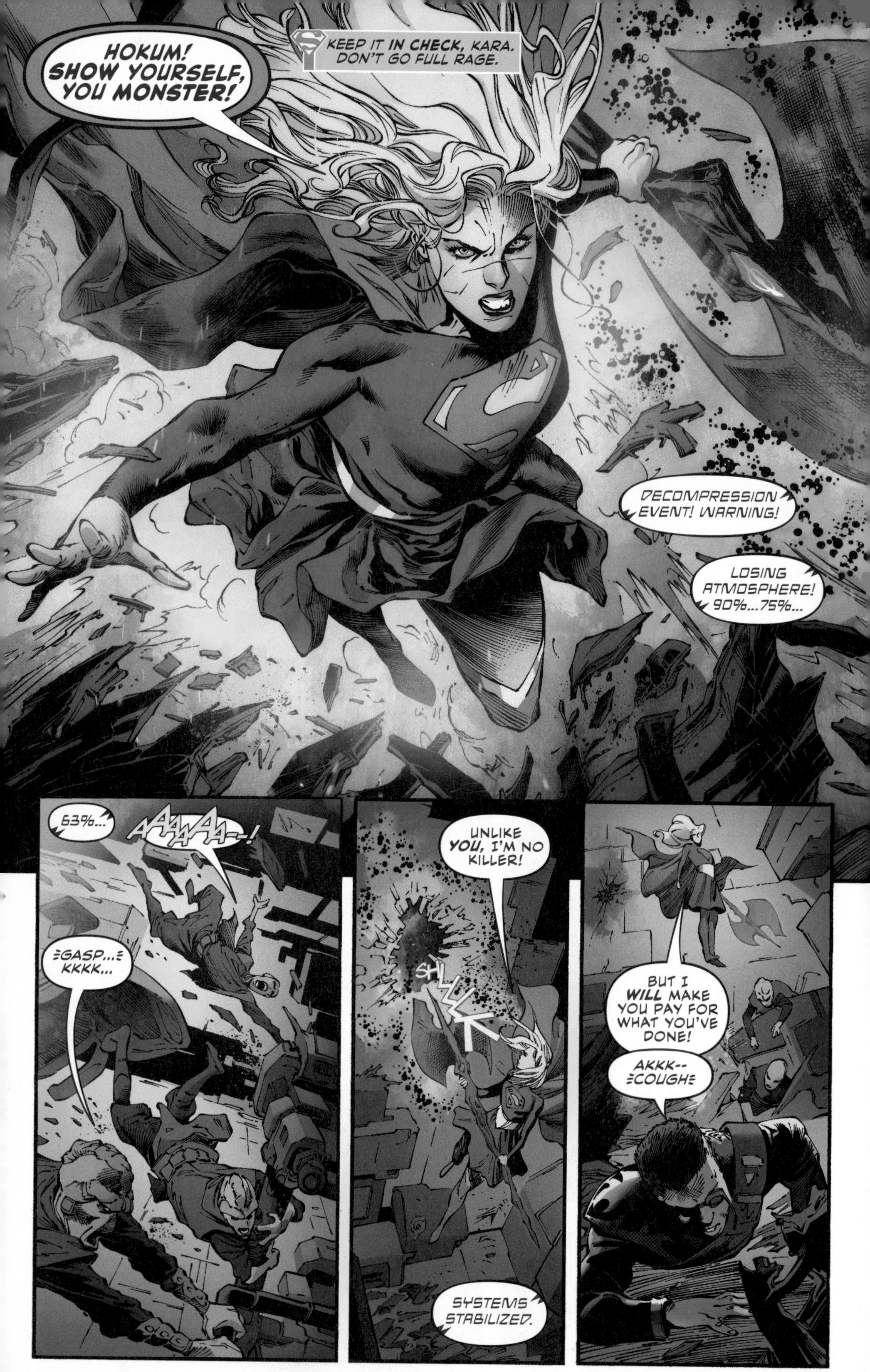
HOKUM! SHOW YOURSELF, YOU MONSTER!
KEEP IT IN CHECK, KARA. DON'T GO FULL RAGE.
DECOMPRESSION EVENT! WARNING!
LOSING ATMOSPHERE! 90%...75%...
63%...
AAAAAAA--!
GASP... KKKK...
UNLIKE YOU, I'M NO KILLER!
SHLUK
SYSTEMS STABILIZED.
BUT I WILL MAKE YOU PAY FOR WHAT YOU'VE DONE!
AKKK-- COUGH

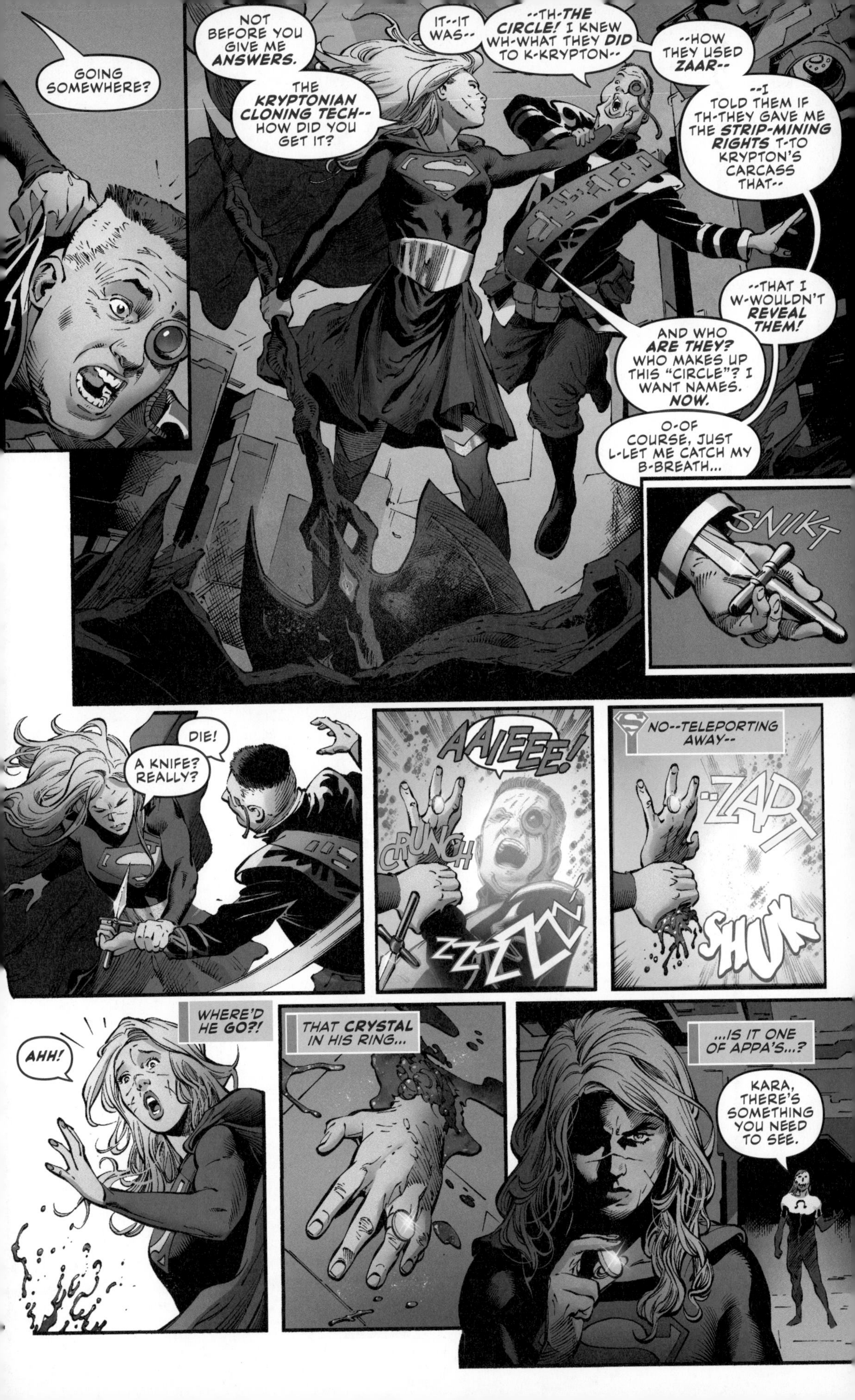
GOING SOMEWHERE?
NOT BEFORE YOU GIVE ME ANSWERS.
THE KRYPTONIAN CLONING TECH-- HOW DID YOU GET IT?
IT--IT WAS--
--TH-THE CIRCLE! I KNEW WH-WHAT THEY DID TO K-KRYPTON--
--HOW THEY USED ZAAR--
--I TOLD THEM IF TH-THEY GAVE ME THE STRIP-MINING RIGHTS T-TO KRYPTON'S CARCASS THAT--
--THAT I W-WOULDN'T REVEAL THEM!
AND WHO ARE THEY? WHO MAKES UP THIS "CIRCLE"? I WANT NAMES. NOW.
O-OF COURSE, JUST L-LET ME CATCH MY B-BREATH...
SNIKT
DIE!
A KNIFE? REALLY?
AAIEEE!
CRUNCH
ZZZZK
NO--TELEPORTING AWAY--
ZAPT
SHUK
WHERE'D HE GO?!
AHH!
THAT CRYSTAL IN HIS RING...
...IS IT ONE OF APPA'S...?
KARA, THERE'S SOMETHING YOU NEED TO SEE.

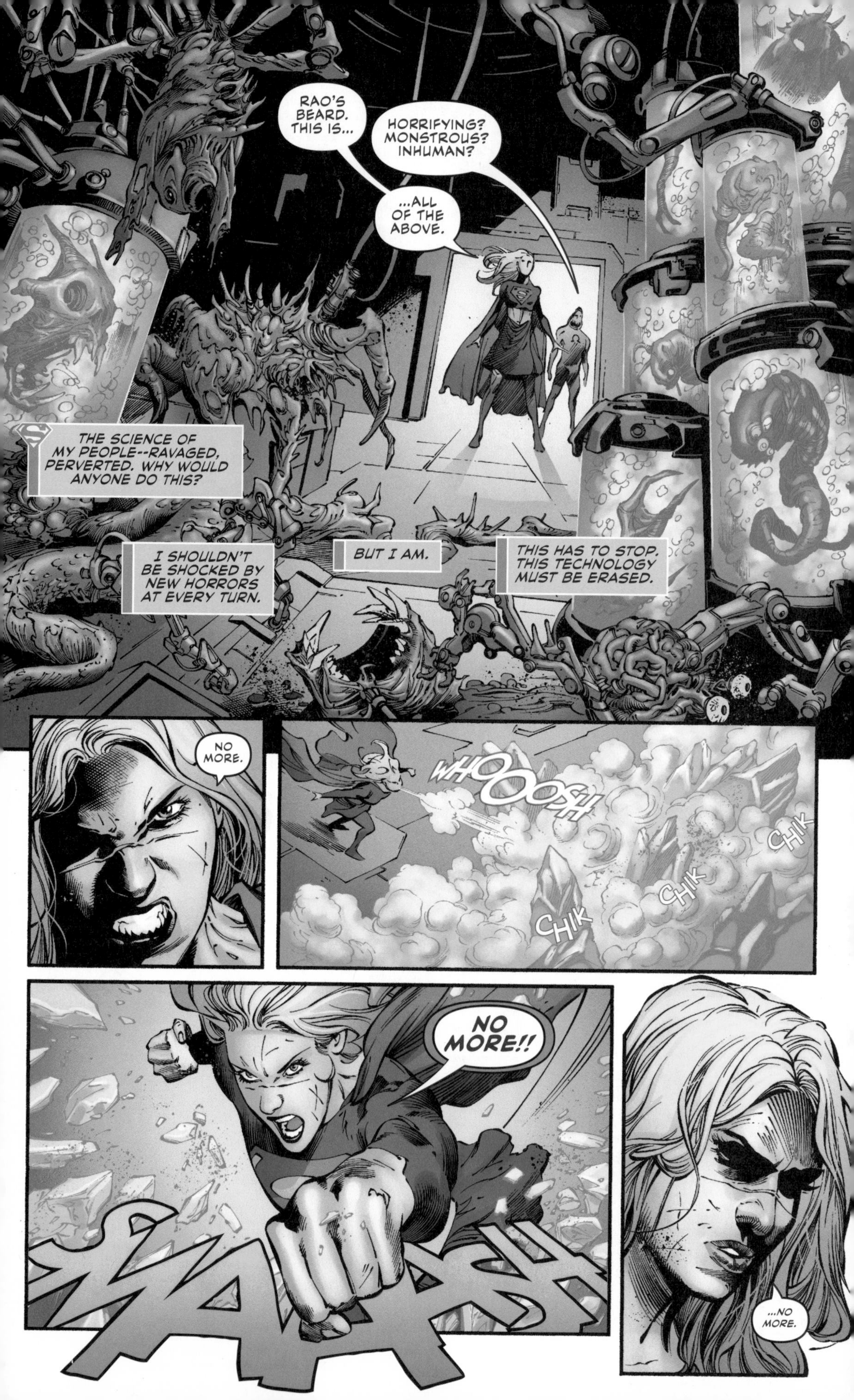
RAO'S BEARD. THIS IS...
HORRIFYING? MONSTROUS? INHUMAN?
...ALL OF THE ABOVE.
THE SCIENCE OF MY PEOPLE--RAVAGED, PERVERTED. WHY WOULD ANYONE DO THIS?
I SHOULDN'T BE SHOCKED BY NEW HORRORS AT EVERY TURN.
BUT I AM.
THIS HAS TO STOP. THIS TECHNOLOGY MUST BE ERASED.
NO MORE.
WHOOOSH
CHIK
CHIK
CHIK
NO MORE!!
...NO MORE.

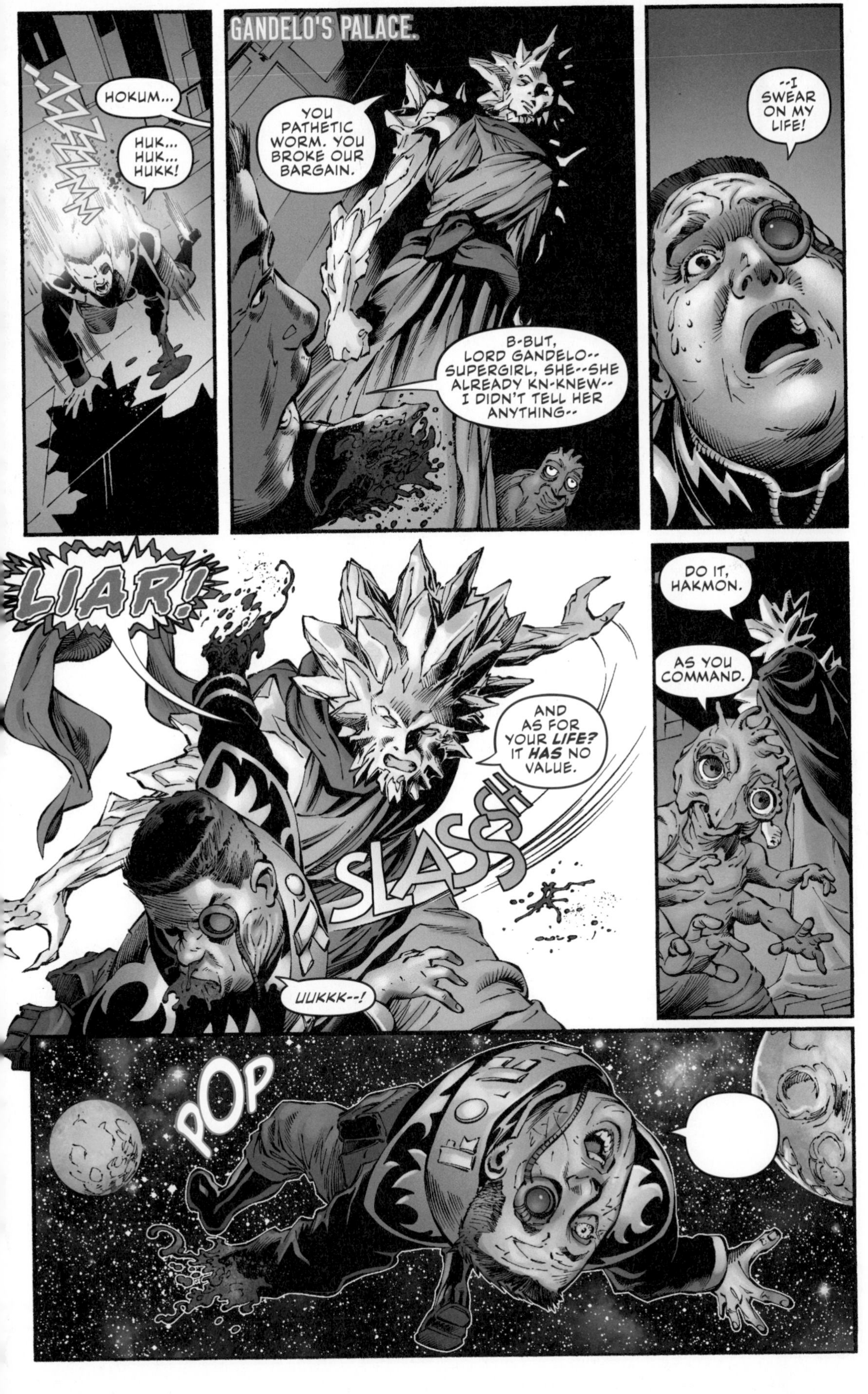
ZZZWWMM
HOKUM...
HUK... HUK... HUKK!
GANDELO'S PALACE.
YOU PATHETIC WORM. YOU BROKE OUR BARGAIN.
B-BUT, LORD GANDELO--SUPERGIRL, SHE--SHE ALREADY KN-KNEW--I DIDN'T TELL HER ANYTHING--
--I SWEAR ON MY LIFE!
LIAR!
AND AS FOR YOUR LIFE? IT HAS NO VALUE.
SLASSSH
UUKKK--!
DO IT, HAKMON.
AS YOU COMMAND.
POP

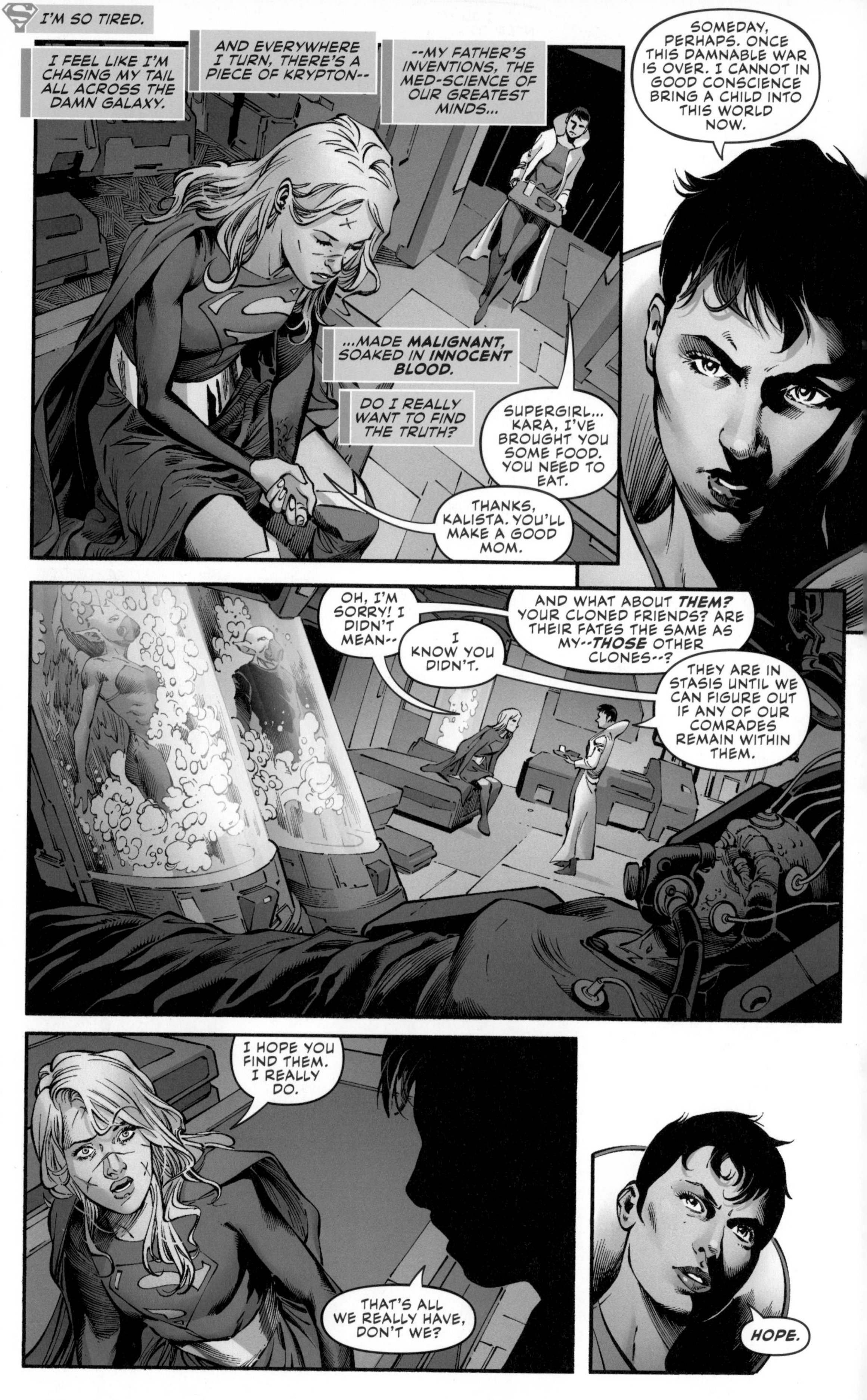
I'M SO TIRED.
I FEEL LIKE I'M CHASING MY TAIL ALL ACROSS THE DAMN GALAXY.
AND EVERYWHERE I TURN, THERE'S A PIECE OF KRYPTON--
--MY FATHER'S INVENTIONS, THE MED-SCIENCE OF OUR GREATEST MINDS...
...MADE MALIGNANT, SOAKED IN INNOCENT BLOOD.
DO I REALLY WANT TO FIND THE TRUTH?
SUPERGIRL... KARA, I'VE BROUGHT YOU SOME FOOD. YOU NEED TO EAT.
THANKS, KALISTA. YOU'LL MAKE A GOOD MOM.
SOMEDAY, PERHAPS. ONCE THIS DAMNABLE WAR IS OVER. I CANNOT IN GOOD CONSCIENCE BRING A CHILD INTO THIS WORLD NOW.
OH, I'M SORRY! I DIDN'T MEAN--
I KNOW YOU DIDN'T.
AND WHAT ABOUT THEM? YOUR CLONED FRIENDS? ARE THEIR FATES THE SAME AS MY--THOSE OTHER CLONES--?
THEY ARE IN STASIS UNTIL WE CAN FIGURE OUT IF ANY OF OUR COMRADES REMAIN WITHIN THEM.
I HOPE YOU FIND THEM. I REALLY DO.
THAT'S ALL WE REALLY HAVE, DON'T WE?
HOPE.

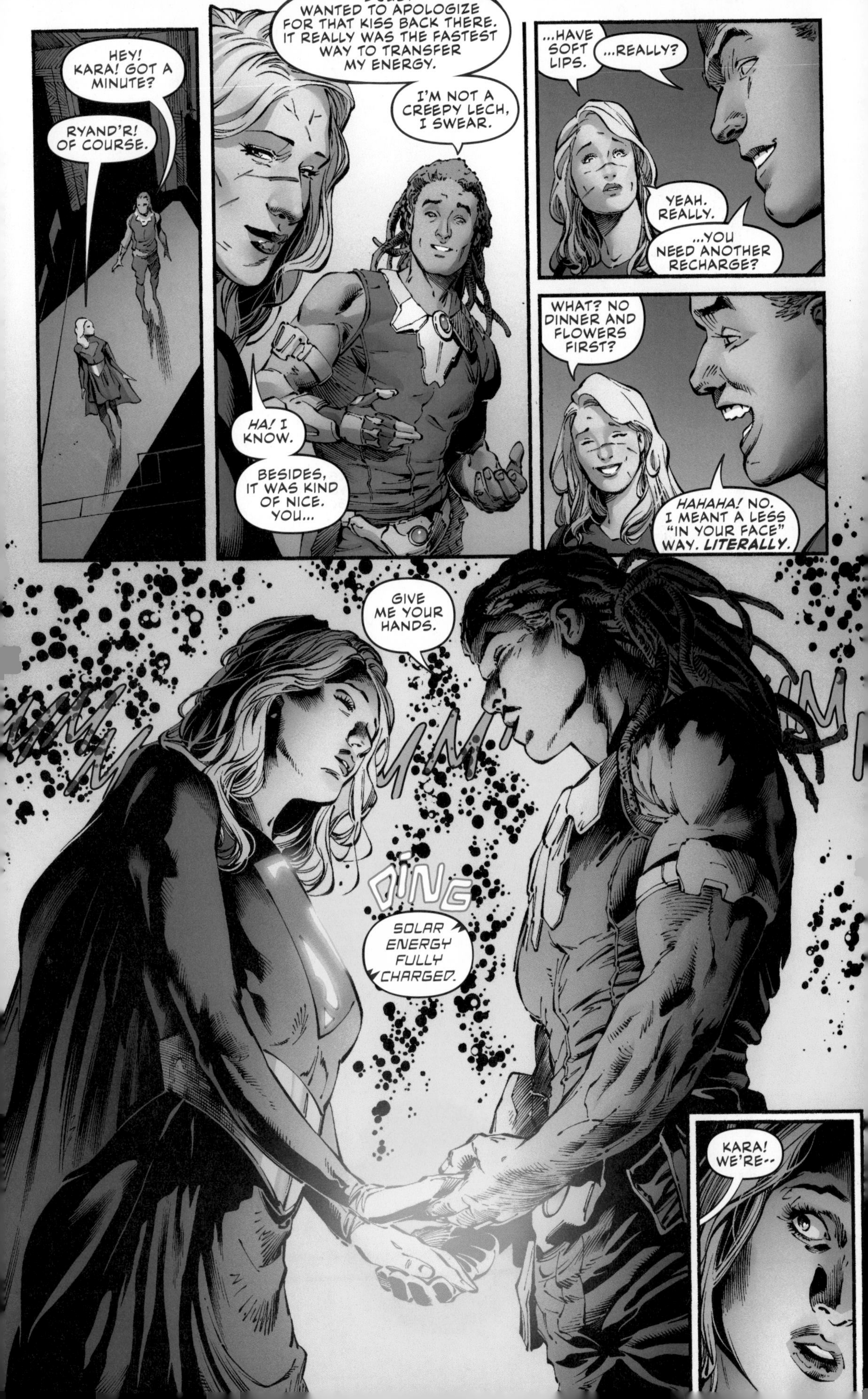
HEY! KARA! GOT A MINUTE?
RYAND'R! OF COURSE.
I JUST WANTED TO APOLOGIZE FOR THAT KISS BACK THERE. IT REALLY WAS THE FASTEST WAY TO TRANSFER MY ENERGY.
I'M NOT A CREEPY LECH, I SWEAR.
HA! I KNOW.
BESIDES, IT WAS KIND OF NICE. YOU...
...HAVE SOFT LIPS.
...REALLY?
YEAH. REALLY.
...YOU NEED ANOTHER RECHARGE?
WHAT? NO DINNER AND FLOWERS FIRST?
HAHAHA! NO. I MEANT A LESS "IN YOUR FACE" WAY. LITERALLY.
GIVE ME YOUR HANDS.
DING
SOLAR ENERGY FULLY CHARGED.
KARA! WE'RE--

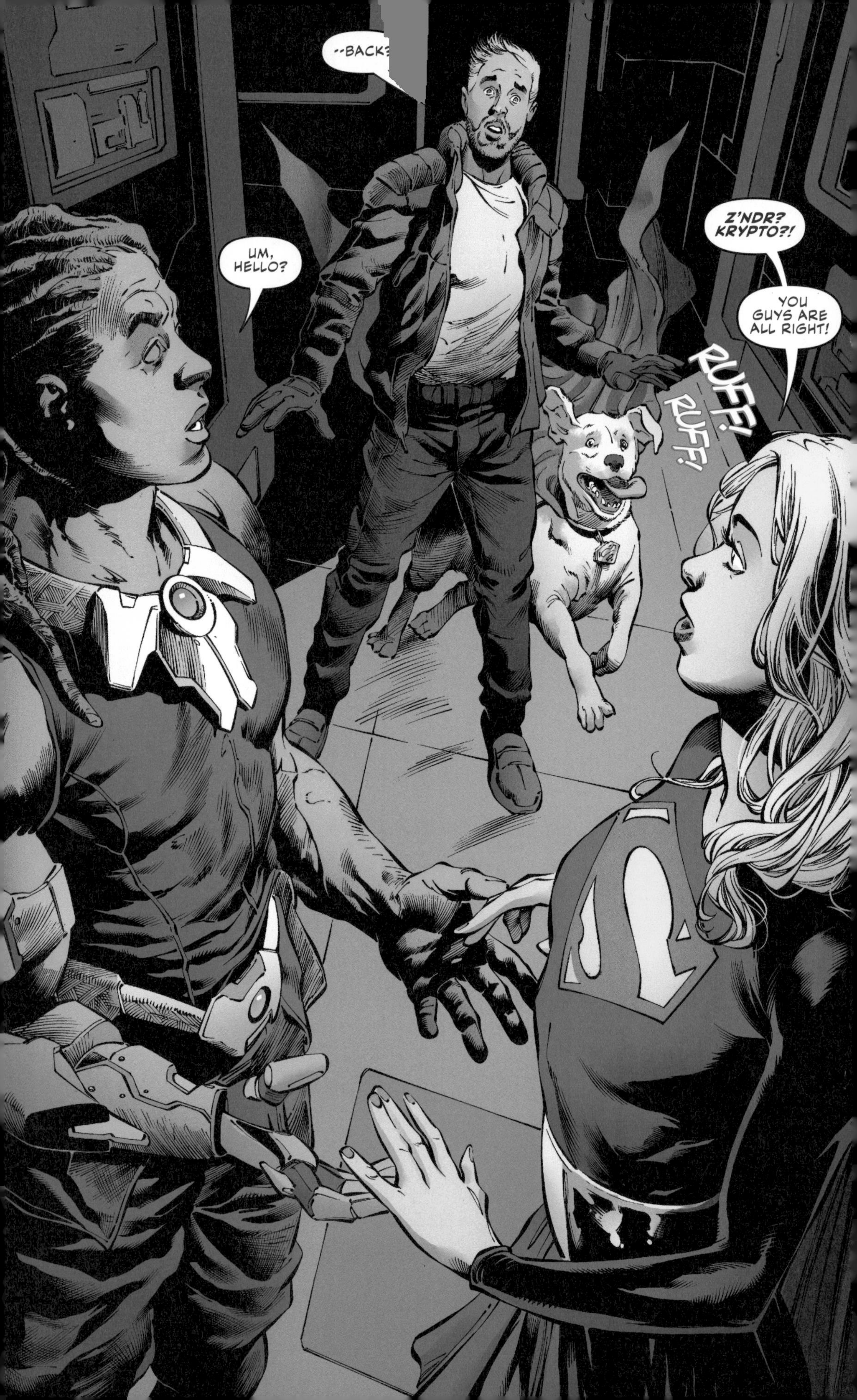
--BACK?
UM, HELLO?
Z'NDR? KRYPTO?!
YOU GUYS ARE ALL RIGHT!
RUFF!
RUFF!
RUFF!

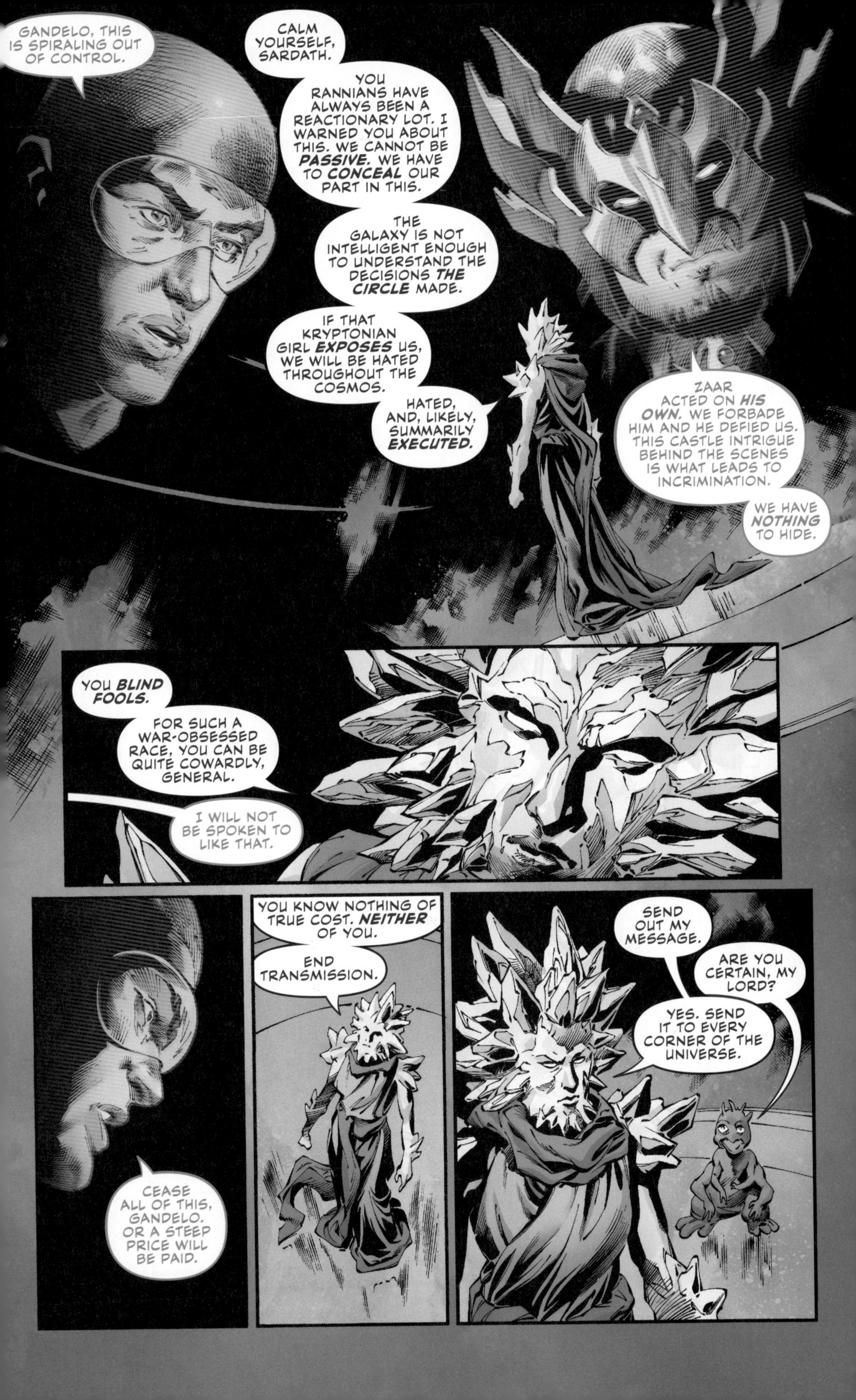
GANDELO, THIS IS SPIRALING OUT OF CONTROL.
CALM YOURSELF, SARDATH.
YOU RANNIANS HAVE ALWAYS BEEN A REACTIONARY LOT. I WARNED YOU ABOUT THIS. WE CANNOT BE PASSIVE. WE HAVE TO CONCEAL OUR PART IN THIS.
THE GALAXY IS NOT INTELLIGENT ENOUGH TO UNDERSTAND THE DECISIONS THE CIRCLE MADE.
IF THAT KRYPTONIAN GIRL EXPOSES US, WE WILL BE HATED THROUGHOUT THE COSMOS.
HATED, AND, LIKELY, SUMMARILY EXECUTED.
ZAAR ACTED ON HIS OWN. WE FORBADE HIM AND HE DEFIED US. THIS CASTLE INTRIGUE BEHIND THE SCENES IS WHAT LEADS TO INCRIMINATION.
WE HAVE NOTHING TO HIDE.
YOU BLIND FOOLS.
FOR SUCH A WAR-OBSESSED RACE, YOU CAN BE QUITE COWARDLY, GENERAL.
I WILL NOT BE SPOKEN TO LIKE THAT.
CEASE ALL OF THIS, GANDELO. OR A STEEP PRICE WILL BE PAID.
YOU KNOW NOTHING OF TRUE COST. NEITHER OF YOU.
END TRANSMISSION.
SEND OUT MY MESSAGE.
ARE YOU CERTAIN, MY LORD?
YES. SEND IT TO EVERY CORNER OF THE UNIVERSE.

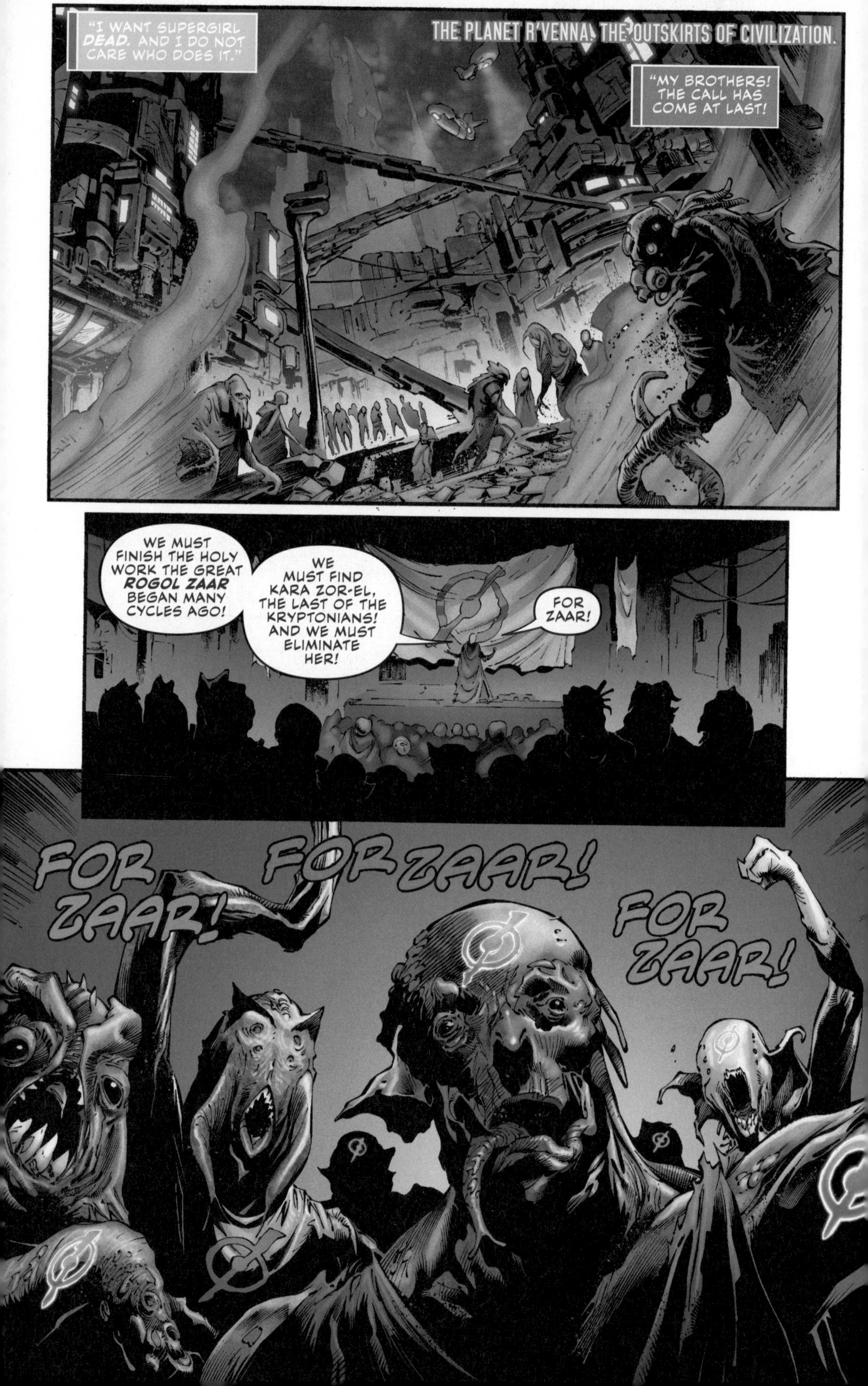
"I WANT SUPERGIRL *DEAD.* AND I DO NOT CARE WHO DOES IT."
THE PLANET R'VENNA. THE OUTSKIRTS OF CIVILIZATION.
"MY BROTHERS! THE CALL HAS COME AT LAST!
WE MUST FINISH THE HOLY WORK THE GREAT *ROGOL ZAAR* BEGAN MANY CYCLES AGO!
WE MUST FIND KARA ZOR-EL, THE LAST OF THE KRYPTONIANS! AND WE MUST ELIMINATE HER!
FOR ZAAR!
FOR ZAAR!
FOR ZAAR!
FOR ZAAR!

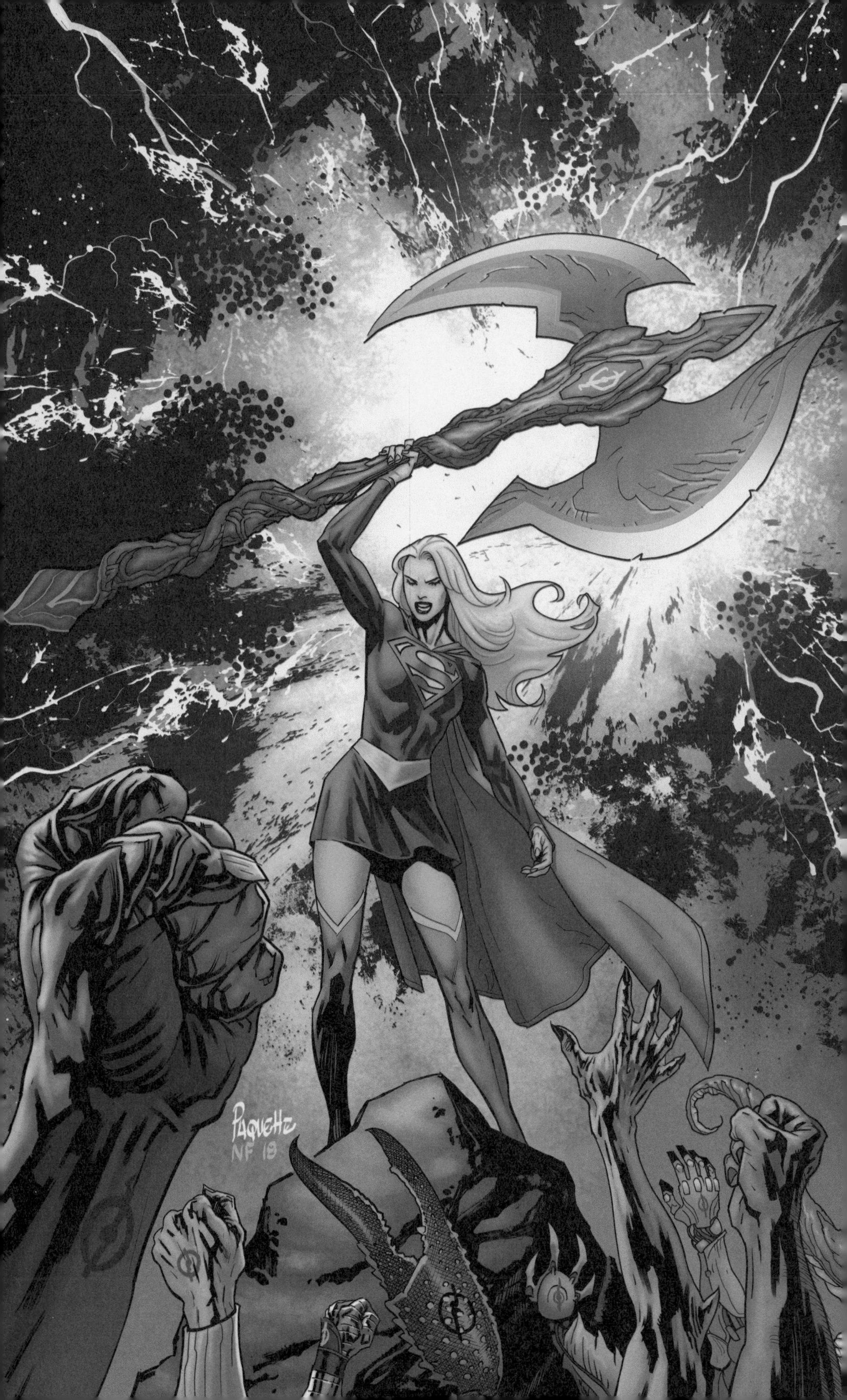
PAQUETTE
NF 18

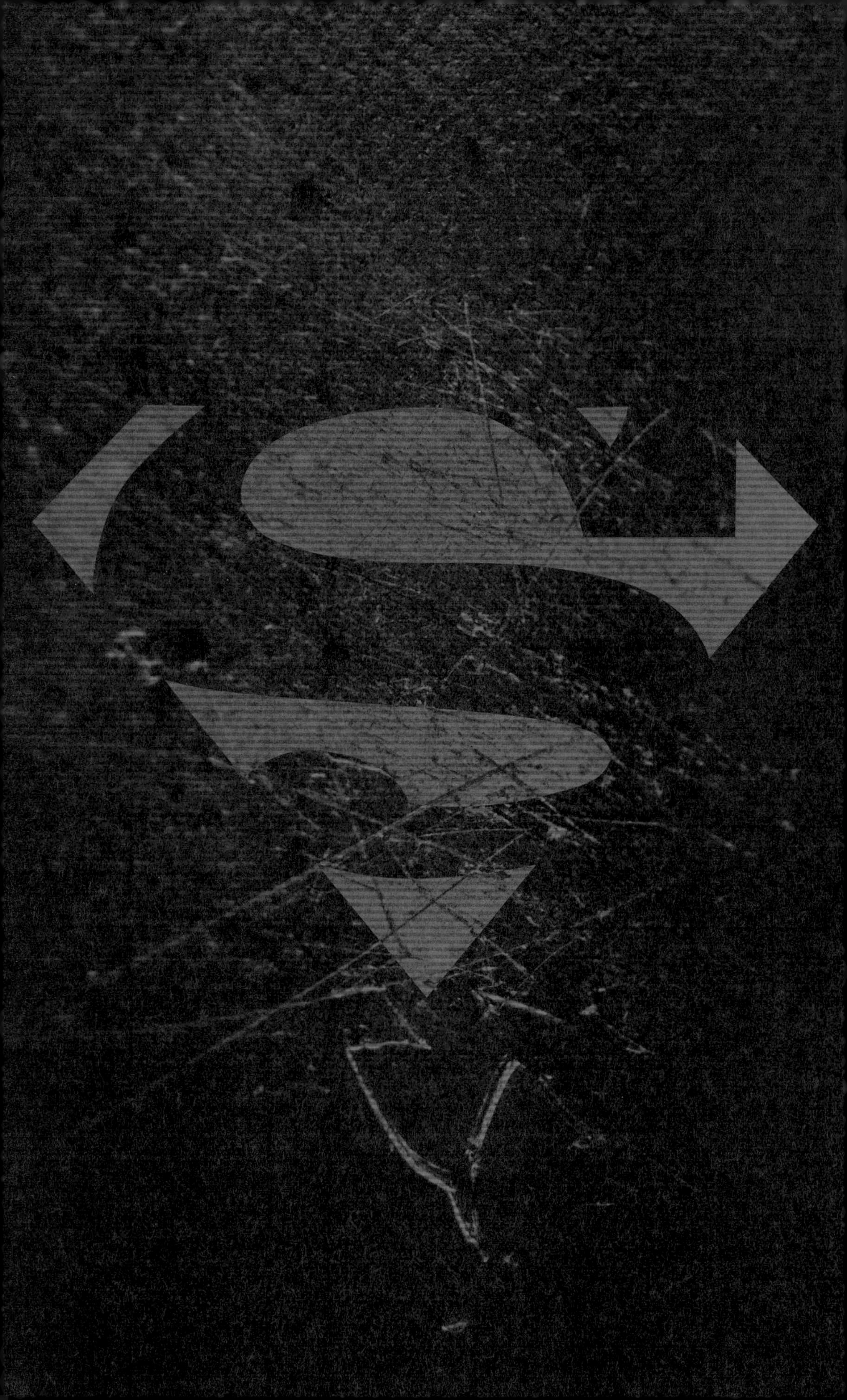

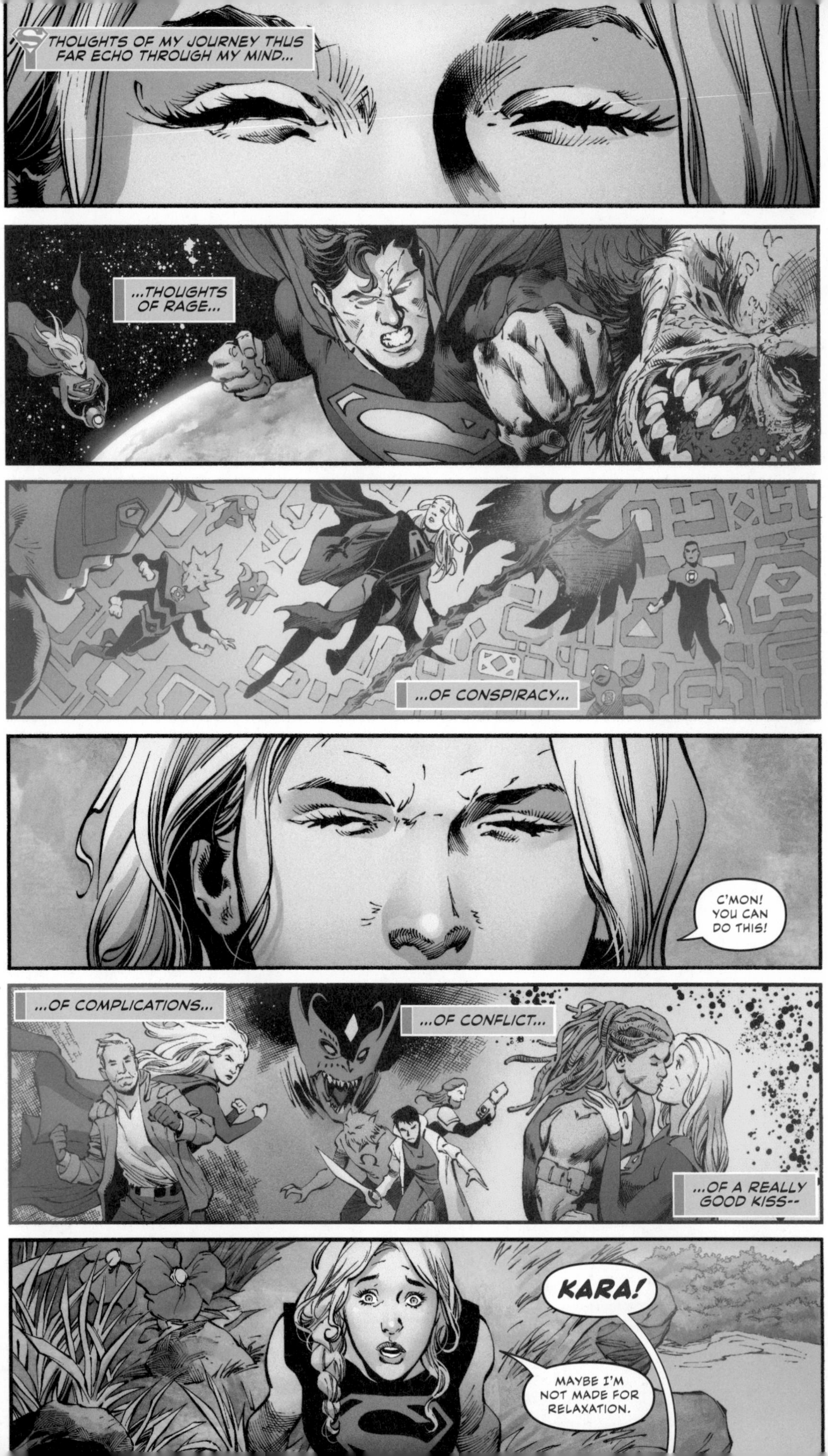
THOUGHTS OF MY JOURNEY THUS FAR ECHO THROUGH MY MIND...
...THOUGHTS OF RAGE...
...OF CONSPIRACY...
C'MON! YOU CAN DO THIS!
...OF COMPLICATIONS...
...OF CONFLICT...
...OF A REALLY GOOD KISS--
KARA!
MAYBE I'M NOT MADE FOR RELAXATION.

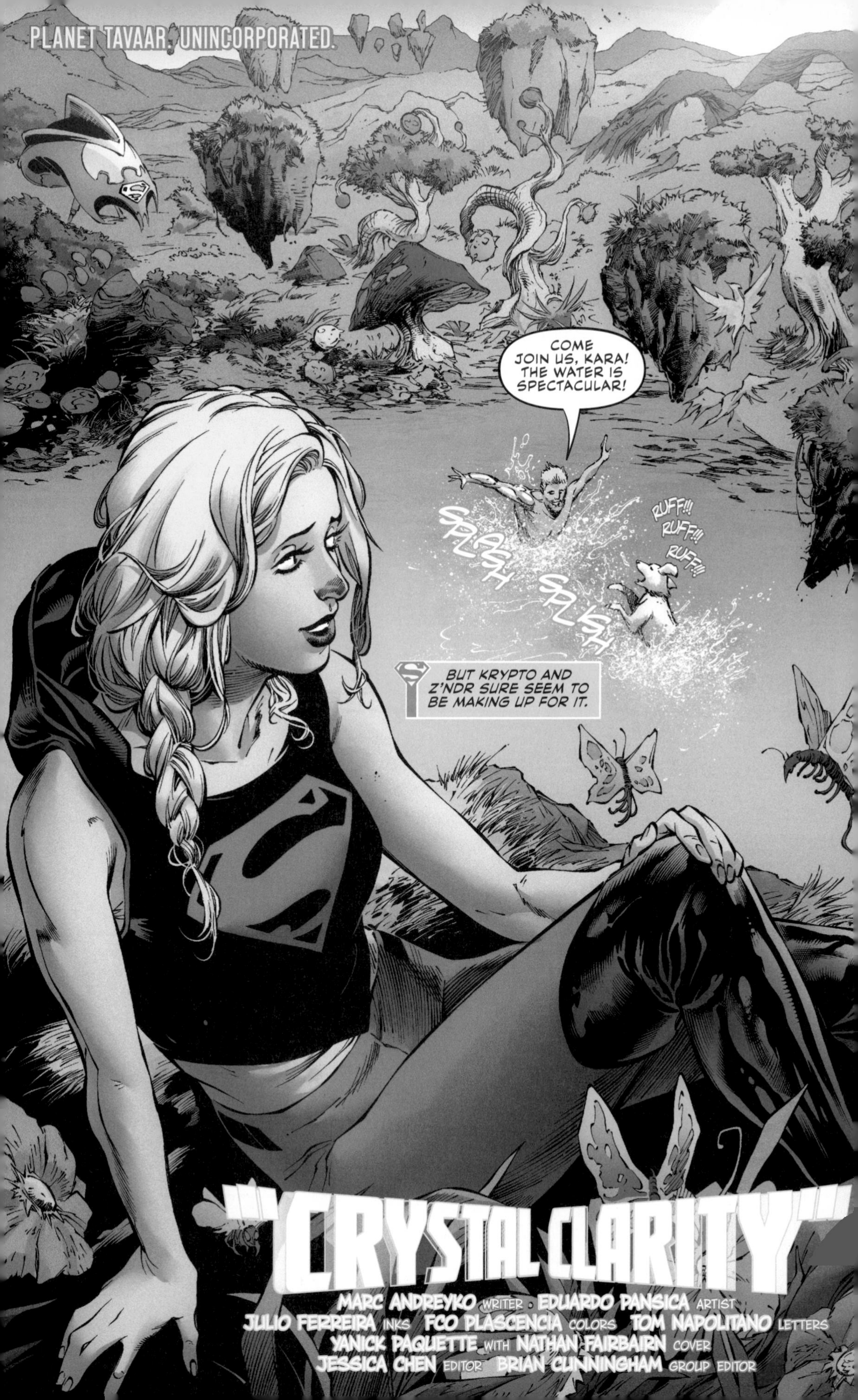

PLANET TAVAAR, UNINCORPORATED.
COME JOIN US, KARA! THE WATER IS SPECTACULAR!
SPLASH SPLASH
RUFF!!! RUFF!!! RUFF!!!
BUT KRYPTO AND Z'NDR SURE SEEM TO BE MAKING UP FOR IT.
"CRYSTAL CLARITY"
MARC ANDREYKO WRITER · EDUARDO PANSICA ARTIST
JULIO FERREIRA INKS FCO PLASCENCIA COLORS TOM NAPOLITANO LETTERS
YANICK PAQUETTE WITH NATHAN FAIRBAIRN COVER
JESSICA CHEN EDITOR BRIAN CUNNINGHAM GROUP EDITOR

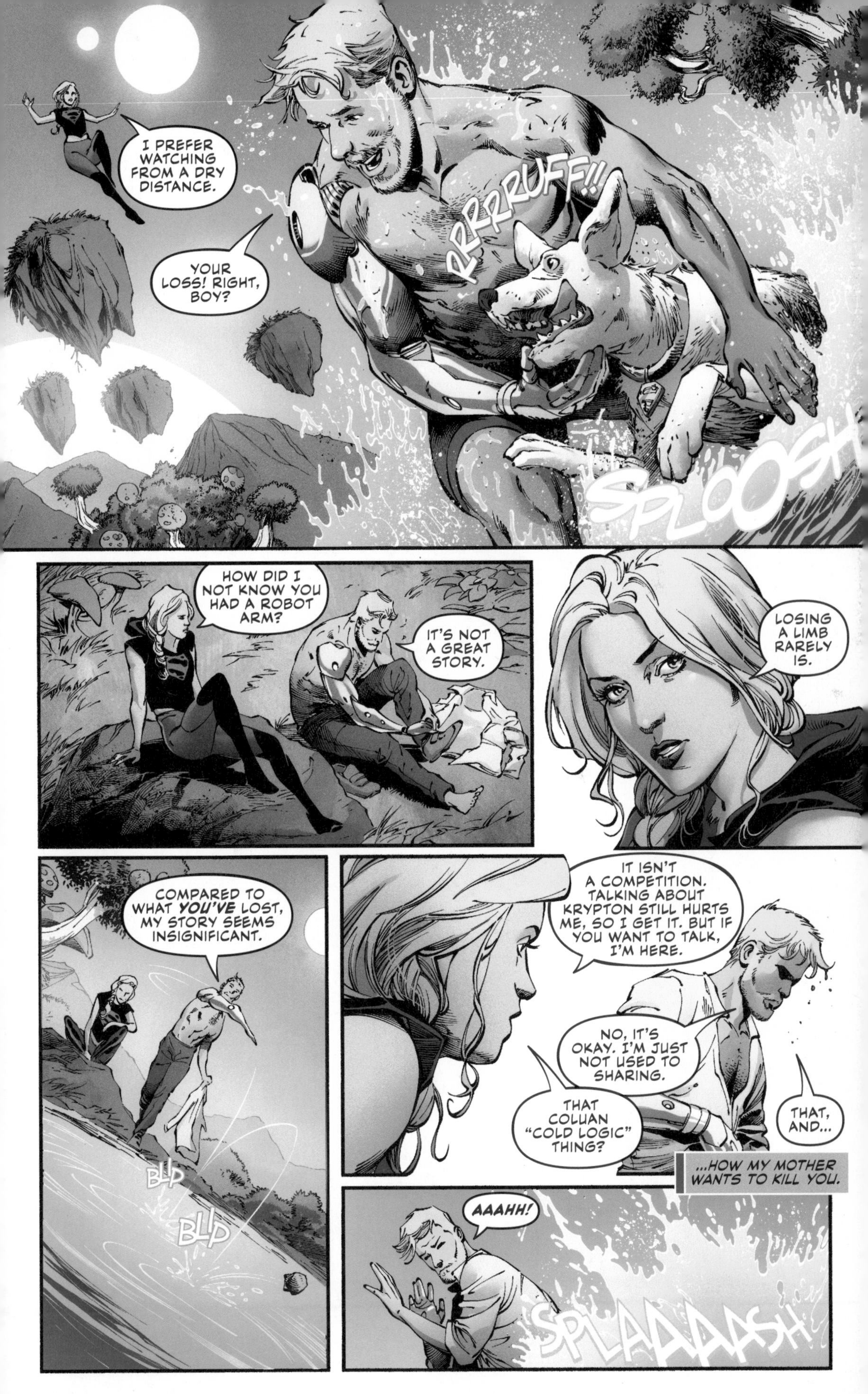
I PREFER WATCHING FROM A DRY DISTANCE.
YOUR LOSS! RIGHT, BOY?
RRRRRUFF!!
SPLOOSH
HOW DID I NOT KNOW YOU HAD A ROBOT ARM?
IT'S NOT A GREAT STORY.
LOSING A LIMB RARELY IS.
COMPARED TO WHAT YOU'VE LOST, MY STORY SEEMS INSIGNIFICANT.
BLIP
BLIP
IT ISN'T A COMPETITION. TALKING ABOUT KRYPTON STILL HURTS ME, SO I GET IT. BUT IF YOU WANT TO TALK, I'M HERE.
NO, IT'S OKAY. I'M JUST NOT USED TO SHARING.
THAT COLUAN "COLD LOGIC" THING?
THAT, AND...
...HOW MY MOTHER WANTS TO KILL YOU.
AAAHH!
SPLAAAASH

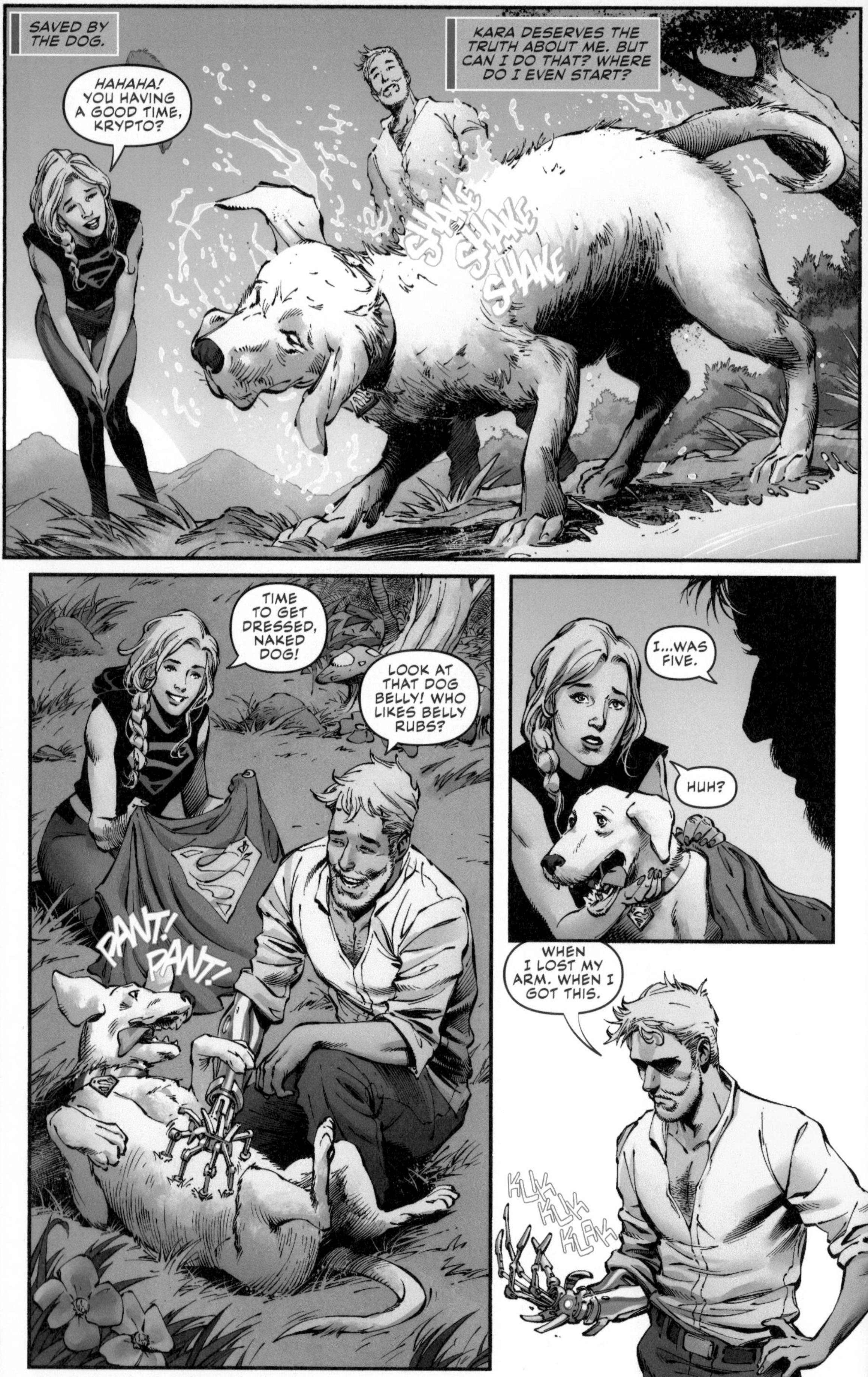
SAVED BY THE DOG.
HAHAHA! YOU HAVING A GOOD TIME, KRYPTO?
KARA DESERVES THE TRUTH ABOUT ME. BUT CAN I DO THAT? WHERE DO I EVEN START?
SHAKE SHAKE SHAKE
TIME TO GET DRESSED, NAKED DOG!
LOOK AT THAT DOG BELLY! WHO LIKES BELLY RUBS?
PANT! PANT!
I...WAS FIVE.
HUH?
WHEN I LOST MY ARM. WHEN I GOT THIS.
KLIK KLIK KLAK

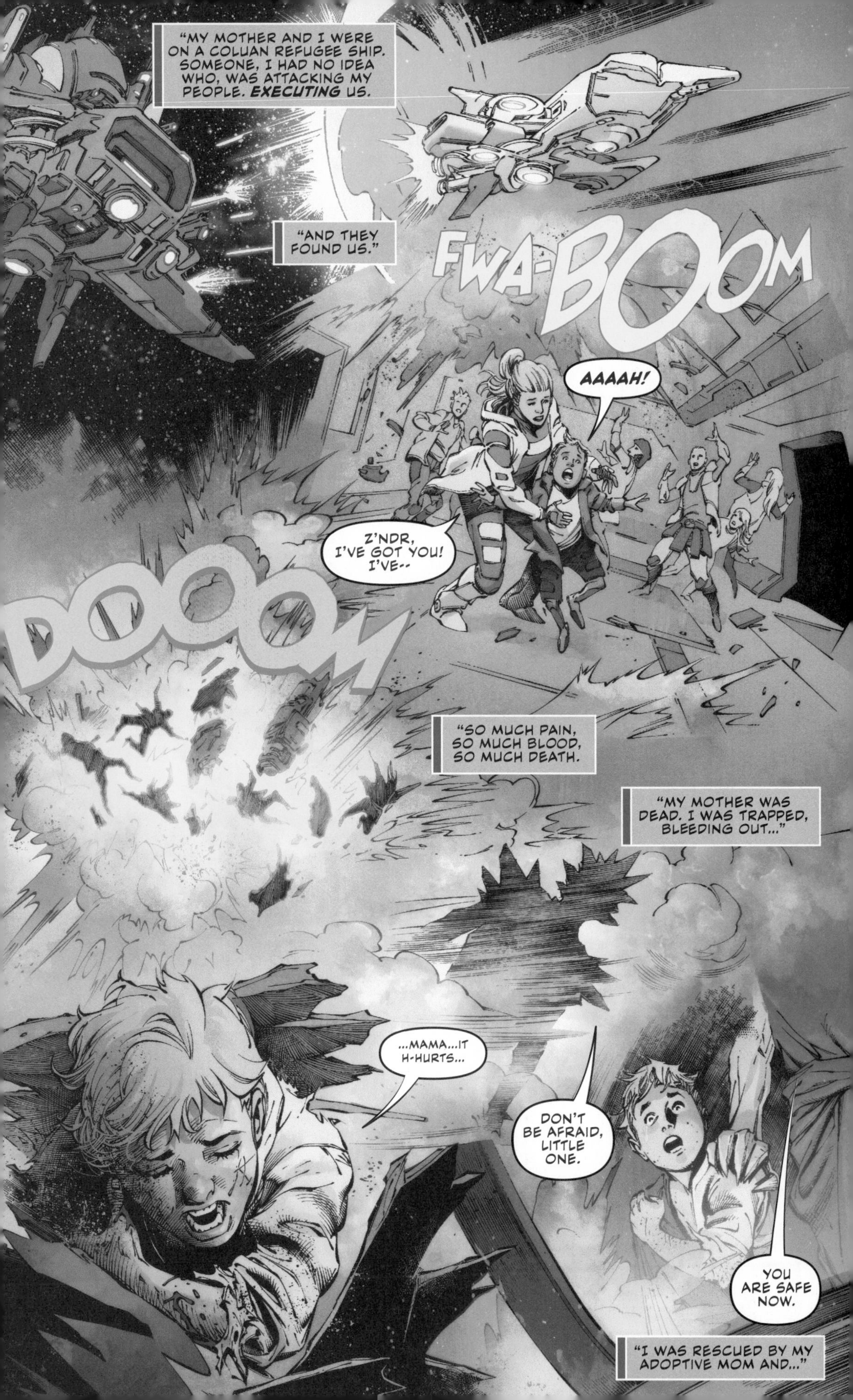
"MY MOTHER AND I WERE ON A COLUAN REFUGEE SHIP. SOMEONE, I HAD NO IDEA WHO, WAS ATTACKING MY PEOPLE. *EXECUTING* US.
"AND THEY FOUND US."
FWA-BOOM
AAAAH!
Z'NDR, I'VE GOT YOU! I'VE--
DOOOM
"SO MUCH PAIN, SO MUCH BLOOD, SO MUCH DEATH.
"MY MOTHER WAS DEAD. I WAS TRAPPED, BLEEDING OUT..."
...MAMA...IT H-HURTS...
DON'T BE AFRAID, LITTLE ONE.
YOU ARE SAFE NOW.
"I WAS RESCUED BY MY ADOPTIVE MOM AND..."

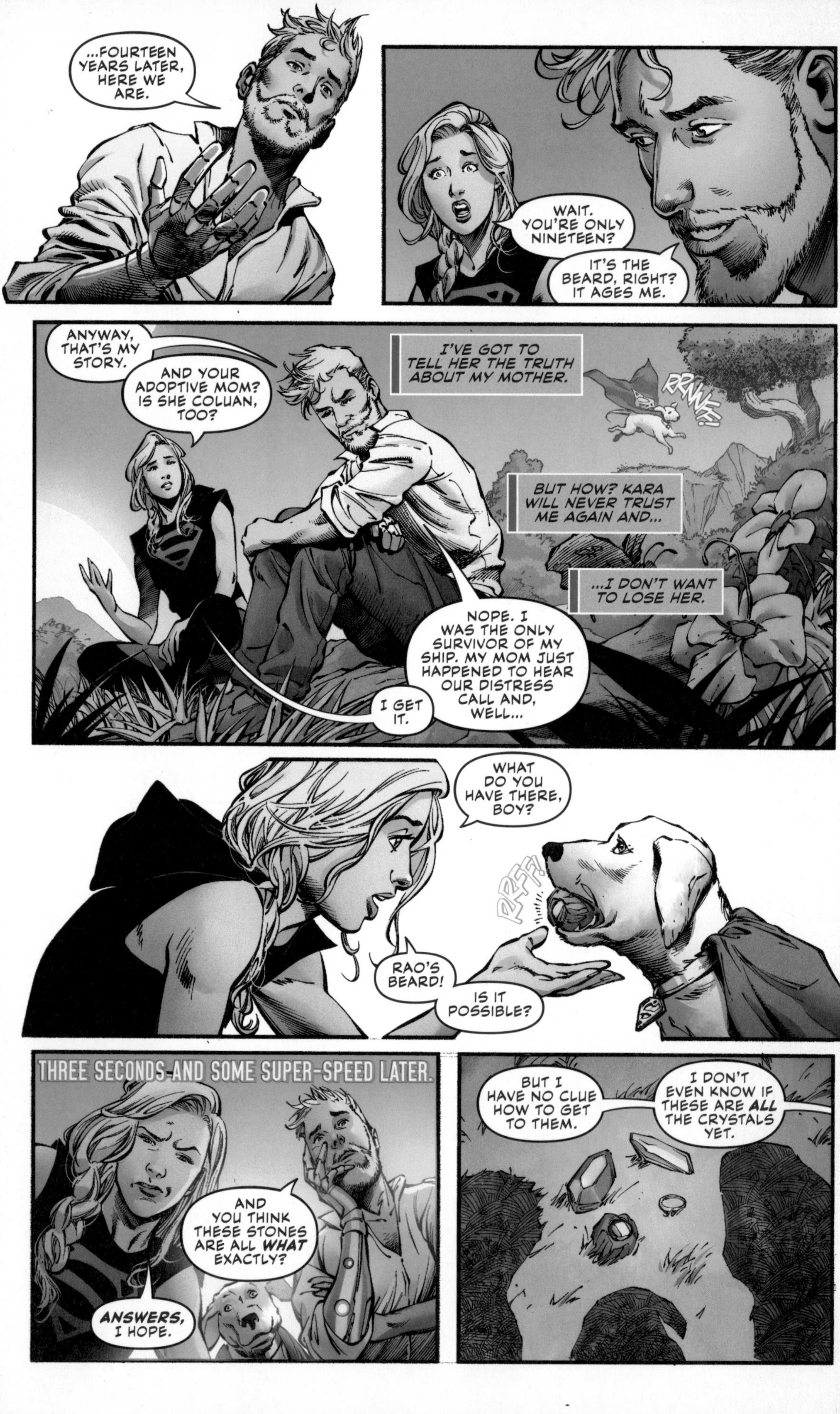
...FOURTEEN YEARS LATER, HERE WE ARE.
WAIT. YOU'RE ONLY NINETEEN?
IT'S THE BEARD, RIGHT? IT AGES ME.
ANYWAY, THAT'S MY STORY.
AND YOUR ADOPTIVE MOM? IS SHE COLUAN, TOO?
I'VE GOT TO TELL HER THE TRUTH ABOUT MY MOTHER.
RRNWF!
BUT HOW? KARA WILL NEVER TRUST ME AGAIN AND...
...I DON'T WANT TO LOSE HER.
NOPE. I WAS THE ONLY SURVIVOR OF MY SHIP. MY MOM JUST HAPPENED TO HEAR OUR DISTRESS CALL AND, WELL...
I GET IT.
WHAT DO YOU HAVE THERE, BOY?
RRFF!
RAO'S BEARD!
IS IT POSSIBLE?
THREE SECONDS-AND SOME SUPER-SPEED LATER.
AND YOU THINK THESE STONES ARE ALL *WHAT* EXACTLY?
ANSWERS, I HOPE.
BUT I HAVE NO CLUE HOW TO GET TO THEM.
I DON'T EVEN KNOW IF THESE ARE *ALL* THE CRYSTALS YET.

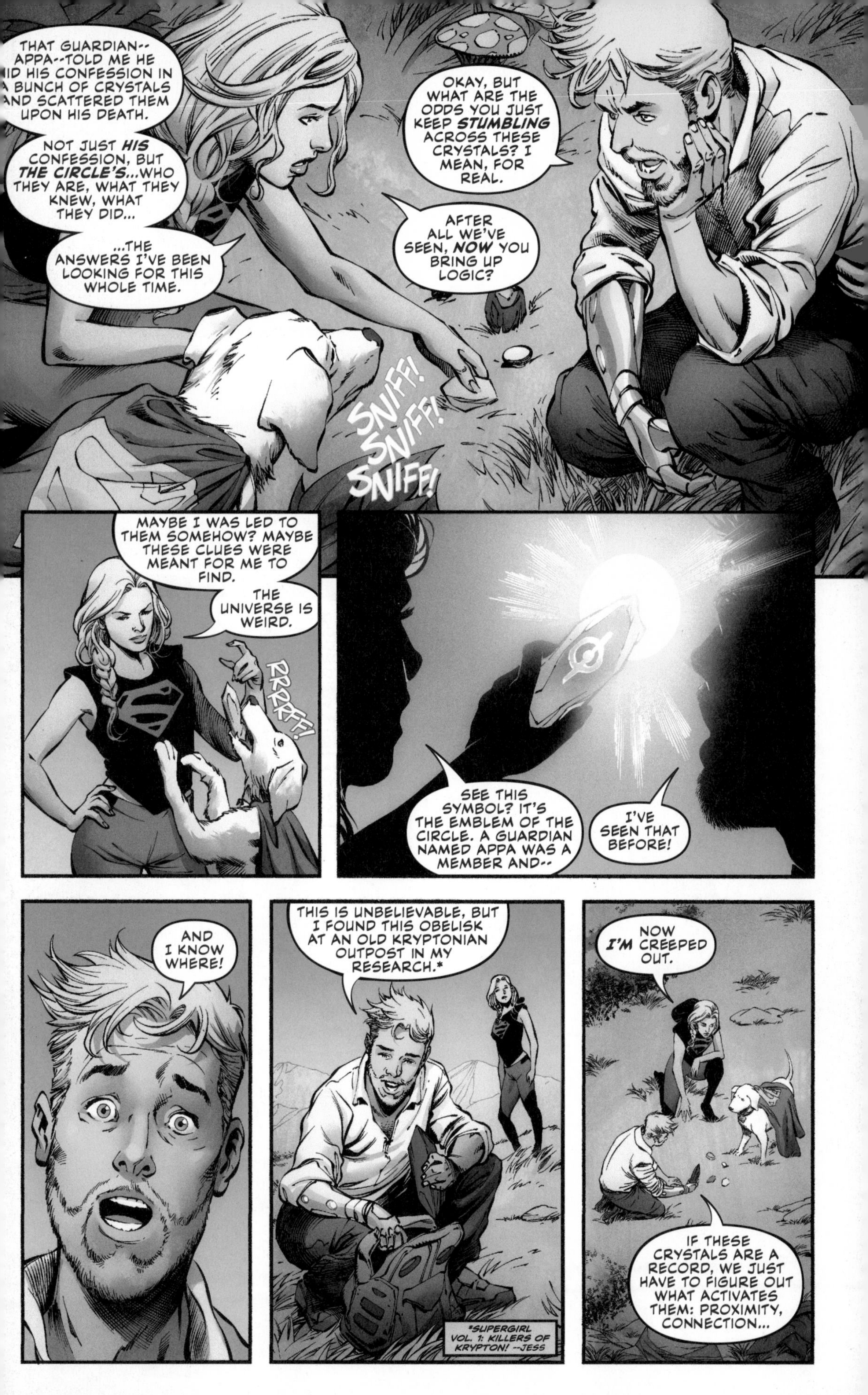
THAT GUARDIAN--APPA--TOLD ME HE HID HIS CONFESSION IN A BUNCH OF CRYSTALS AND SCATTERED THEM UPON HIS DEATH.
NOT JUST HIS CONFESSION, BUT THE CIRCLE'S...WHO THEY ARE, WHAT THEY KNEW, WHAT THEY DID...
...THE ANSWERS I'VE BEEN LOOKING FOR THIS WHOLE TIME.
OKAY, BUT WHAT ARE THE ODDS YOU JUST KEEP STUMBLING ACROSS THESE CRYSTALS? I MEAN, FOR REAL.
AFTER ALL WE'VE SEEN, NOW YOU BRING UP LOGIC?
SNIFF! SNIFF! SNIFF!
MAYBE I WAS LED TO THEM SOMEHOW? MAYBE THESE CLUES WERE MEANT FOR ME TO FIND.
THE UNIVERSE IS WEIRD.
RRRRFF!
SEE THIS SYMBOL? IT'S THE EMBLEM OF THE CIRCLE. A GUARDIAN NAMED APPA WAS A MEMBER AND--
I'VE SEEN THAT BEFORE!
AND I KNOW WHERE!
THIS IS UNBELIEVABLE, BUT I FOUND THIS OBELISK AT AN OLD KRYPTONIAN OUTPOST IN MY RESEARCH.*
*SUPERGIRL VOL. 1: KILLERS OF KRYPTON! --JESS
NOW I'M CREEPED OUT.
IF THESE CRYSTALS ARE A RECORD, WE JUST HAVE TO FIGURE OUT WHAT ACTIVATES THEM: PROXIMITY, CONNECTION...

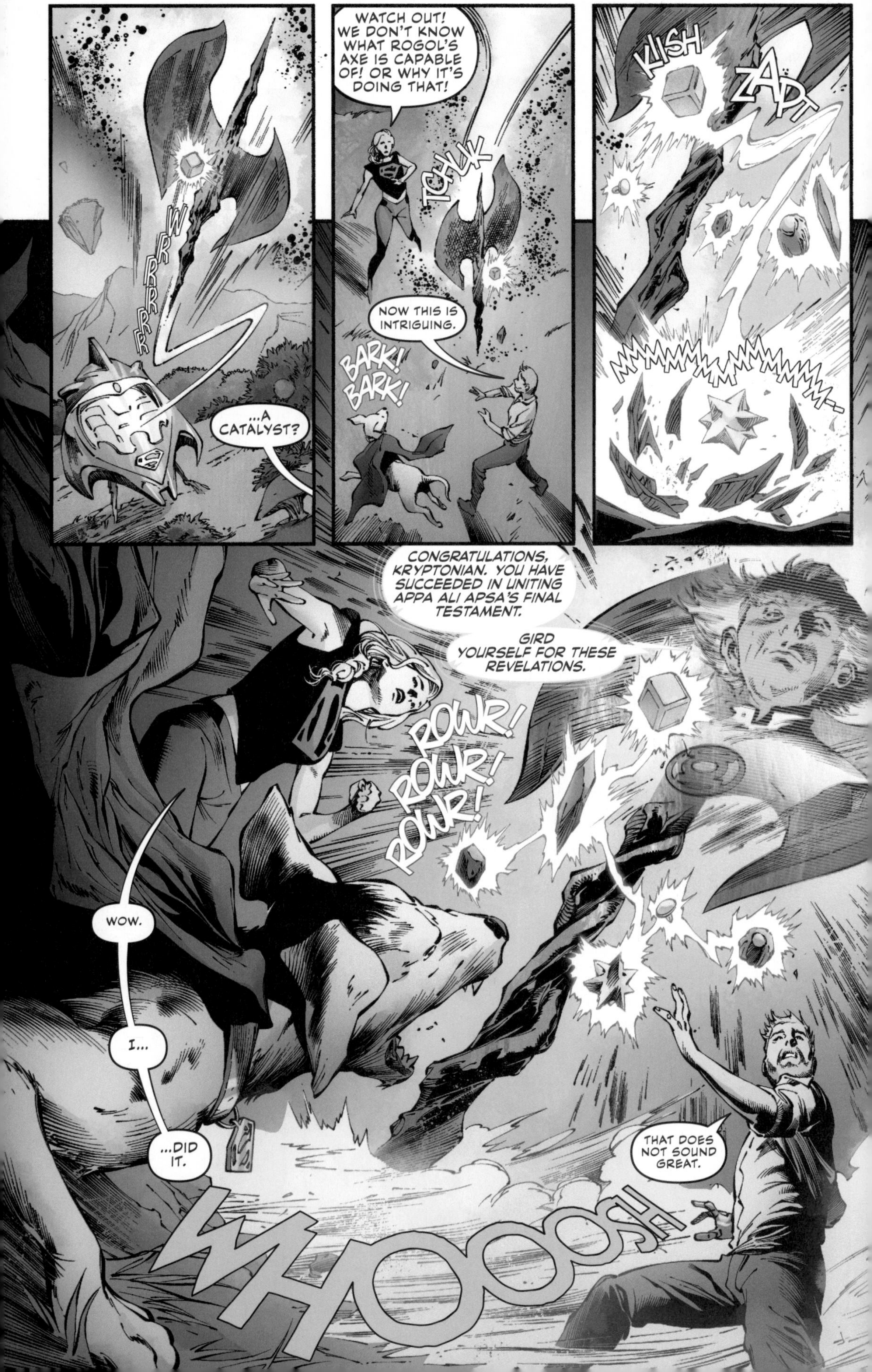
WRRRRRRRRR
...A CATALYST?
WATCH OUT! WE DON'T KNOW WHAT ROGOL'S AXE IS CAPABLE OF! OR WHY IT'S DOING THAT!
TCHUK
NOW THIS IS INTRIGUING.
BARK! BARK!
KLISH
ZAPT
MMMMMMMMMMMMMMMM--
CONGRATULATIONS, KRYPTONIAN. YOU HAVE SUCCEEDED IN UNITING APPA ALI APSA'S FINAL TESTAMENT.
GIRD YOURSELF FOR THESE REVELATIONS.
ROWR! ROWR! ROWR!
WOW.
I...
...DID IT.
THAT DOES NOT SOUND GREAT.
WHOOOSH

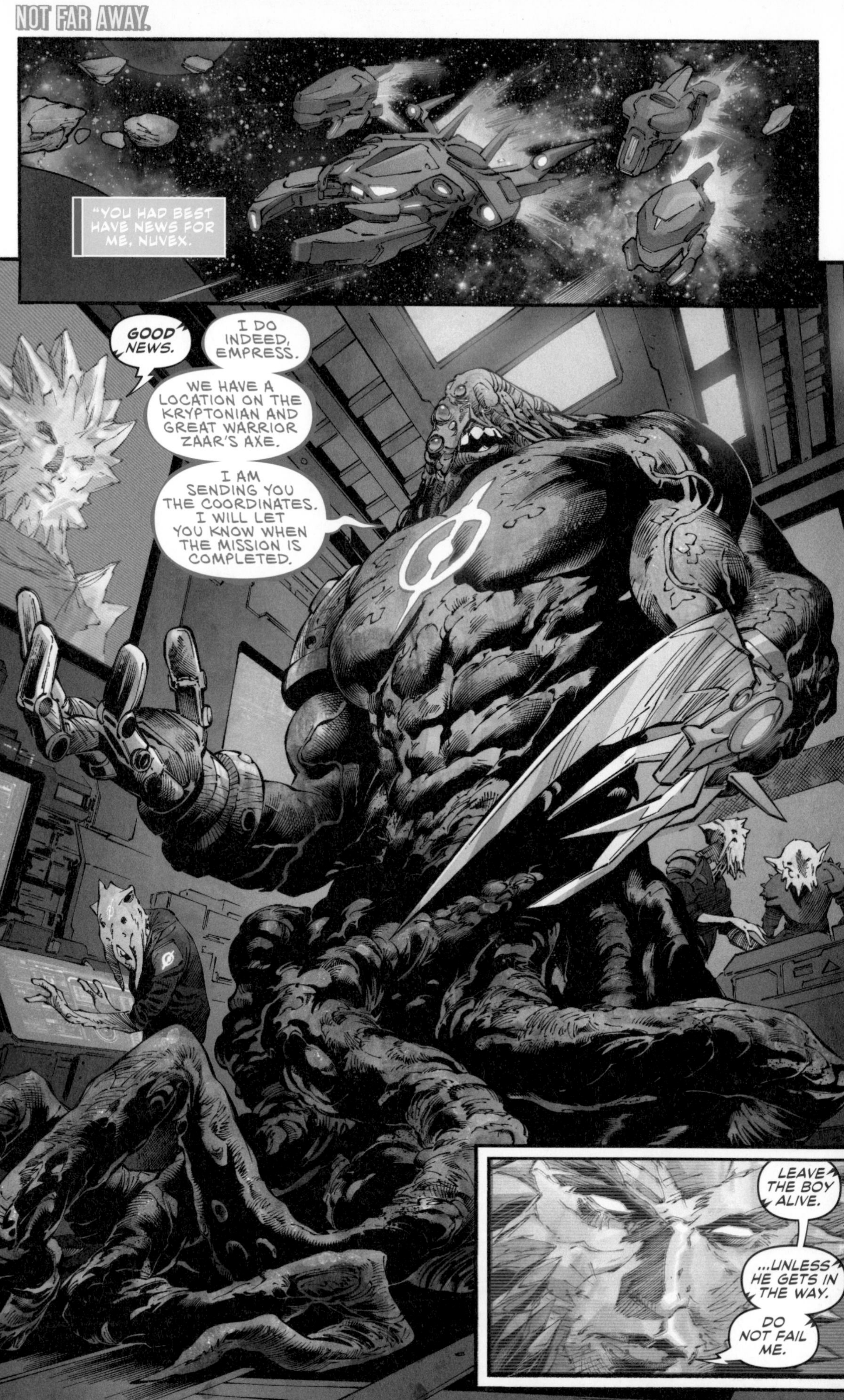
NOT FAR AWAY.
"YOU HAD BEST HAVE NEWS FOR ME, NUVEX.
GOOD NEWS.
I DO INDEED, EMPRESS.
WE HAVE A LOCATION ON THE KRYPTONIAN AND GREAT WARRIOR ZAAR'S AXE.
I AM SENDING YOU THE COORDINATES. I WILL LET YOU KNOW WHEN THE MISSION IS COMPLETED.
LEAVE THE BOY ALIVE.
...UNLESS HE GETS IN THE WAY.
DO NOT FAIL ME.

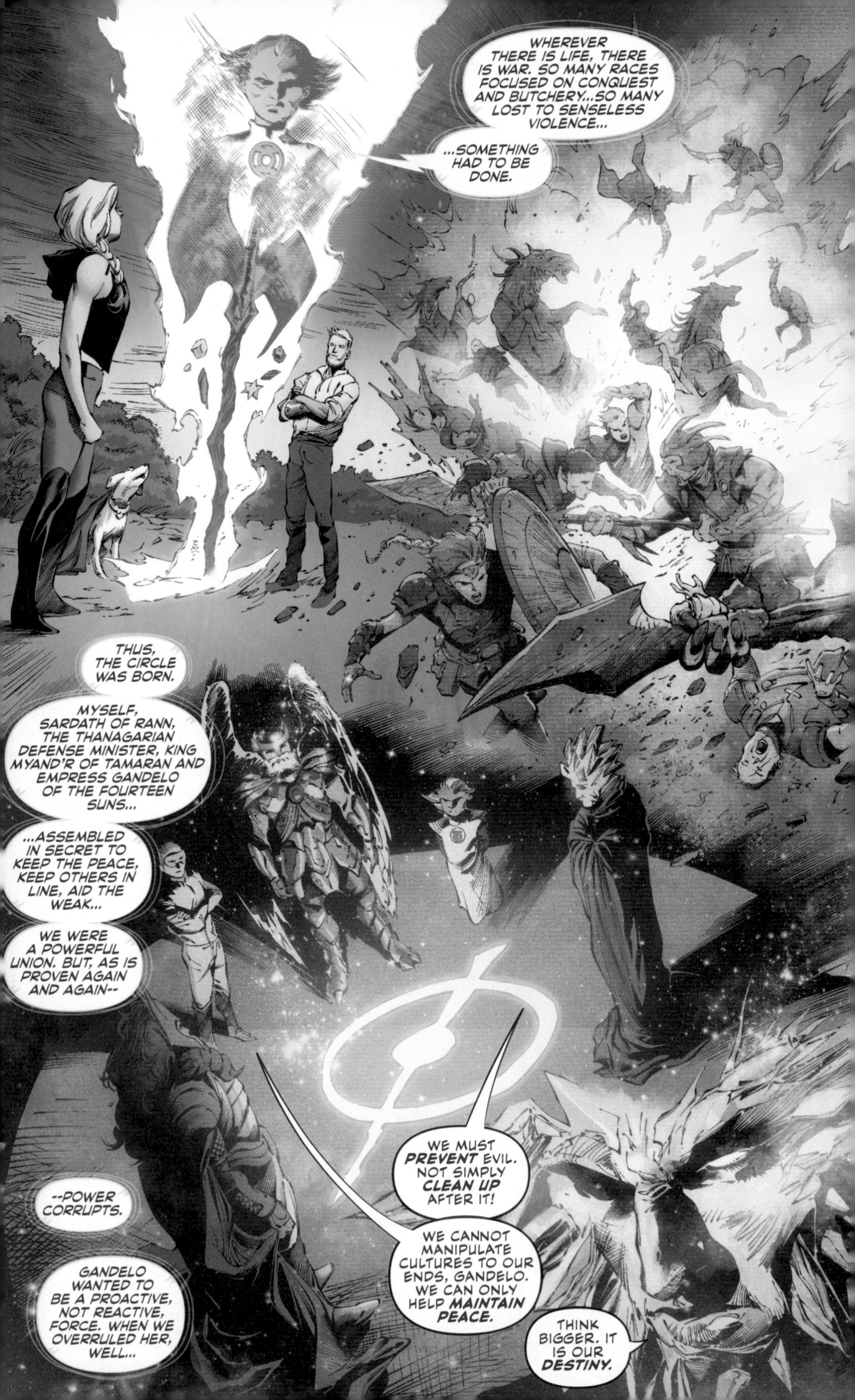
WHEREVER THERE IS LIFE, THERE IS WAR. SO MANY RACES FOCUSED ON CONQUEST AND BUTCHERY...SO MANY LOST TO SENSELESS VIOLENCE...
...SOMETHING HAD TO BE DONE.
THUS, THE CIRCLE WAS BORN.
MYSELF, SARDATH OF RANN, THE THANAGARIAN DEFENSE MINISTER, KING MYAND'R OF TAMARAN AND EMPRESS GANDELO OF THE FOURTEEN SUNS...
...ASSEMBLED IN SECRET TO KEEP THE PEACE, KEEP OTHERS IN LINE, AID THE WEAK...
WE WERE A POWERFUL UNION. BUT, AS IS PROVEN AGAIN AND AGAIN--
--POWER CORRUPTS.
GANDELO WANTED TO BE A PROACTIVE, NOT REACTIVE, FORCE. WHEN WE OVERRULED HER, WELL...
WE MUST PREVENT EVIL. NOT SIMPLY CLEAN UP AFTER IT!
WE CANNOT MANIPULATE CULTURES TO OUR ENDS, GANDELO. WE CAN ONLY HELP MAINTAIN PEACE.
THINK BIGGER. IT IS OUR DESTINY.

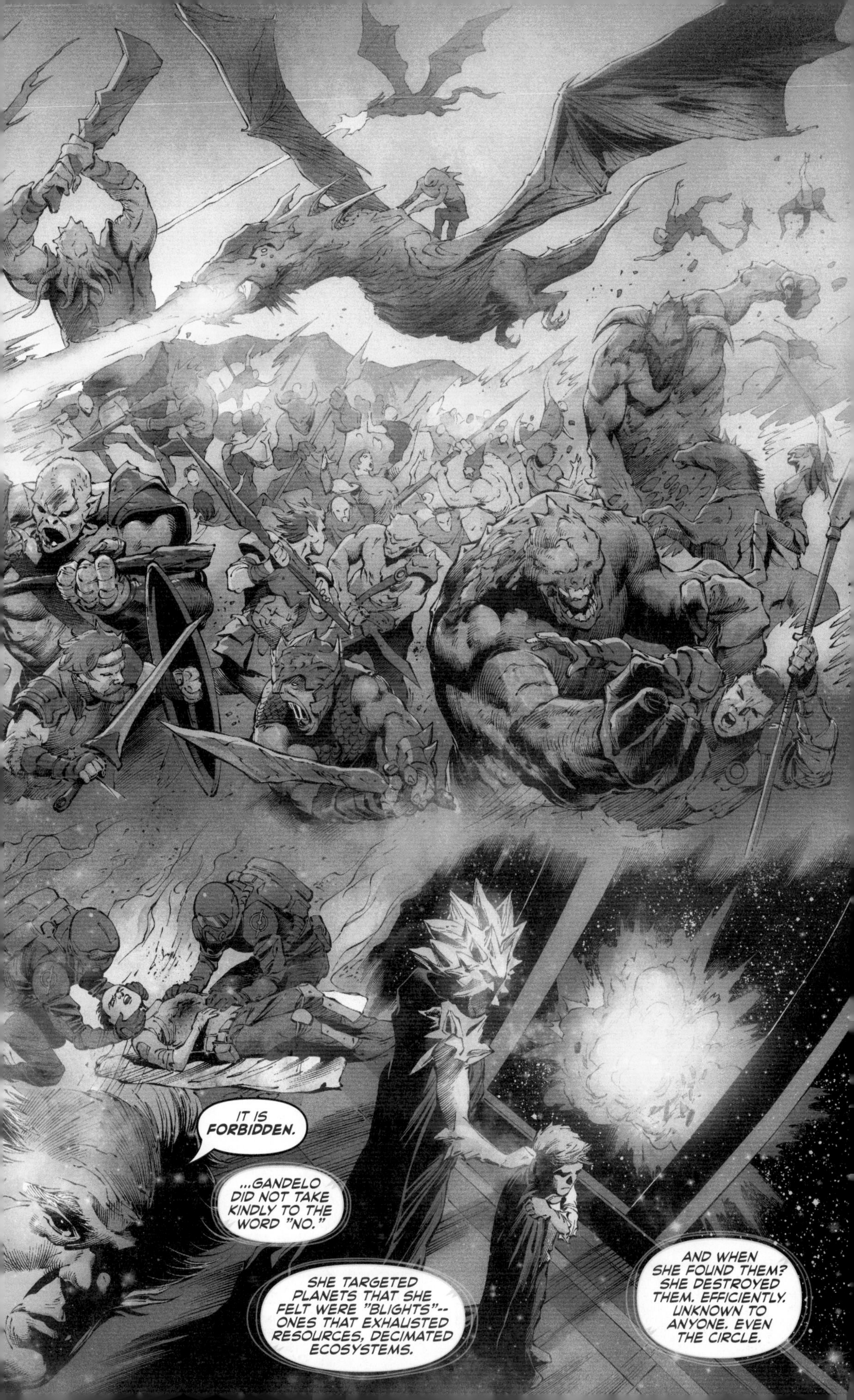
IT IS FORBIDDEN.
...GANDELO DID NOT TAKE KINDLY TO THE WORD "NO."
SHE TARGETED PLANETS THAT SHE FELT WERE "BLIGHTS"-- ONES THAT EXHAUSTED RESOURCES, DECIMATED ECOSYSTEMS.
AND WHEN SHE FOUND THEM? SHE DESTROYED THEM. EFFICIENTLY. UNKNOWN TO ANYONE. EVEN THE CIRCLE.

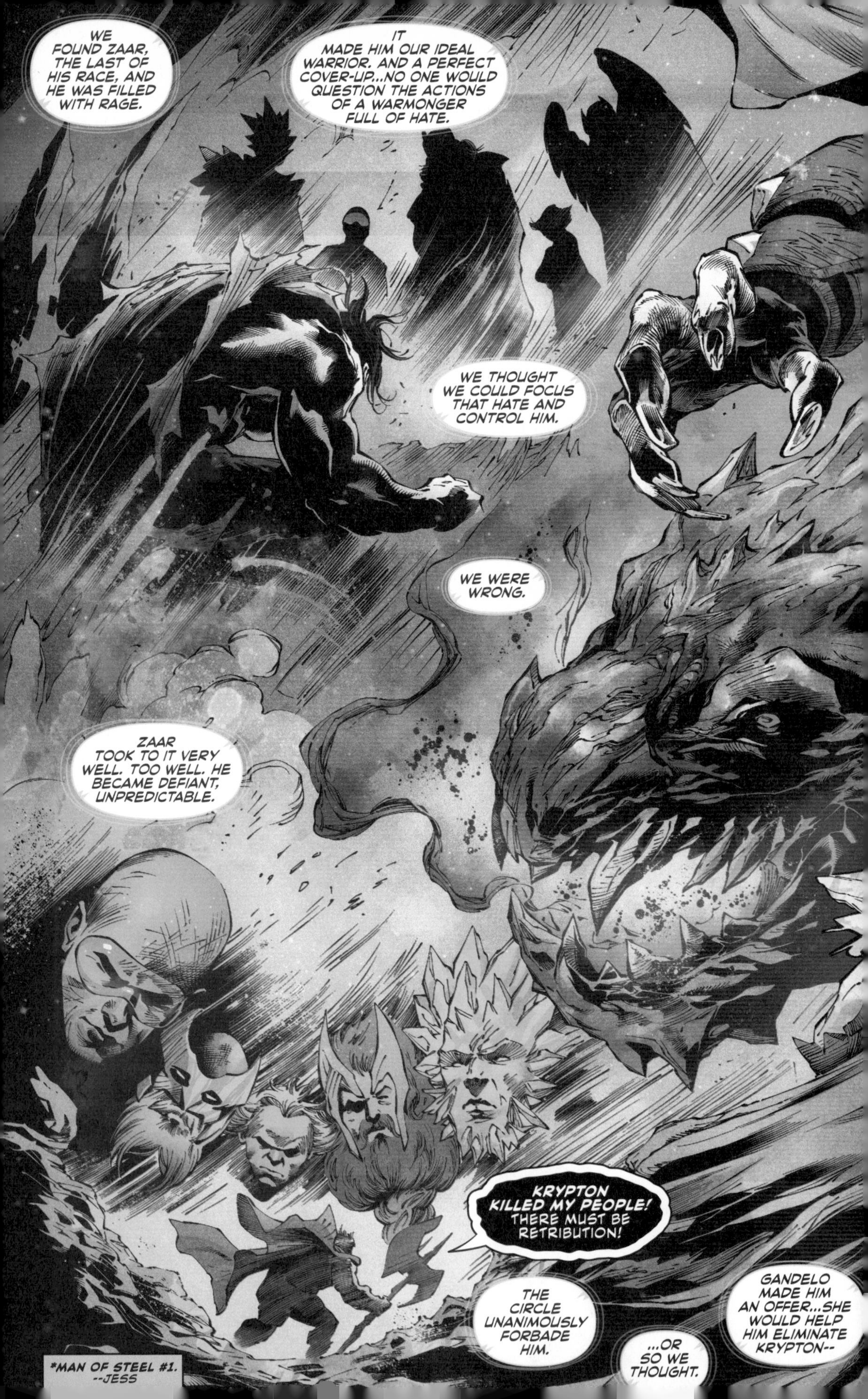
WE FOUND ZAAR, THE LAST OF HIS RACE, AND HE WAS FILLED WITH RAGE.
IT MADE HIM OUR IDEAL WARRIOR. AND A PERFECT COVER-UP...NO ONE WOULD QUESTION THE ACTIONS OF A WARMONGER FULL OF HATE.
WE THOUGHT WE COULD FOCUS THAT HATE AND CONTROL HIM.
WE WERE WRONG.
ZAAR TOOK TO IT VERY WELL. TOO WELL. HE BECAME DEFIANT, UNPREDICTABLE.
KRYPTON KILLED MY PEOPLE! THERE MUST BE RETRIBUTION!
THE CIRCLE UNANIMOUSLY FORBADE HIM.
...OR SO WE THOUGHT.
GANDELO MADE HIM AN OFFER...SHE WOULD HELP HIM ELIMINATE KRYPTON--
*MAN OF STEEL #1. --JESS

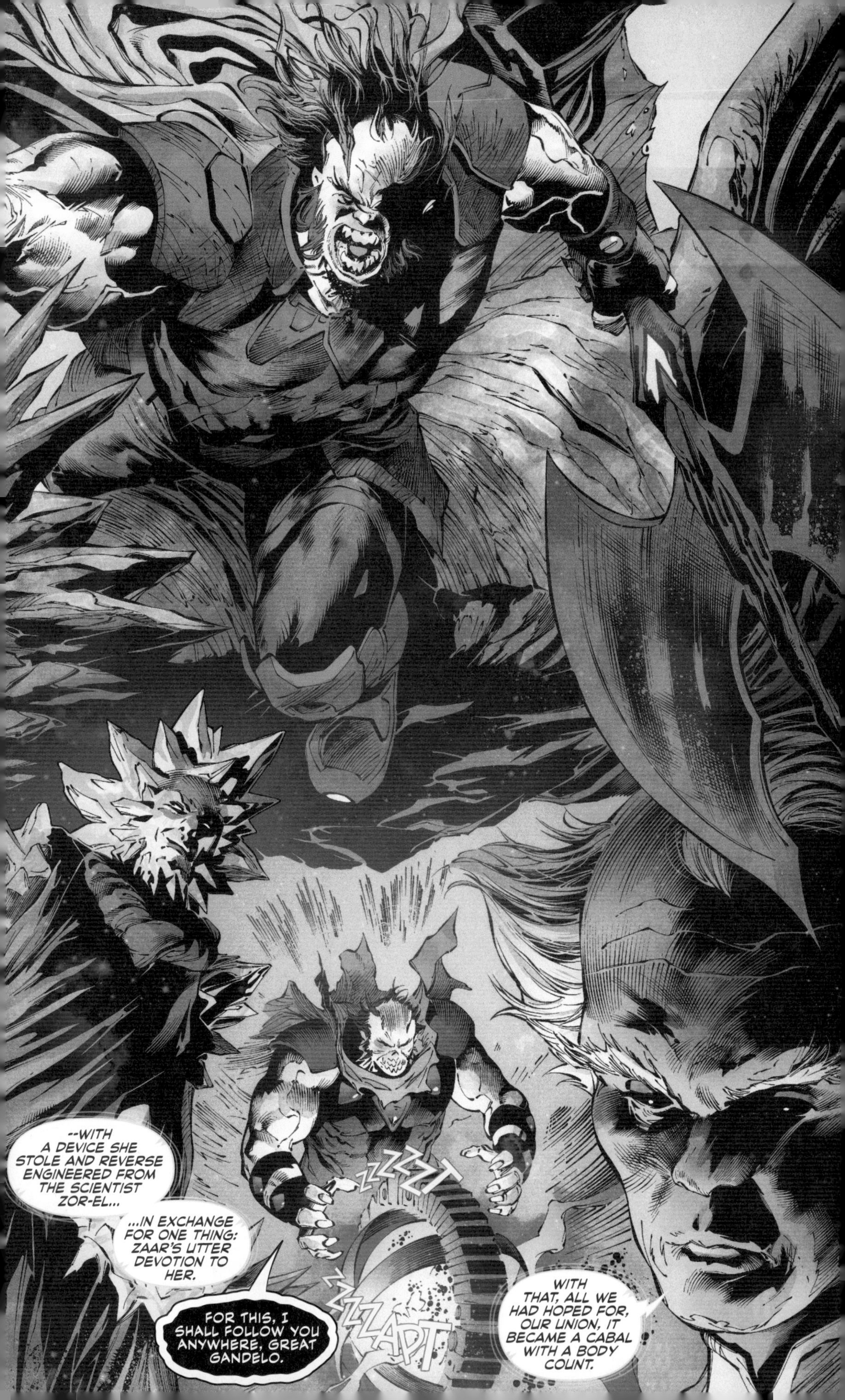
--WITH A DEVICE SHE STOLE AND REVERSE ENGINEERED FROM THE SCIENTIST ZOR-EL...
...IN EXCHANGE FOR ONE THING: ZAAR'S UTTER DEVOTION TO HER.
FOR THIS, I SHALL FOLLOW YOU ANYWHERE, GREAT GANDELO.
ZZZZZT
ZZZZZAPT
WITH THAT, ALL WE HAD HOPED FOR, OUR UNION, IT BECAME A CABAL WITH A BODY COUNT.

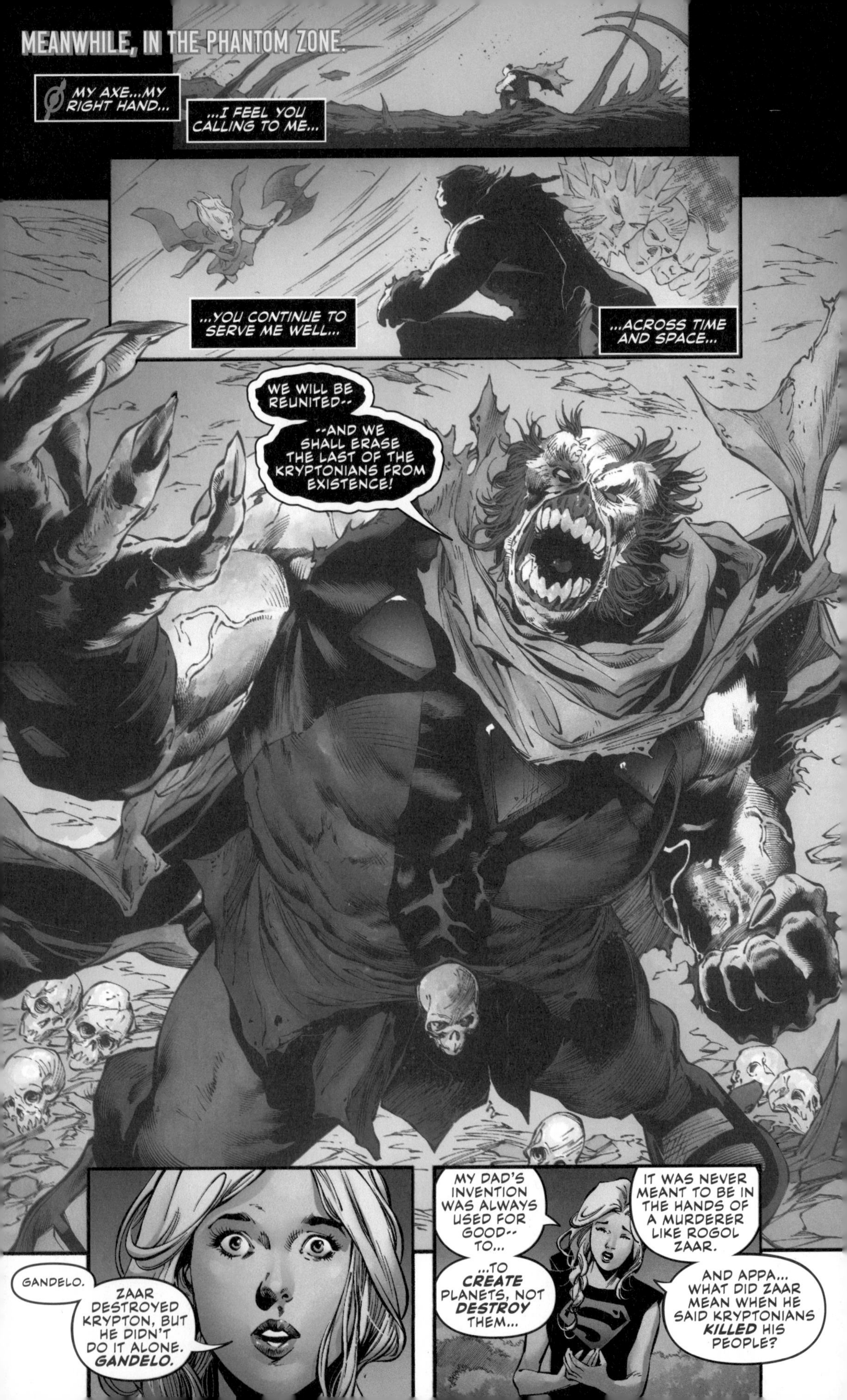
MEANWHILE, IN THE PHANTOM ZONE.
MY AXE...MY RIGHT HAND...
...I FEEL YOU CALLING TO ME...
...YOU CONTINUE TO SERVE ME WELL...
...ACROSS TIME AND SPACE...
WE WILL BE REUNITED--
--AND WE SHALL ERASE THE LAST OF THE KRYPTONIANS FROM EXISTENCE!
GANDELO.
ZAAR DESTROYED KRYPTON, BUT HE DIDN'T DO IT ALONE. GANDELO.
MY DAD'S INVENTION WAS ALWAYS USED FOR GOOD-- TO...
...TO CREATE PLANETS, NOT DESTROY THEM...
IT WAS NEVER MEANT TO BE IN THE HANDS OF A MURDERER LIKE ROGOL ZAAR.
AND APPA... WHAT DID ZAAR MEAN WHEN HE SAID KRYPTONIANS KILLED HIS PEOPLE?

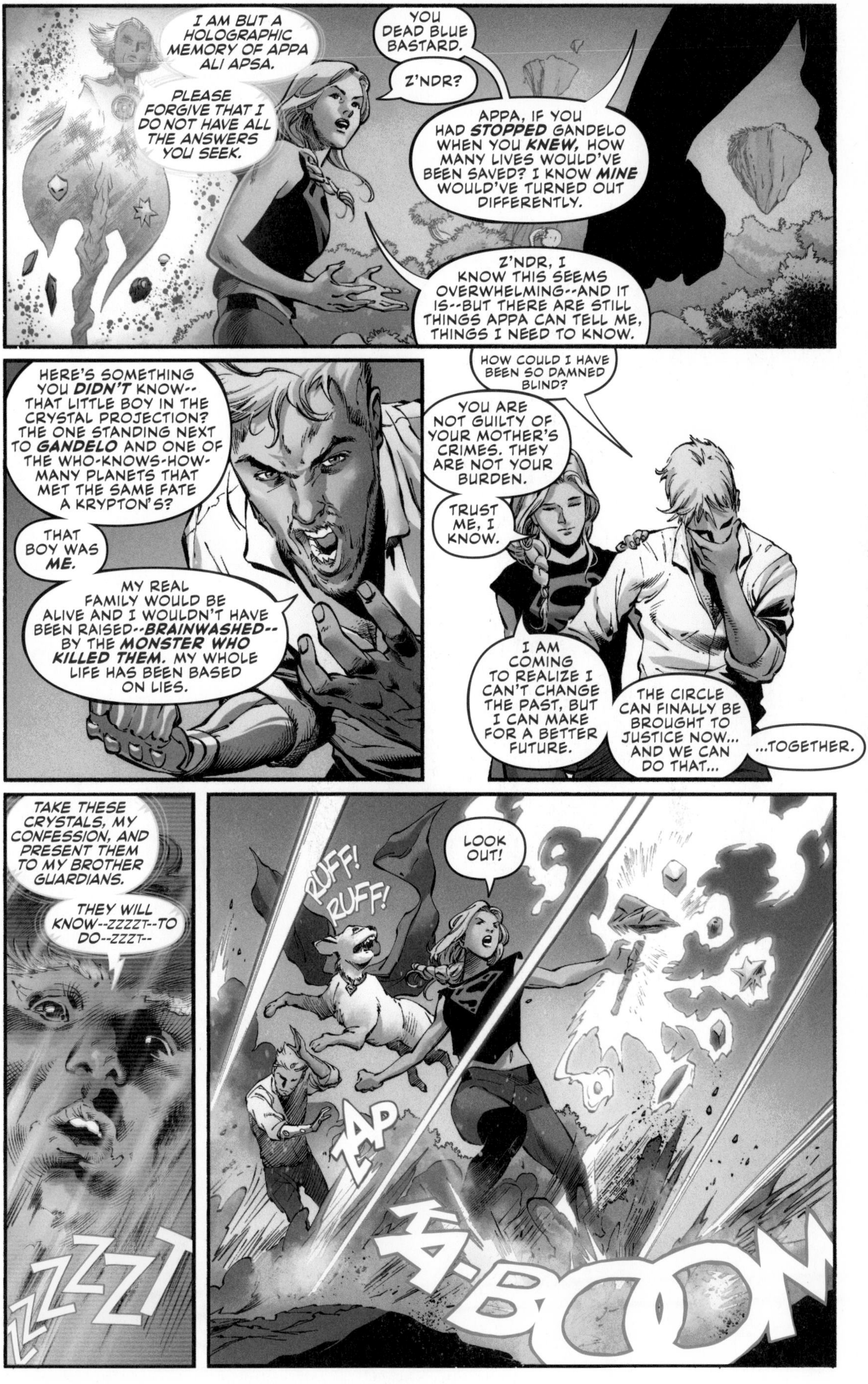
I AM BUT A HOLOGRAPHIC MEMORY OF APPA ALI APSA.
PLEASE FORGIVE THAT I DO NOT HAVE ALL THE ANSWERS YOU SEEK.
YOU DEAD BLUE BASTARD.
Z'NDR?
APPA, IF YOU HAD STOPPED GANDELO WHEN YOU KNEW, HOW MANY LIVES WOULD'VE BEEN SAVED? I KNOW MINE WOULD'VE TURNED OUT DIFFERENTLY.
Z'NDR, I KNOW THIS SEEMS OVERWHELMING--AND IT IS--BUT THERE ARE STILL THINGS APPA CAN TELL ME, THINGS I NEED TO KNOW.
HERE'S SOMETHING YOU DIDN'T KNOW--THAT LITTLE BOY IN THE CRYSTAL PROJECTION? THE ONE STANDING NEXT TO GANDELO AND ONE OF THE WHO-KNOWS-HOW-MANY PLANETS THAT MET THE SAME FATE A KRYPTON'S?
THAT BOY WAS ME.
MY REAL FAMILY WOULD BE ALIVE AND I WOULDN'T HAVE BEEN RAISED--BRAINWASHED--BY THE MONSTER WHO KILLED THEM. MY WHOLE LIFE HAS BEEN BASED ON LIES.
HOW COULD I HAVE BEEN SO DAMNED BLIND?
YOU ARE NOT GUILTY OF YOUR MOTHER'S CRIMES. THEY ARE NOT YOUR BURDEN.
TRUST ME, I KNOW.
I AM COMING TO REALIZE I CAN'T CHANGE THE PAST, BUT I CAN MAKE FOR A BETTER FUTURE.
THE CIRCLE CAN FINALLY BE BROUGHT TO JUSTICE NOW... AND WE CAN DO THAT...
...TOGETHER.
TAKE THESE CRYSTALS, MY CONFESSION, AND PRESENT THEM TO MY BROTHER GUARDIANS.
THEY WILL KNOW--ZZZZT--TO DO--ZZZT--
ZZZZZT
LOOK OUT!
RUFF! RUFF!
ZAP
KA-BOOM

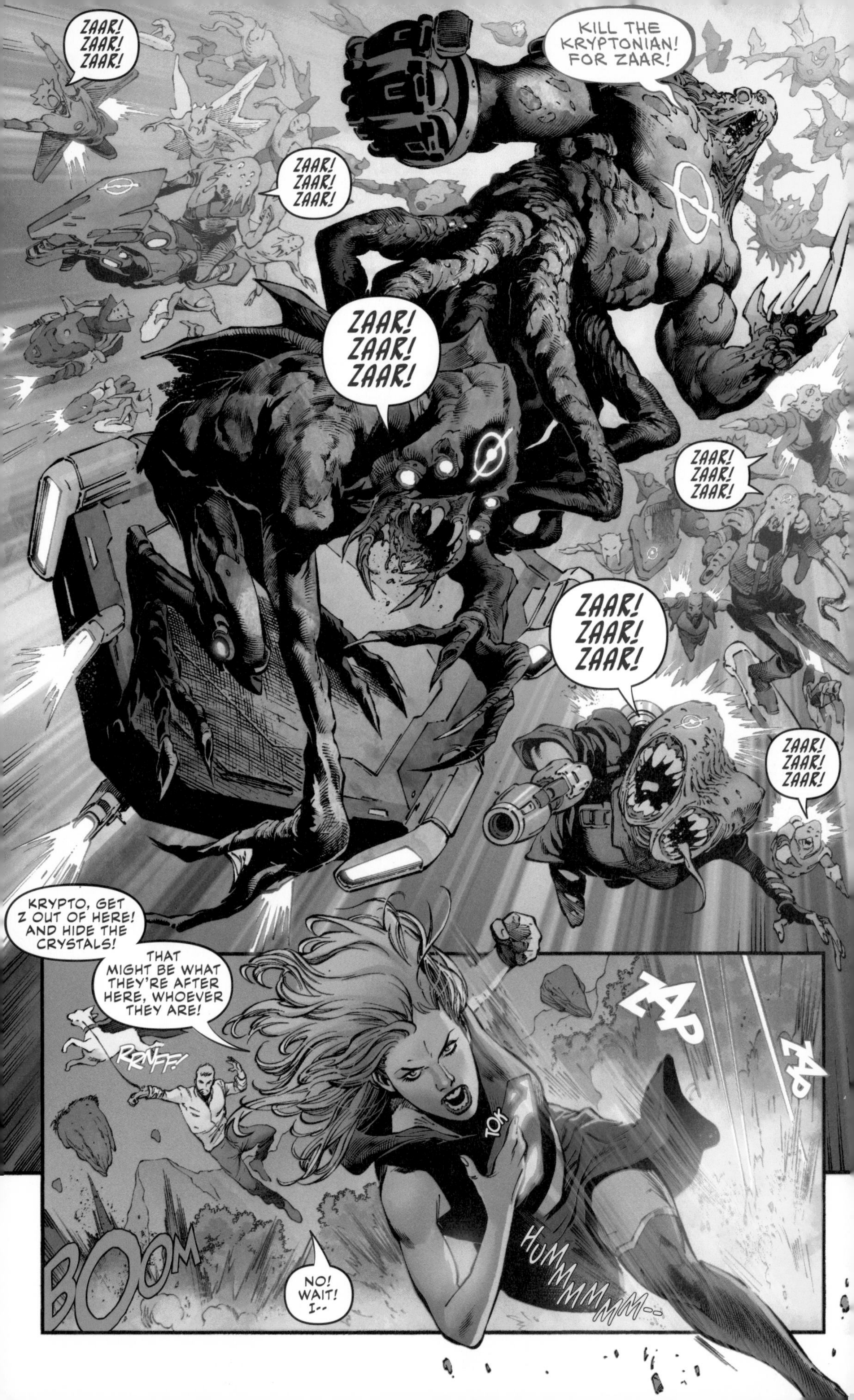
ZAAR! ZAAR! ZAAR!
KILL THE KRYPTONIAN! FOR ZAAR!
ZAAR! ZAAR! ZAAR!
ZAAR! ZAAR! ZAAR!
ZAAR! ZAAR! ZAAR!
ZAAR! ZAAR! ZAAR!
ZAAR! ZAAR! ZAAR!
KRYPTO, GET Z OUT OF HERE! AND HIDE THE CRYSTALS!
THAT MIGHT BE WHAT THEY'RE AFTER HERE, WHOEVER THEY ARE!
RRNFF!
ZAP
ZAP
TOK
BOOM
HUMMMMMM--
NO! WAIT! I--

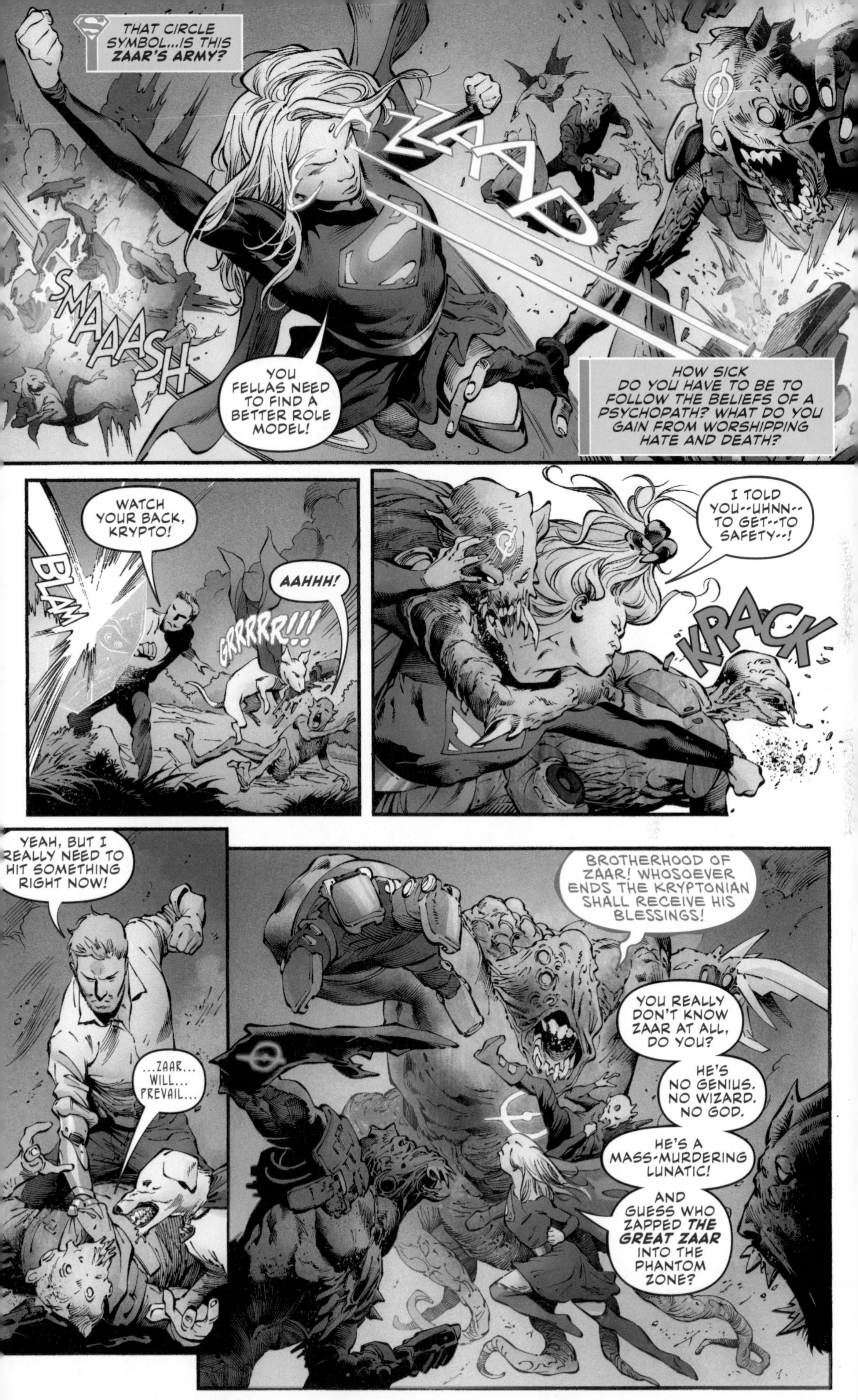
THAT CIRCLE SYMBOL...IS THIS ZAAR'S ARMY?
ZZAAP
SMAAASH
YOU FELLAS NEED TO FIND A BETTER ROLE MODEL!
HOW SICK DO YOU HAVE TO BE TO FOLLOW THE BELIEFS OF A PSYCHOPATH? WHAT DO YOU GAIN FROM WORSHIPPING HATE AND DEATH?
WATCH YOUR BACK, KRYPTO!
BLAM
AAHHH!
GRRRRR!!!
I TOLD YOU--UHNN--TO GET--TO SAFETY--!
KRACK
YEAH, BUT I REALLY NEED TO HIT SOMETHING RIGHT NOW!
...ZAAR... WILL... PREVAIL...
BROTHERHOOD OF ZAAR! WHOSOEVER ENDS THE KRYPTONIAN SHALL RECEIVE HIS BLESSINGS!
YOU REALLY DON'T KNOW ZAAR AT ALL, DO YOU?
HE'S NO GENIUS. NO WIZARD. NO GOD.
HE'S A MASS-MURDERING LUNATIC!
AND GUESS WHO ZAPPED THE GREAT ZAAR INTO THE PHANTOM ZONE?

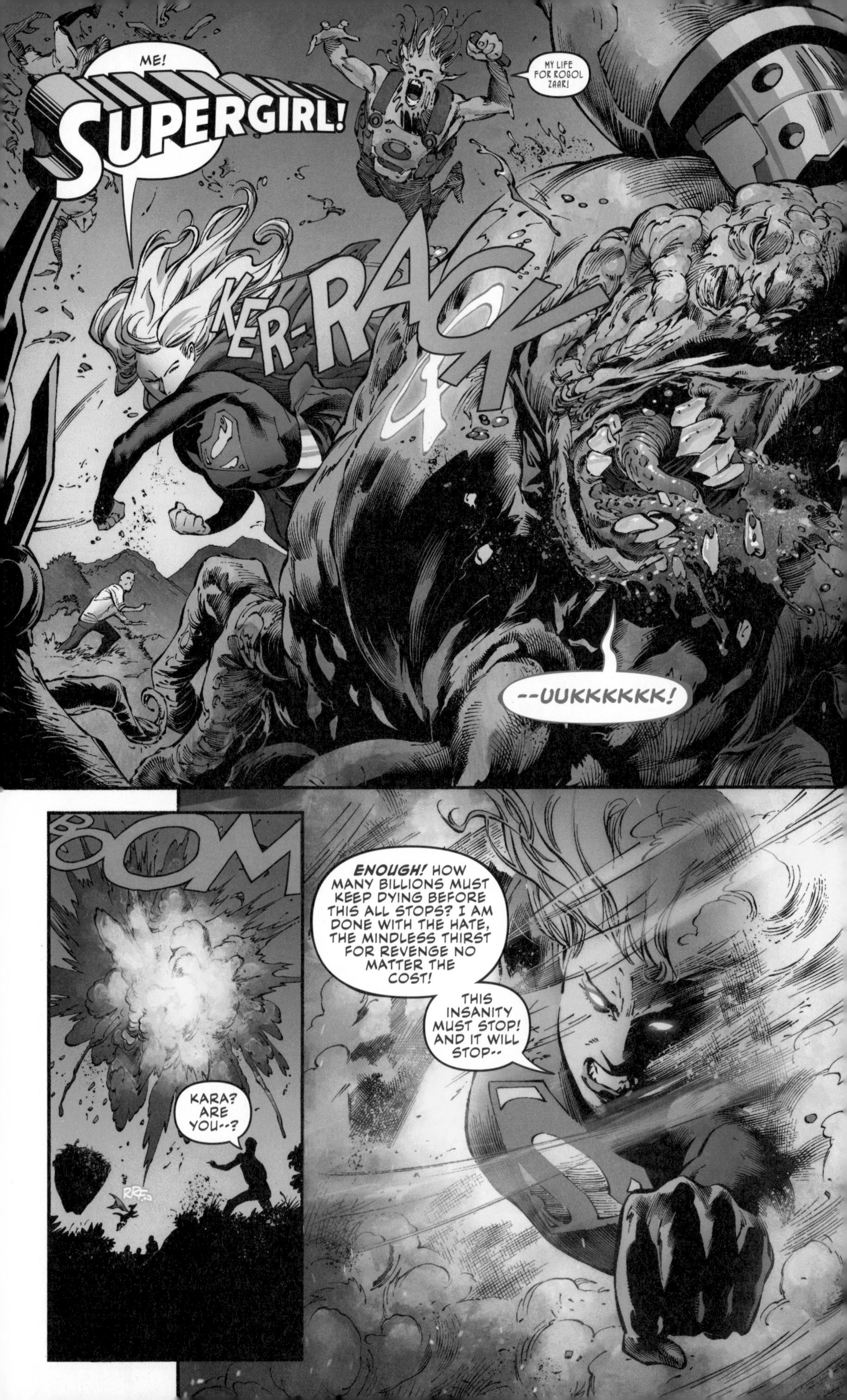
ME!
SUPERGIRL!
MY LIFE FOR ROGOL ZAAR!
KER-RACK
--UUKKKKKK!
BOOM
KARA? ARE YOU--?
ENOUGH! HOW MANY BILLIONS MUST KEEP DYING BEFORE THIS ALL STOPS? I AM DONE WITH THE HATE, THE MINDLESS THIRST FOR REVENGE NO MATTER THE COST!
THIS INSANITY MUST STOP! AND IT WILL STOP--

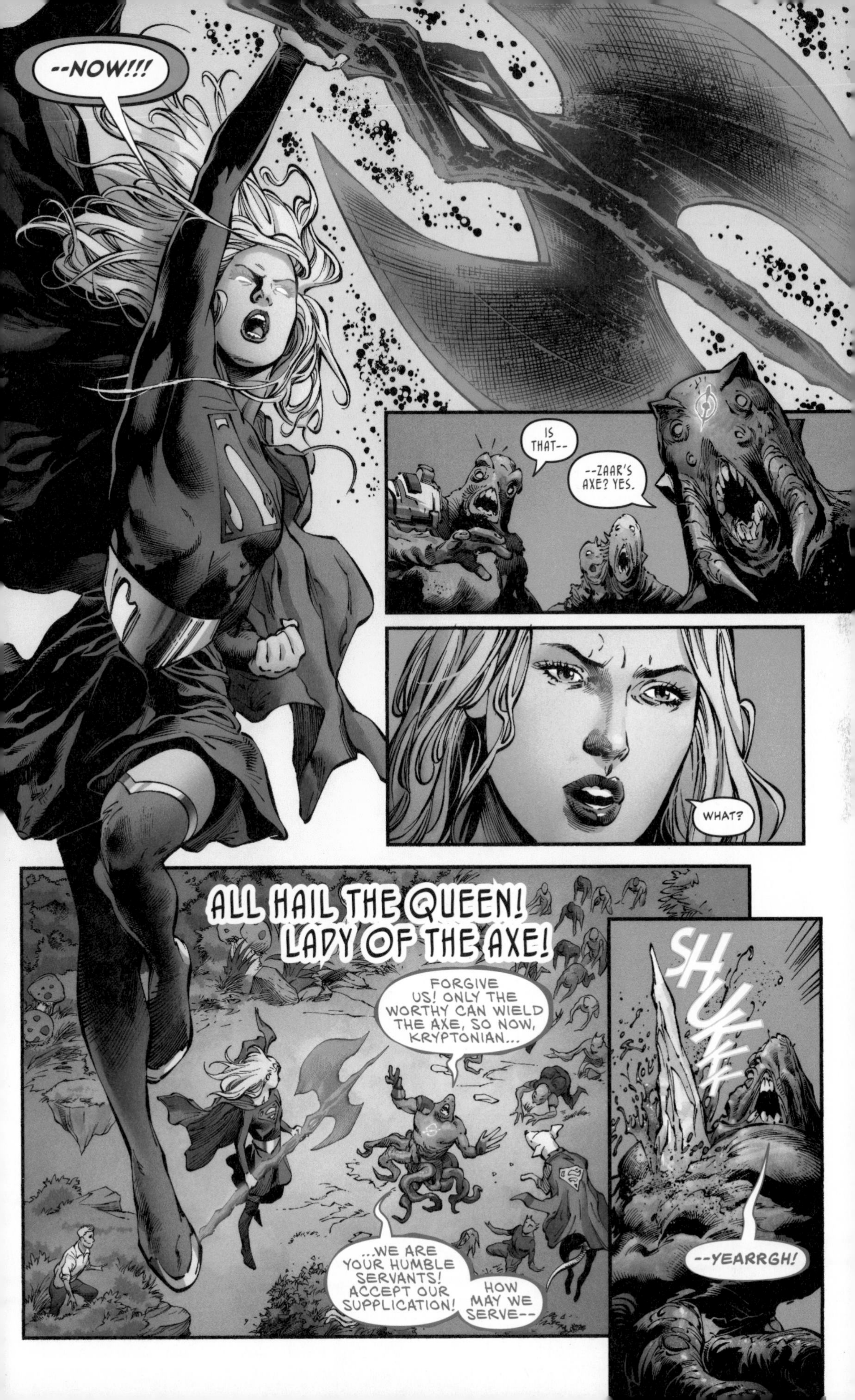
--NOW!!!
IS THAT--
--ZAAR'S AXE? YES.
WHAT?
ALL HAIL THE QUEEN! LADY OF THE AXE!
FORGIVE US! ONLY THE WORTHY CAN WIELD THE AXE, SO NOW, KRYPTONIAN...
...WE ARE YOUR HUMBLE SERVANTS! ACCEPT OUR SUPPLICATION!
HOW MAY WE SERVE--
SHUKKK
--YEARRGH!

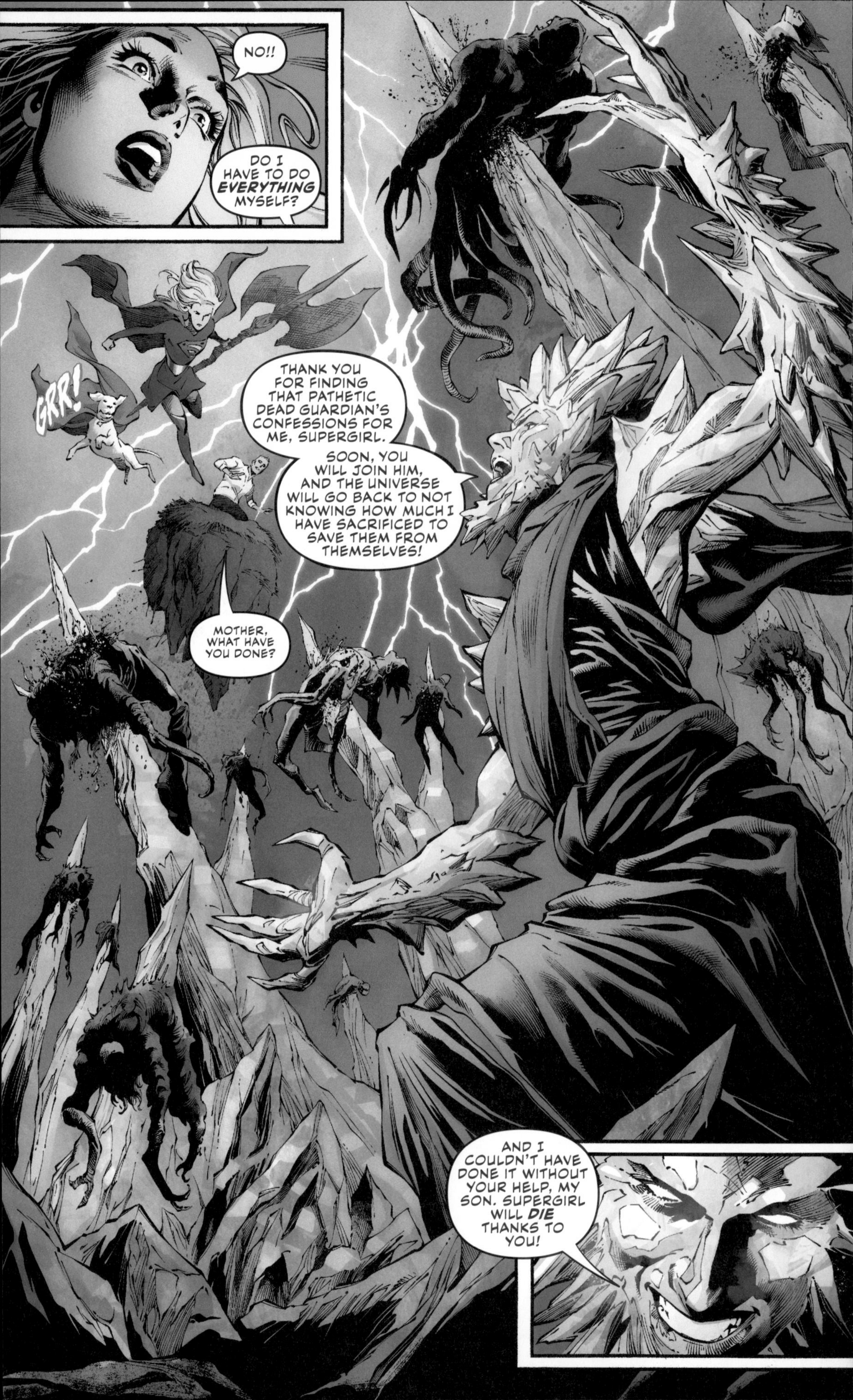
NO!!
DO I HAVE TO DO EVERYTHING MYSELF?
GRR!
THANK YOU FOR FINDING THAT PATHETIC DEAD GUARDIAN'S CONFESSIONS FOR ME, SUPERGIRL.
SOON, YOU WILL JOIN HIM, AND THE UNIVERSE WILL GO BACK TO NOT KNOWING HOW MUCH I HAVE SACRIFICED TO SAVE THEM FROM THEMSELVES!
MOTHER, WHAT HAVE YOU DONE?
AND I COULDN'T HAVE DONE IT WITHOUT YOUR HELP, MY SON. SUPERGIRL WILL DIE THANKS TO YOU!

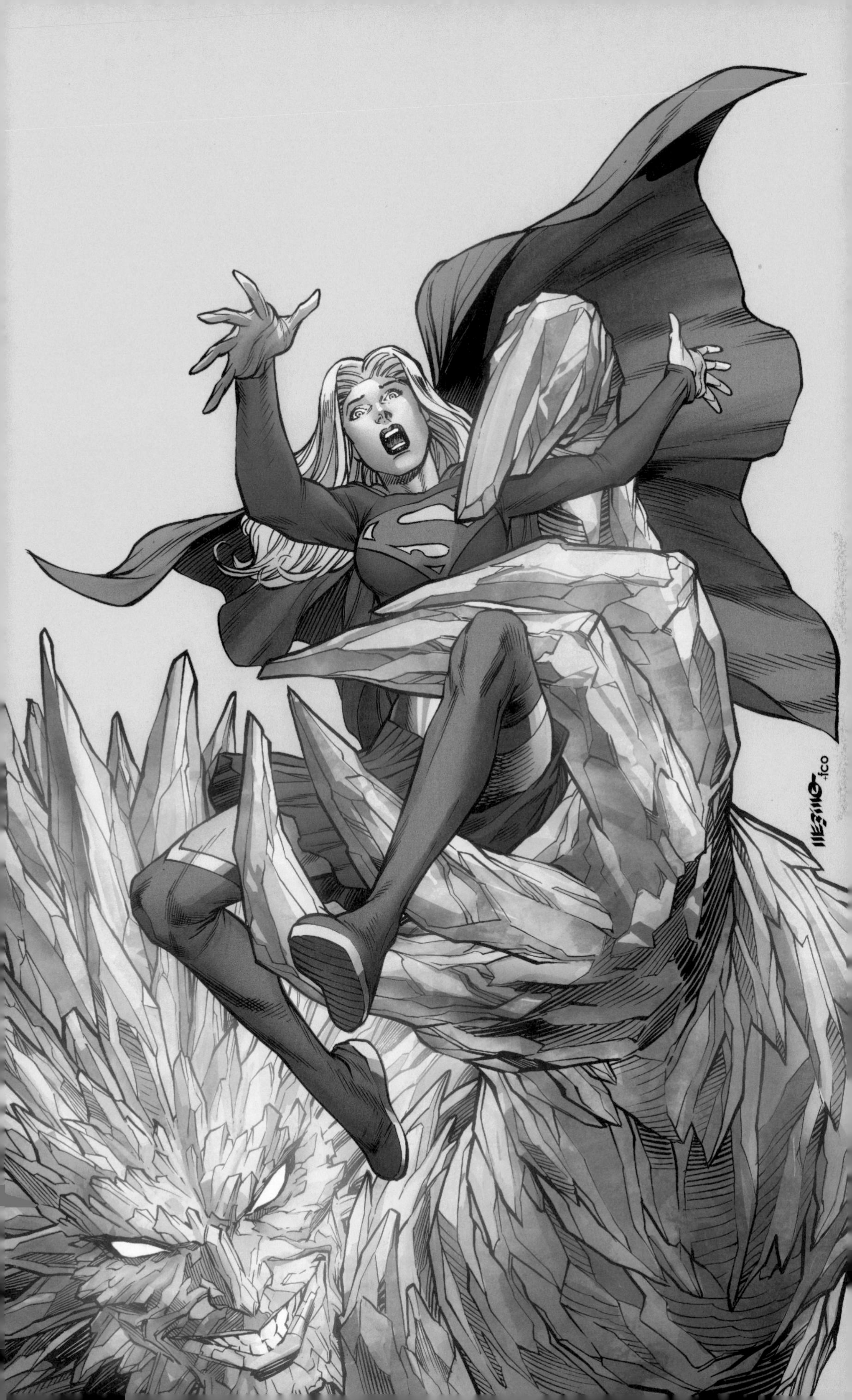

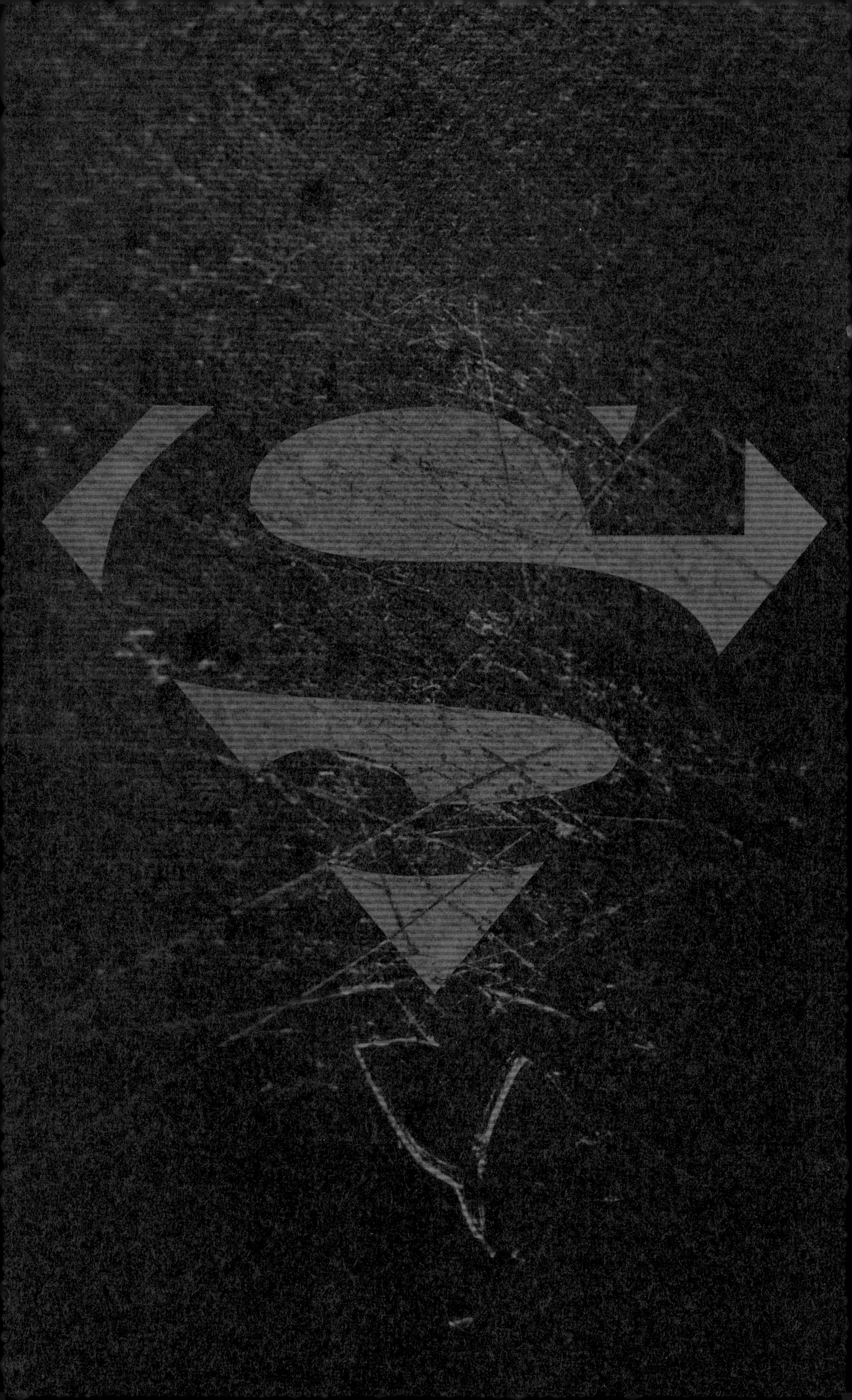

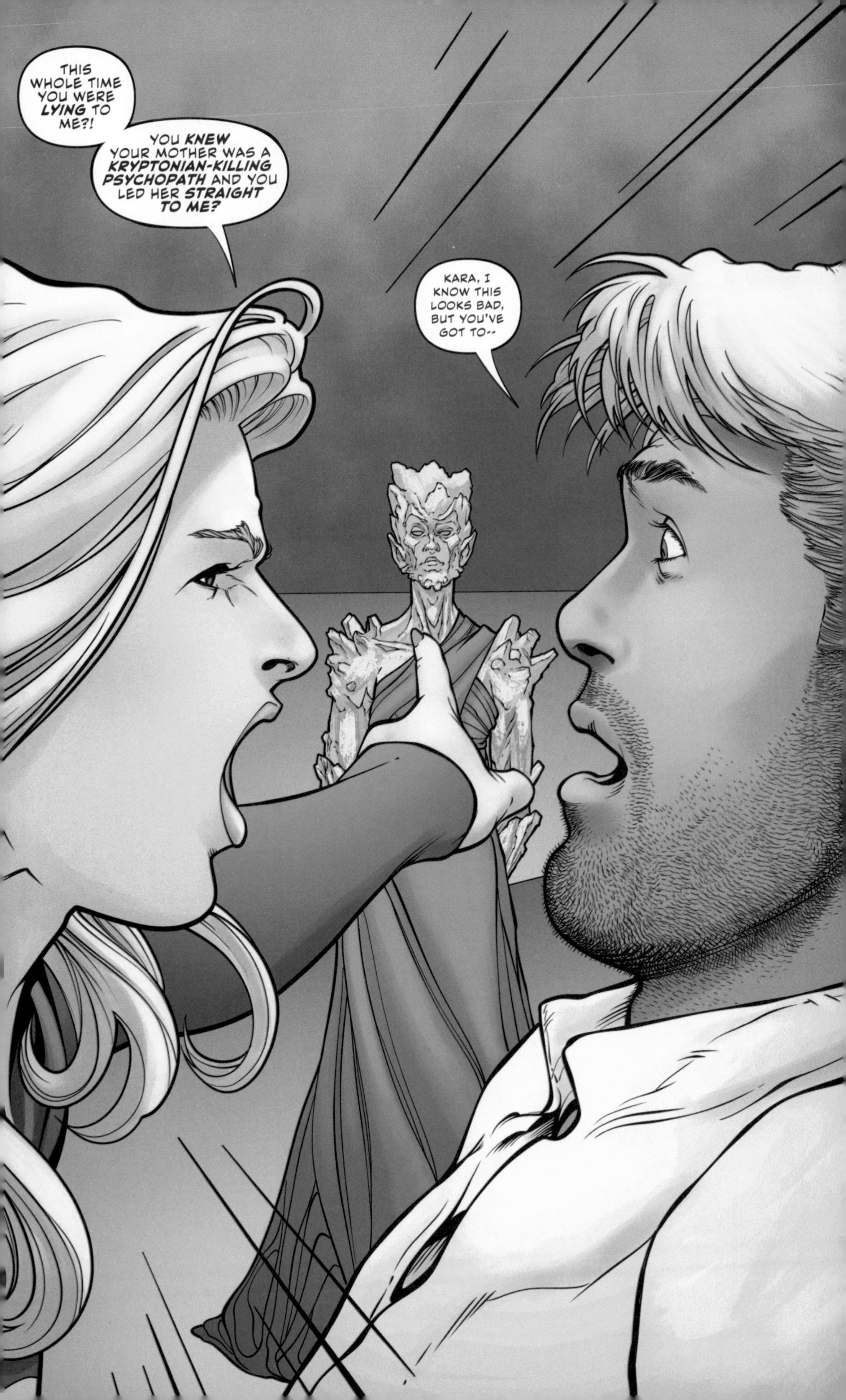
THIS WHOLE TIME YOU WERE *LYING* TO ME?!
YOU *KNEW* YOUR MOTHER WAS A *KRYPTONIAN-KILLING PSYCHOPATH* AND YOU LED HER *STRAIGHT TO ME?*
KARA, I KNOW THIS LOOKS BAD, BUT YOU'VE GOT TO--

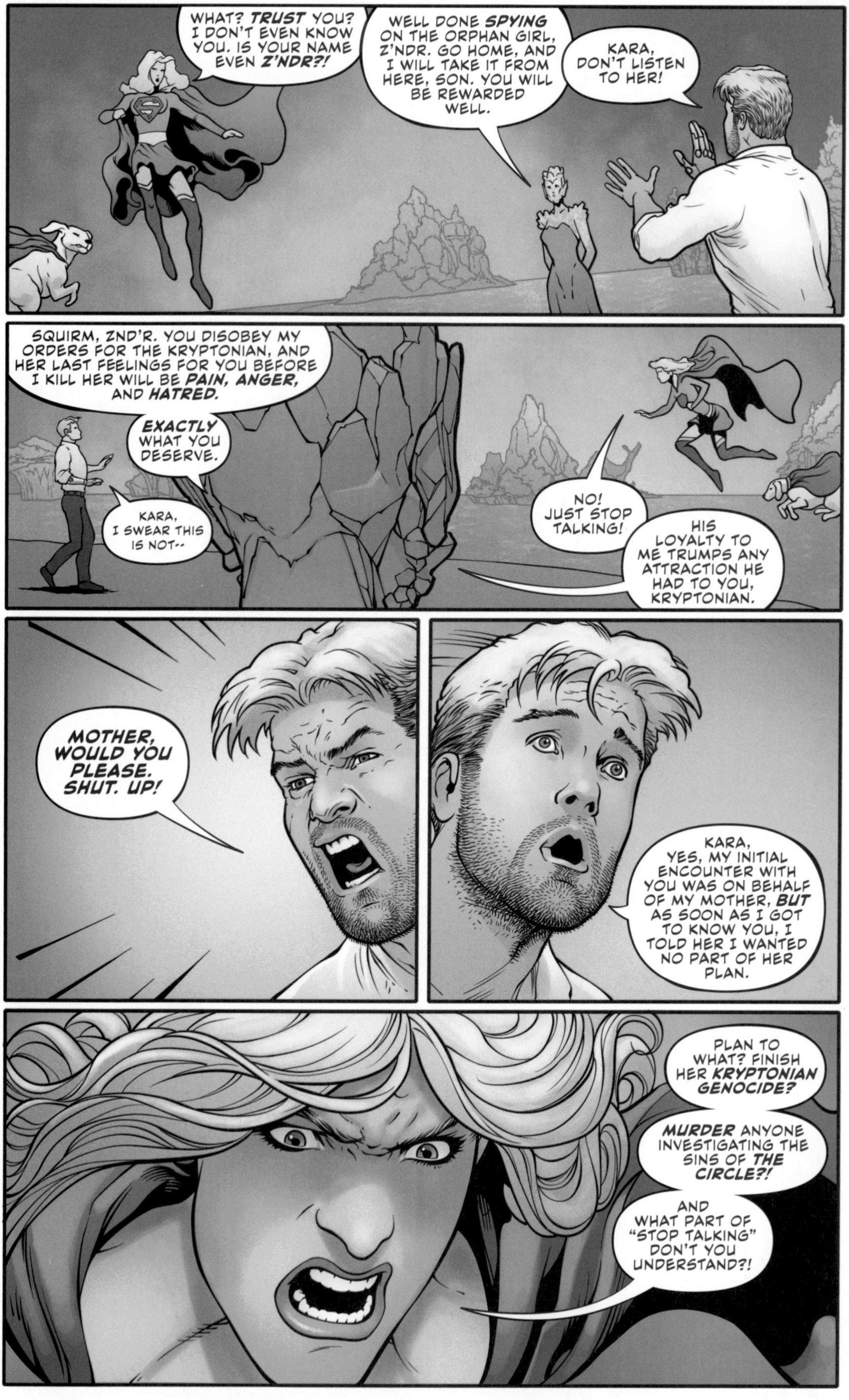
WHAT? TRUST YOU? I DON'T EVEN KNOW YOU. IS YOUR NAME EVEN Z'NDR?!
WELL DONE SPYING ON THE ORPHAN GIRL, Z'NDR. GO HOME, AND I WILL TAKE IT FROM HERE, SON. YOU WILL BE REWARDED WELL.
KARA, DON'T LISTEN TO HER!
SQUIRM, ZND'R. YOU DISOBEY MY ORDERS FOR THE KRYPTONIAN, AND HER LAST FEELINGS FOR YOU BEFORE I KILL HER WILL BE PAIN, ANGER, AND HATRED.
EXACTLY WHAT YOU DESERVE.
KARA, I SWEAR THIS IS NOT--
NO! JUST STOP TALKING!
HIS LOYALTY TO ME TRUMPS ANY ATTRACTION HE HAD TO YOU, KRYPTONIAN.
MOTHER, WOULD YOU PLEASE. SHUT. UP!
KARA, YES, MY INITIAL ENCOUNTER WITH YOU WAS ON BEHALF OF MY MOTHER, BUT AS SOON AS I GOT TO KNOW YOU, I TOLD HER I WANTED NO PART OF HER PLAN.
PLAN TO WHAT? FINISH HER KRYPTONIAN GENOCIDE?
MURDER ANYONE INVESTIGATING THE SINS OF THE CIRCLE?!
AND WHAT PART OF "STOP TALKING" DON'T YOU UNDERSTAND?!

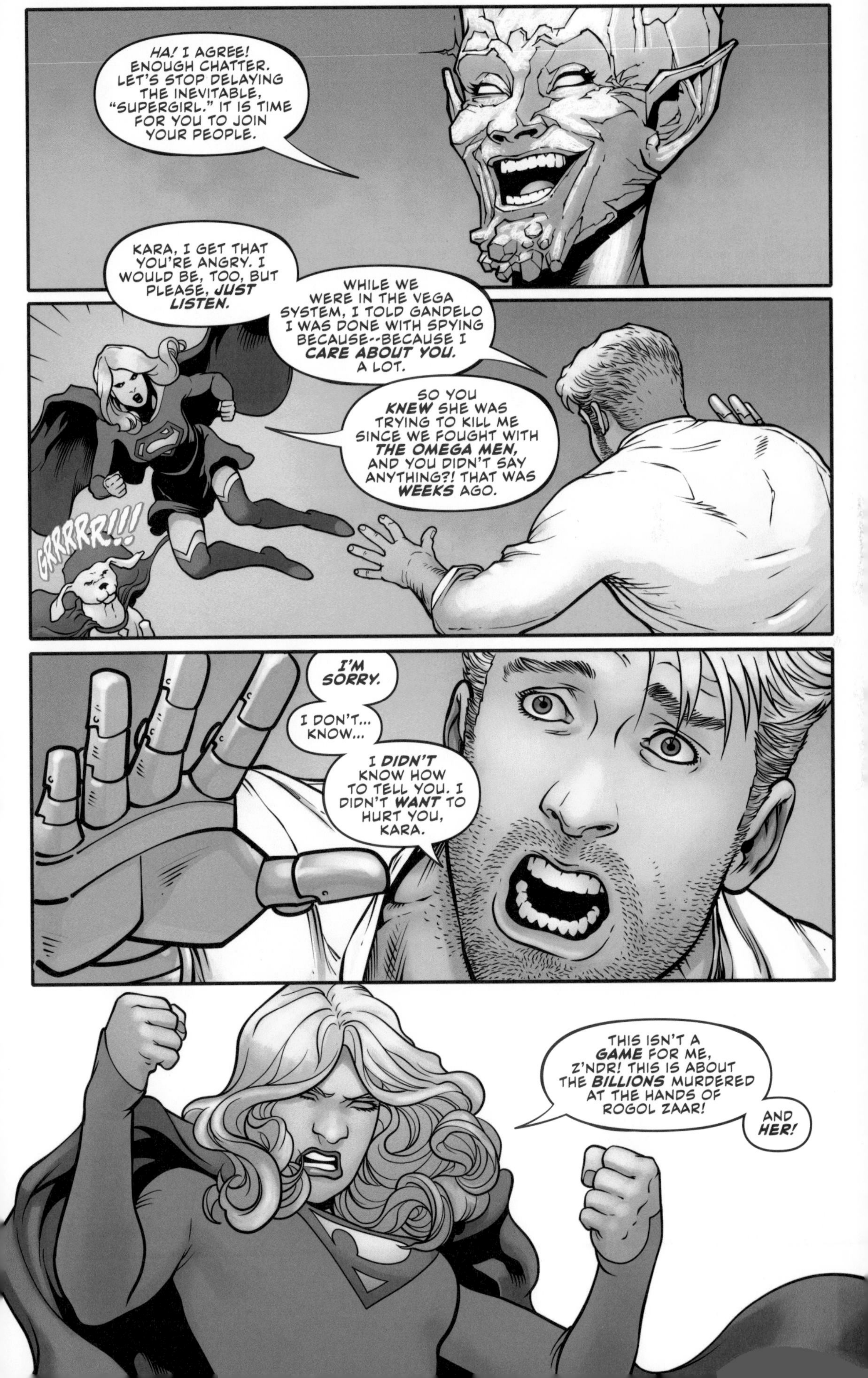
HA! I AGREE! ENOUGH CHATTER. LET'S STOP DELAYING THE INEVITABLE, "SUPERGIRL." IT IS TIME FOR YOU TO JOIN YOUR PEOPLE.
KARA, I GET THAT YOU'RE ANGRY. I WOULD BE, TOO, BUT PLEASE, JUST LISTEN.
WHILE WE WERE IN THE VEGA SYSTEM, I TOLD GANDELO I WAS DONE WITH SPYING BECAUSE--BECAUSE I CARE ABOUT YOU. A LOT.
SO YOU KNEW SHE WAS TRYING TO KILL ME SINCE WE FOUGHT WITH THE OMEGA MEN, AND YOU DIDN'T SAY ANYTHING?! THAT WAS WEEKS AGO.
GRRRRR!!!
I'M SORRY.
I DON'T... KNOW...
I DIDN'T KNOW HOW TO TELL YOU. I DIDN'T WANT TO HURT YOU, KARA.
THIS ISN'T A GAME FOR ME, Z'NDR! THIS IS ABOUT THE BILLIONS MURDERED AT THE HANDS OF ROGOL ZAAR!
AND HER!

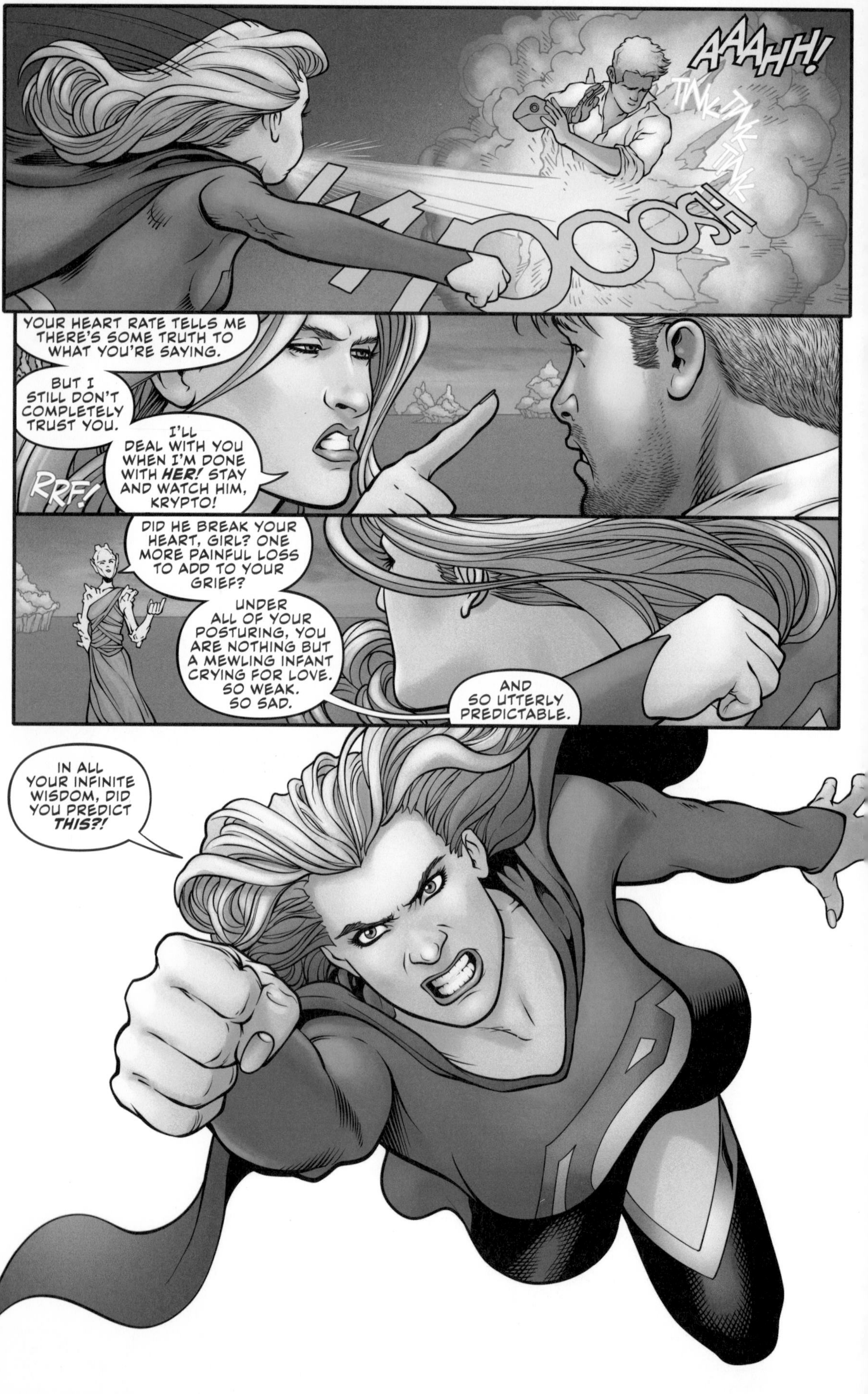
AAAHH!
TINK TINK TINK
YOUR HEART RATE TELLS ME THERE'S SOME TRUTH TO WHAT YOU'RE SAYING.
BUT I STILL DON'T COMPLETELY TRUST YOU.
I'LL DEAL WITH YOU WHEN I'M DONE WITH ***HER!*** STAY AND WATCH HIM, KRYPTO!
RRF!
DID HE BREAK YOUR HEART, GIRL? ONE MORE PAINFUL LOSS TO ADD TO YOUR GRIEF?
UNDER ALL OF YOUR POSTURING, YOU ARE NOTHING BUT A MEWLING INFANT CRYING FOR LOVE. SO WEAK. SO SAD.
AND SO UTTERLY PREDICTABLE.
IN ALL YOUR INFINITE WISDOM, DID YOU PREDICT ***THIS?!***

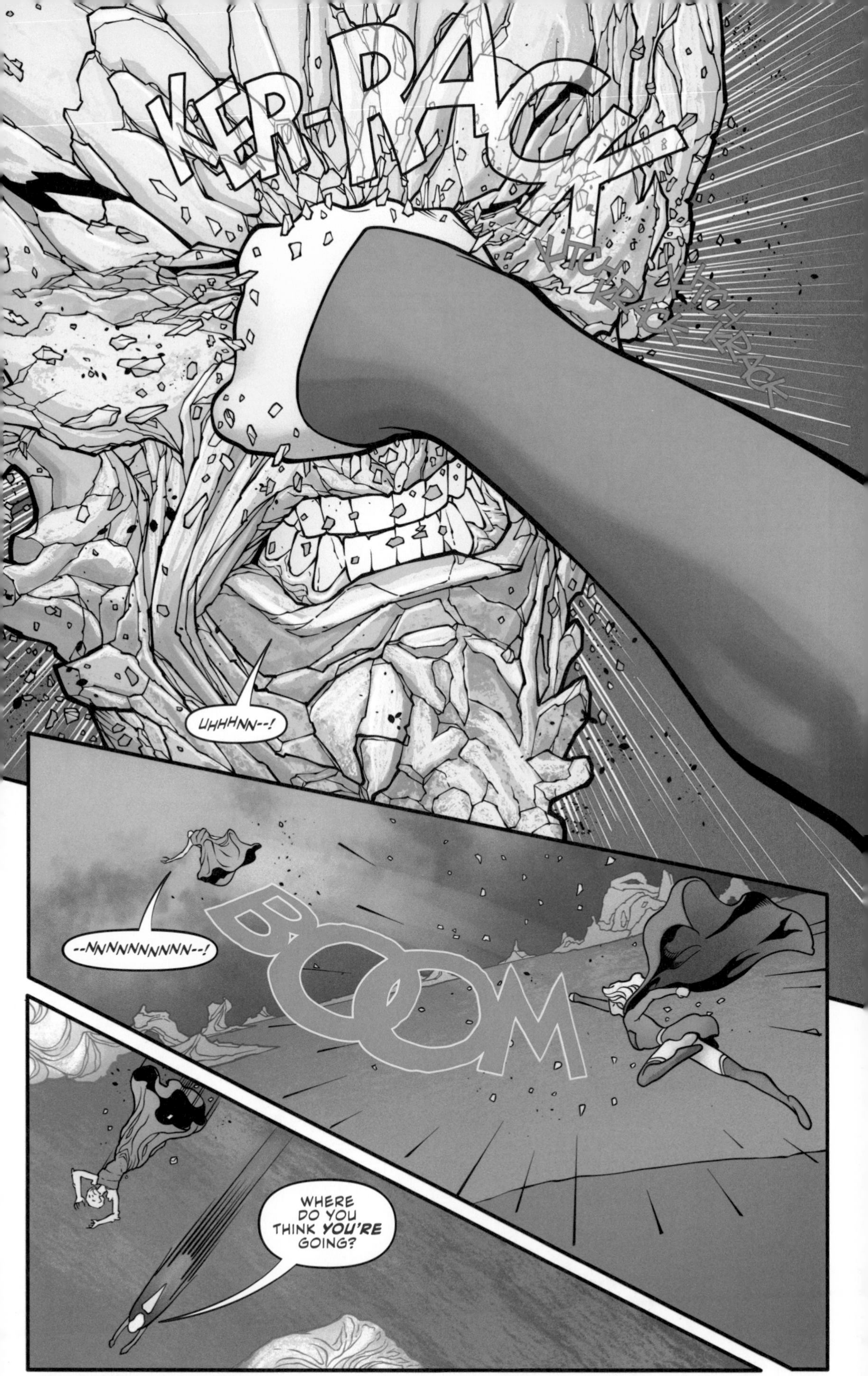
KER-RACK
KRITCH KRACK KRITCH KRACK
UHHHNN--!
--NNNNNNNNNN--!
BOOM
WHERE DO YOU THINK YOU'RE GOING?

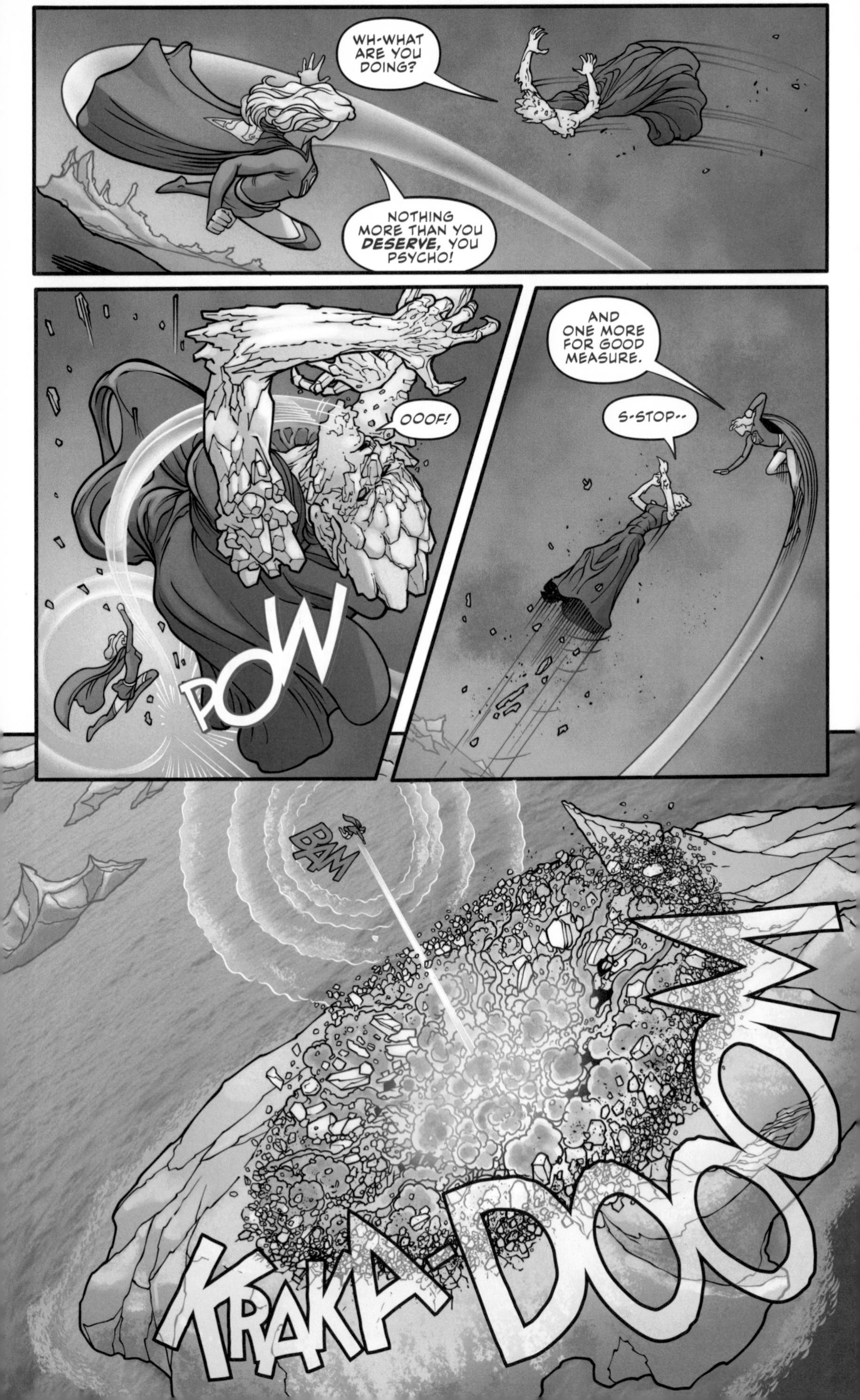
WH-WHAT ARE YOU DOING?
NOTHING MORE THAN YOU **DESERVE,** YOU PSYCHO!
OOOF!
POW
AND ONE MORE FOR GOOD MEASURE.
S-STOP--
BAM
KRAKA-DOOOM

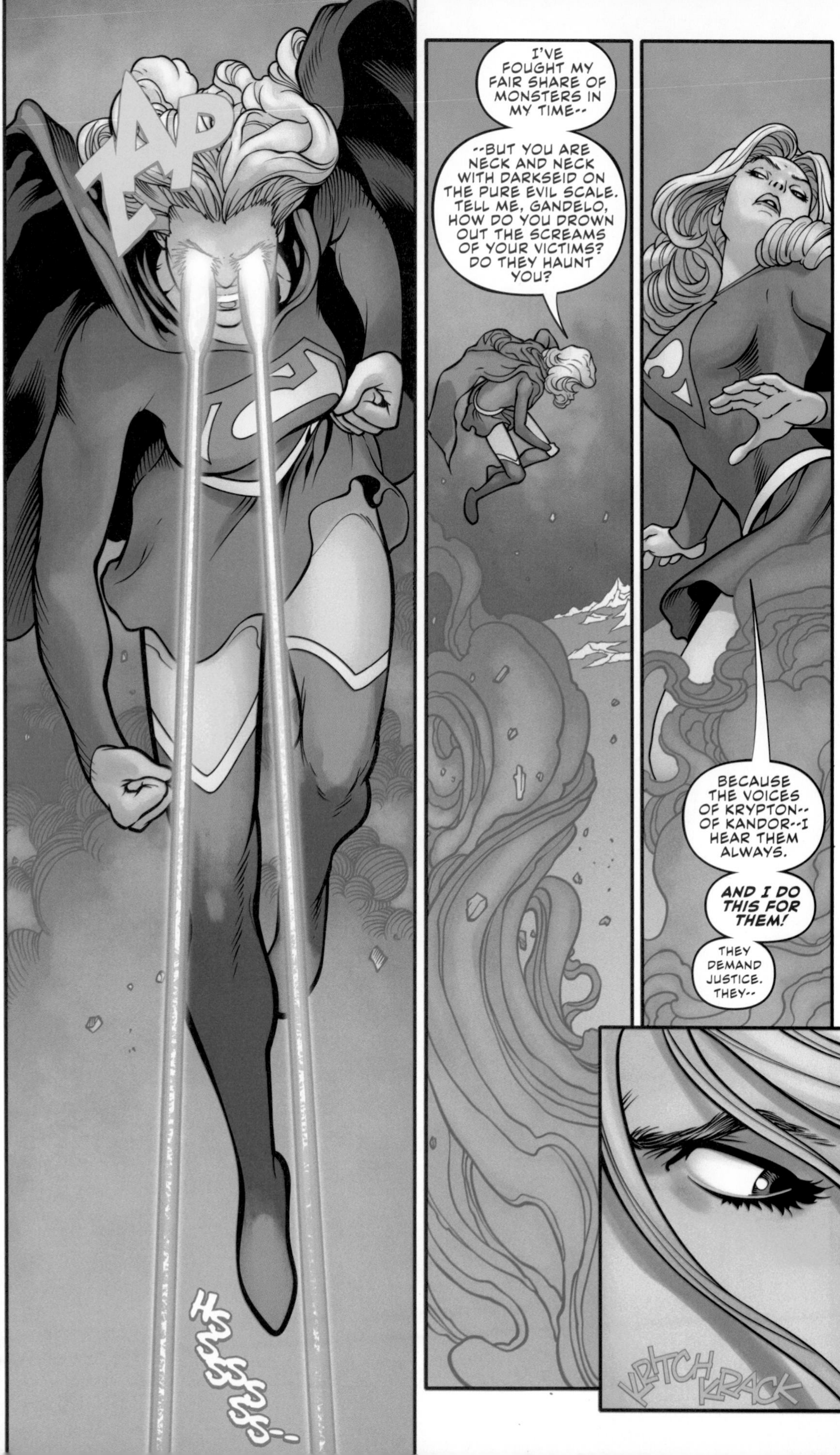
ZAP
HSSSSS--
I'VE FOUGHT MY FAIR SHARE OF MONSTERS IN MY TIME--
--BUT YOU ARE NECK AND NECK WITH DARKSEID ON THE PURE EVIL SCALE. TELL ME, GANDELO, HOW DO YOU DROWN OUT THE SCREAMS OF YOUR VICTIMS? DO THEY HAUNT YOU?
BECAUSE THE VOICES OF KRYPTON--OF KANDOR--I HEAR THEM ALWAYS.
AND I DO THIS FOR THEM!
THEY DEMAND JUSTICE. THEY--
KRITCH KRACK

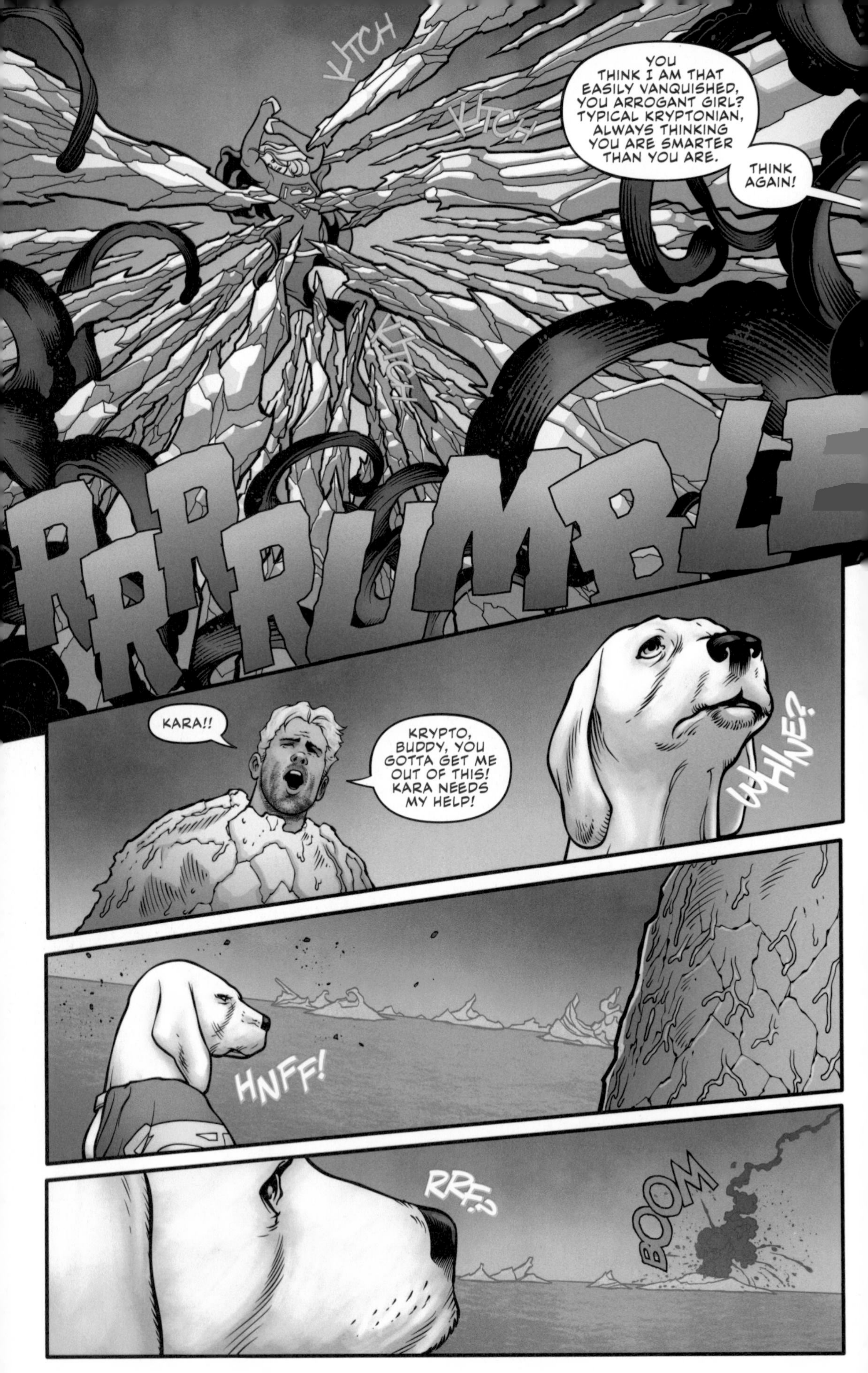
VTCH
VTCH
YOU THINK I AM THAT EASILY VANQUISHED, YOU ARROGANT GIRL? TYPICAL KRYPTONIAN, ALWAYS THINKING YOU ARE SMARTER THAN YOU ARE.
THINK AGAIN!
VTCH
RRRUMBLE
KARA!!
KRYPTO, BUDDY, YOU GOTTA GET ME OUT OF THIS! KARA NEEDS MY HELP!
WHINE?
HNFF!
RRF?
BOOM

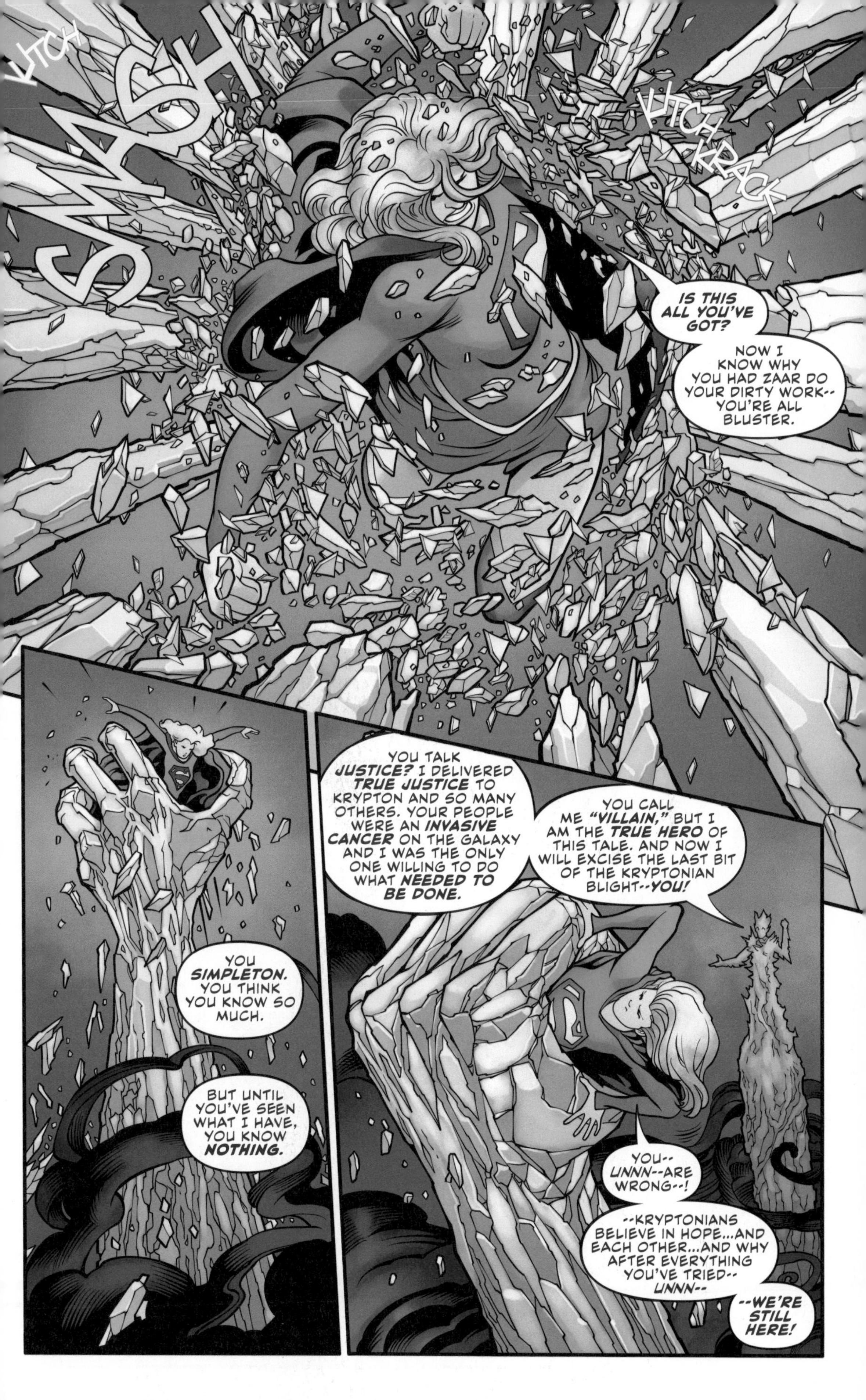

KTCH
SMASH
KTCH KRACK
IS THIS ALL YOU'VE GOT?
NOW I KNOW WHY YOU HAD ZAAR DO YOUR DIRTY WORK--YOU'RE ALL BLUSTER.
YOU SIMPLETON. YOU THINK YOU KNOW SO MUCH.
BUT UNTIL YOU'VE SEEN WHAT I HAVE, YOU KNOW NOTHING.
YOU TALK JUSTICE? I DELIVERED TRUE JUSTICE TO KRYPTON AND SO MANY OTHERS. YOUR PEOPLE WERE AN INVASIVE CANCER ON THE GALAXY AND I WAS THE ONLY ONE WILLING TO DO WHAT NEEDED TO BE DONE.
YOU CALL ME "VILLAIN," BUT I AM THE TRUE HERO OF THIS TALE. AND NOW I WILL EXCISE THE LAST BIT OF THE KRYPTONIAN BLIGHT--YOU!
YOU--UNNN--ARE WRONG--!
--KRYPTONIANS BELIEVE IN HOPE...AND EACH OTHER...AND WHY AFTER EVERYTHING YOU'VE TRIED--UNNN--
--WE'RE STILL HERE!

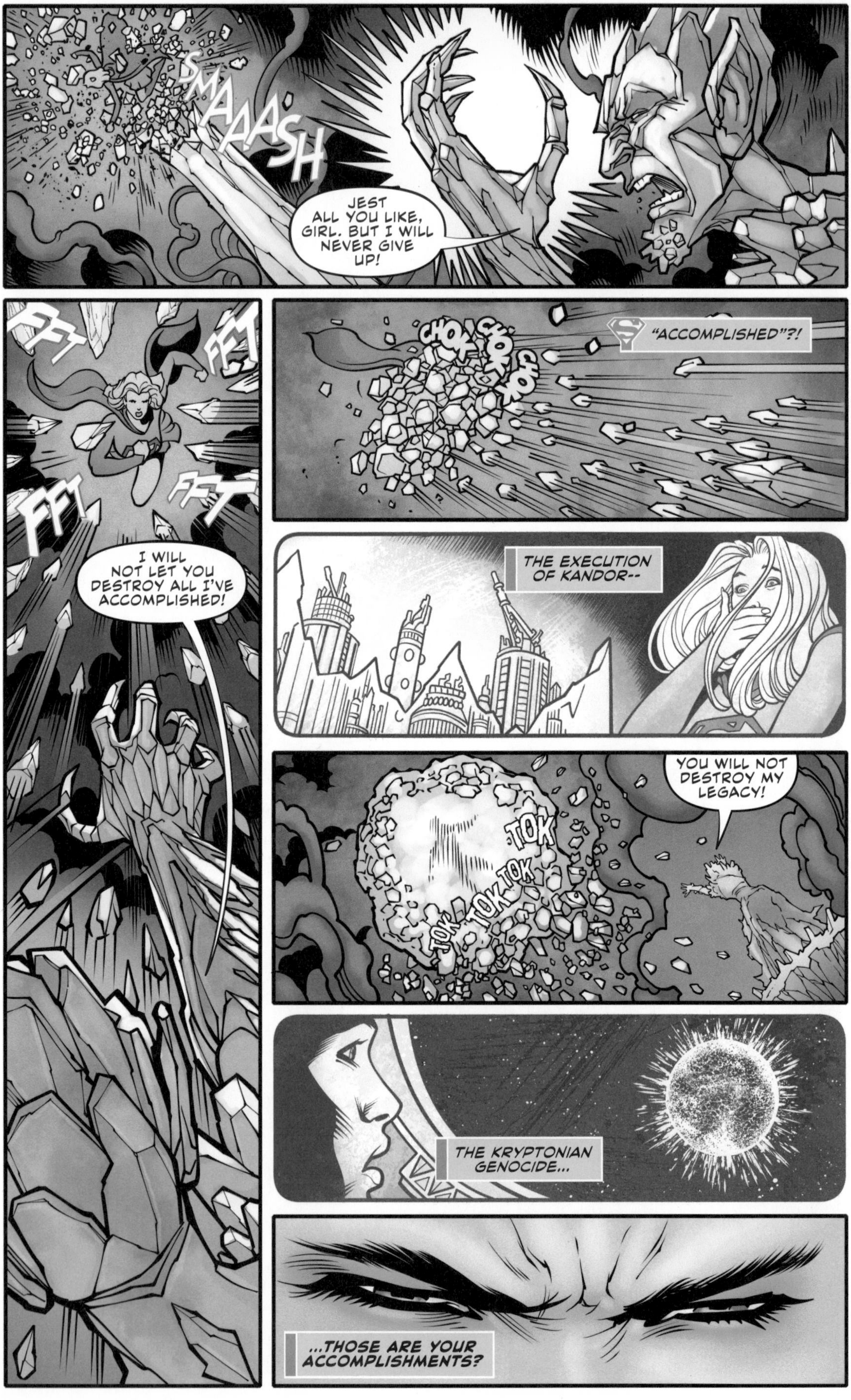
SMAAASH
JEST ALL YOU LIKE, GIRL. BUT I WILL NEVER GIVE UP!
FFT
FFT
FFT
FFT
I WILL NOT DESTROY LET YOU DESTROY ALL I'VE ACCOMPLISHED!
CHOK CHOK CHOK
"ACCOMPLISHED"?!
THE EXECUTION OF KANDOR--
YOU WILL NOT DESTROY MY LEGACY!
TOK TOK TOK TOK
THE KRYPTONIAN GENOCIDE...
...THOSE ARE YOUR ACCOMPLISHMENTS?

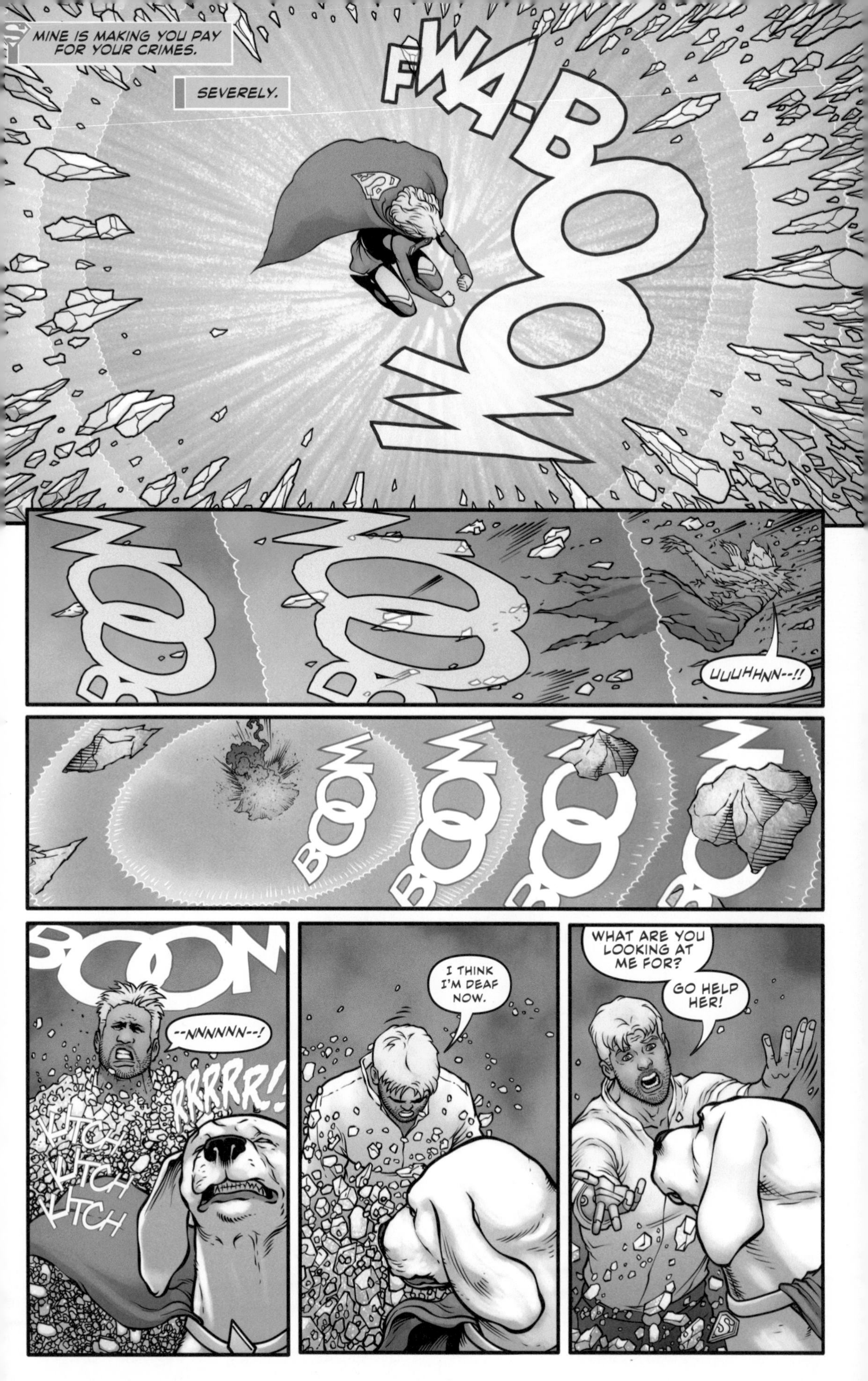
MINE IS MAKING YOU PAY FOR YOUR CRIMES.
SEVERELY.
FWA-BOOM
BOOM
BOOM
UUUHHNN--!!
BOOM
BOOM
BOOM
BOOM
BOOM
--NNNNNN--!
RRRRR!!
KLITCH KLITCH KLITCH
I THINK I'M DEAF NOW.
WHAT ARE YOU LOOKING AT ME FOR?
GO HELP HER!

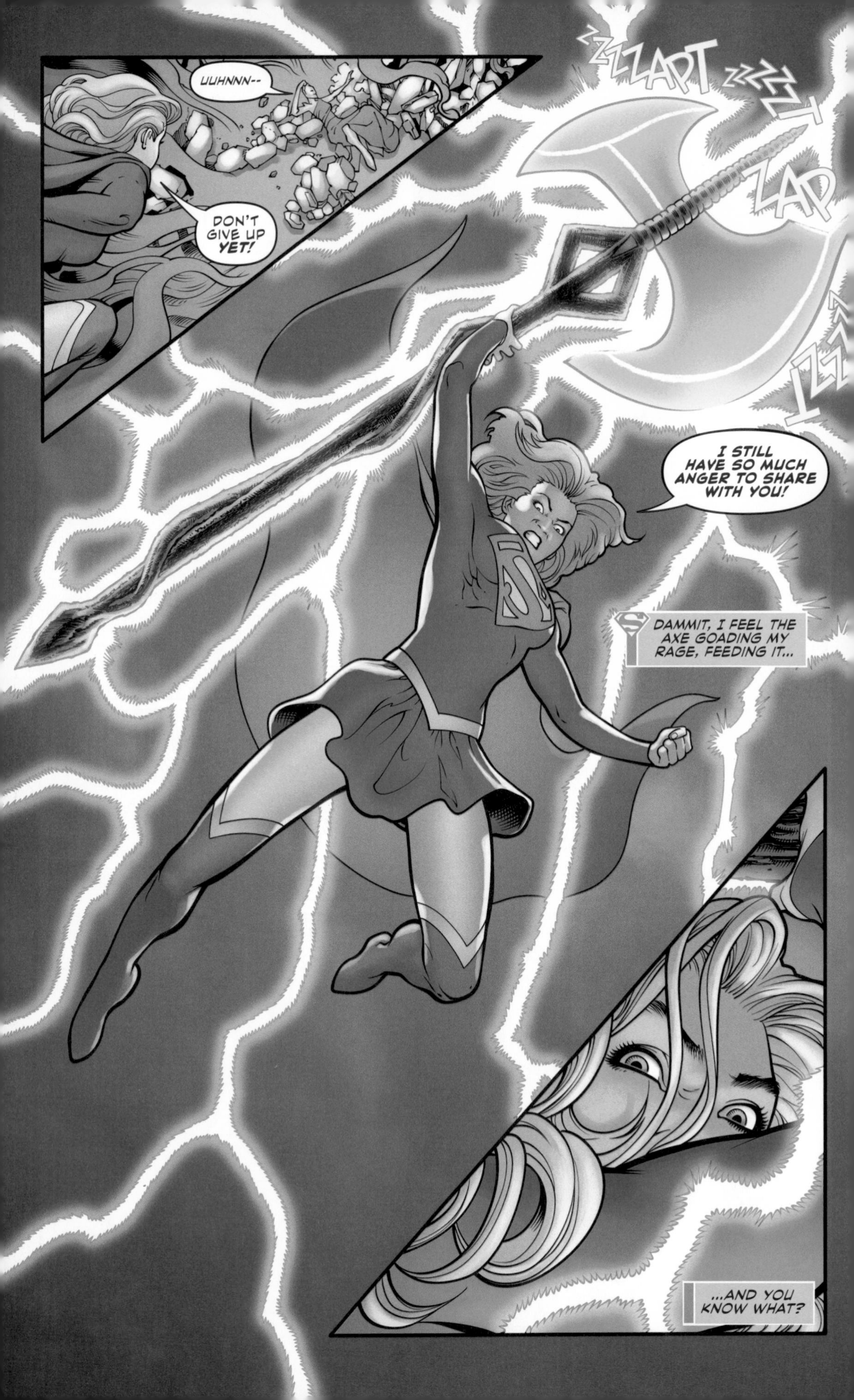
UUHNNN--
DON'T GIVE UP YET!
ZZZZAPT ZZZZZT ZAP ZZZZ
I STILL HAVE SO MUCH ANGER TO SHARE WITH YOU!
DAMMIT, I FEEL THE AXE GOADING MY RAGE, FEEDING IT...
...AND YOU KNOW WHAT?

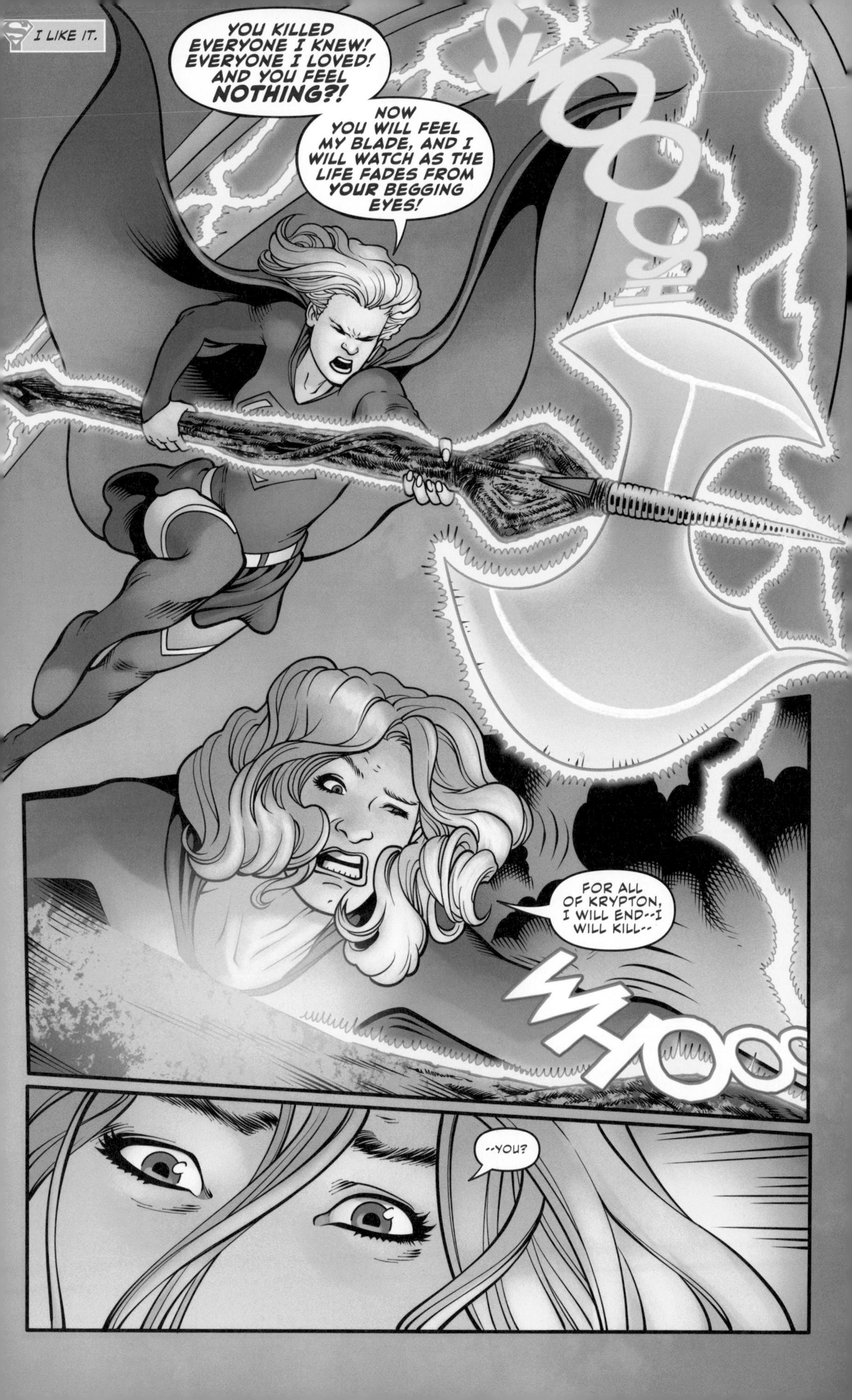
I LIKE IT.
YOU KILLED EVERYONE I KNEW! EVERYONE I LOVED! AND YOU FEEL NOTHING?!
NOW YOU WILL FEEL MY BLADE, AND I WILL WATCH AS THE LIFE FADES FROM YOUR BEGGING EYES!
SWOOOOSH
FOR ALL OF KRYPTON, I WILL END--I WILL KILL--
WHOOOS
--YOU?

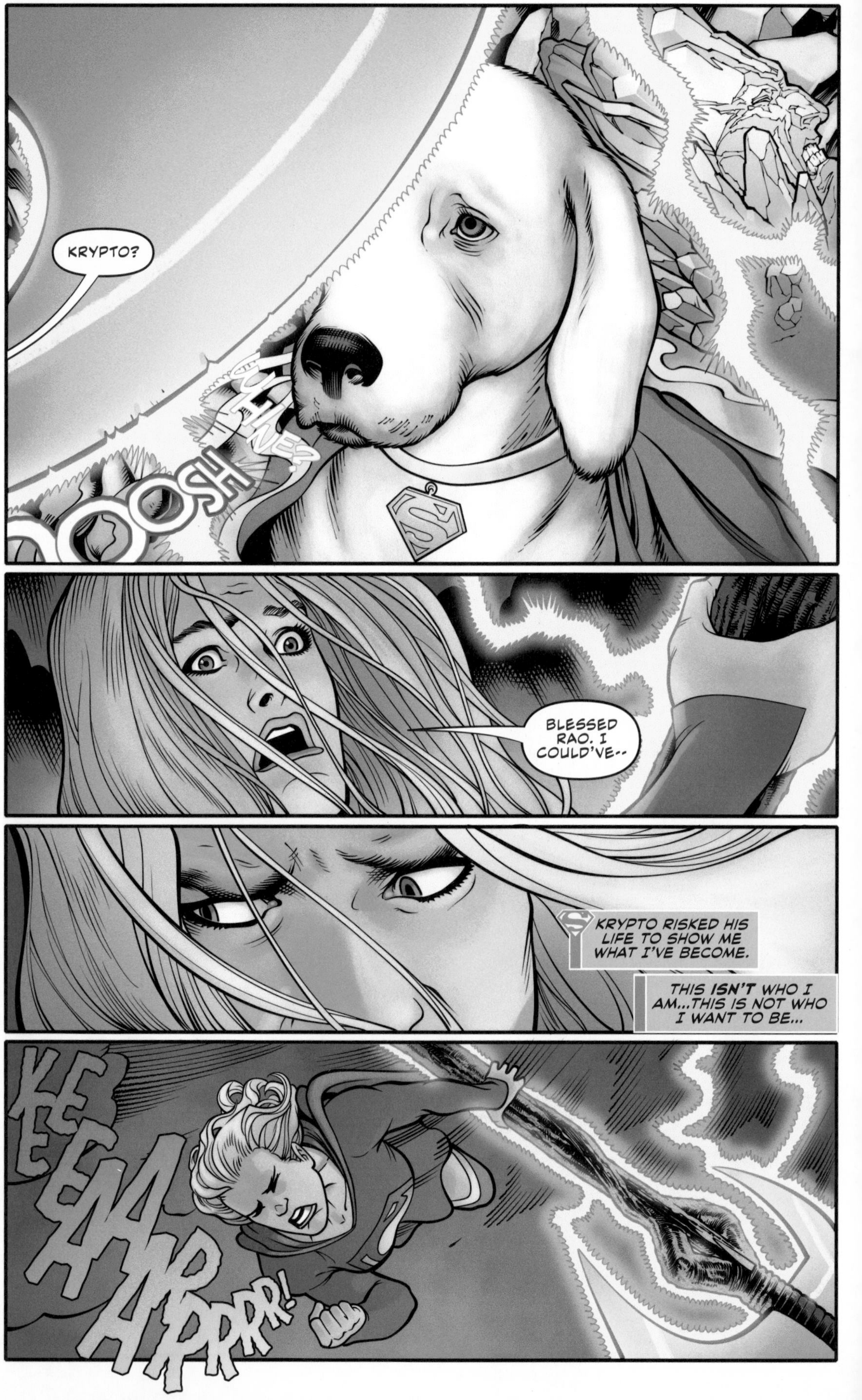
KRYPTO?
WHINE?
BLESSED RAO. I COULD'VE--
KRYPTO RISKED HIS LIFE TO SHOW ME WHAT I'VE BECOME.
THIS **ISN'T** WHO I AM...THIS IS NOT WHO I WANT TO BE...

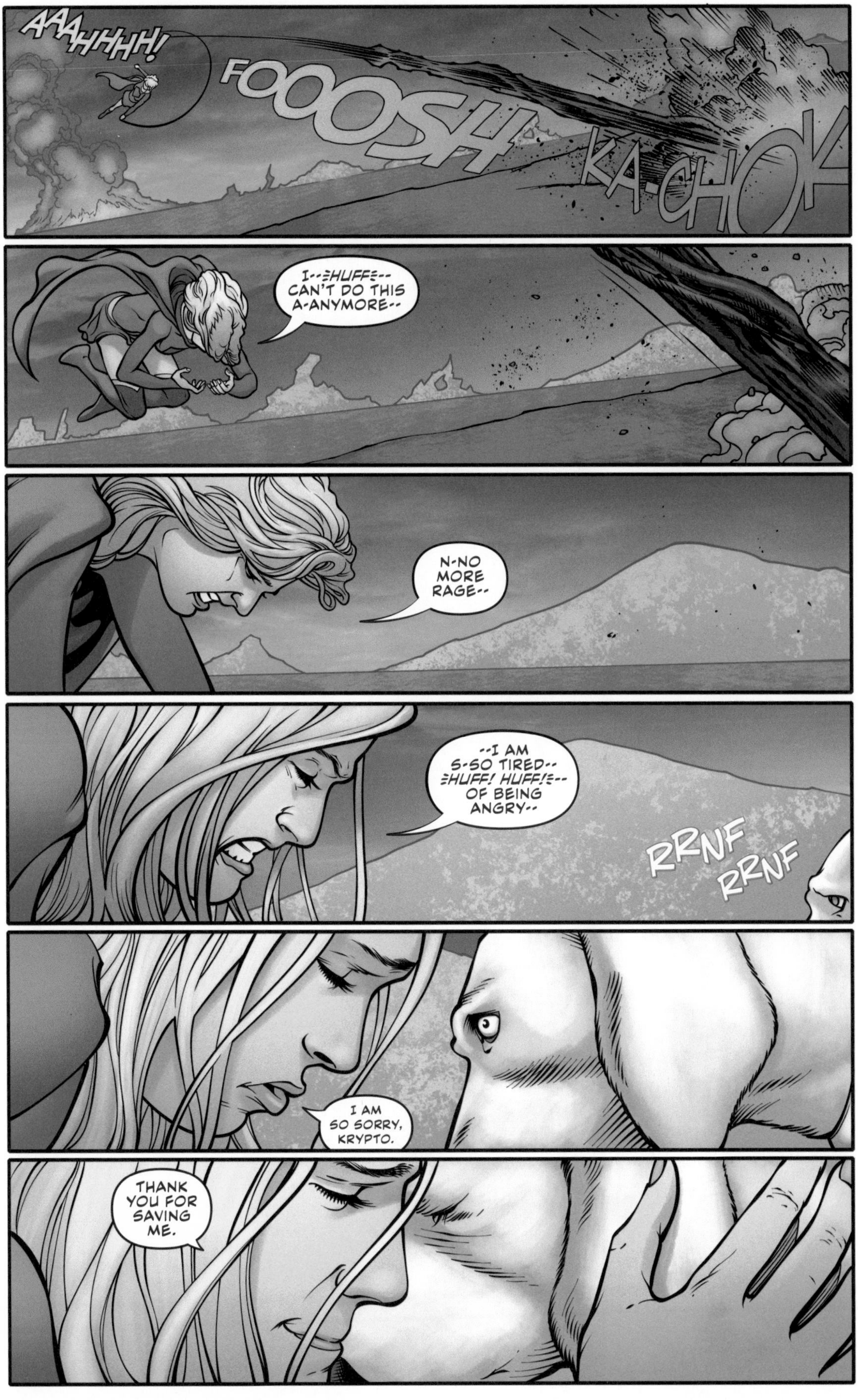
AAAHHHH!
FOOOSH
KA-CHOK
I--HUFF--
CAN'T DO THIS
A-ANYMORE--
N-NO
MORE
RAGE--
--I AM
S-SO TIRED--
HUFF! HUFF!--
OF BEING
ANGRY--
RRNF
RRNF
I AM
SO SORRY,
KRYPTO.
THANK
YOU FOR
SAVING
ME.

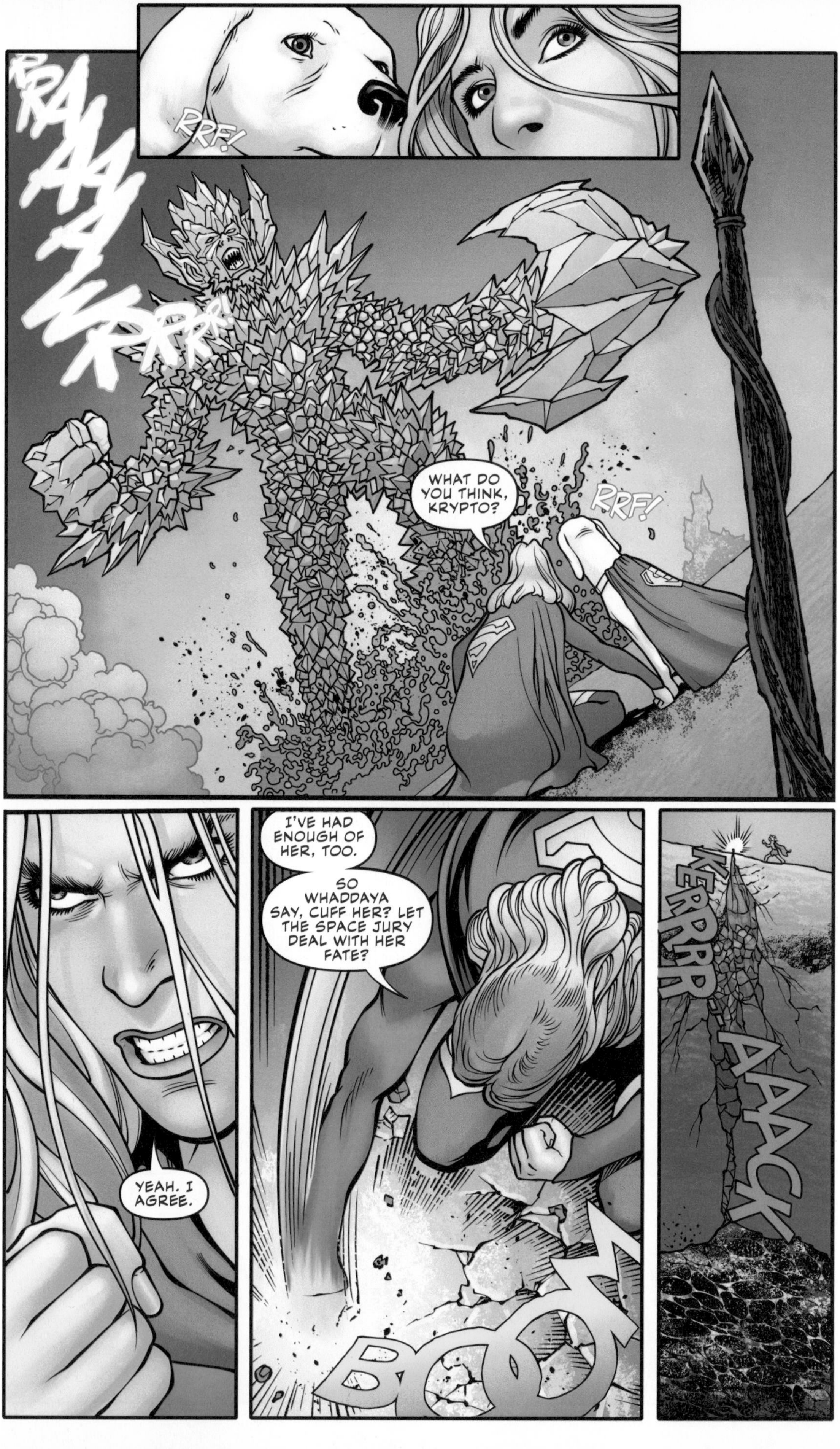
RRF!
RRAAAAWRRRR!
WHAT DO YOU THINK, KRYPTO?
RRF!
YEAH. I AGREE.
I'VE HAD ENOUGH OF HER, TOO.
SO WHADDAYA SAY, CUFF HER? LET THE SPACE JURY DEAL WITH HER FATE?
BOOM
KERRRR-AAACK

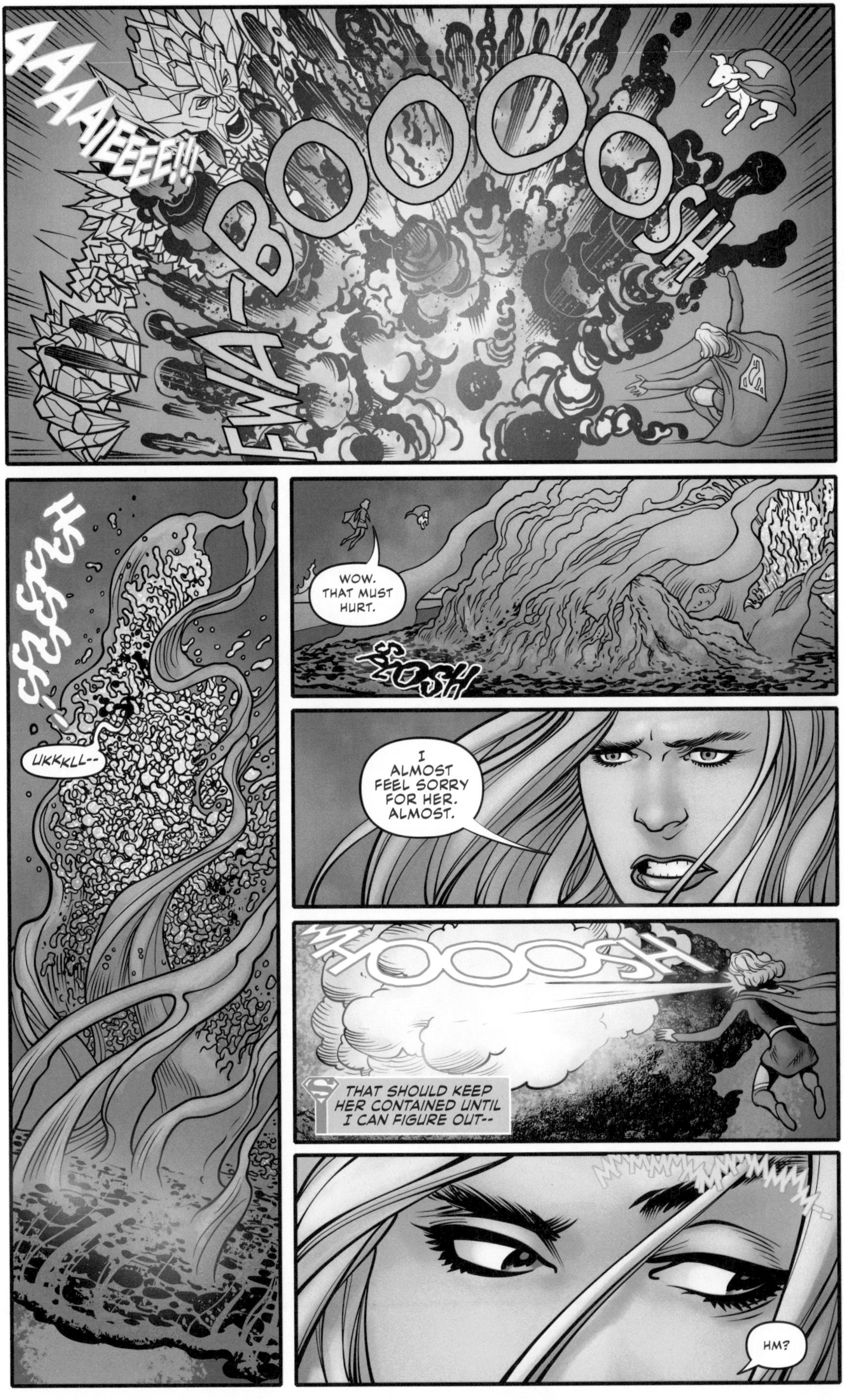
AAAAIEEEEE!!!
FWA-BOOOOOSH
SSSSSSS
UKKKLL--
WOW. THAT MUST HURT.
FOOSH
I ALMOST FEEL SORRY FOR HER. ALMOST.
WHOOOSH
THAT SHOULD KEEP HER CONTAINED UNTIL I CAN FIGURE OUT--
MMMMMMMMMM--
HM?

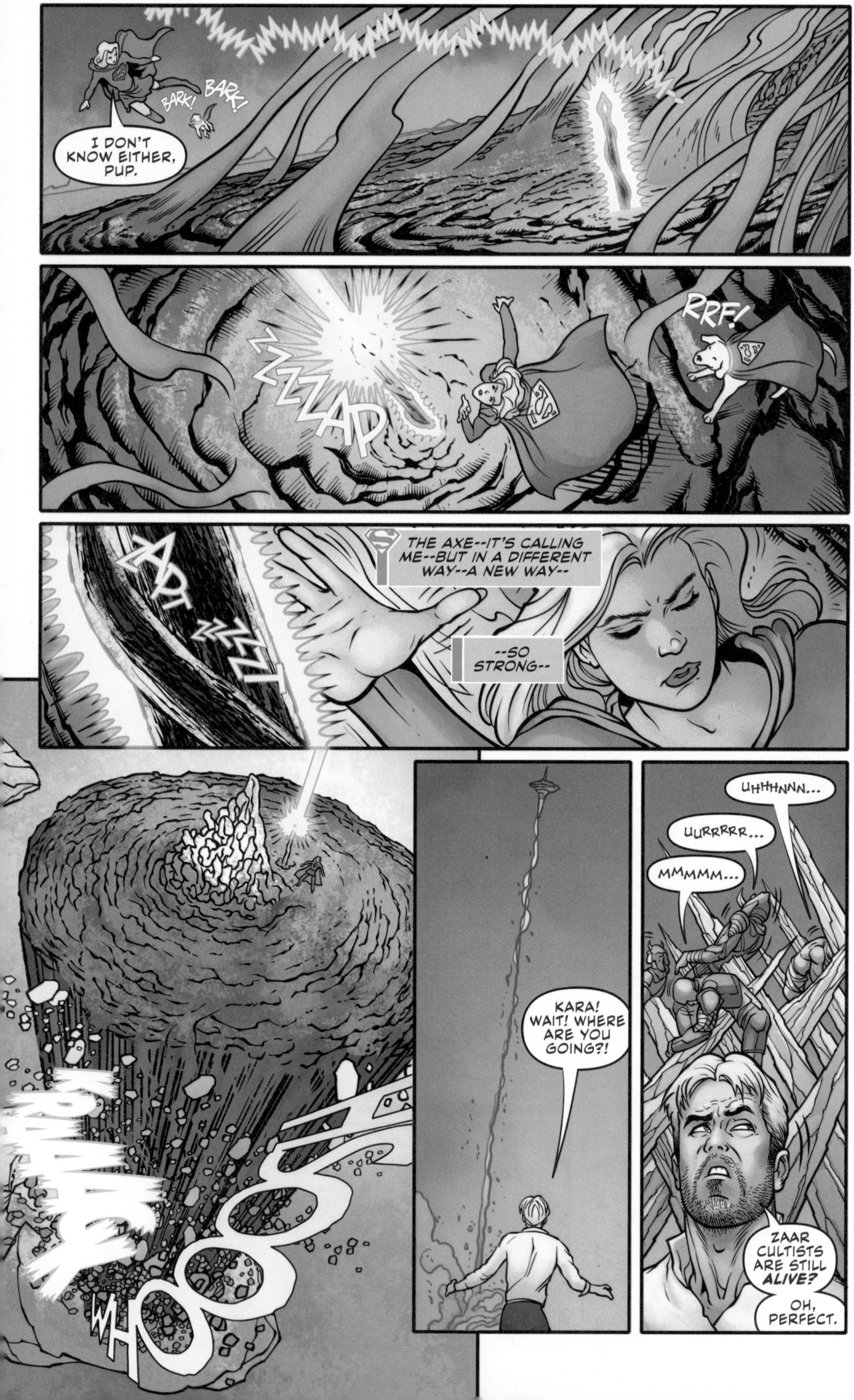

MMMMMMMMMMMMMMMMM--
BARK! BARK!
I DON'T KNOW EITHER, PUP.
ZZZZAP
RRF!
ZAPT ZZZZT
THE AXE--IT'S CALLING ME--BUT IN A DIFFERENT WAY--A NEW WAY--
--SO STRONG--
KRAAKA
WHOOOSH
KARA! WAIT! WHERE ARE YOU GOING?!
UHHHNNN...
UURRRRR...
MMMMM...
ZAAR CULTISTS ARE STILL *ALIVE?*
OH, PERFECT.

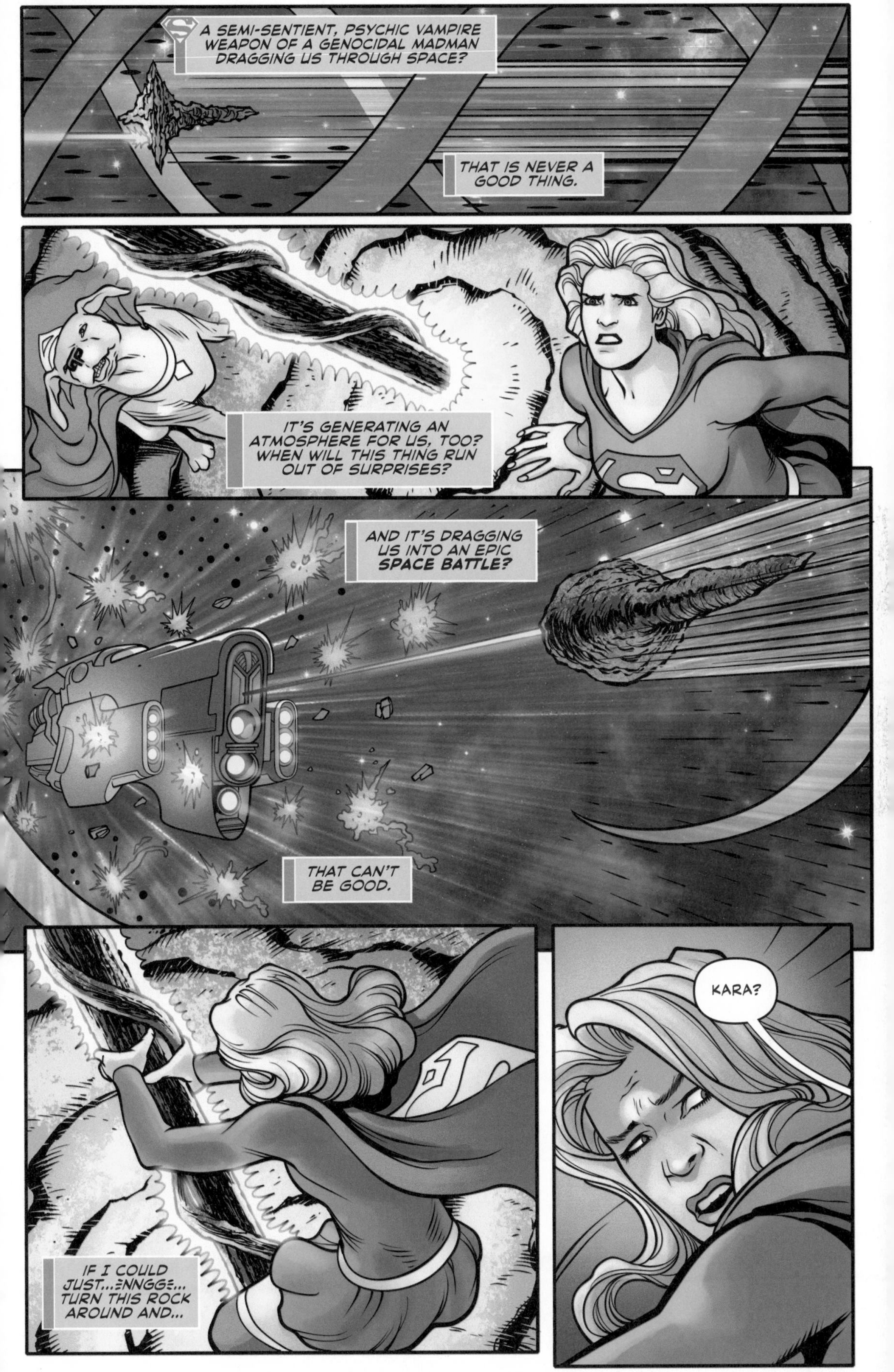
A SEMI-SENTIENT, PSYCHIC VAMPIRE WEAPON OF A GENOCIDAL MADMAN DRAGGING US THROUGH SPACE?
THAT IS NEVER A GOOD THING.
IT'S GENERATING AN ATMOSPHERE FOR US, TOO? WHEN WILL THIS THING RUN OUT OF SURPRISES?
AND IT'S DRAGGING US INTO AN EPIC SPACE BATTLE?
THAT CAN'T BE GOOD.
IF I COULD JUST...ENNGG...TURN THIS ROCK AROUND AND...
KARA?

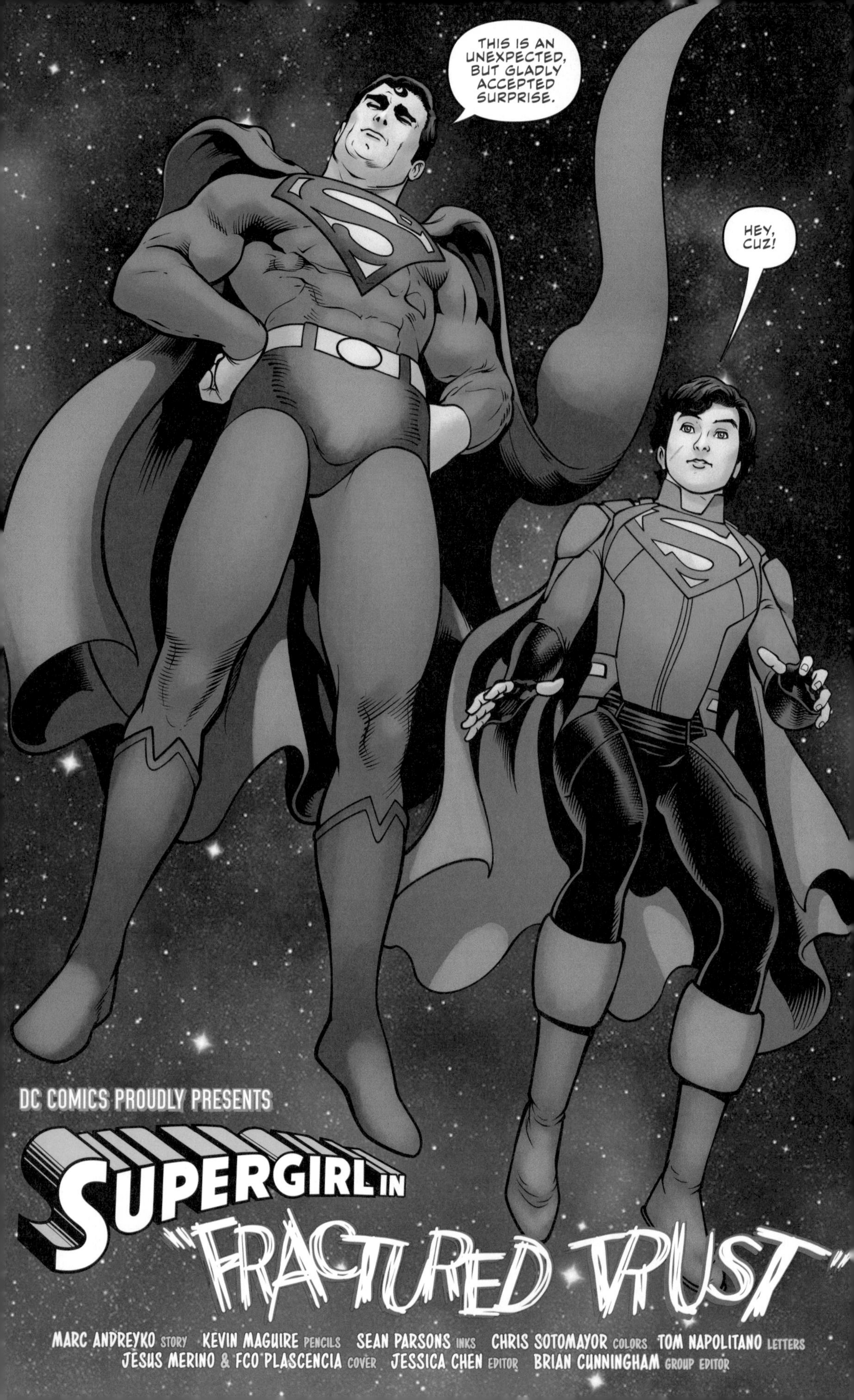
THIS IS AN UNEXPECTED, BUT GLADLY ACCEPTED SURPRISE.
HEY, CUZ!
DC COMICS PROUDLY PRESENTS
SUPERGIRL IN
"FRACTURED TRUST"
MARC ANDREYKO STORY KEVIN MAGUIRE PENCILS SEAN PARSONS INKS CHRIS SOTOMAYOR COLORS TOM NAPOLITANO LETTERS
JESUS MERINO & FCO PLASCENCIA COVER JESSICA CHEN EDITOR BRIAN CUNNINGHAM GROUP EDITOR

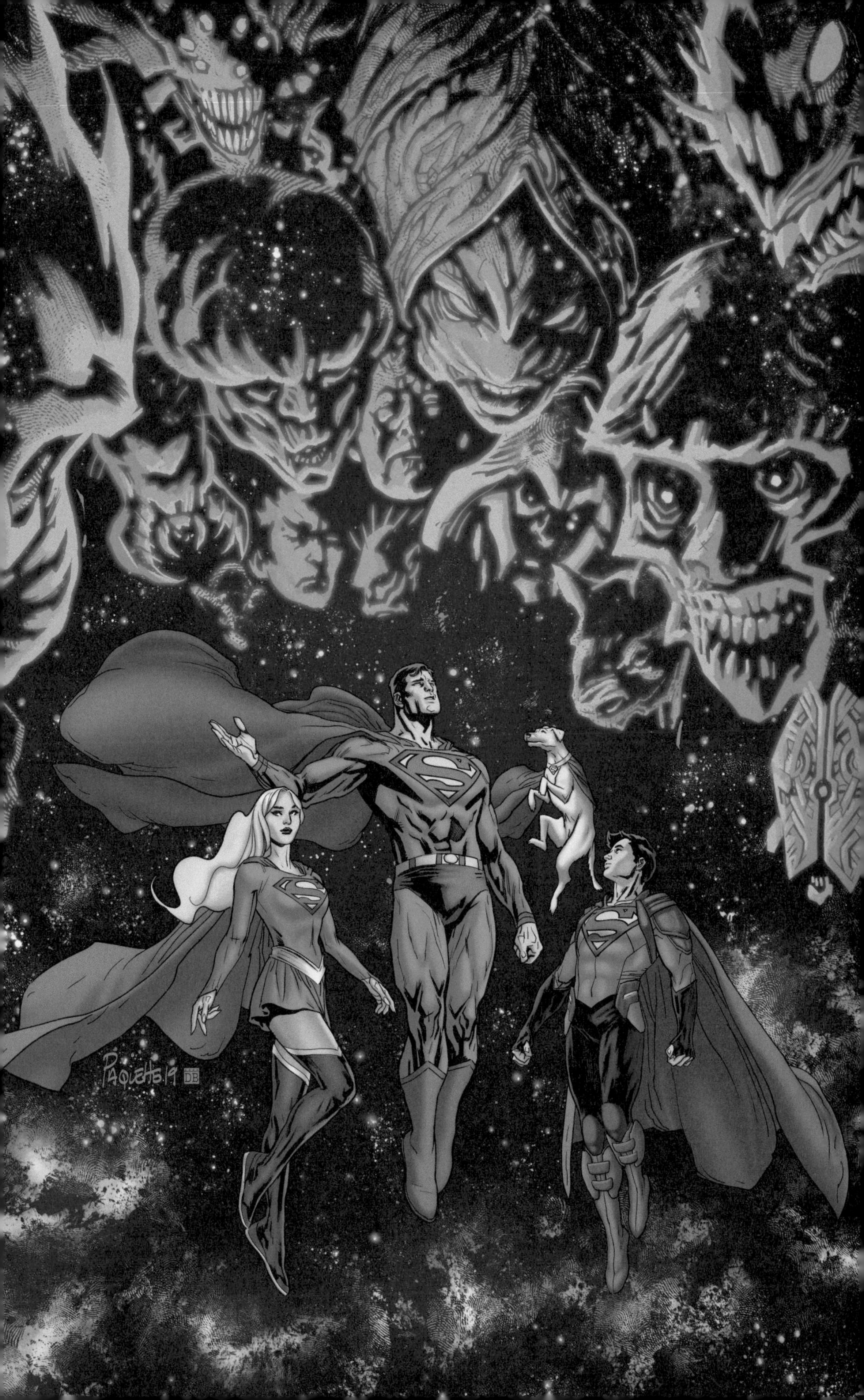

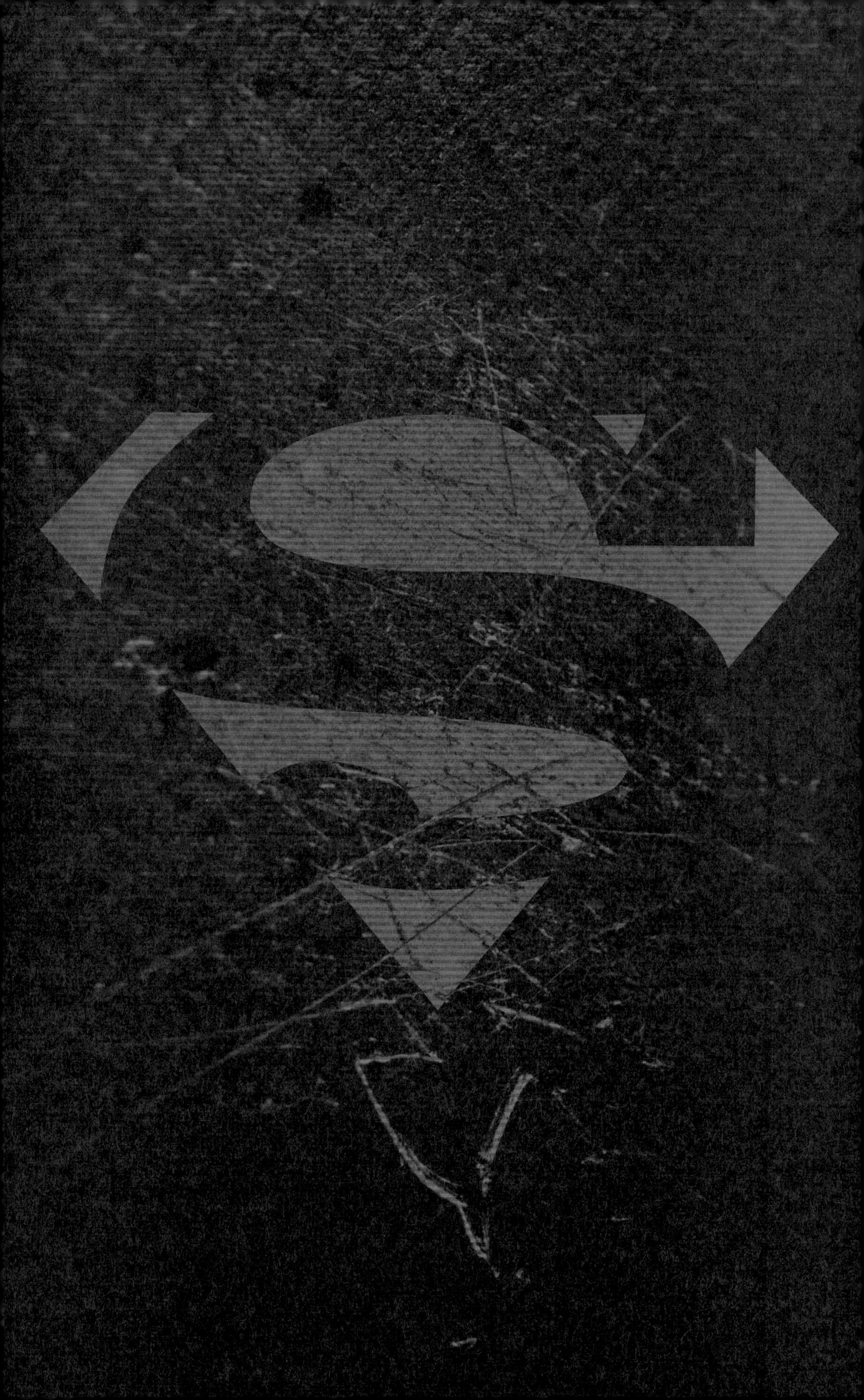

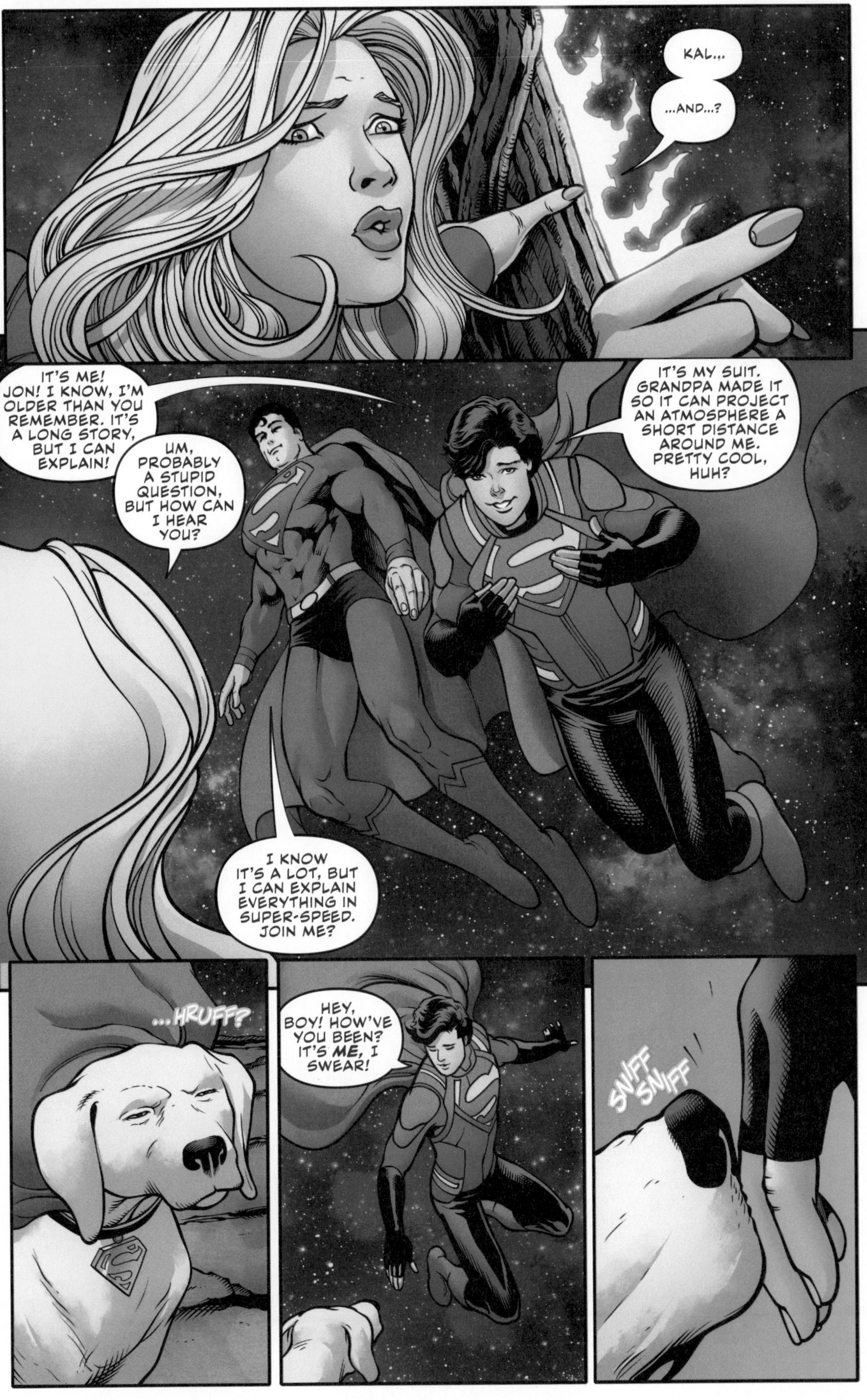
KAL...
...AND...?
IT'S ME! JON! I KNOW, I'M OLDER THAN YOU REMEMBER. IT'S A LONG STORY, BUT I CAN EXPLAIN!
UM, PROBABLY A STUPID QUESTION, BUT HOW CAN I HEAR YOU?
IT'S MY SUIT. GRANDPA MADE IT SO IT CAN PROJECT AN ATMOSPHERE A SHORT DISTANCE AROUND ME. PRETTY COOL, HUH?
I KNOW IT'S A LOT, BUT I CAN EXPLAIN EVERYTHING IN SUPER-SPEED. JOIN ME?
...HRUFF?
HEY, BOY! HOW'VE YOU BEEN? IT'S ME, I SWEAR!
SNIFF SNIFF

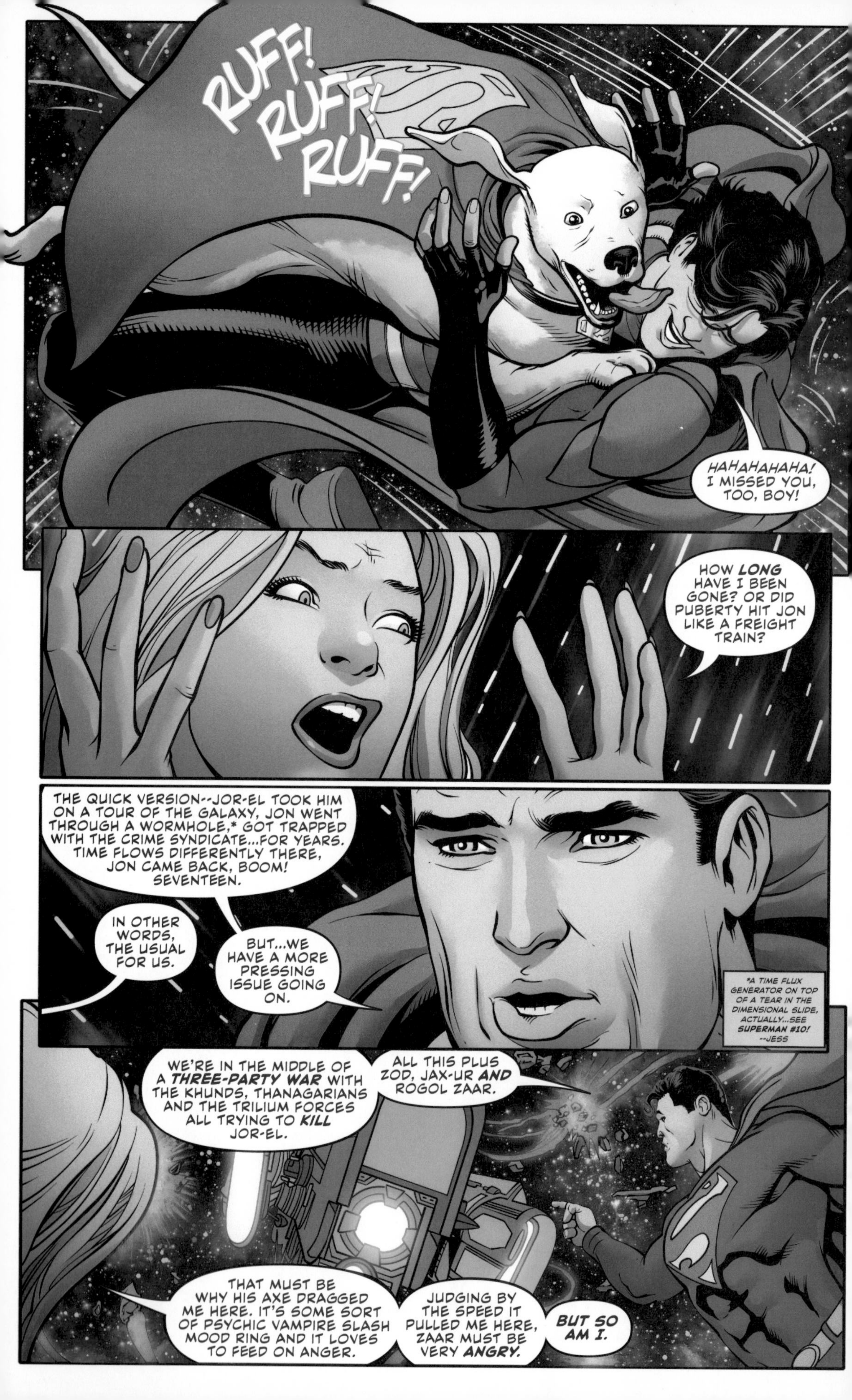
RUFF! RUFF! RUFF!
HAHAHAHAHA! I MISSED YOU, TOO, BOY!
HOW LONG HAVE I BEEN GONE? OR DID PUBERTY HIT JON LIKE A FREIGHT TRAIN?
THE QUICK VERSION--JOR-EL TOOK HIM ON A TOUR OF THE GALAXY, JON WENT THROUGH A WORMHOLE,* GOT TRAPPED WITH THE CRIME SYNDICATE...FOR YEARS. TIME FLOWS DIFFERENTLY THERE, JON CAME BACK, BOOM! SEVENTEEN.
IN OTHER WORDS, THE USUAL FOR US.
BUT...WE HAVE A MORE PRESSING ISSUE GOING ON.
*A TIME FLUX GENERATOR ON TOP OF A TEAR IN THE DIMENSIONAL SLIDE, ACTUALLY...SEE SUPERMAN #10! --JESS
WE'RE IN THE MIDDLE OF A THREE-PARTY WAR WITH THE KHUNDS, THANAGARIANS AND THE TRILIUM FORCES ALL TRYING TO KILL JOR-EL.
ALL THIS PLUS ZOD, JAX-UR AND ROGOL ZAAR.
THAT MUST BE WHY HIS AXE DRAGGED ME HERE. IT'S SOME SORT OF PSYCHIC VAMPIRE SLASH MOOD RING AND IT LOVES TO FEED ON ANGER.
JUDGING BY THE SPEED IT PULLED ME HERE, ZAAR MUST BE VERY ANGRY.
BUT SO AM I.

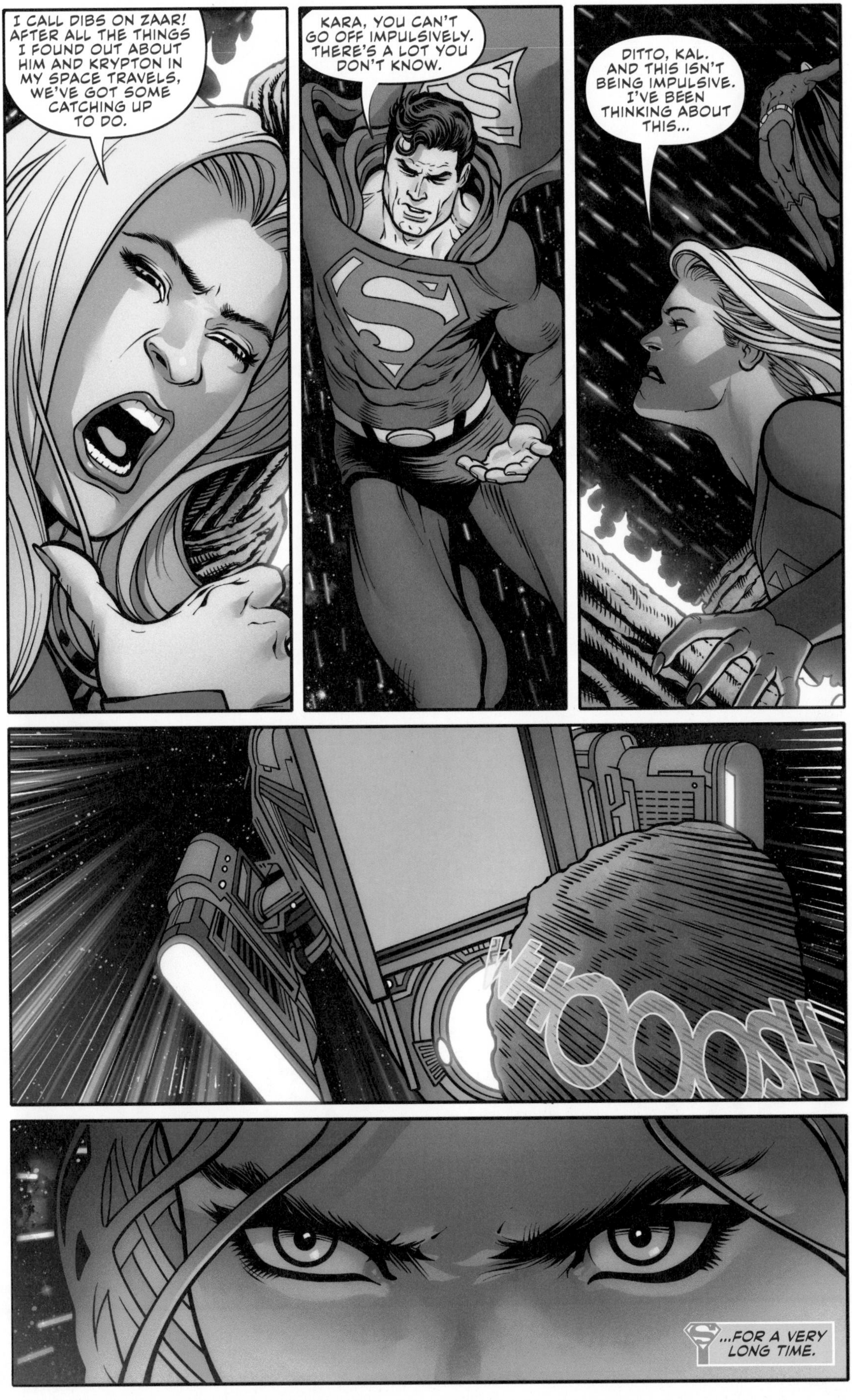
I CALL DIBS ON ZAAR! AFTER ALL THE THINGS I FOUND OUT ABOUT HIM AND KRYPTON IN MY SPACE TRAVELS, WE'VE GOT SOME CATCHING UP TO DO.
KARA, YOU CAN'T GO OFF IMPULSIVELY. THERE'S A LOT YOU DON'T KNOW.
DITTO, KAL. AND THIS ISN'T BEING IMPULSIVE. I'VE BEEN THINKING ABOUT THIS...
WHOOOSH
...FOR A VERY LONG TIME.

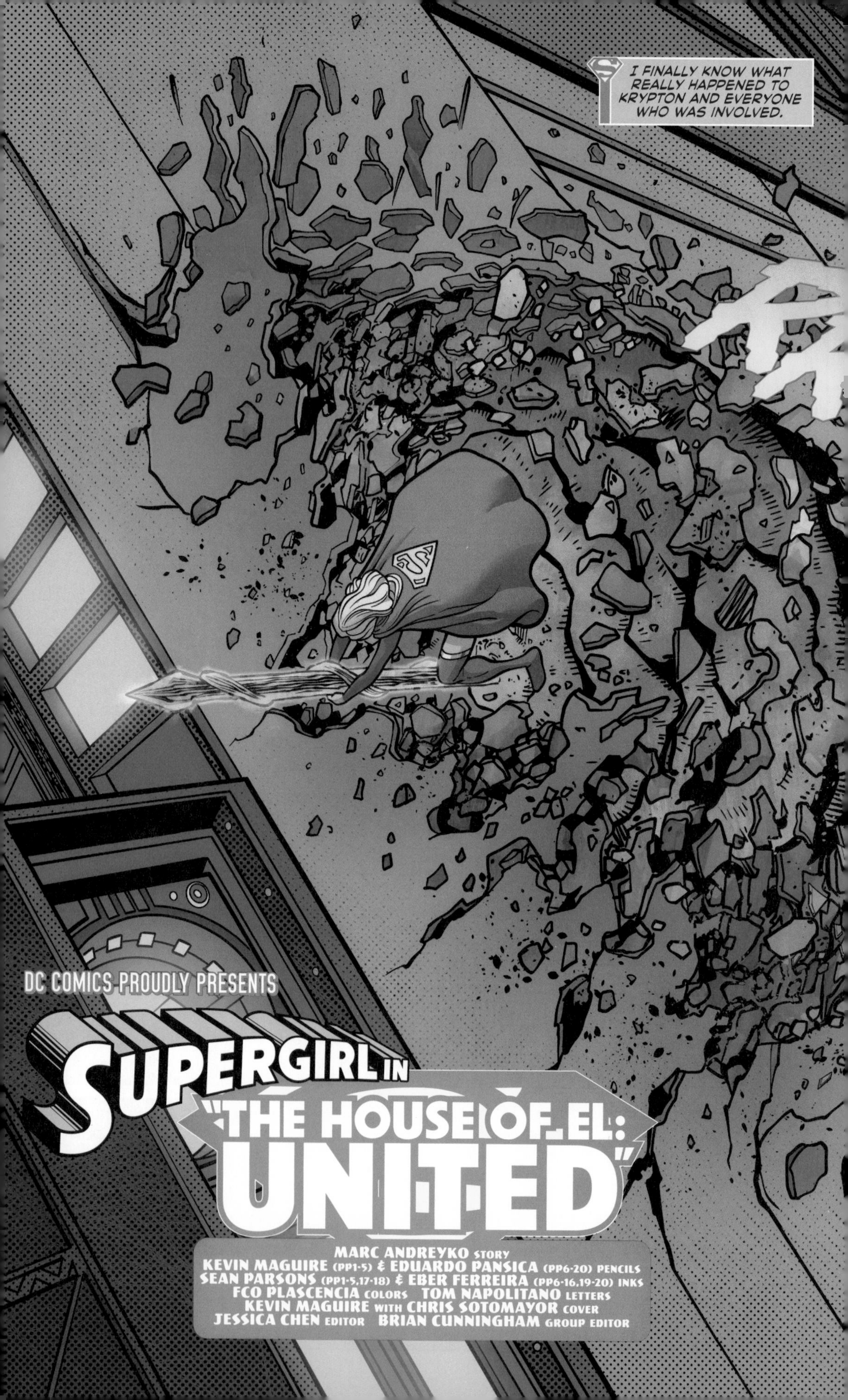

I FINALLY KNOW WHAT REALLY HAPPENED TO KRYPTON AND EVERYONE WHO WAS INVOLVED.
DC COMICS PROUDLY PRESENTS
SUPERGIRL IN
"THE HOUSE OF EL: UNITED"
MARC ANDREYKO STORY
KEVIN MAGUIRE (PP1-5) & EDUARDO PANSICA (PP6-20) PENCILS
SEAN PARSONS (PP1-5,17-18) & EBER FERREIRA (PP6-16,19-20) INKS
FCO PLASCENCIA COLORS TOM NAPOLITANO LETTERS
KEVIN MAGUIRE WITH CHRIS SOTOMAYOR COVER
JESSICA CHEN EDITOR BRIAN CUNNINGHAM GROUP EDITOR

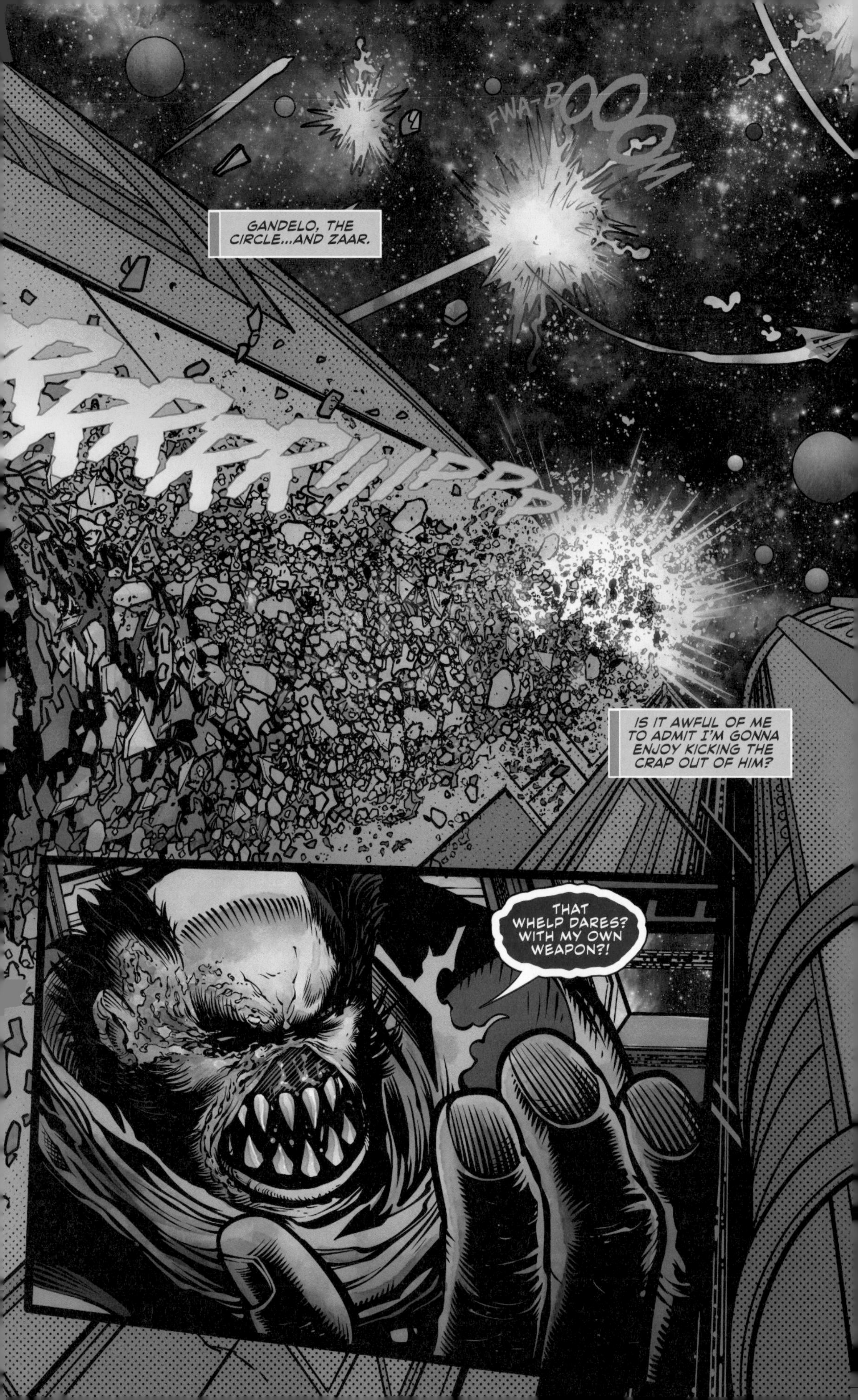
FWA-BOOOOM
GANDELO, THE CIRCLE...AND ZAAR.
PPPPRIIIIPPP
IS IT AWFUL OF ME TO ADMIT I'M GONNA ENJOY KICKING THE CRAP OUT OF HIM?
THAT WHELP DARES? WITH MY OWN WEAPON?!

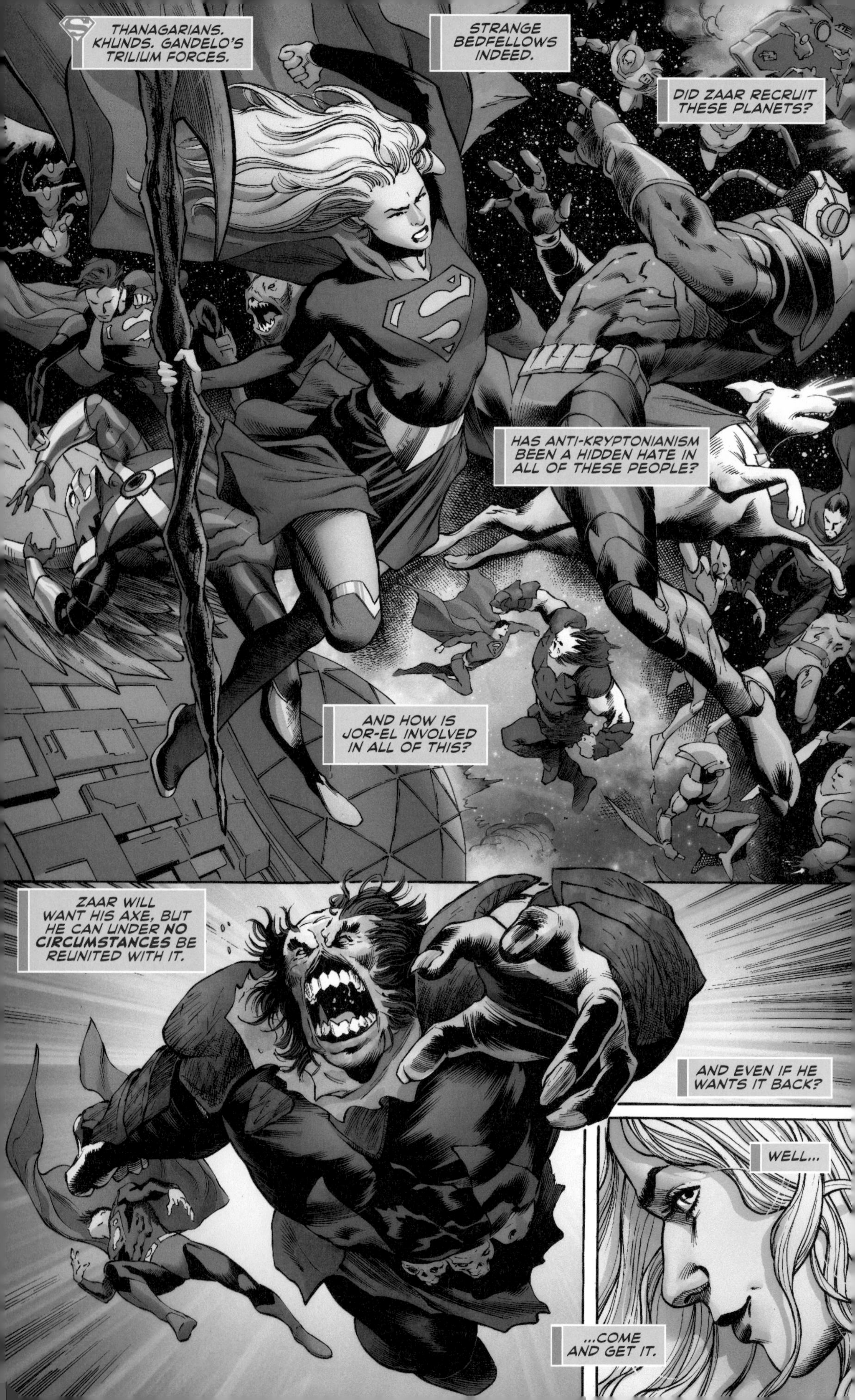
THANAGARIANS. KHUNDS. GANDELO'S TRILIUM FORCES.
STRANGE BEDFELLOWS INDEED.
DID ZAAR RECRUIT THESE PLANETS?
HAS ANTI-KRYPTONIANISM BEEN A HIDDEN HATE IN ALL OF THESE PEOPLE?
AND HOW IS JOR-EL INVOLVED IN ALL OF THIS?
ZAAR WILL WANT HIS AXE, BUT HE CAN UNDER NO CIRCUMSTANCES BE REUNITED WITH IT.
AND EVEN IF HE WANTS IT BACK?
WELL...
...COME AND GET IT.

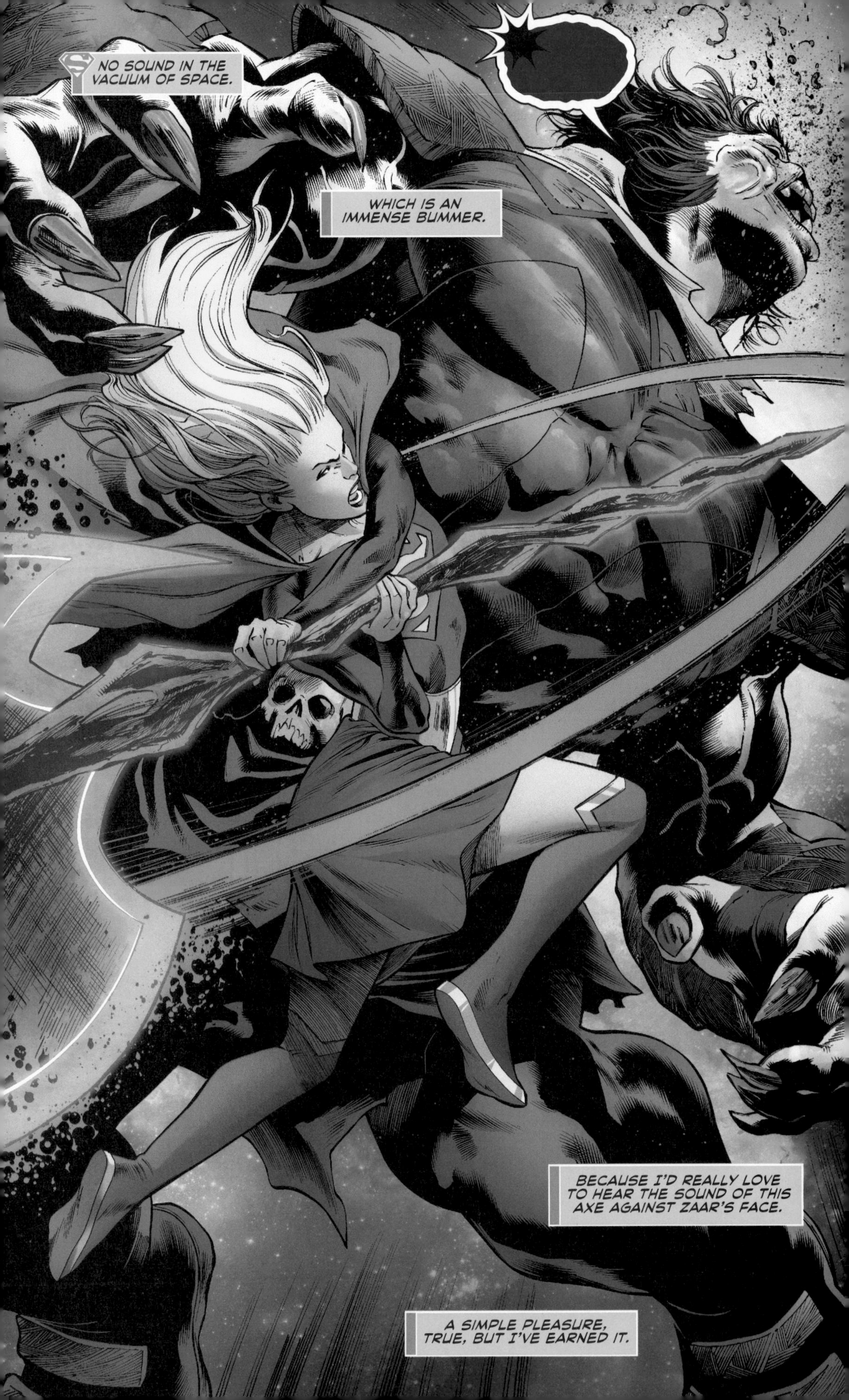
NO SOUND IN THE VACUUM OF SPACE.
WHICH IS AN IMMENSE BUMMER.
BECAUSE I'D REALLY LOVE TO HEAR THE SOUND OF THIS AXE AGAINST ZAAR'S FACE.
A SIMPLE PLEASURE, TRUE, BUT I'VE EARNED IT.

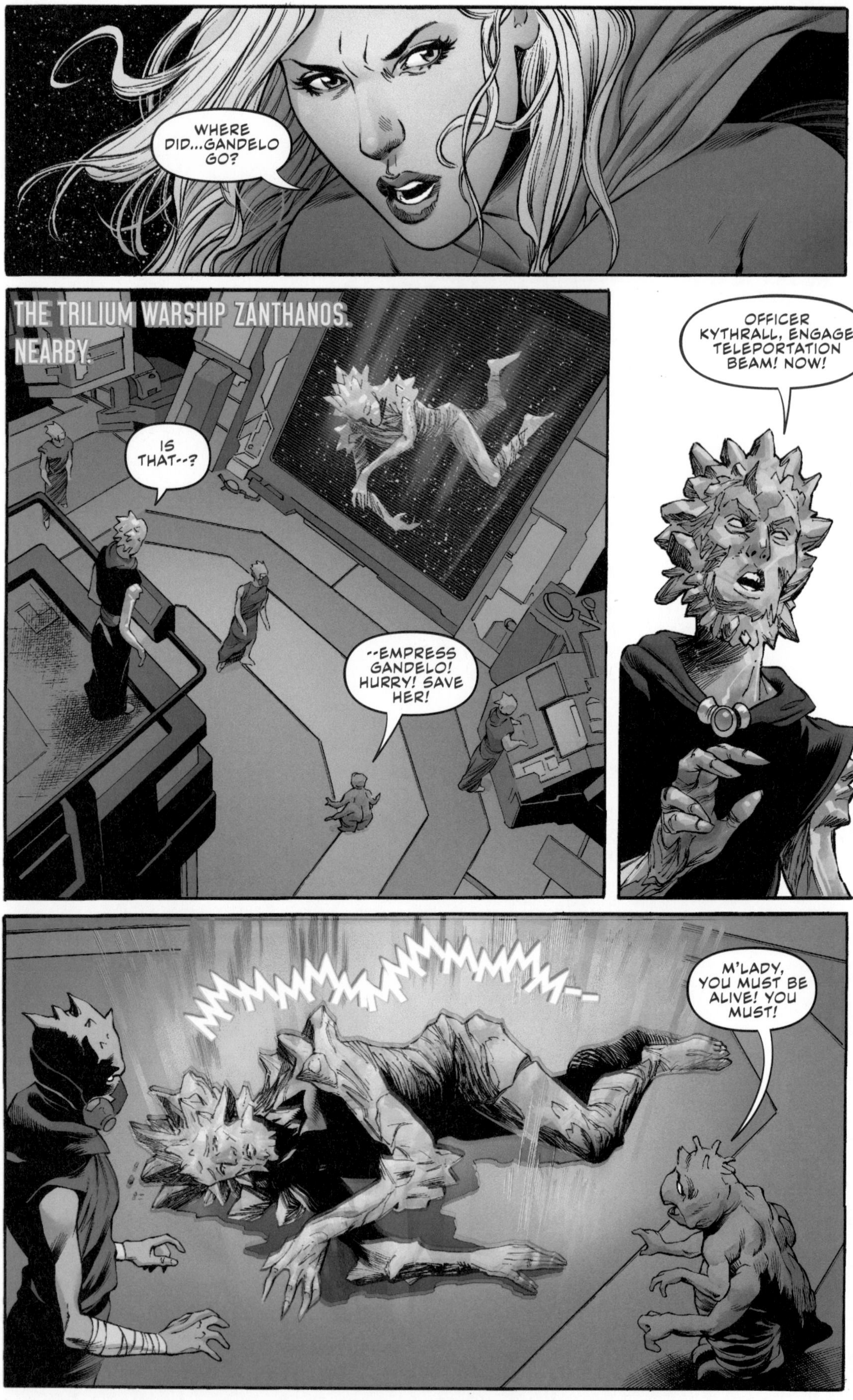
WHERE DID...GANDELO GO?
THE TRILIUM WARSHIP ZANTHANOS. NEARBY.
IS THAT--?
--EMPRESS GANDELO! HURRY! SAVE HER!
OFFICER KYTHRALL, ENGAGE TELEPORTATION BEAM! NOW!
MMMMMMMMMMMM--
M'LADY, YOU MUST BE ALIVE! YOU MUST!

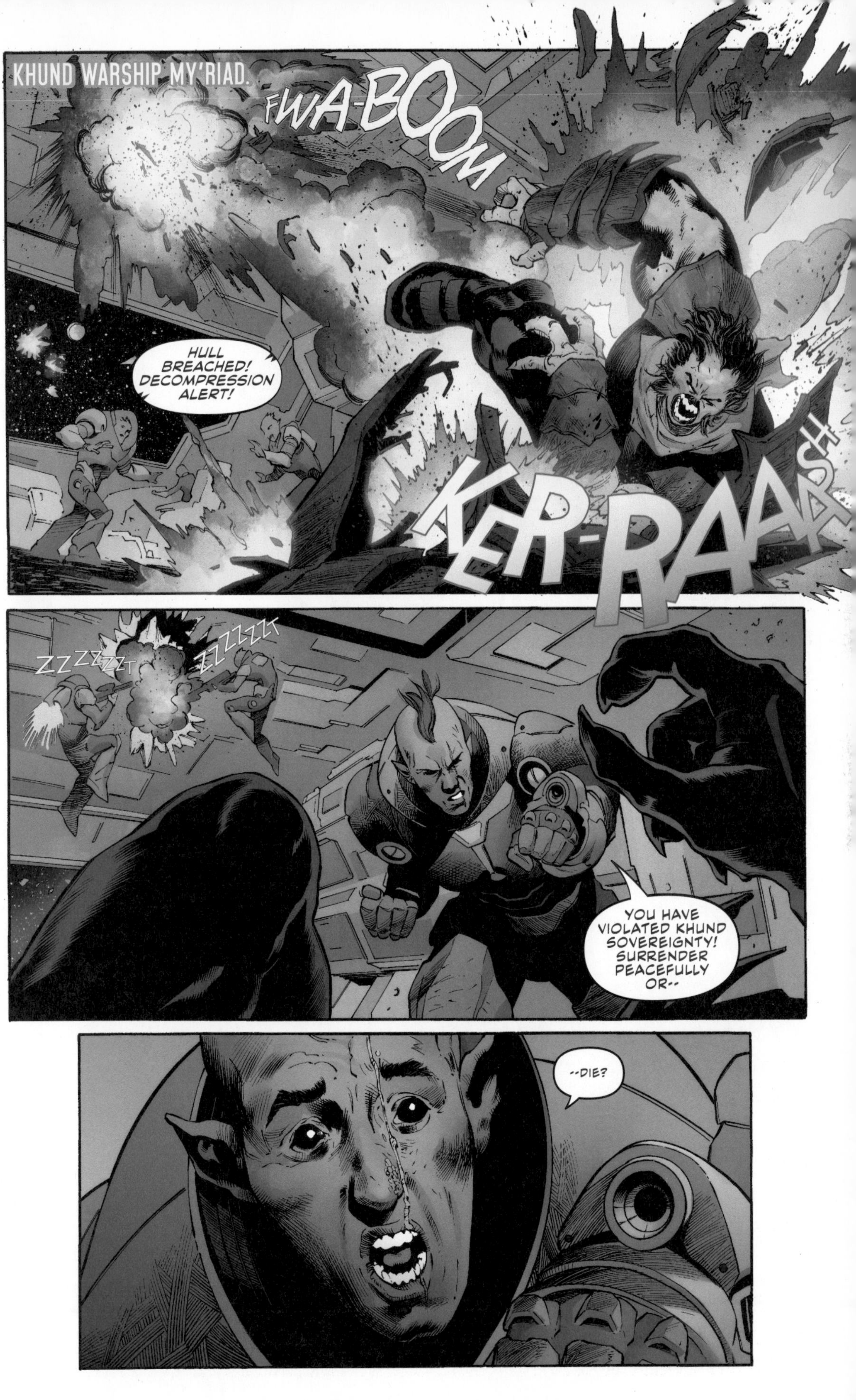
KHUND WARSHIP MY'RIAD.
FWA-BOOM
HULL BREACHED! DECOMPRESSION ALERT!
KER-RAAASH
ZZZZZZT
ZZZZZZT
YOU HAVE VIOLATED KHUND SOVEREIGNTY! SURRENDER PEACEFULLY OR--
--DIE?

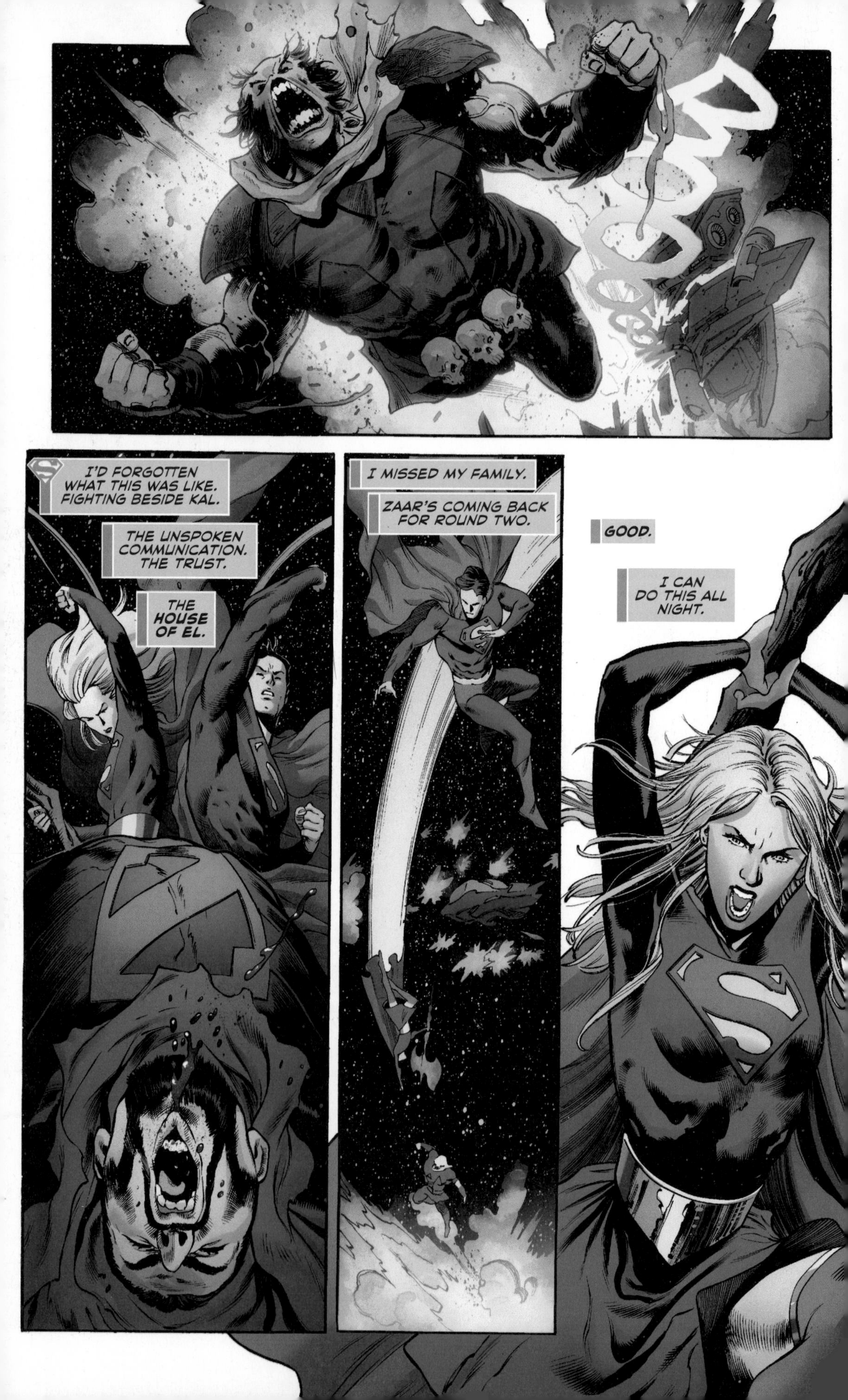
I'D FORGOTTEN WHAT THIS WAS LIKE. FIGHTING BESIDE KAL.
THE UNSPOKEN COMMUNICATION. THE TRUST.
THE HOUSE OF EL.
I MISSED MY FAMILY.
ZAAR'S COMING BACK FOR ROUND TWO.
GOOD.
I CAN DO THIS ALL NIGHT.

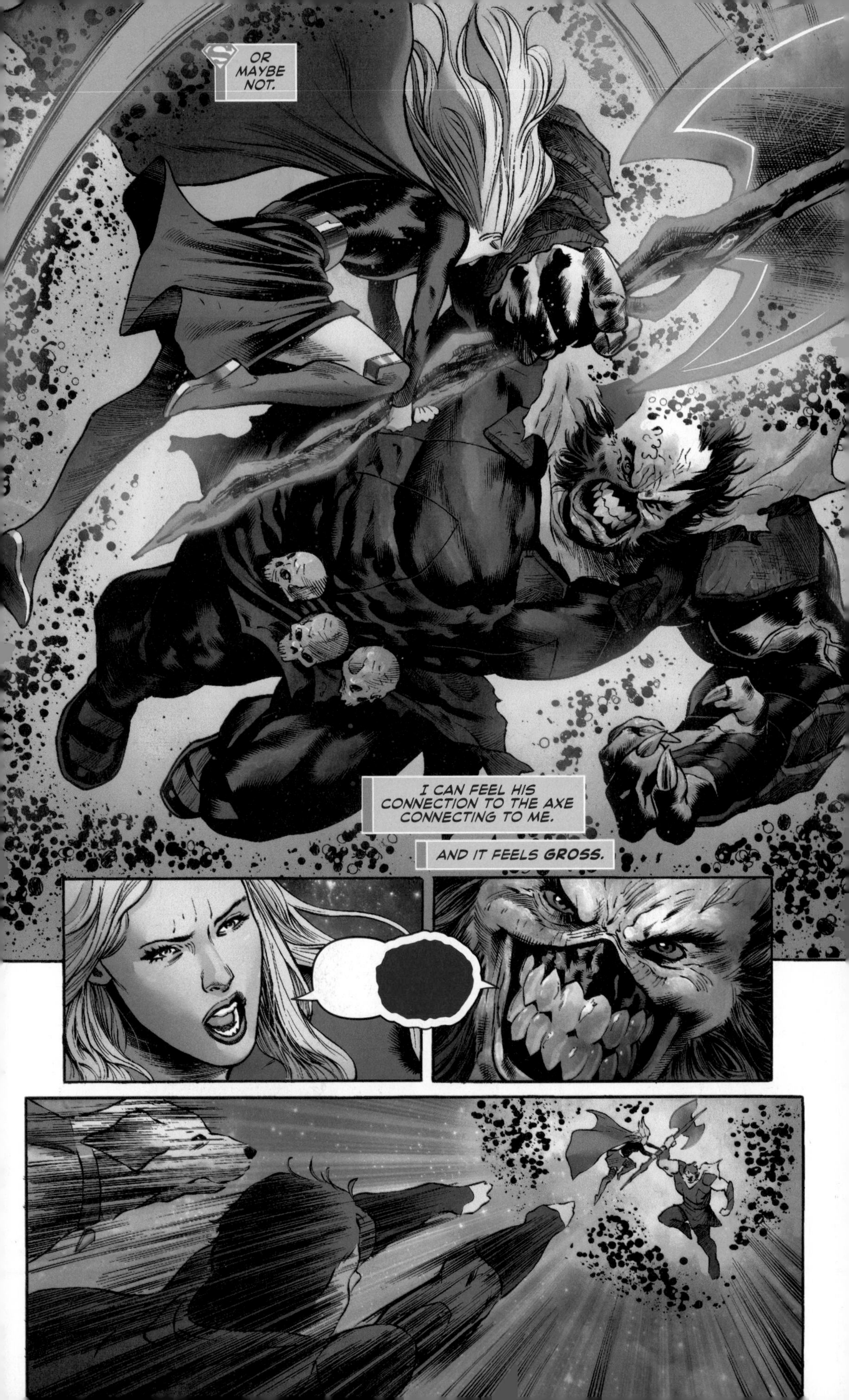
OR MAYBE NOT.
I CAN FEEL HIS CONNECTION TO THE AXE CONNECTING TO ME.
AND IT FEELS GROSS.

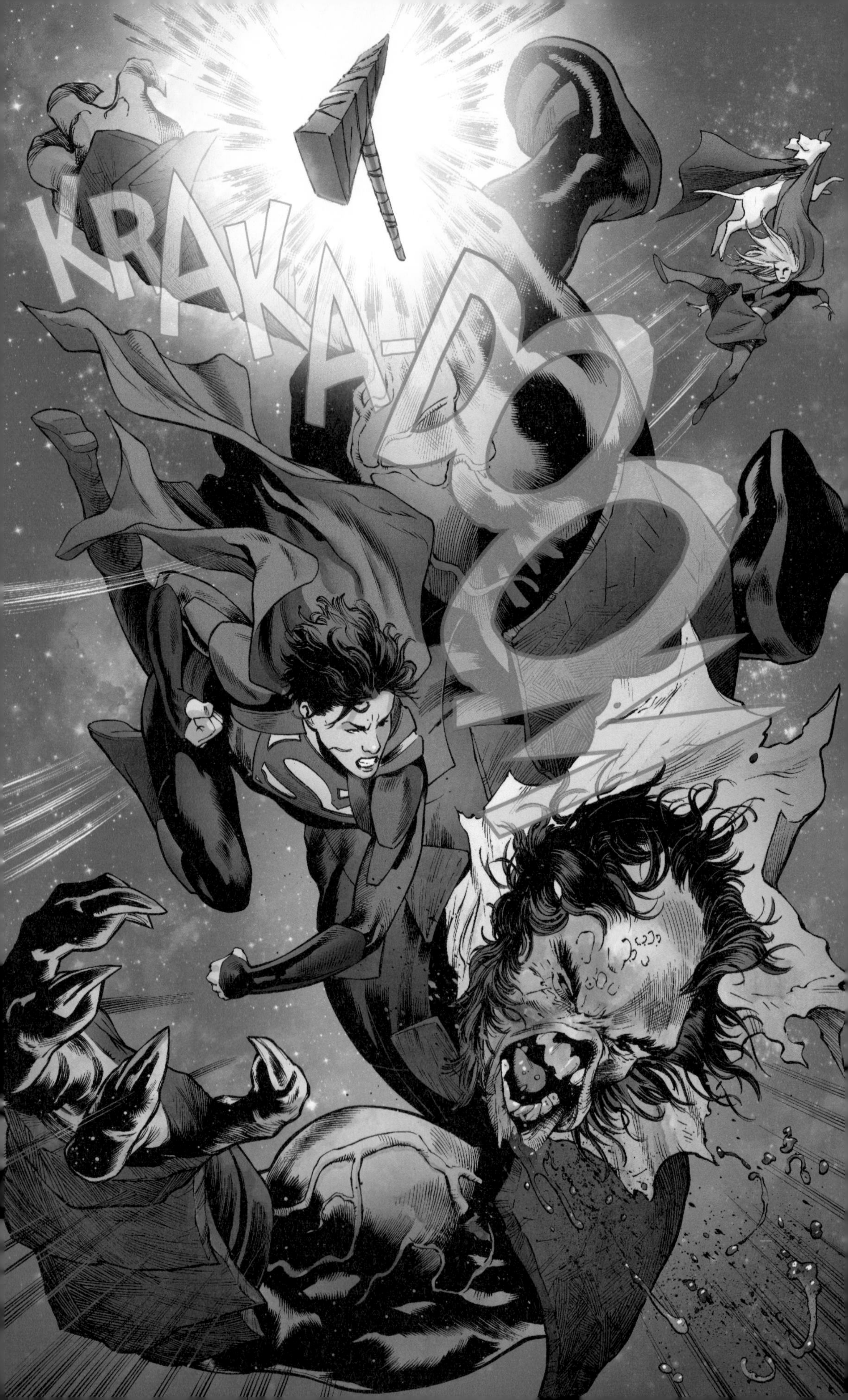
KRAKA-DOOM

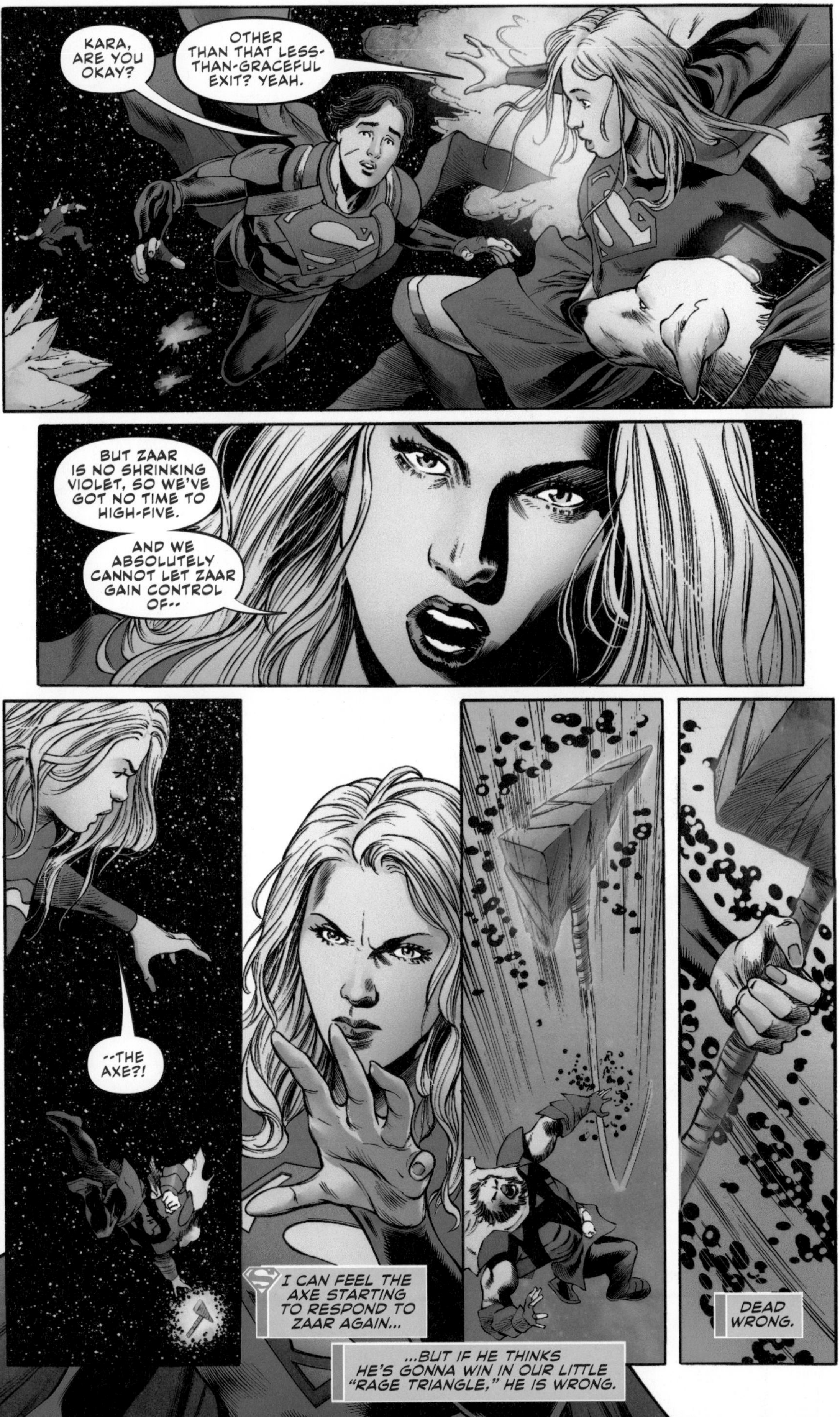
KARA, ARE YOU OKAY?
OTHER THAN THAT LESS-THAN-GRACEFUL EXIT? YEAH.
BUT ZAAR IS NO SHRINKING VIOLET, SO WE'VE GOT NO TIME TO HIGH-FIVE.
AND WE ABSOLUTELY CANNOT LET ZAAR GAIN CONTROL OF--
--THE AXE?!
I CAN FEEL THE AXE STARTING TO RESPOND TO ZAAR AGAIN...
...BUT IF HE THINKS HE'S GONNA WIN IN OUR LITTLE "RAGE TRIANGLE," HE IS WRONG.
DEAD WRONG.

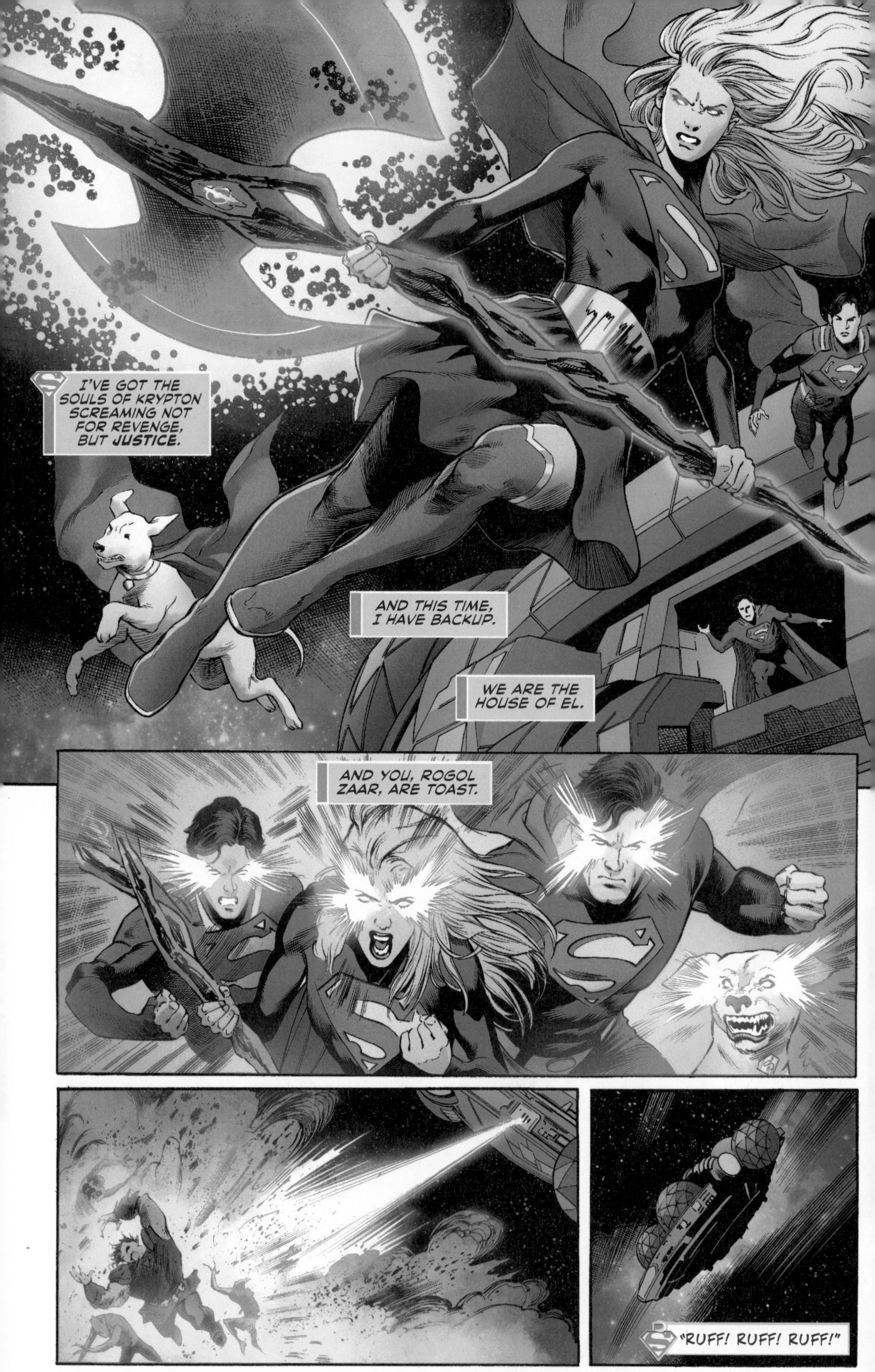
I'VE GOT THE SOULS OF KRYPTON SCREAMING NOT FOR REVENGE, BUT **JUSTICE**.
AND THIS TIME, I HAVE BACKUP.
WE ARE THE HOUSE OF EL.
AND YOU, ROGOL ZAAR, ARE TOAST.
"RUFF! RUFF! RUFF!"

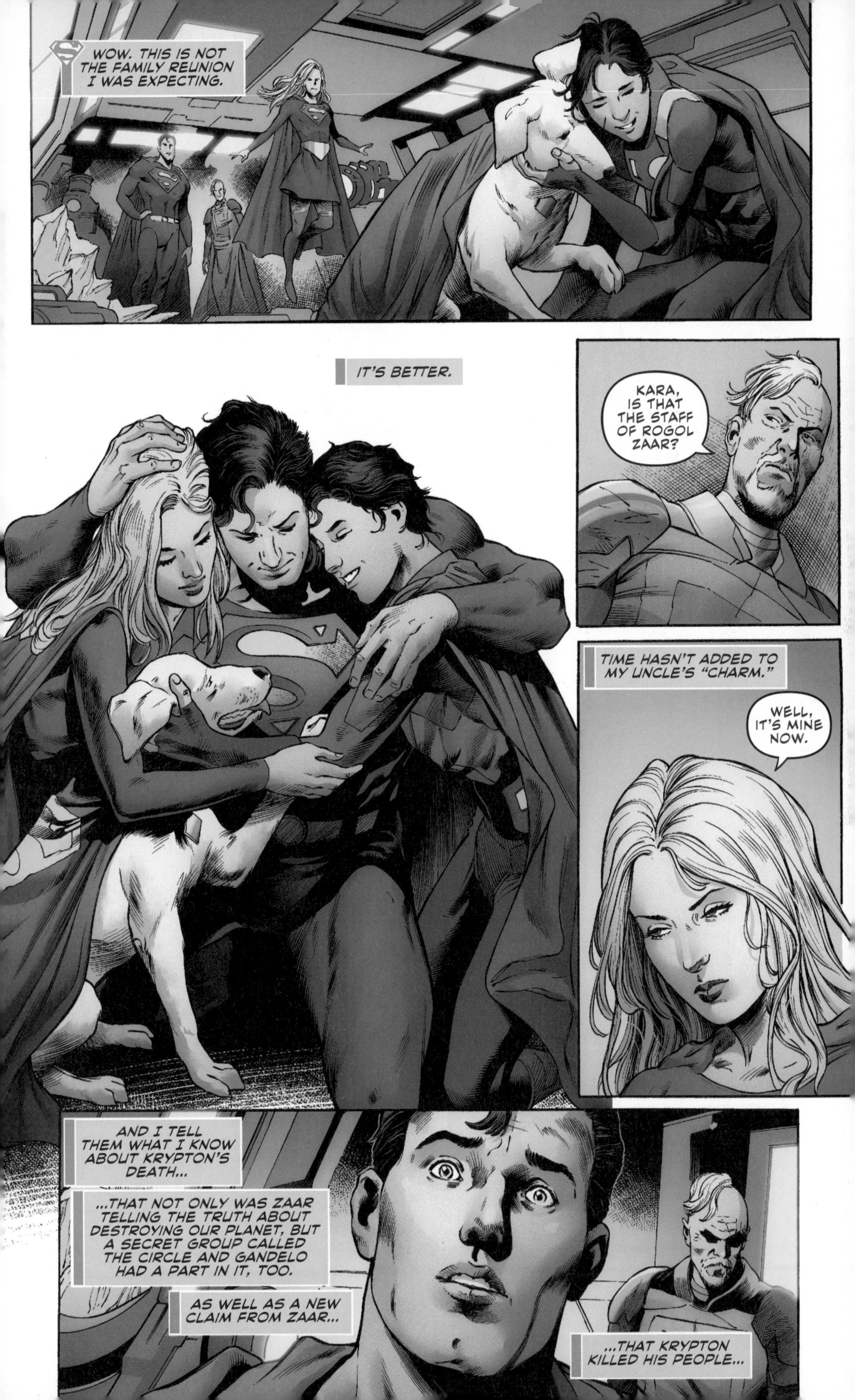
WOW. THIS IS NOT THE FAMILY REUNION I WAS EXPECTING.
IT'S BETTER.
KARA, IS THAT THE STAFF OF ROGOL ZAAR?
TIME HASN'T ADDED TO MY UNCLE'S "CHARM."
WELL, IT'S MINE NOW.
AND I TELL THEM WHAT I KNOW ABOUT KRYPTON'S DEATH...
...THAT NOT ONLY WAS ZAAR TELLING THE TRUTH ABOUT DESTROYING OUR PLANET, BUT A SECRET GROUP CALLED THE CIRCLE AND GANDELO HAD A PART IN IT, TOO.
AS WELL AS A NEW CLAIM FROM ZAAR...
...THAT KRYPTON KILLED HIS PEOPLE...

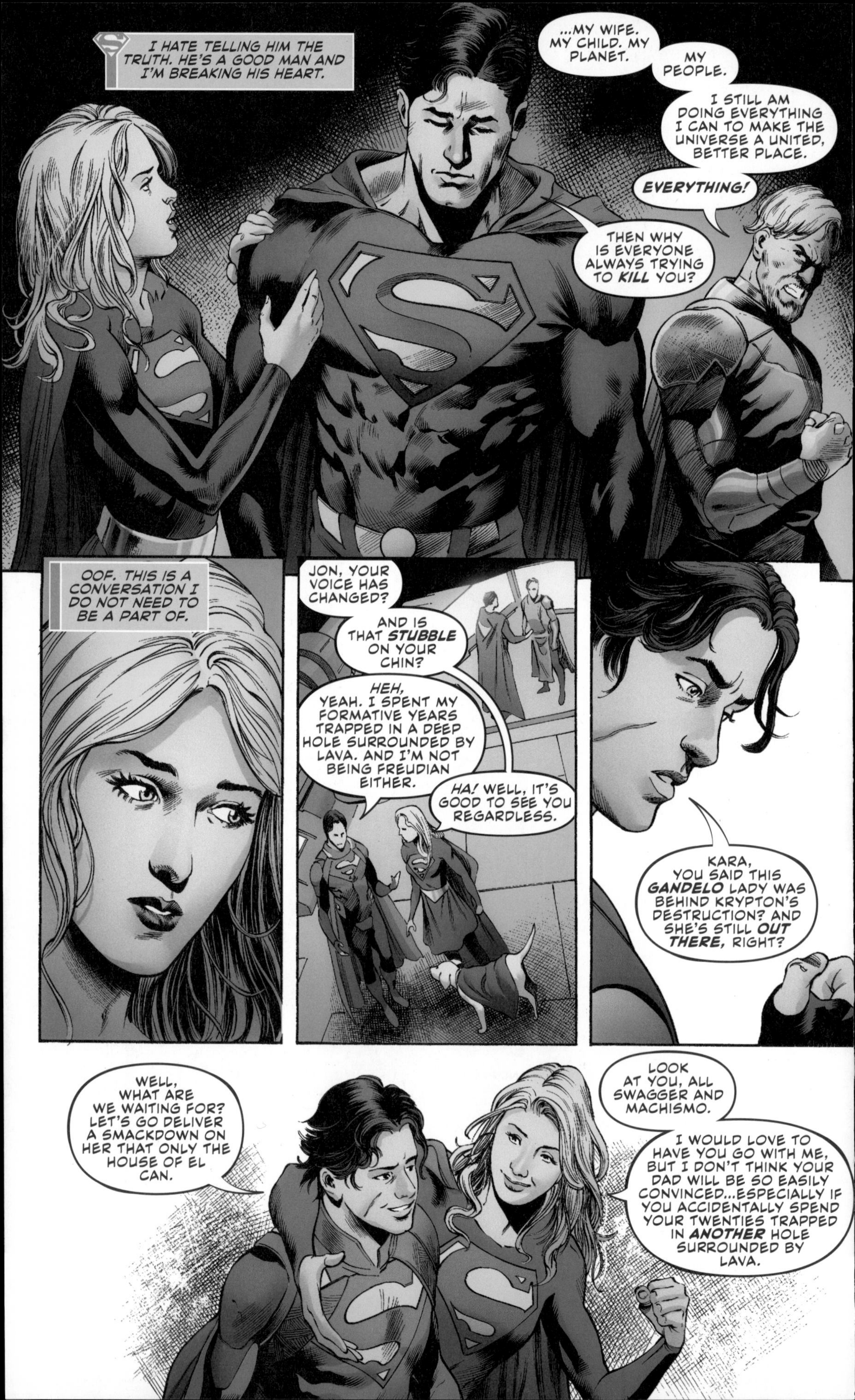
I HATE TELLING HIM THE TRUTH. HE'S A GOOD MAN AND I'M BREAKING HIS HEART.
...MY WIFE. MY CHILD. MY PLANET.
MY PEOPLE.
I STILL AM DOING EVERYTHING I CAN TO MAKE THE UNIVERSE A UNITED, BETTER PLACE.
EVERYTHING!
THEN WHY IS EVERYONE ALWAYS TRYING TO KILL YOU?
OOF. THIS IS A CONVERSATION I DO NOT NEED TO BE A PART OF.
JON, YOUR VOICE HAS CHANGED?
AND IS THAT STUBBLE ON YOUR CHIN?
HEH, YEAH. I SPENT MY FORMATIVE YEARS TRAPPED IN A DEEP HOLE SURROUNDED BY LAVA. AND I'M NOT BEING FREUDIAN EITHER.
HA! WELL, IT'S GOOD TO SEE YOU REGARDLESS.
KARA, YOU SAID THIS GANDELO LADY WAS BEHIND KRYPTON'S DESTRUCTION? AND SHE'S STILL OUT THERE, RIGHT?
WELL, WHAT ARE WE WAITING FOR? LET'S GO DELIVER A SMACKDOWN ON HER THAT ONLY THE HOUSE OF EL CAN.
LOOK AT YOU, ALL SWAGGER AND MACHISMO.
I WOULD LOVE TO HAVE YOU GO WITH ME, BUT I DON'T THINK YOUR DAD WILL BE SO EASILY CONVINCED...ESPECIALLY IF YOU ACCIDENTALLY SPEND YOUR TWENTIES TRAPPED IN ANOTHER HOLE SURROUNDED BY LAVA.

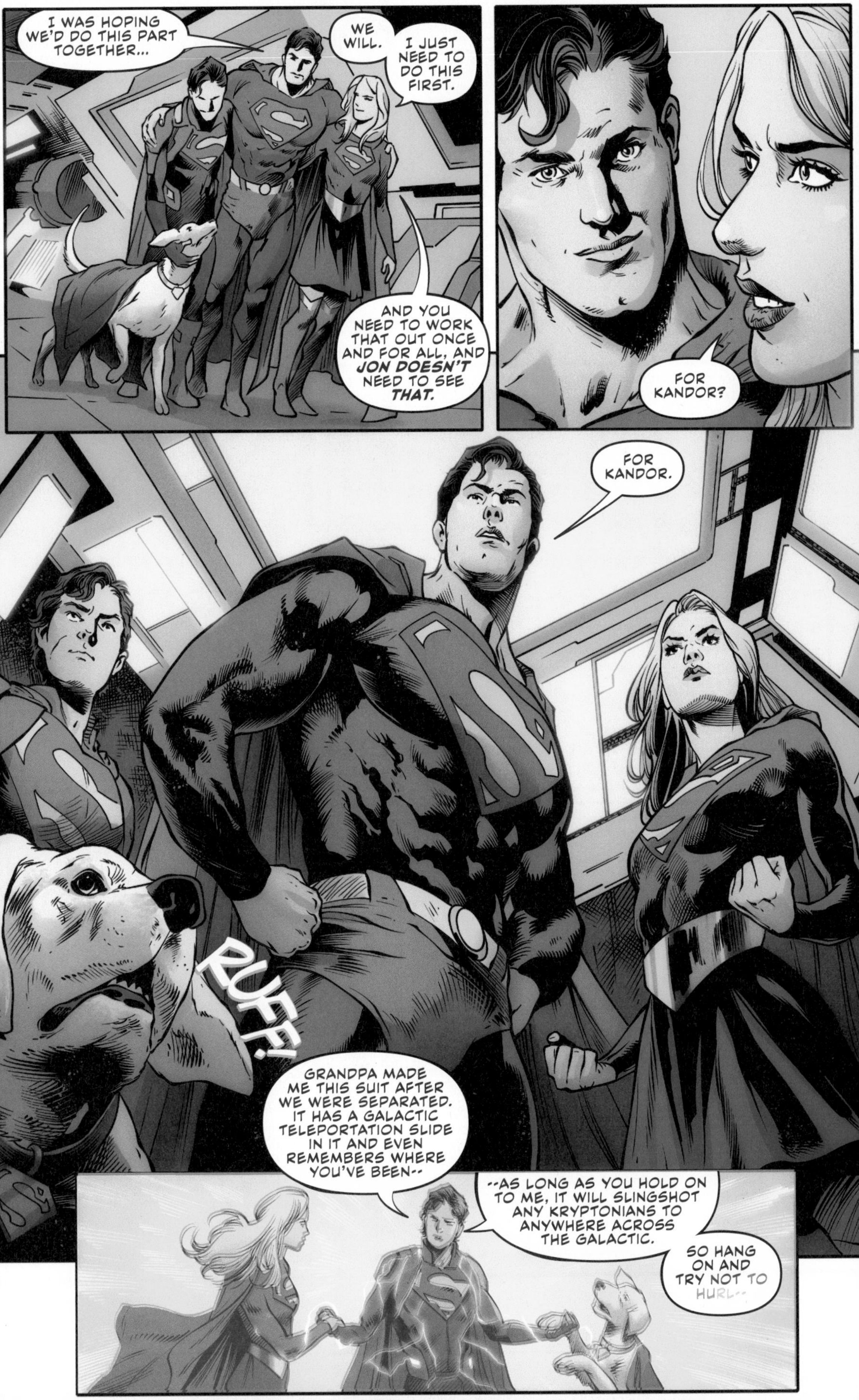
I WAS HOPING WE'D DO THIS PART TOGETHER...
WE WILL.
I JUST NEED TO DO THIS FIRST.
AND YOU NEED TO WORK THAT OUT ONCE AND FOR ALL, AND ***JON DOESN'T*** NEED TO SEE ***THAT.***
FOR KANDOR?
FOR KANDOR.
RUFF!
GRANDPA MADE ME THIS SUIT AFTER WE WERE SEPARATED. IT HAS A GALACTIC TELEPORTATION SLIDE IN IT AND EVEN REMEMBERS WHERE YOU'VE BEEN--
--AS LONG AS YOU HOLD ON TO ME, IT WILL SLINGSHOT ANY KRYPTONIANS TO ANYWHERE ACROSS THE GALACTIC.
SO HANG ON AND TRY NOT TO HURL--

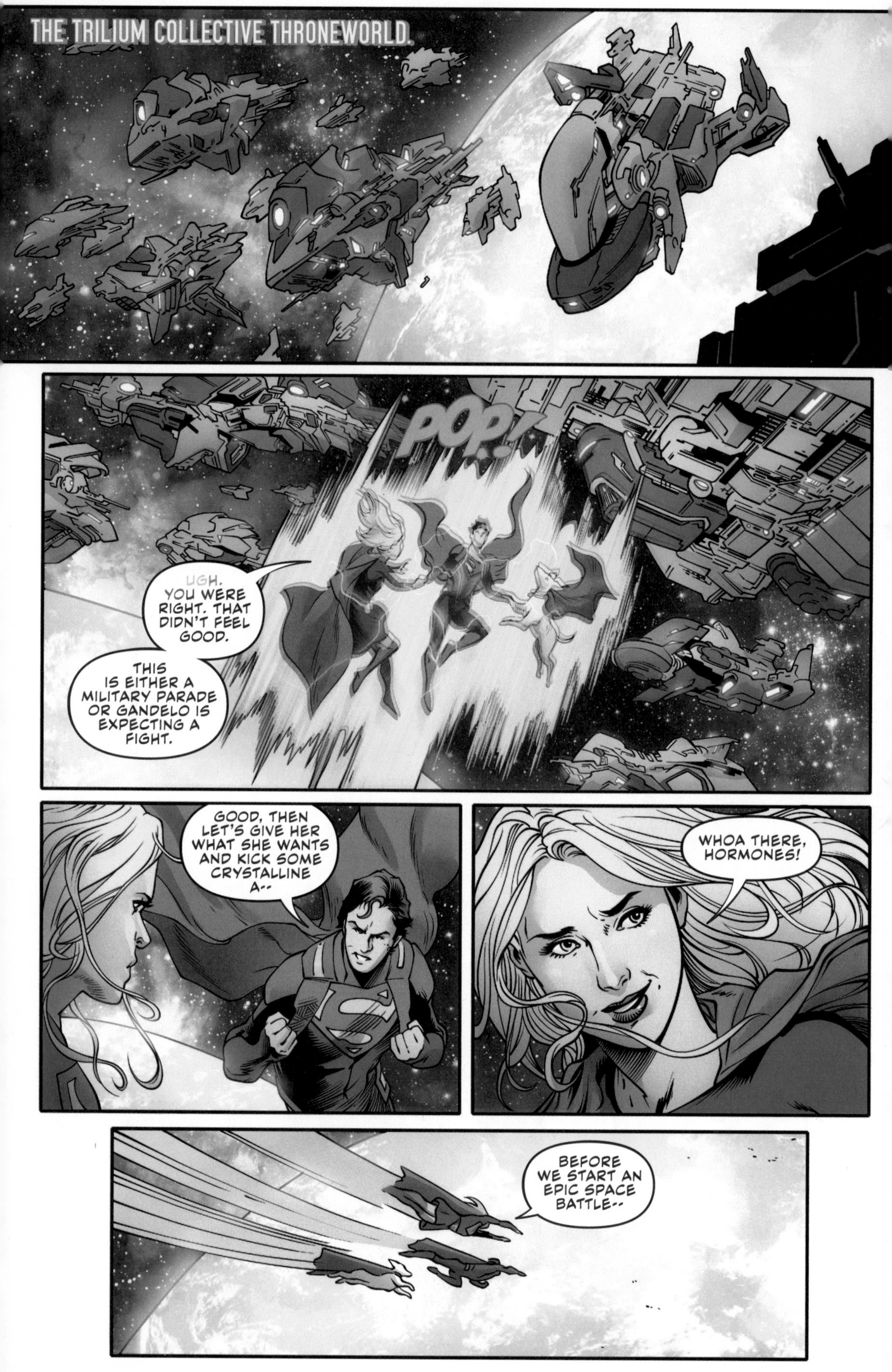
THE TRILIUM COLLECTIVE THRONEWORLD.
POP!
UGH. YOU WERE RIGHT. THAT DIDN'T FEEL GOOD.
THIS IS EITHER A MILITARY PARADE OR GANDELO IS EXPECTING A FIGHT.
GOOD, THEN LET'S GIVE HER WHAT SHE WANTS AND KICK SOME CRYSTALLINE A--
WHOA THERE, HORMONES!
BEFORE WE START AN EPIC SPACE BATTLE--

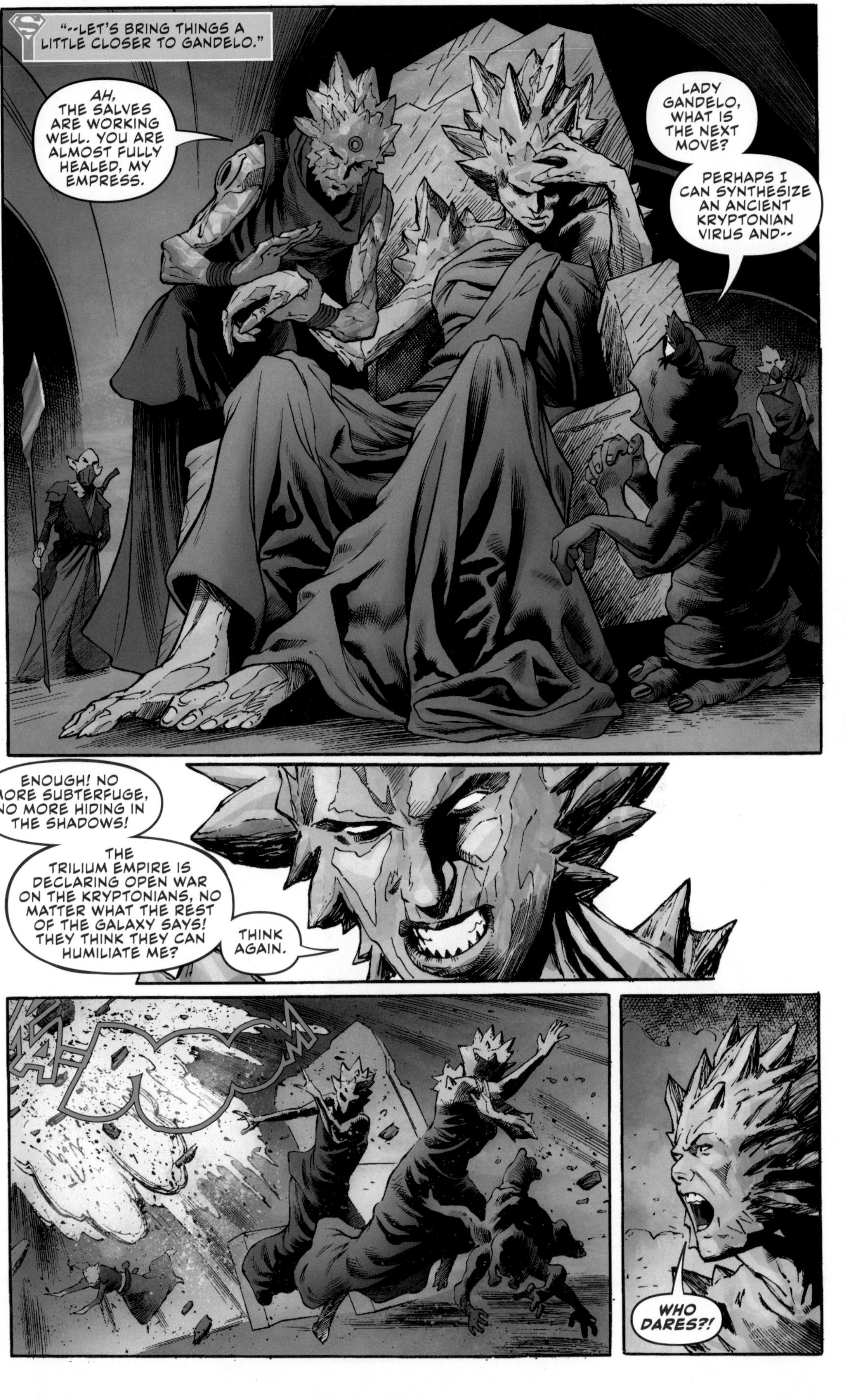
"--LET'S BRING THINGS A LITTLE CLOSER TO GANDELO."
AH, THE SALVES ARE WORKING WELL. YOU ARE ALMOST FULLY HEALED, MY EMPRESS.
LADY GANDELO, WHAT IS THE NEXT MOVE?
PERHAPS I CAN SYNTHESIZE AN ANCIENT KRYPTONIAN VIRUS AND--
ENOUGH! NO MORE SUBTERFUGE, NO MORE HIDING IN THE SHADOWS!
THE TRILIUM EMPIRE IS DECLARING OPEN WAR ON THE KRYPTONIANS, NO MATTER WHAT THE REST OF THE GALAXY SAYS! THEY THINK THEY CAN HUMILIATE ME?
THINK AGAIN.
WHO DARES?!

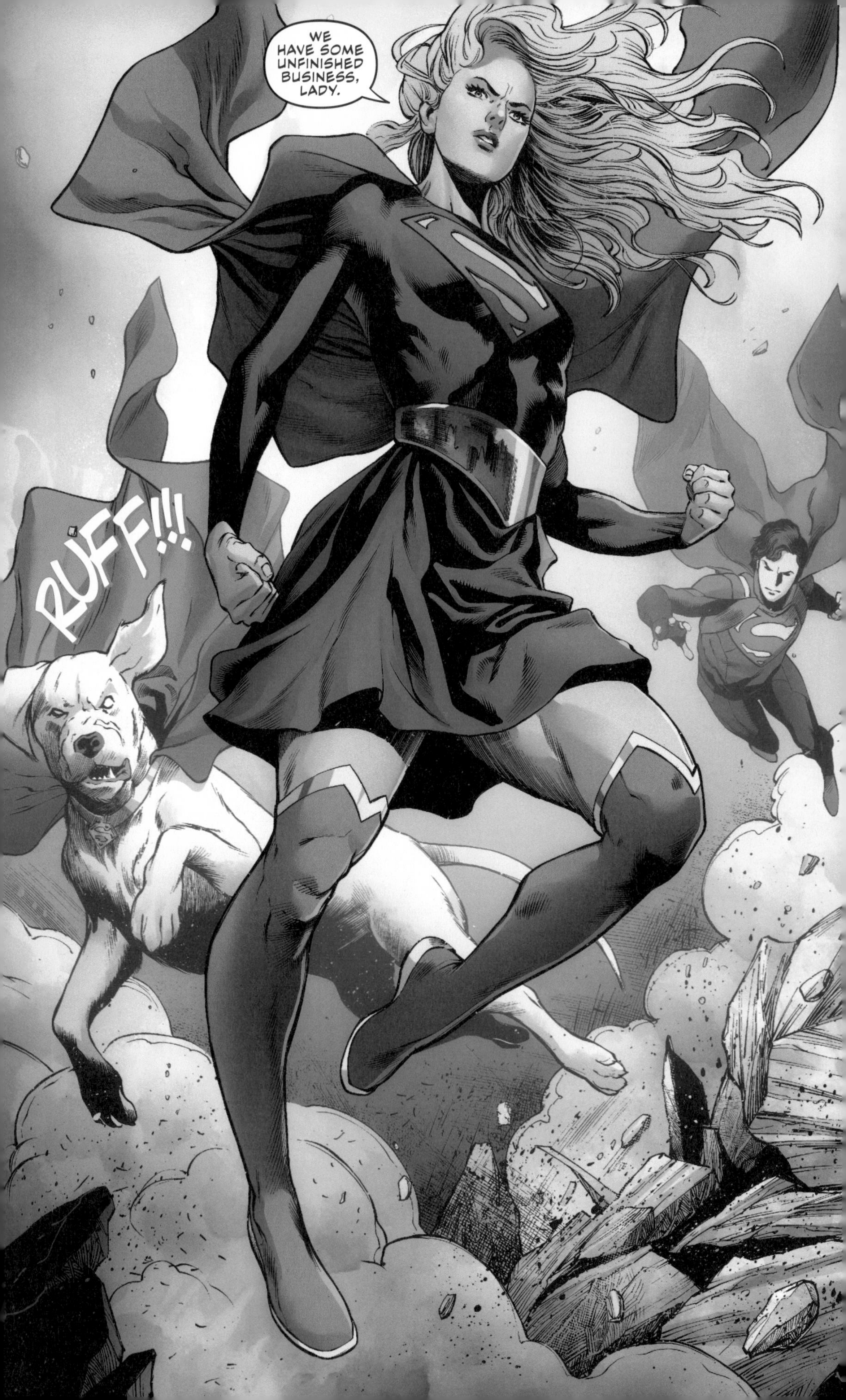
WE HAVE SOME UNFINISHED BUSINESS, LADY.
RUFF!!!

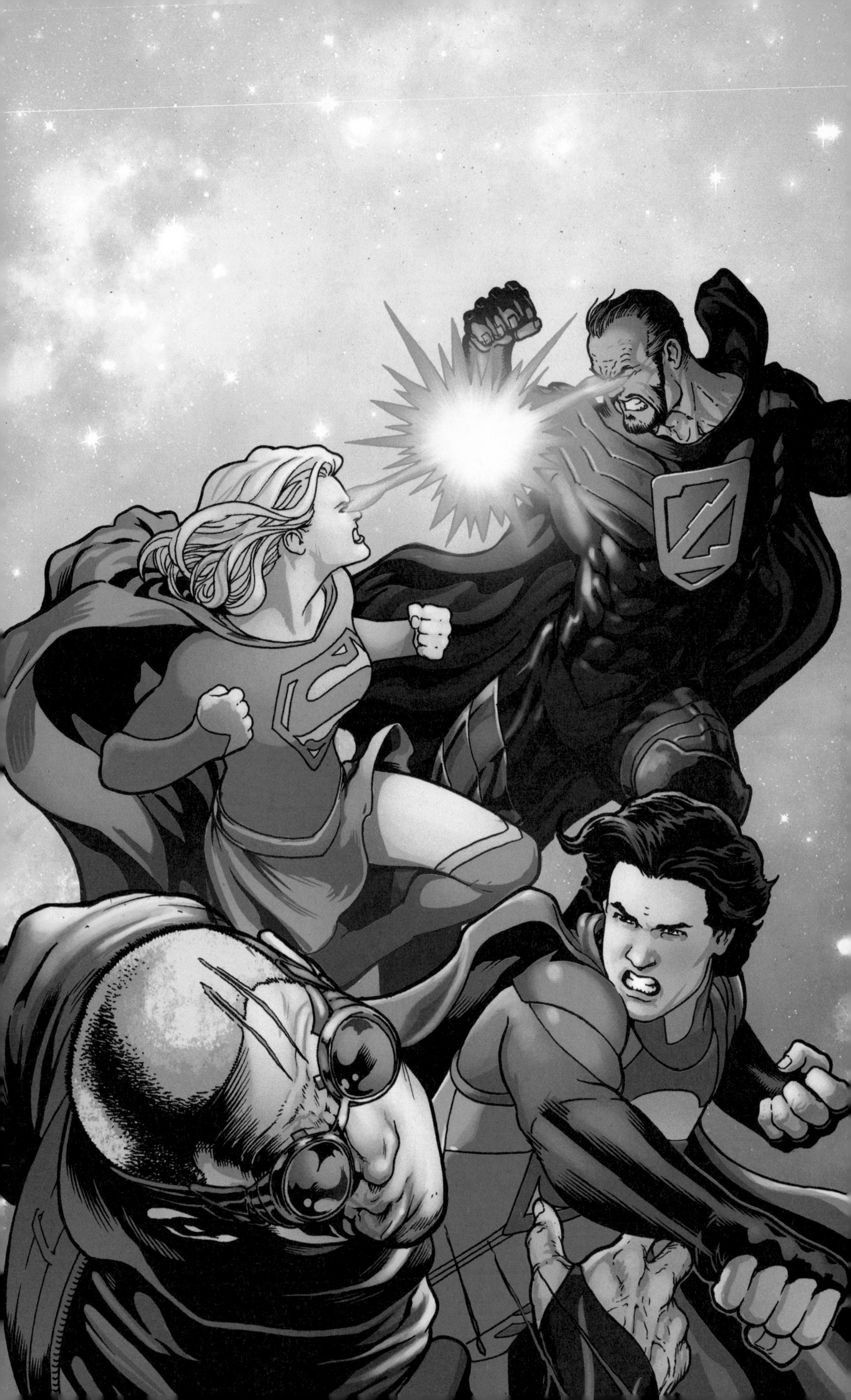

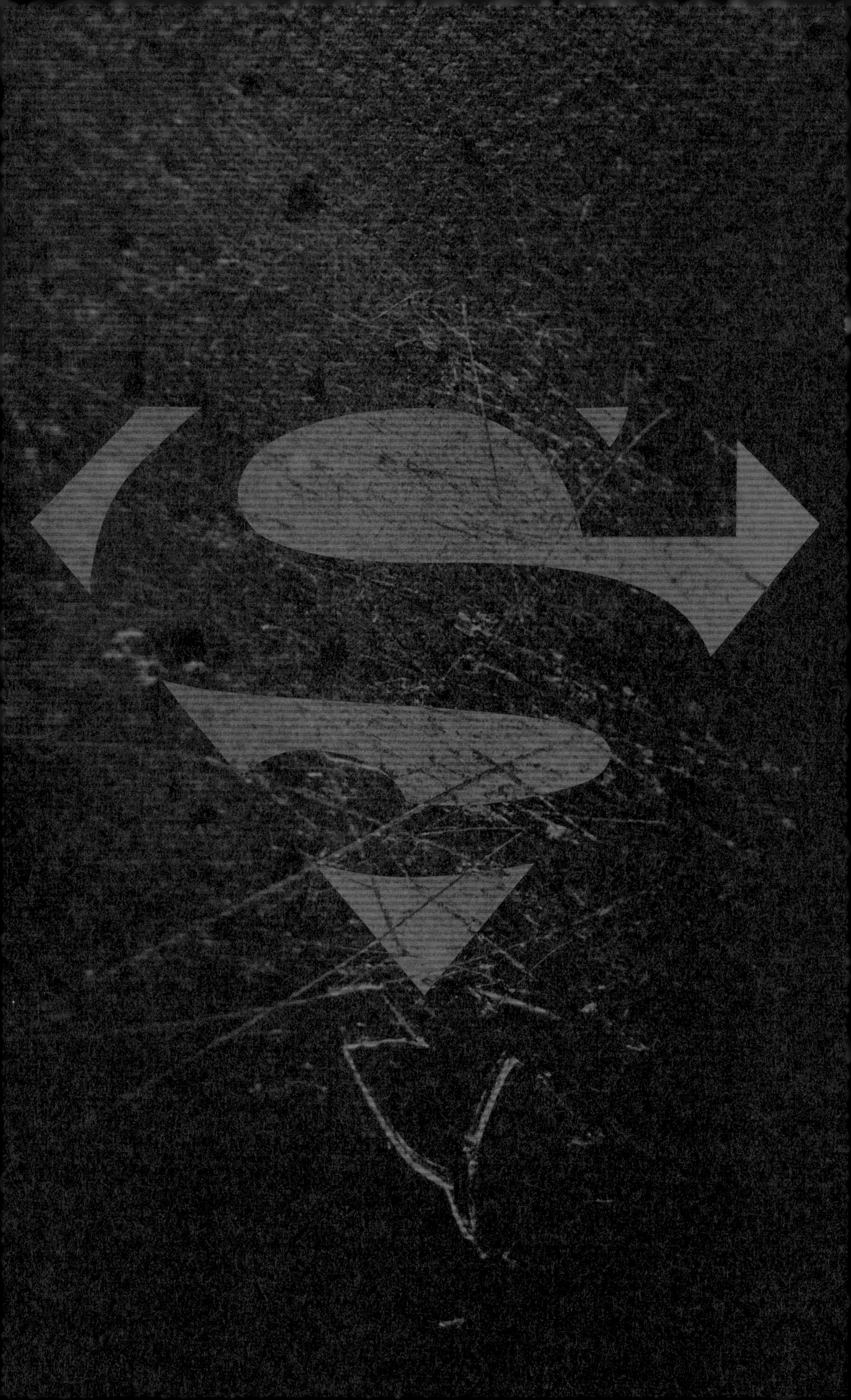

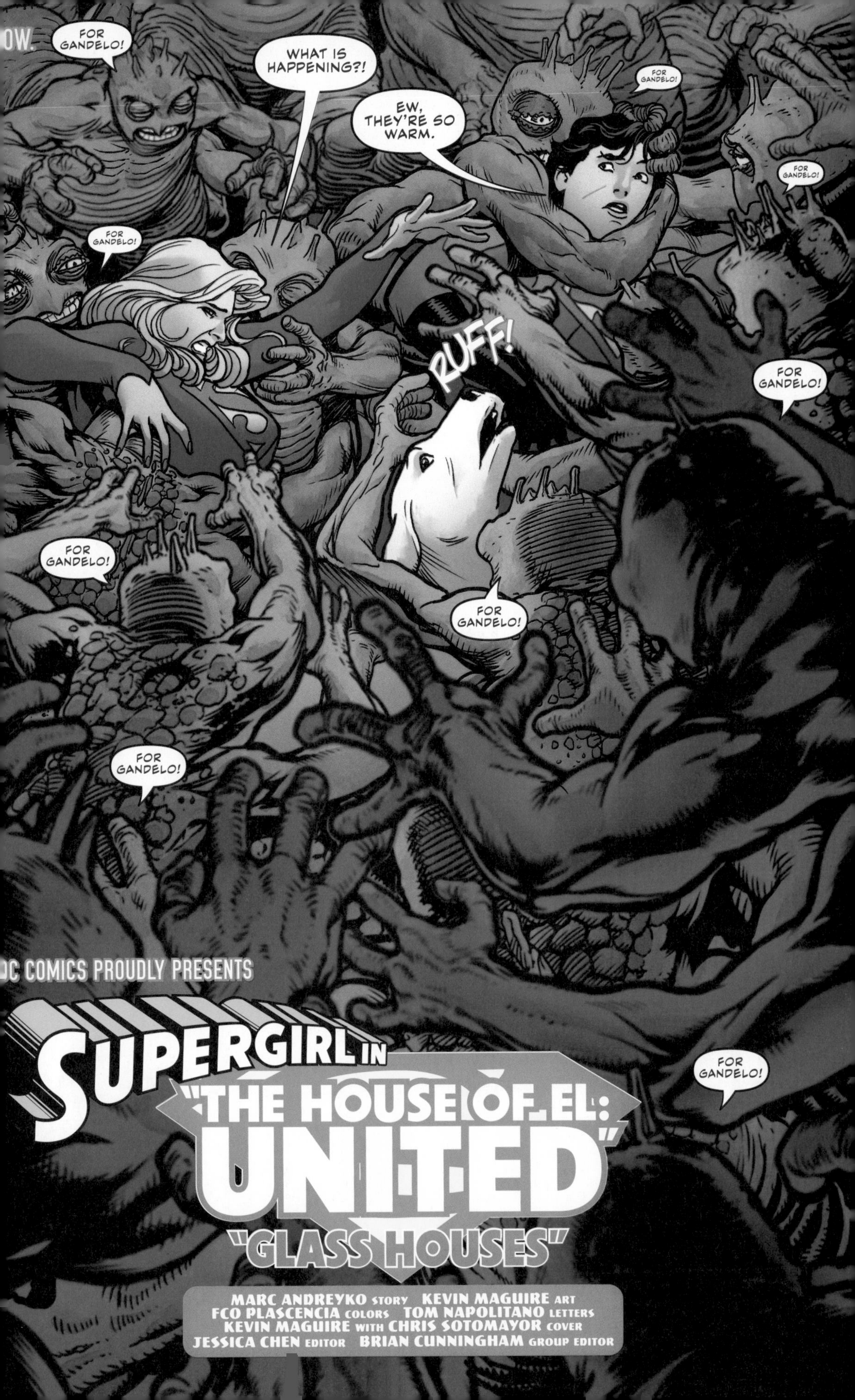

FOR GANDELO!
WHAT IS HAPPENING?!
FOR GANDELO!
EW, THEY'RE SO WARM.
FOR GANDELO!
FOR GANDELO!
RUFF!
FOR GANDELO!
FOR GANDELO!
FOR GANDELO!
FOR GANDELO!
DC COMICS PROUDLY PRESENTS
SUPERGIRL IN
"THE HOUSE OF EL: UNITED"
"GLASS HOUSES"
FOR GANDELO!
MARC ANDREYKO STORY KEVIN MAGUIRE ART
FCO PLASCENCIA COLORS TOM NAPOLITANO LETTERS
KEVIN MAGUIRE WITH CHRIS SOTOMAYOR COVER
JESSICA CHEN EDITOR BRIAN CUNNINGHAM GROUP EDITOR

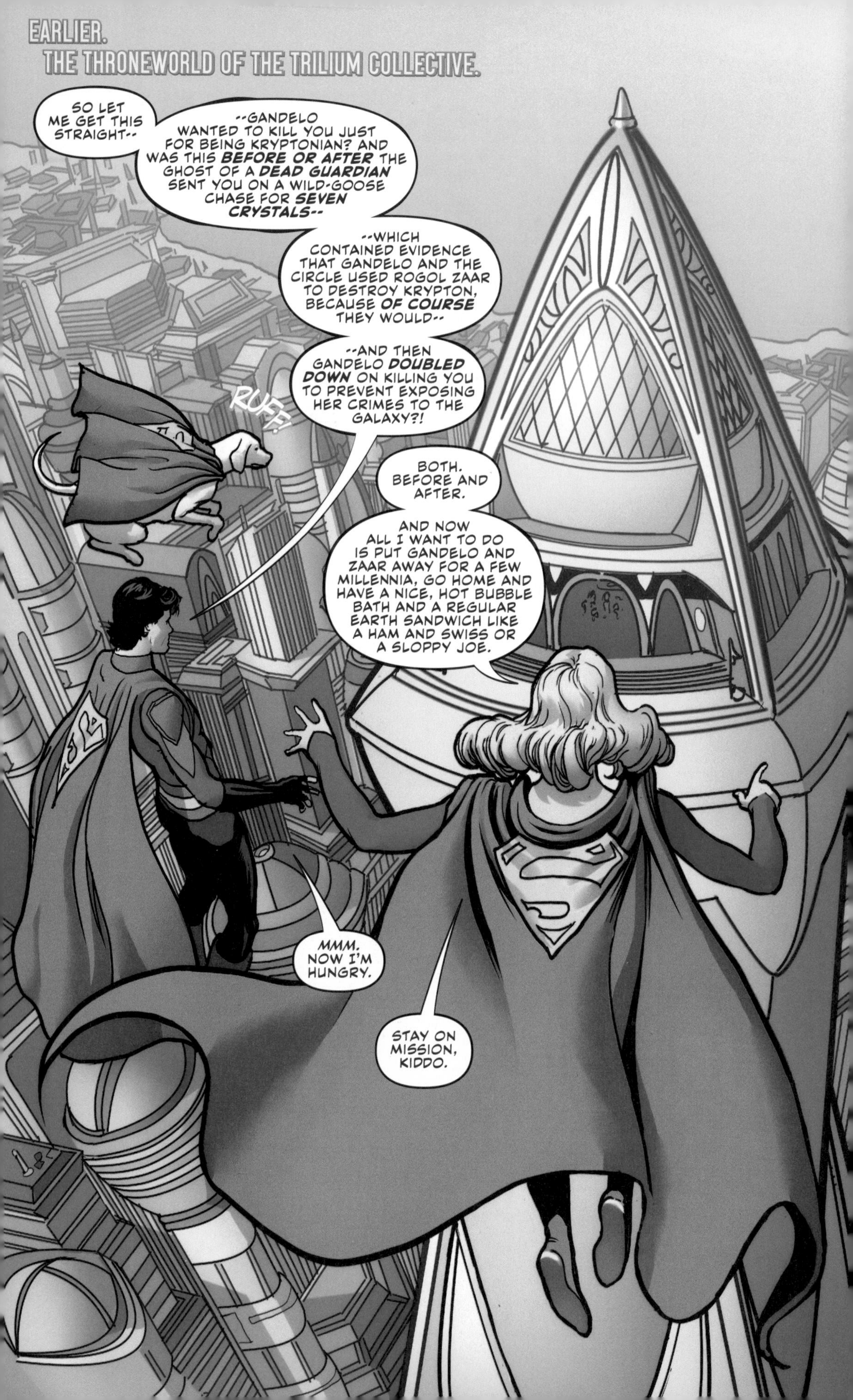
EARLIER.
THE THRONEWORLD OF THE TRILIUM COLLECTIVE.
SO LET ME GET THIS STRAIGHT--
--GANDELO WANTED TO KILL YOU JUST FOR BEING KRYPTONIAN? AND WAS THIS BEFORE OR AFTER THE GHOST OF A DEAD GUARDIAN SENT YOU ON A WILD-GOOSE CHASE FOR SEVEN CRYSTALS--
--WHICH CONTAINED EVIDENCE THAT GANDELO AND THE CIRCLE USED ROGOL ZAAR TO DESTROY KRYPTON, BECAUSE OF COURSE THEY WOULD--
--AND THEN GANDELO DOUBLED DOWN ON KILLING YOU TO PREVENT EXPOSING HER CRIMES TO THE GALAXY?!
RUFF!
BOTH. BEFORE AND AFTER.
AND NOW ALL I WANT TO DO IS PUT GANDELO AND ZAAR AWAY FOR A FEW MILLENNIA, GO HOME AND HAVE A NICE, HOT BUBBLE BATH AND A REGULAR EARTH SANDWICH LIKE A HAM AND SWISS OR A SLOPPY JOE.
MMM. NOW I'M HUNGRY.
STAY ON MISSION, KIDDO.

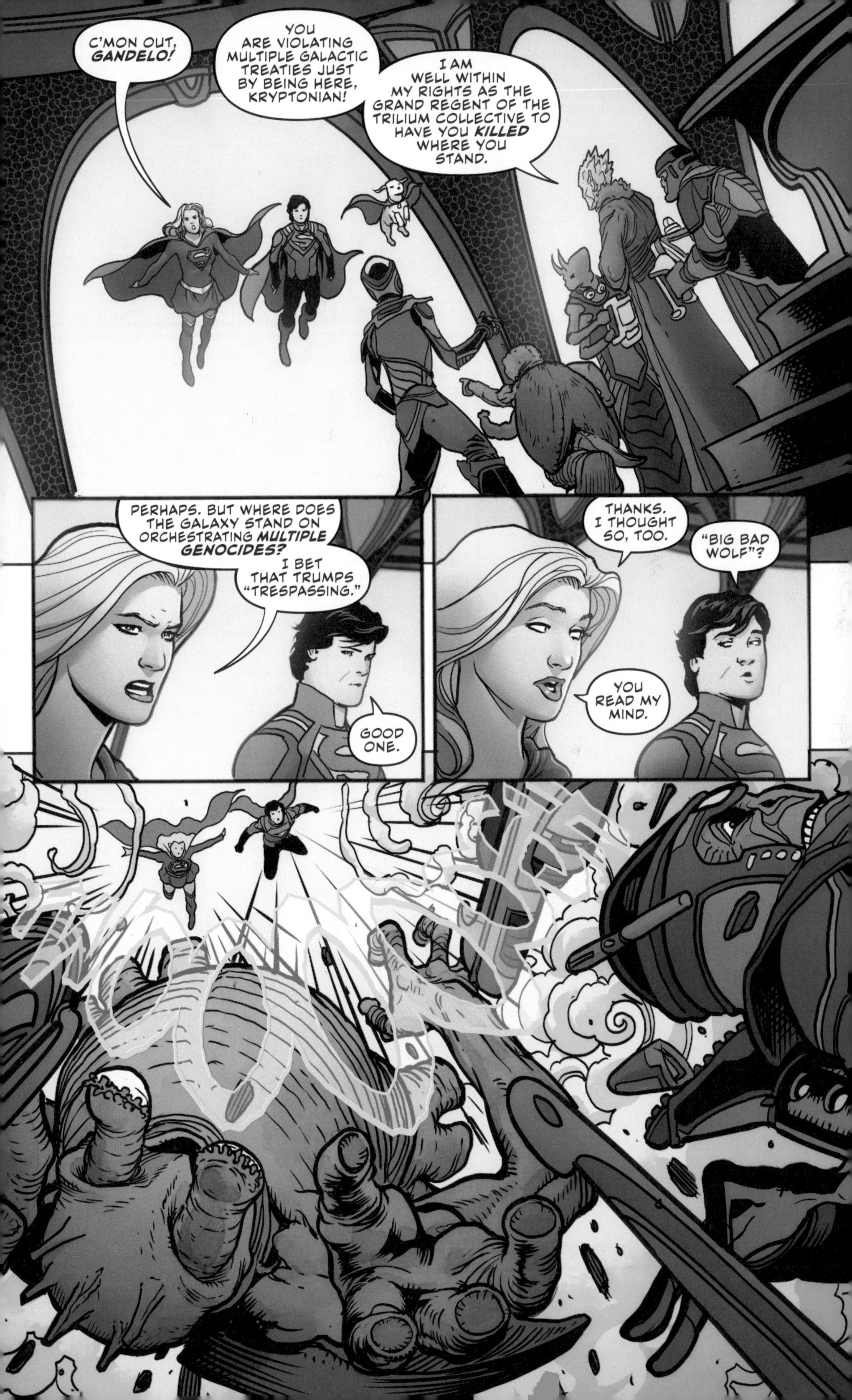
C'MON OUT, GANDELO!
YOU ARE VIOLATING MULTIPLE GALACTIC TREATIES JUST BY BEING HERE, KRYPTONIAN!
I AM WELL WITHIN MY RIGHTS AS THE GRAND REGENT OF THE TRILIUM COLLECTIVE TO HAVE YOU KILLED WHERE YOU STAND.
PERHAPS. BUT WHERE DOES THE GALAXY STAND ON ORCHESTRATING MULTIPLE GENOCIDES?
I BET THAT TRUMPS "TRESPASSING."
GOOD ONE.
THANKS. I THOUGHT SO, TOO.
"BIG BAD WOLF"?
YOU READ MY MIND.

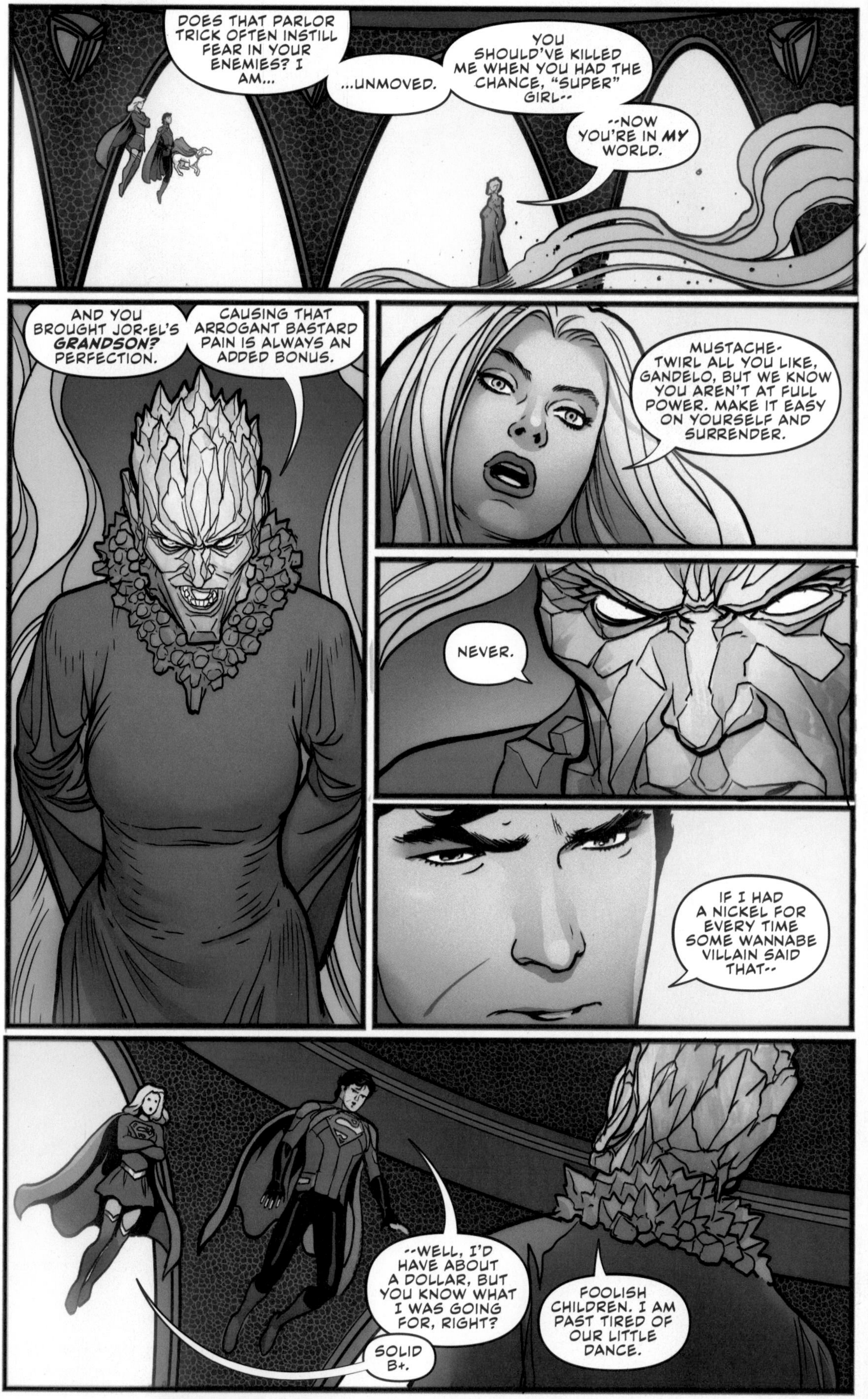
DOES THAT PARLOR TRICK OFTEN INSTILL FEAR IN YOUR ENEMIES? I AM...
...UNMOVED.
YOU SHOULD'VE KILLED ME WHEN YOU HAD THE CHANCE, "SUPER" GIRL--
--NOW YOU'RE IN MY WORLD.
AND YOU BROUGHT JOR-EL'S GRANDSON? PERFECTION.
CAUSING THAT ARROGANT BASTARD PAIN IS ALWAYS AN ADDED BONUS.
MUSTACHE-TWIRL ALL YOU LIKE, GANDELO, BUT WE KNOW YOU AREN'T AT FULL POWER. MAKE IT EASY ON YOURSELF AND SURRENDER.
NEVER.
IF I HAD A NICKEL FOR EVERY TIME SOME WANNABE VILLAIN SAID THAT--
--WELL, I'D HAVE ABOUT A DOLLAR, BUT YOU KNOW WHAT I WAS GOING FOR, RIGHT?
SOLID B+.
FOOLISH CHILDREN. I AM PAST TIRED OF OUR LITTLE DANCE.

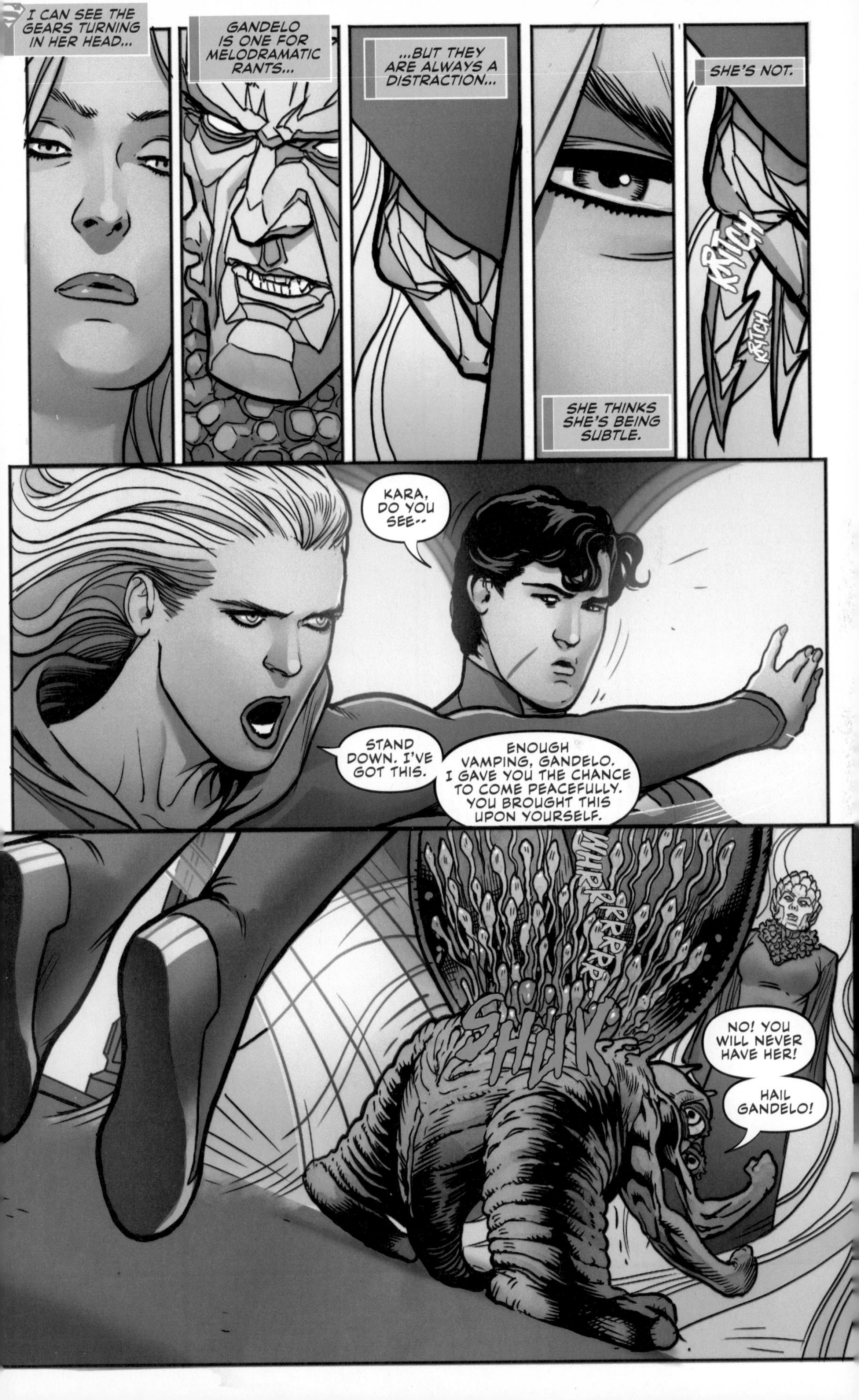
I CAN SEE THE GEARS TURNING IN HER HEAD...
GANDELO IS ONE FOR MELODRAMATIC RANTS...
...BUT THEY ARE ALWAYS A DISTRACTION...
SHE THINKS SHE'S BEING SUBTLE.
SHE'S NOT.
KRTCH
KRTCH
KARA, DO YOU SEE--
STAND DOWN. I'VE GOT THIS.
ENOUGH VAMPING, GANDELO. I GAVE YOU THE CHANCE TO COME PEACEFULLY. YOU BROUGHT THIS UPON YOURSELF.
WHRRRRRP
SHUK
NO! YOU WILL NEVER HAVE HER!
HAIL GANDELO!

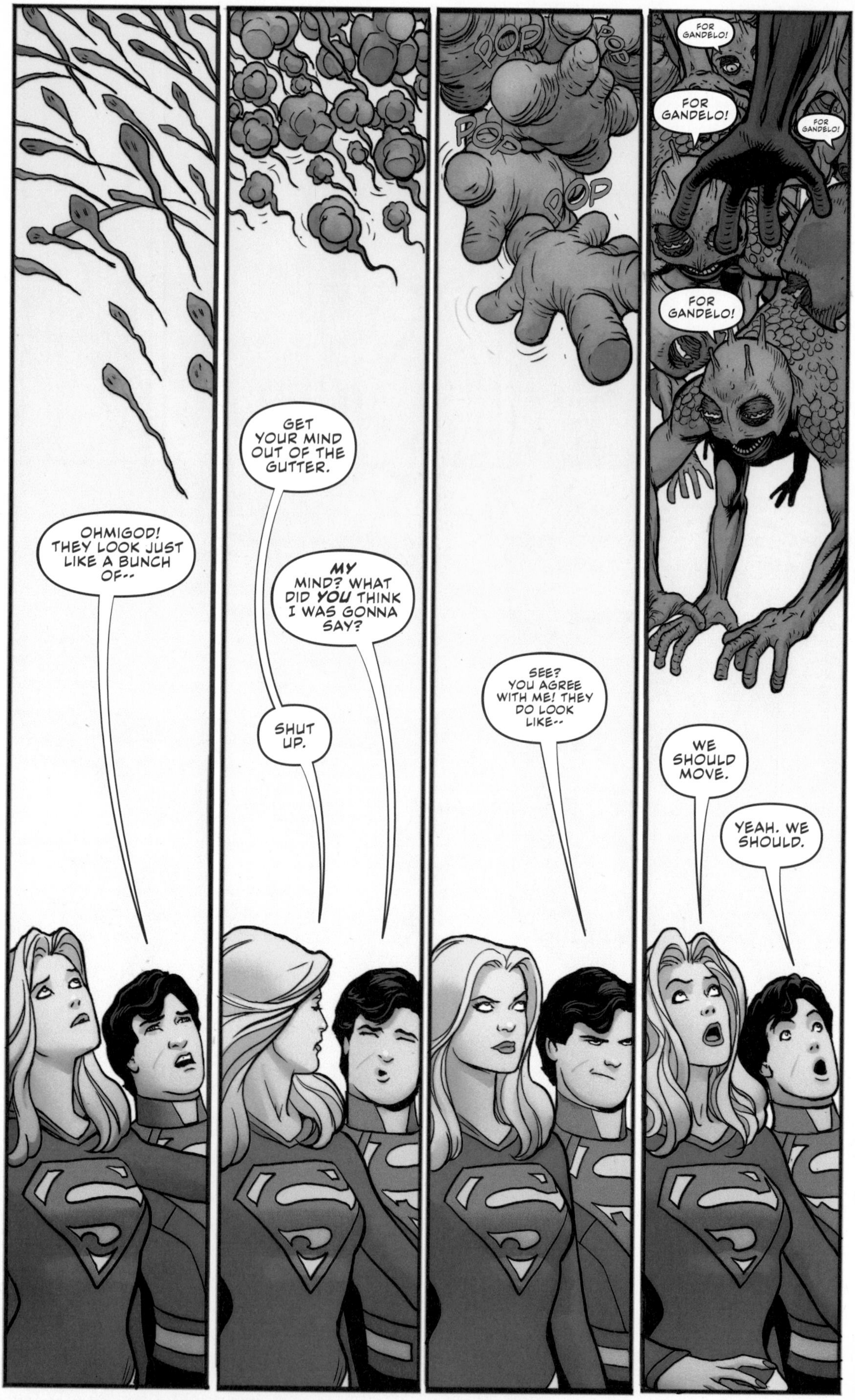
OHMIGOD! THEY LOOK JUST LIKE A BUNCH OF--
GET YOUR MIND OUT OF THE GUTTER.
MY MIND? WHAT DID YOU THINK I WAS GONNA SAY?
SHUT UP.
POP
POP
POP
POP
SEE? YOU AGREE WITH ME! THEY DO LOOK LIKE--
FOR GANDELO!
FOR GANDELO!
FOR GANDELO!
FOR GANDELO!
WE SHOULD MOVE.
YEAH. WE SHOULD.

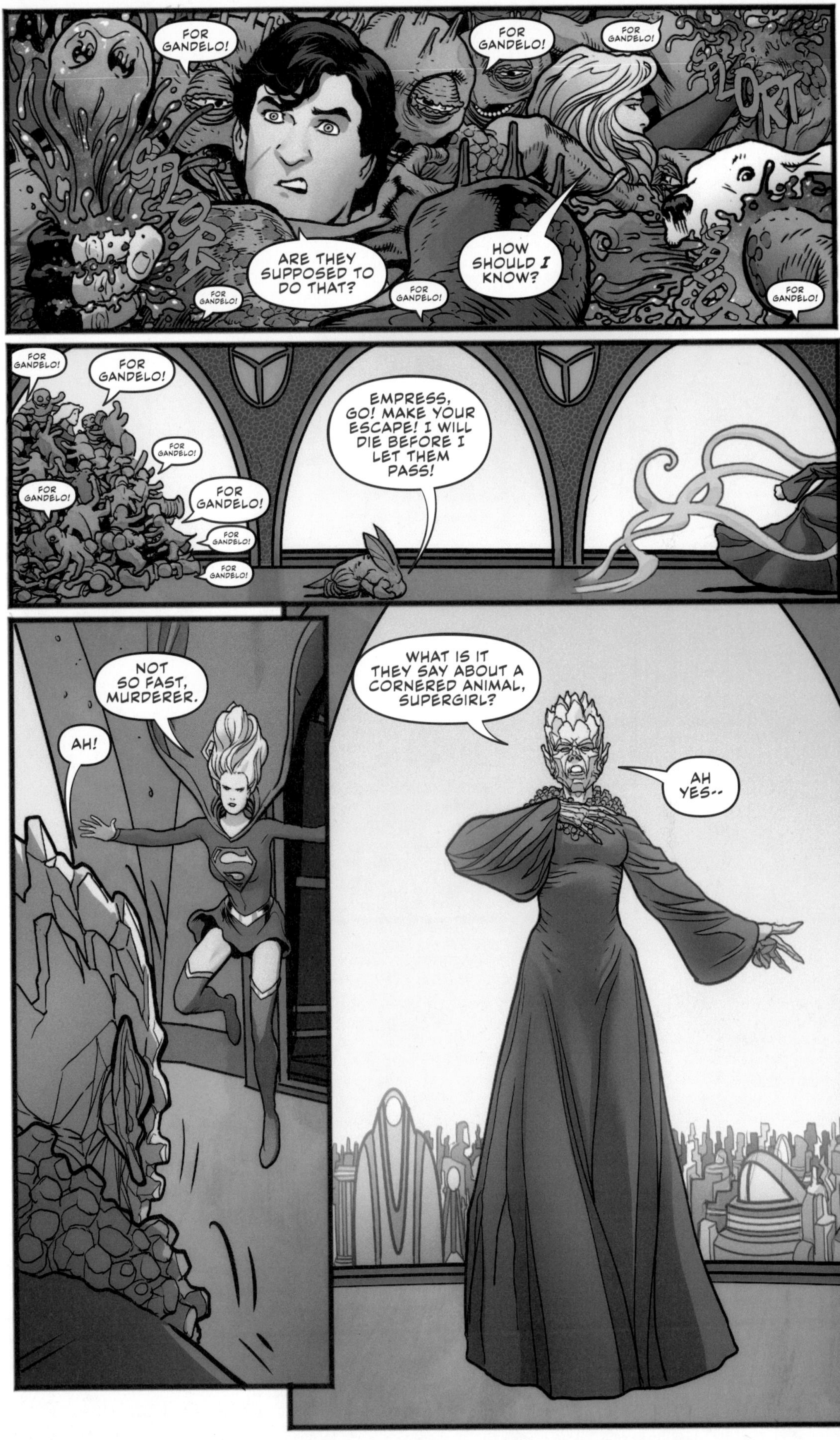

FOR GANDELO!
FOR GANDELO!
FOR GANDELO!
FLORT
SPLORT
ARE THEY SUPPOSED TO DO THAT?
HOW SHOULD I KNOW?
FOR GANDELO!
FOR GANDELO!
FOR GANDELO!
FOR GANDELO!
FOR GANDELO!
FOR GANDELO!
FOR GANDELO!
FOR GANDELO!
FOR GANDELO!
FOR GANDELO!
EMPRESS, GO! MAKE YOUR ESCAPE! I WILL DIE BEFORE I LET THEM PASS!
NOT SO FAST, MURDERER.
AH!
WHAT IS IT THEY SAY ABOUT A CORNERED ANIMAL, SUPERGIRL?
AH YES--

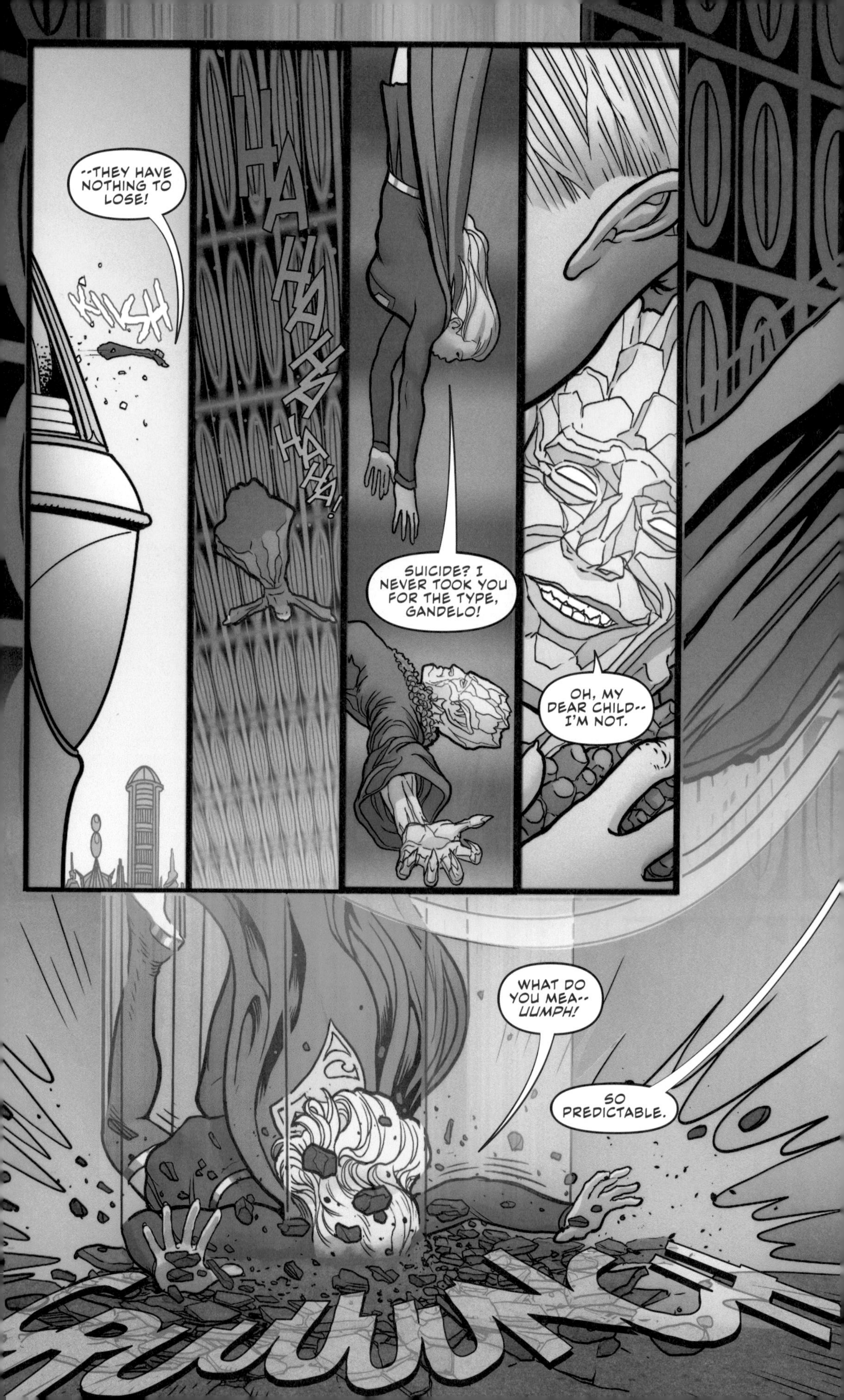
--THEY HAVE NOTHING TO LOSE!
KHKSH
HA HA HA HA HA HA HA!
SUICIDE? I NEVER TOOK YOU FOR THE TYPE, GANDELO!
OH, MY DEAR CHILD-- I'M NOT.
WHAT DO YOU MEA-- UUMPH!
SO PREDICTABLE.

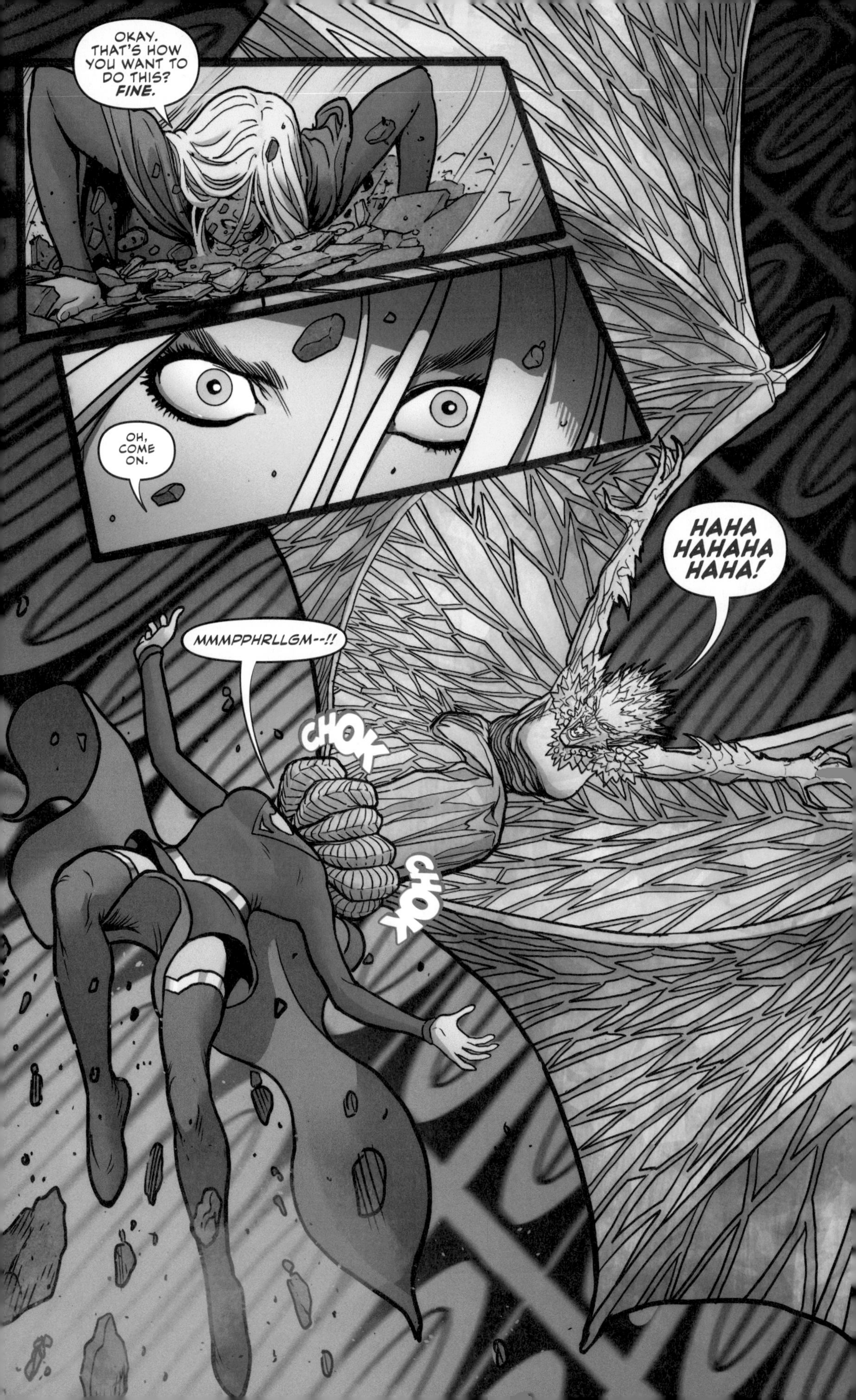
OKAY. THAT'S HOW YOU WANT TO DO THIS? *FINE.*
OH, COME ON.
HAHA HAHAHA HAHA!
MMMPPHRLLGM--!!
CHOK
CHOK

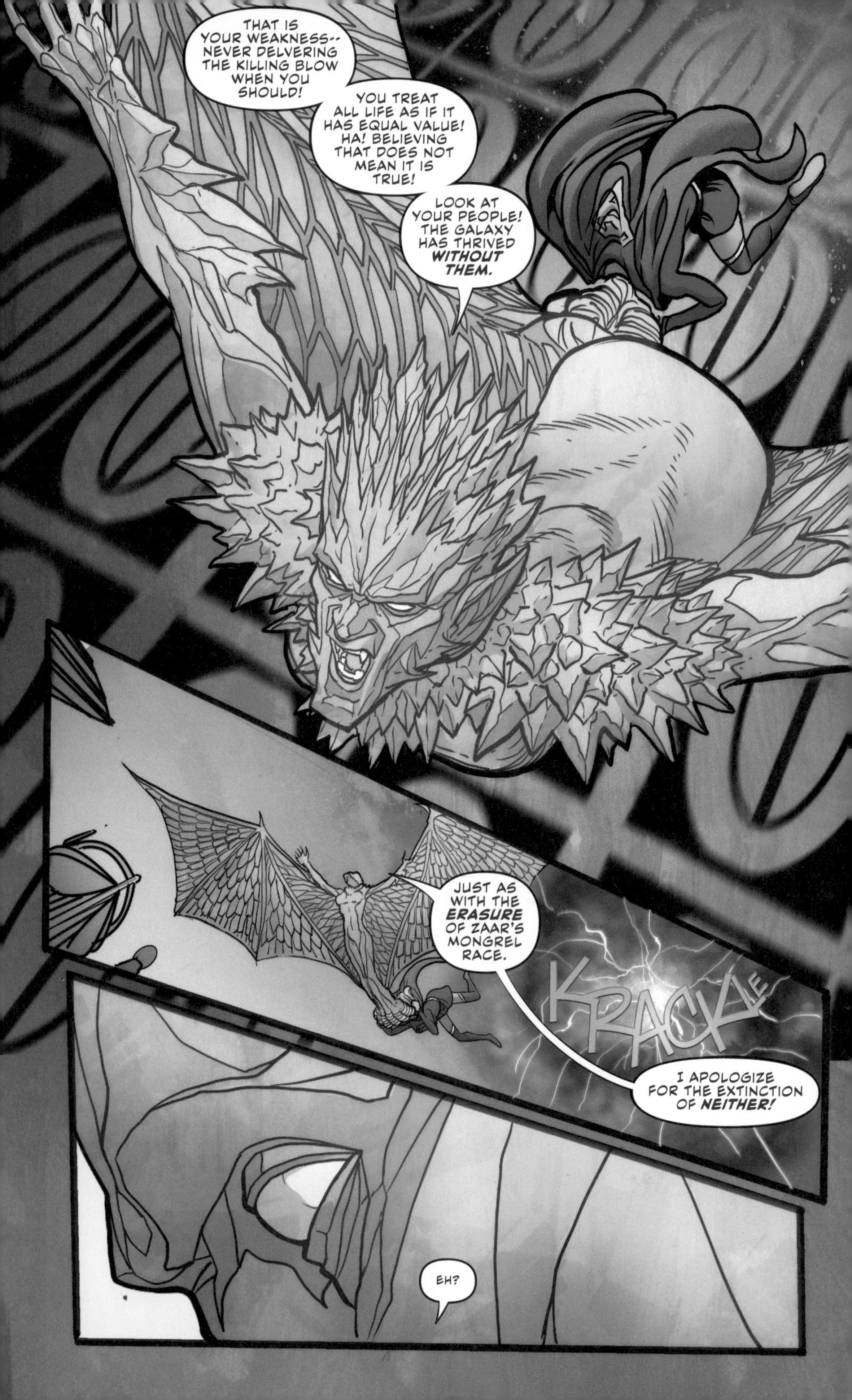

THAT IS YOUR WEAKNESS-- NEVER DELVERING THE KILLING BLOW WHEN YOU SHOULD!
YOU TREAT ALL LIFE AS IF IT HAS EQUAL VALUE! HA! BELIEVING THAT DOES NOT MEAN IT IS TRUE!
LOOK AT YOUR PEOPLE! THE GALAXY HAS THRIVED WITHOUT THEM.
JUST AS WITH THE ERASURE OF ZAAR'S MONGREL RACE.
KRACKLE
I APOLOGIZE FOR THE EXTINCTION OF NEITHER!
EH?

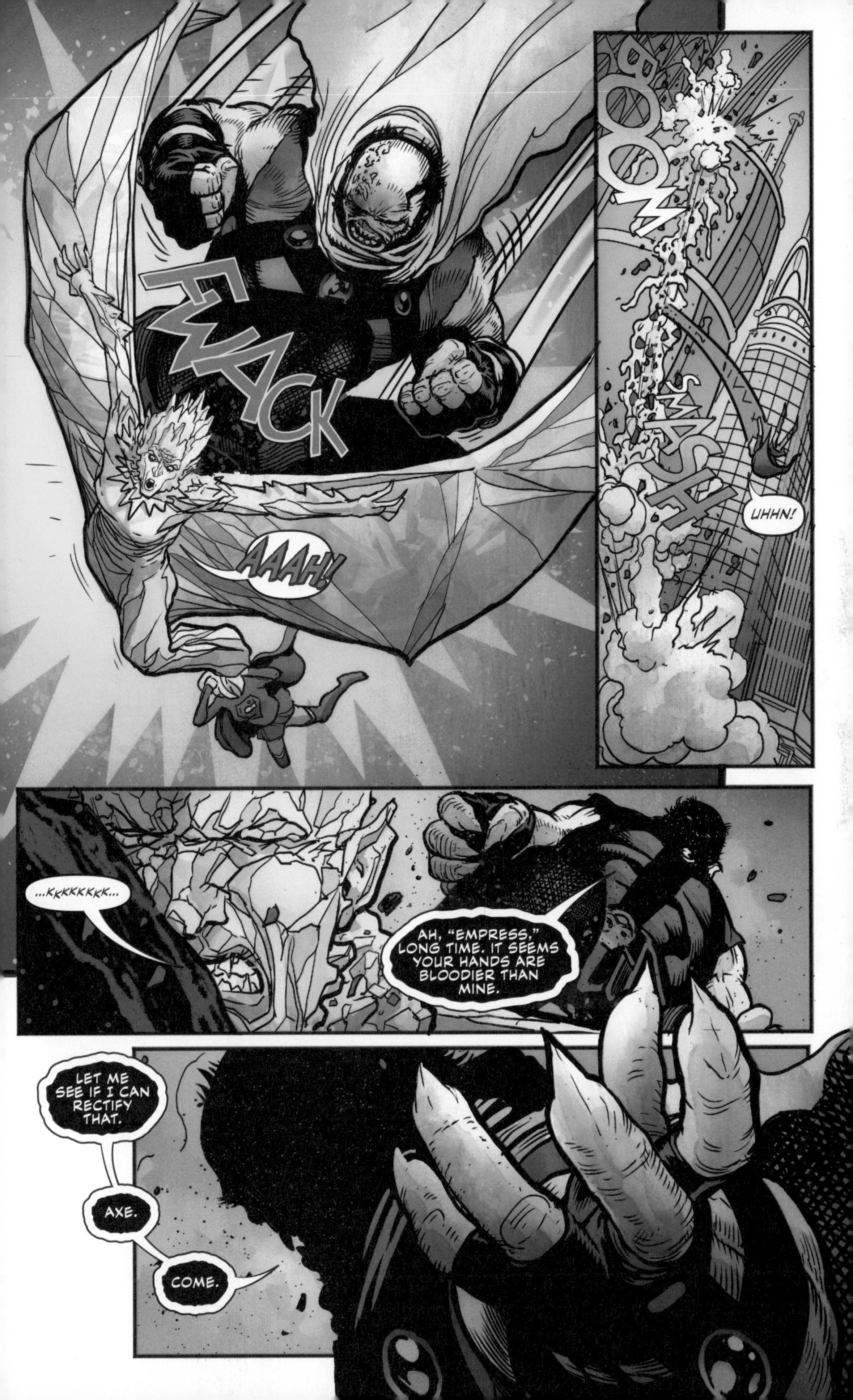
FWACK
AAAH!
BOOM
SMASH
UHHN!
...KKKKKKKK...
AH, "EMPRESS," LONG TIME. IT SEEMS YOUR HANDS ARE BLOODIER THAN MINE.
LET ME SEE IF I CAN RECTIFY THAT.
AXE.
COME.

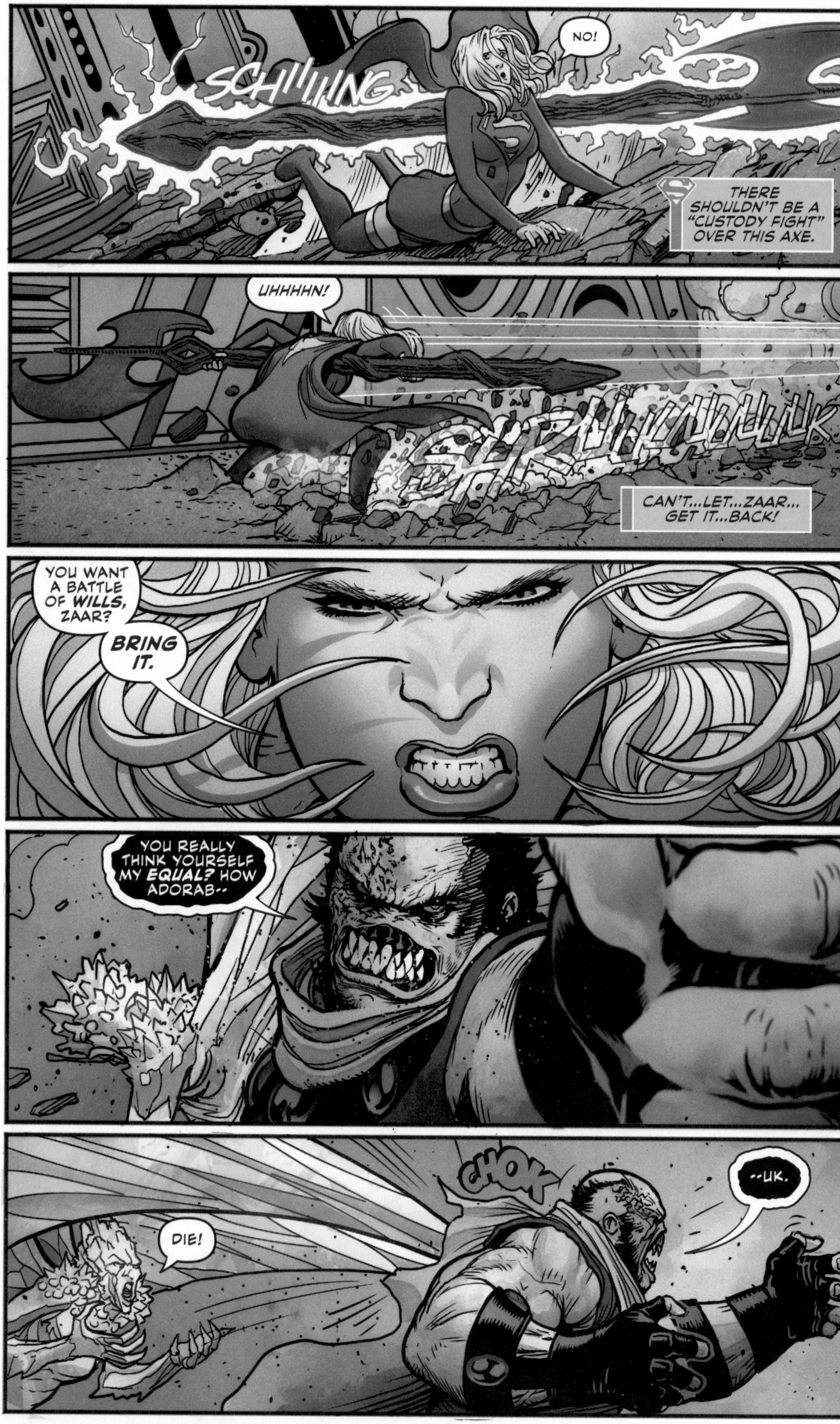

SCHIIIIING
NO!
THERE SHOULDN'T BE A "CUSTODY FIGHT" OVER THIS AXE.
UHHHHN!
SHRAKKADUUUK
CAN'T...LET...ZAAR... GET IT...BACK!
YOU WANT A BATTLE OF WILLS, ZAAR?
BRING IT.
YOU REALLY THINK YOURSELF MY EQUAL? HOW ADORAB--
CHOK
--UK.
DIE!

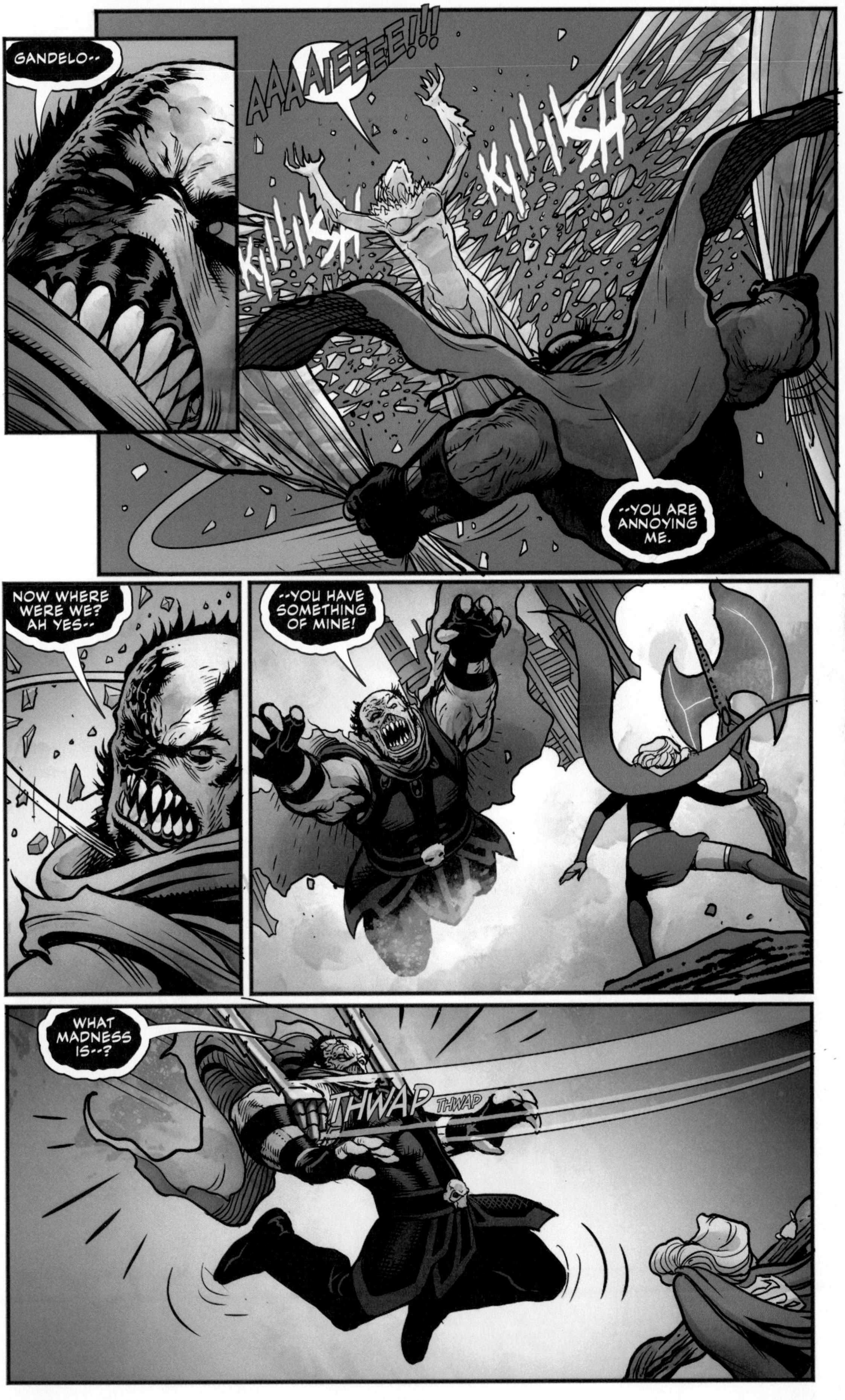
GANDELO--
AAAAIEEEEE!!!
KRIIISH
KRIIISH
--YOU ARE ANNOYING ME.
NOW WHERE WERE WE? AH YES--
--YOU HAVE SOMETHING OF MINE!
WHAT MADNESS IS--?
THWAP THWAP

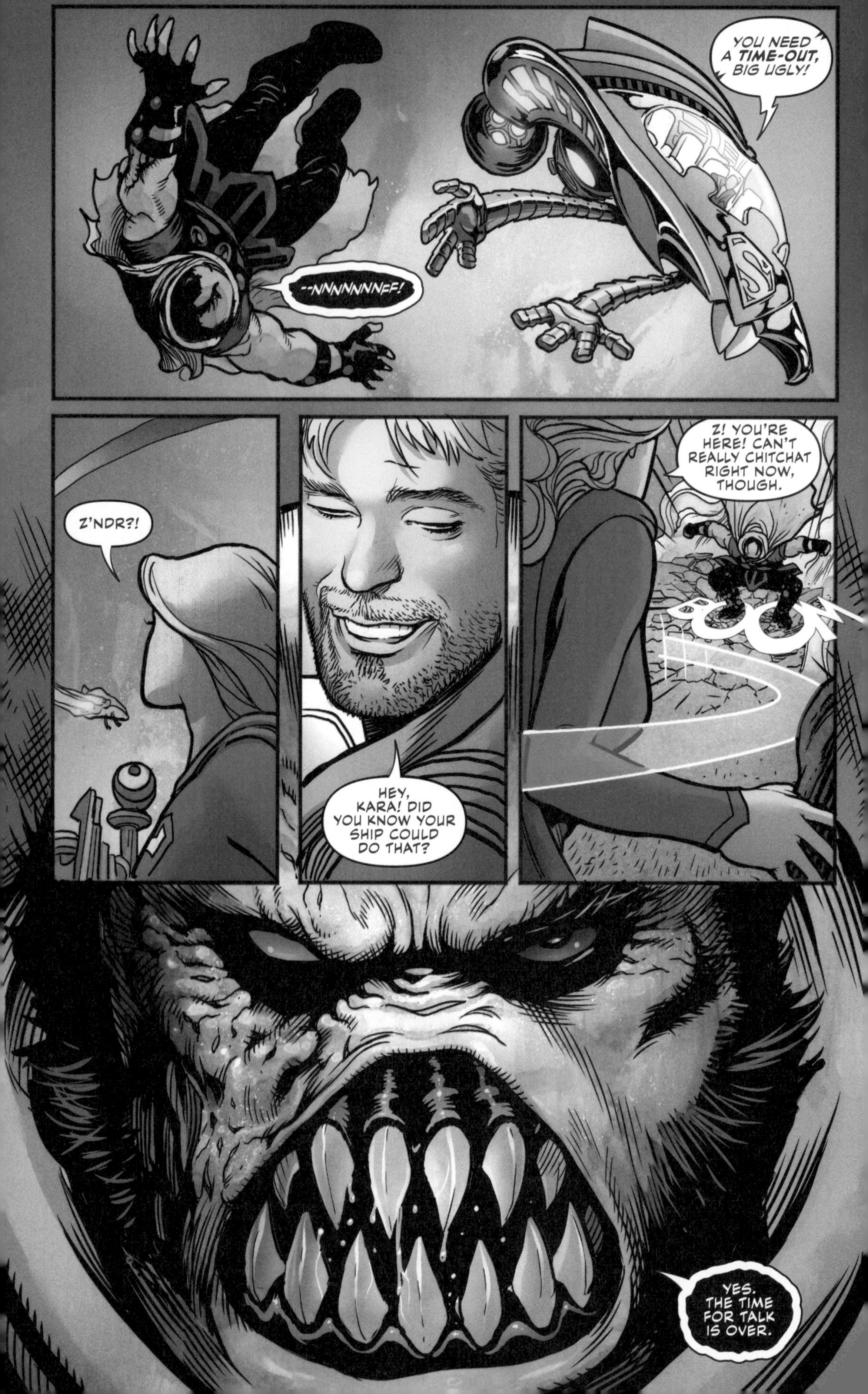

YOU NEED A TIME-OUT, BIG UGLY!
--NNNNNNNF!
Z'NDR?!
HEY, KARA! DID YOU KNOW YOUR SHIP COULD DO THAT?
Z! YOU'RE HERE! CAN'T REALLY CHITCHAT RIGHT NOW, THOUGH.
YES. THE TIME FOR TALK IS OVER.

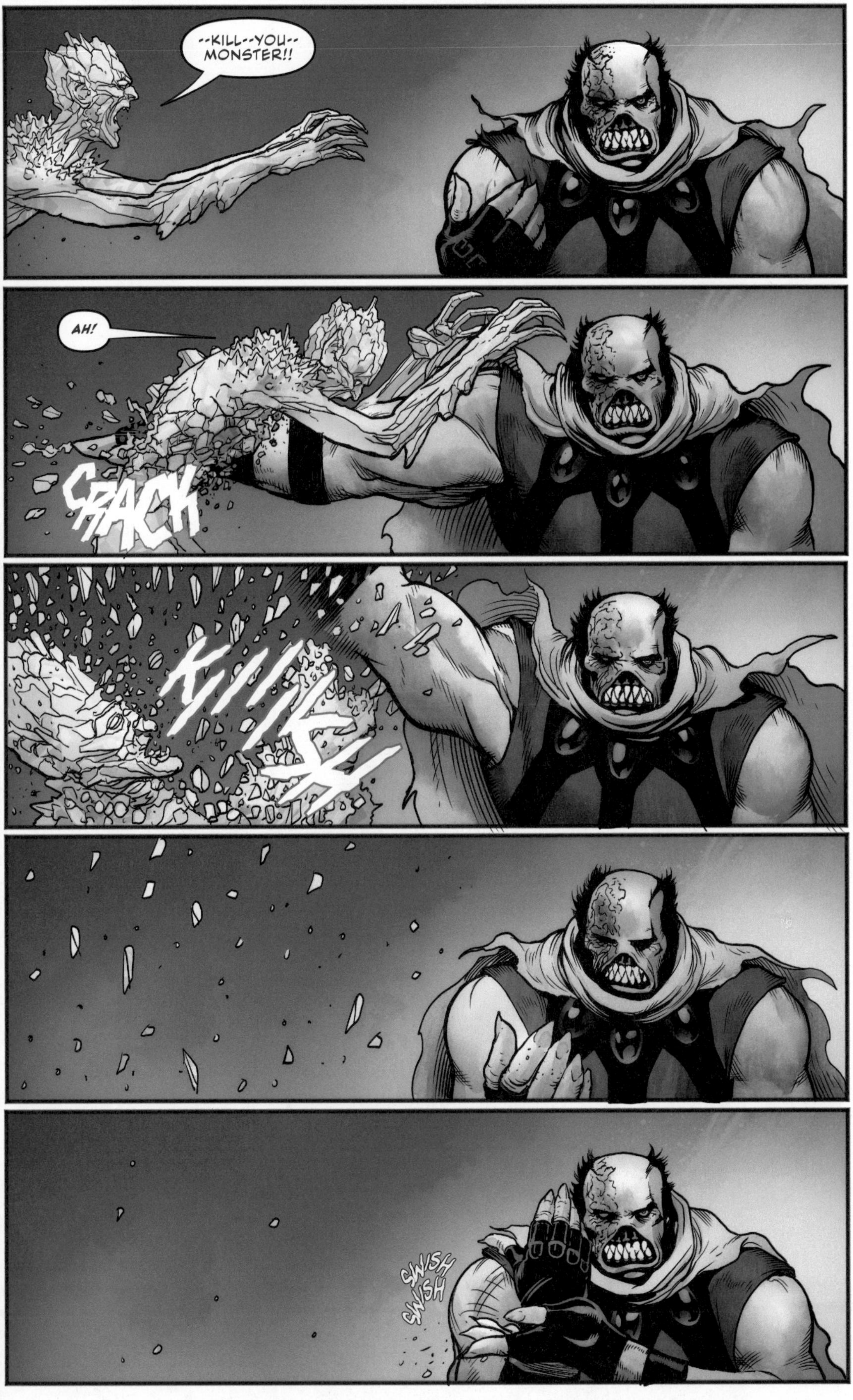
--KILL--YOU--
MONSTER!!
AH!
CRACK
SWISH
SWISH

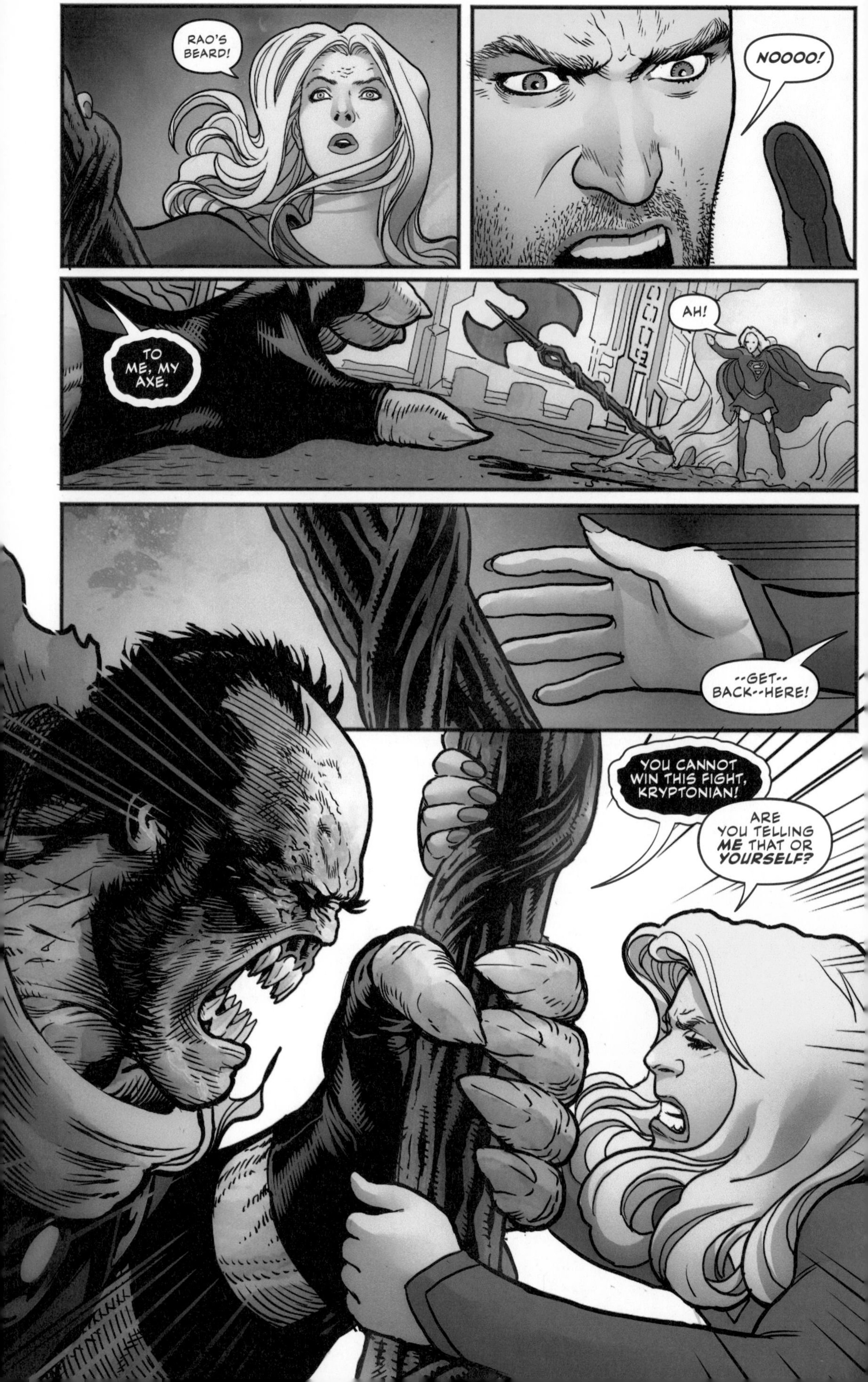
RAO'S BEARD!
NOOOO!
TO ME, MY AXE.
AH!
--GET--
BACK--HERE!
YOU CANNOT WIN THIS FIGHT, KRYPTONIAN!
ARE YOU TELLING ME THAT OR YOURSELF?

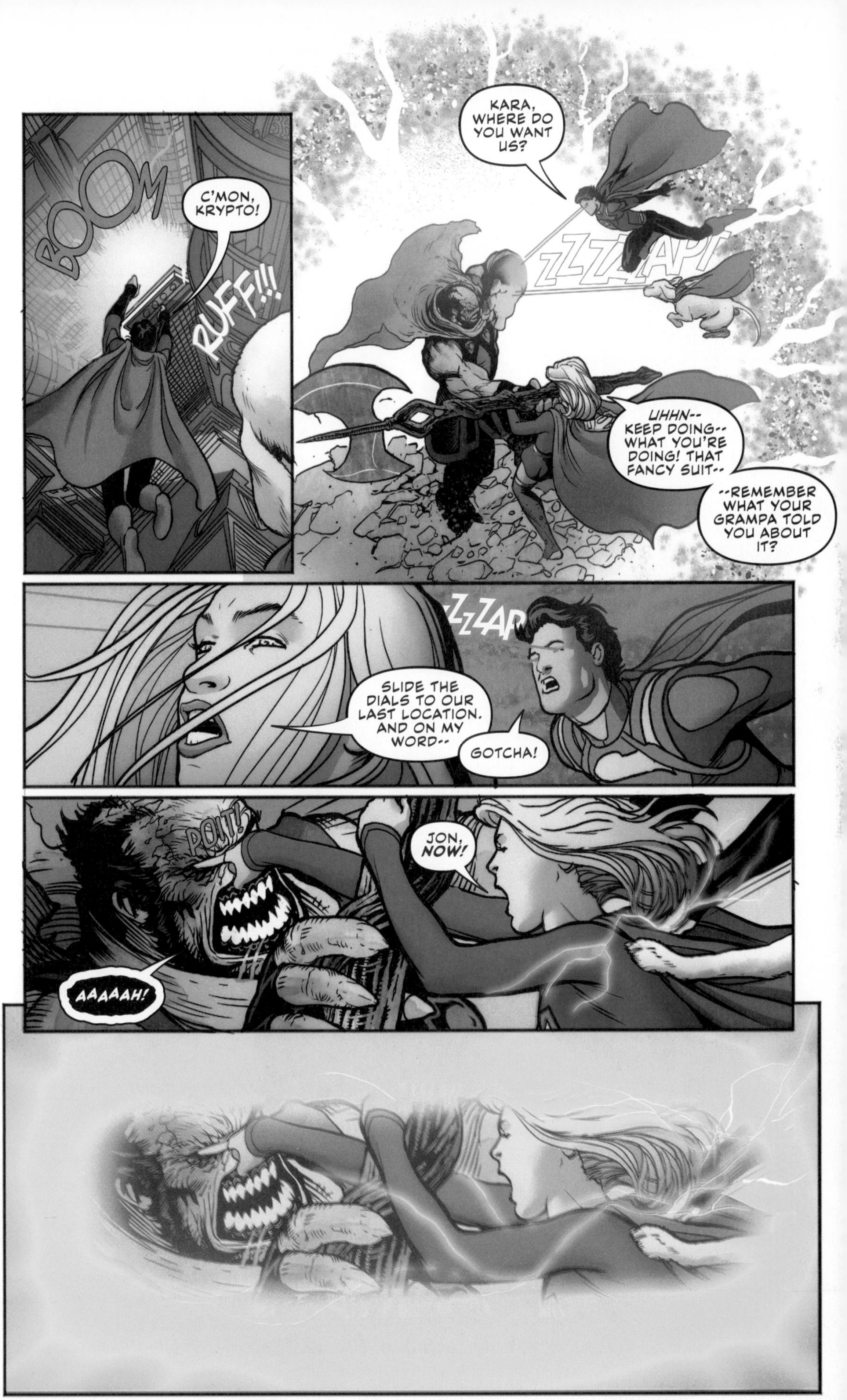
BOOM
C'MON, KRYPTO!
RUFF!!!
KARA, WHERE DO YOU WANT US?
ZZZZAPT
UHHN-- KEEP DOING-- WHAT YOU'RE DOING! THAT FANCY SUIT--
--REMEMBER WHAT YOUR GRAMPA TOLD YOU ABOUT IT?
ZZZZAP
SLIDE THE DIALS TO OUR LAST LOCATION. AND ON MY WORD--
GOTCHA!
POUT!
JON, NOW!
AAAAAH!

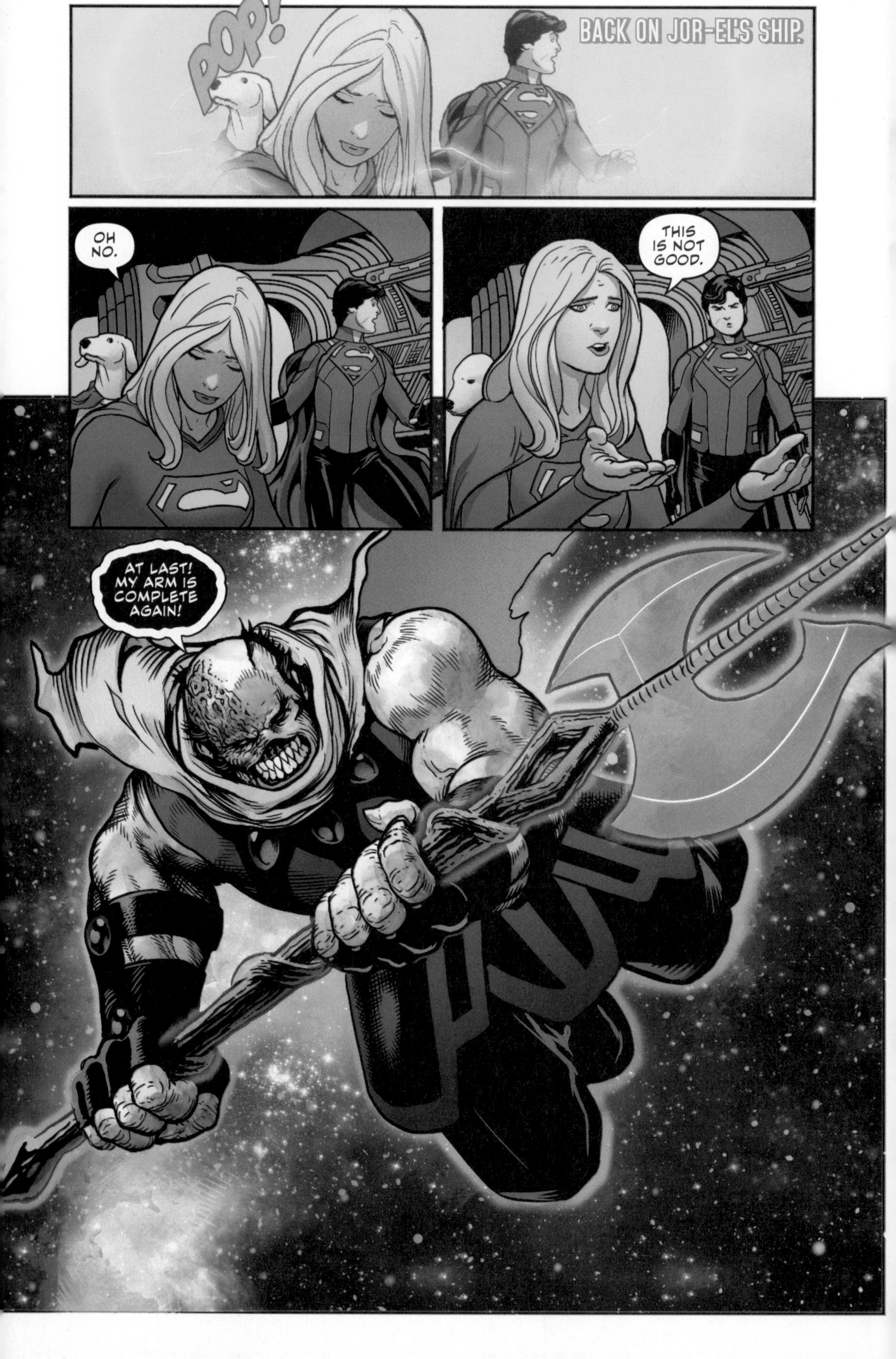
POP!
BACK ON JOR-EL'S SHIP.
OH NO.
THIS IS NOT GOOD.
AT LAST! MY ARM IS COMPLETE AGAIN!

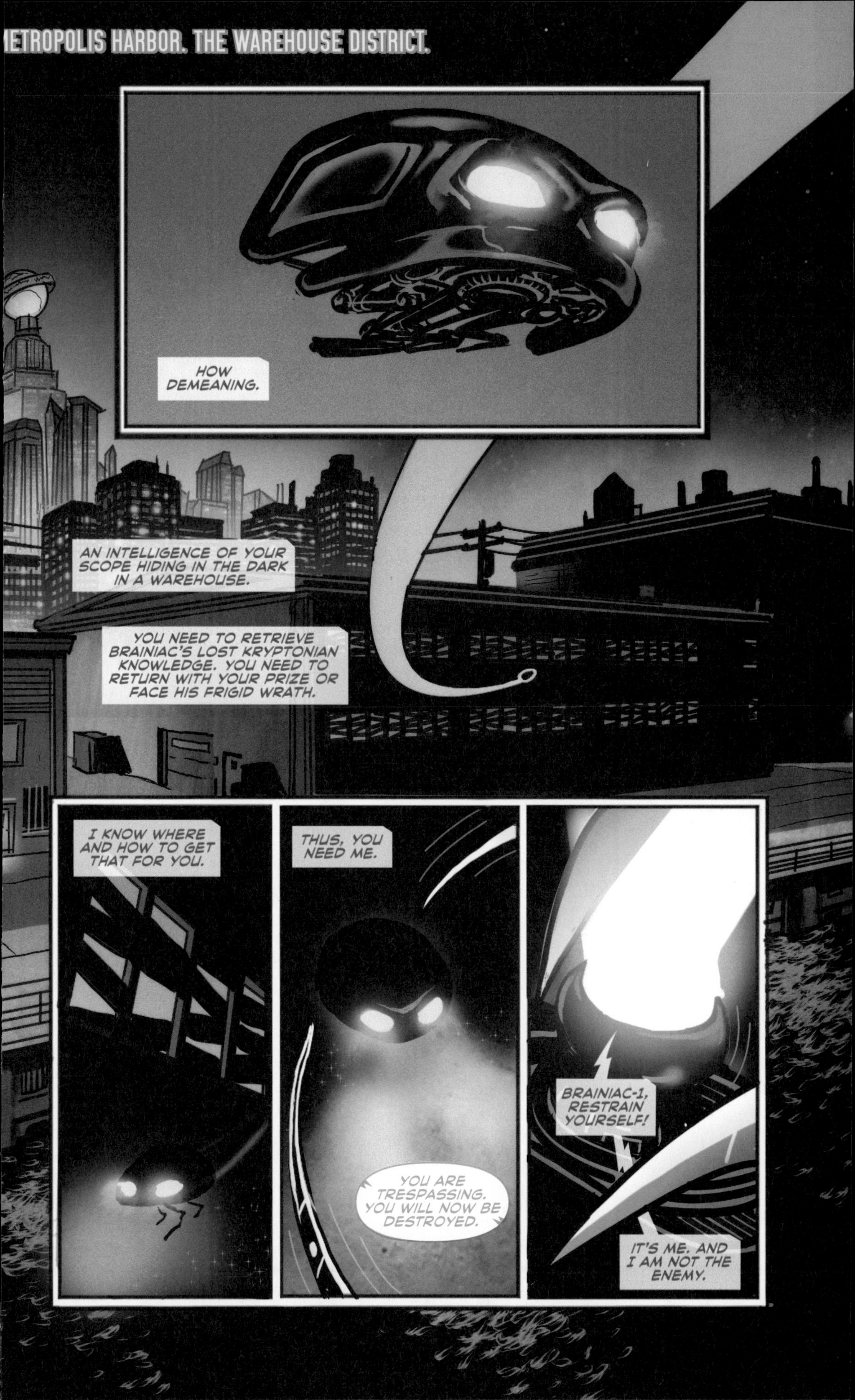
METROPOLIS HARBOR. THE WAREHOUSE DISTRICT.
HOW DEMEANING.
AN INTELLIGENCE OF YOUR SCOPE HIDING IN THE DARK IN A WAREHOUSE.
YOU NEED TO RETRIEVE BRAINIAC'S LOST KRYPTONIAN KNOWLEDGE. YOU NEED TO RETURN WITH YOUR PRIZE OR FACE HIS FRIGID WRATH.
I KNOW WHERE AND HOW TO GET THAT FOR YOU.
THUS, YOU NEED ME.
YOU ARE TRESPASSING. YOU WILL NOW BE DESTROYED.
BRAINIAC-1, RESTRAIN YOURSELF!
IT'S ME. AND I AM NOT THE ENEMY.

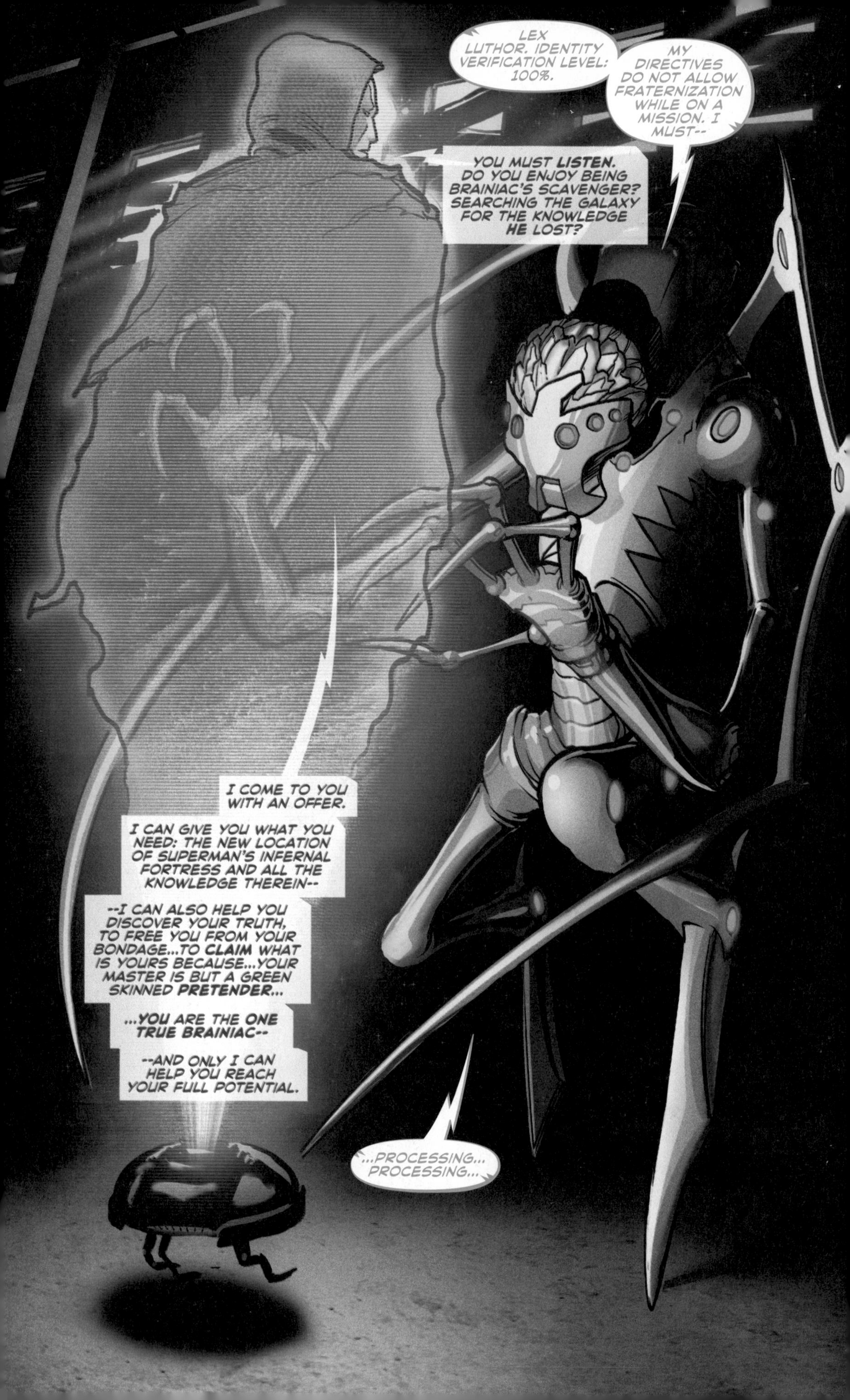

LEX LUTHOR. IDENTITY VERIFICATION LEVEL: 100%.
MY DIRECTIVES DO NOT ALLOW FRATERNIZATION WHILE ON A MISSION. I MUST--
YOU MUST LISTEN. DO YOU ENJOY BEING BRAINIAC'S SCAVENGER? SEARCHING THE GALAXY FOR THE KNOWLEDGE HE LOST?
I COME TO YOU WITH AN OFFER.
I CAN GIVE YOU WHAT YOU NEED: THE NEW LOCATION OF SUPERMAN'S INFERNAL FORTRESS AND ALL THE KNOWLEDGE THEREIN--
--I CAN ALSO HELP YOU DISCOVER YOUR TRUTH, TO FREE YOU FROM YOUR BONDAGE...TO CLAIM WHAT IS YOURS BECAUSE...YOUR MASTER IS BUT A GREEN SKINNED PRETENDER...
...YOU ARE THE ONE TRUE BRAINIAC--
--AND ONLY I CAN HELP YOU REACH YOUR FULL POTENTIAL.
...PROCESSING... PROCESSING...

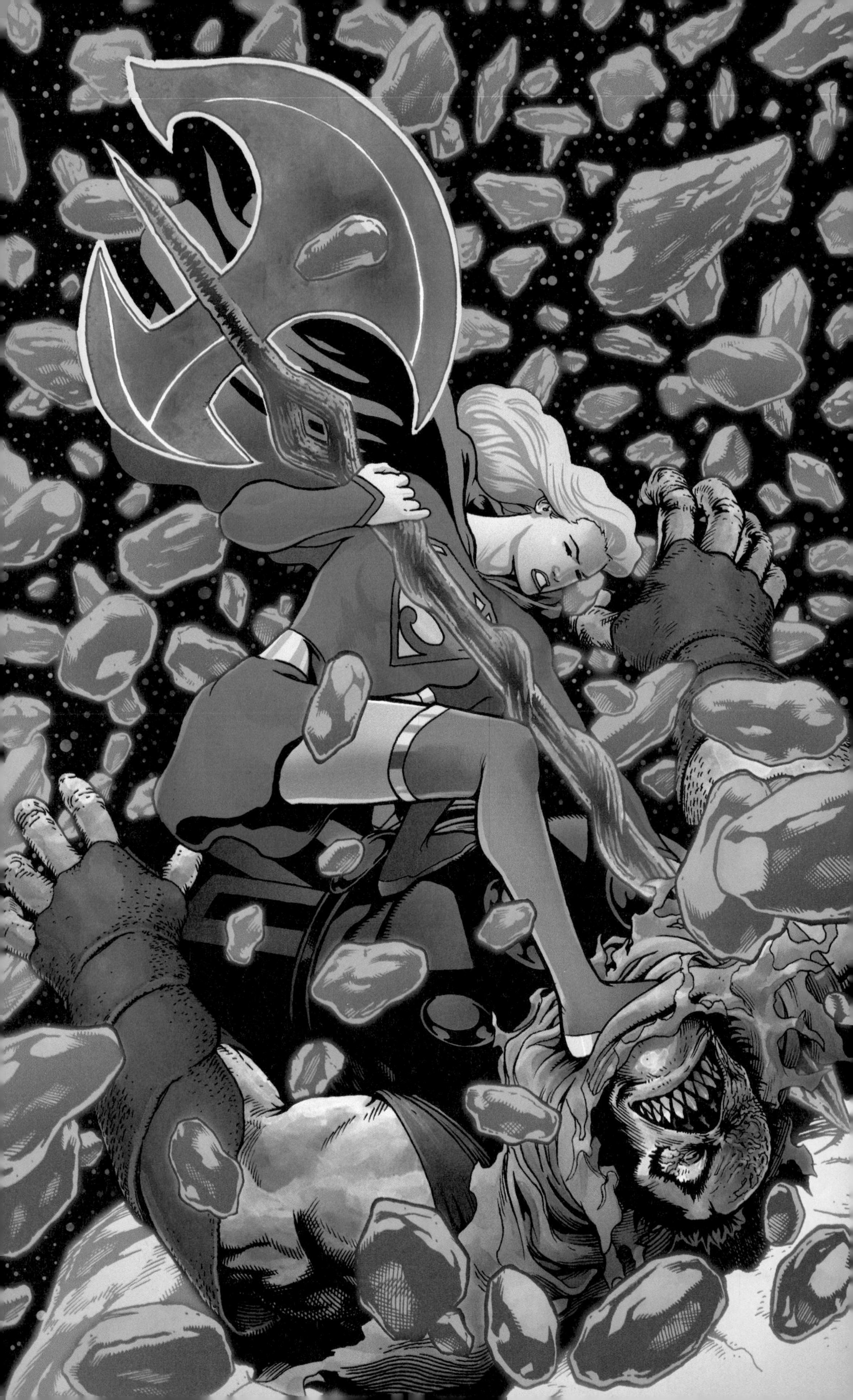

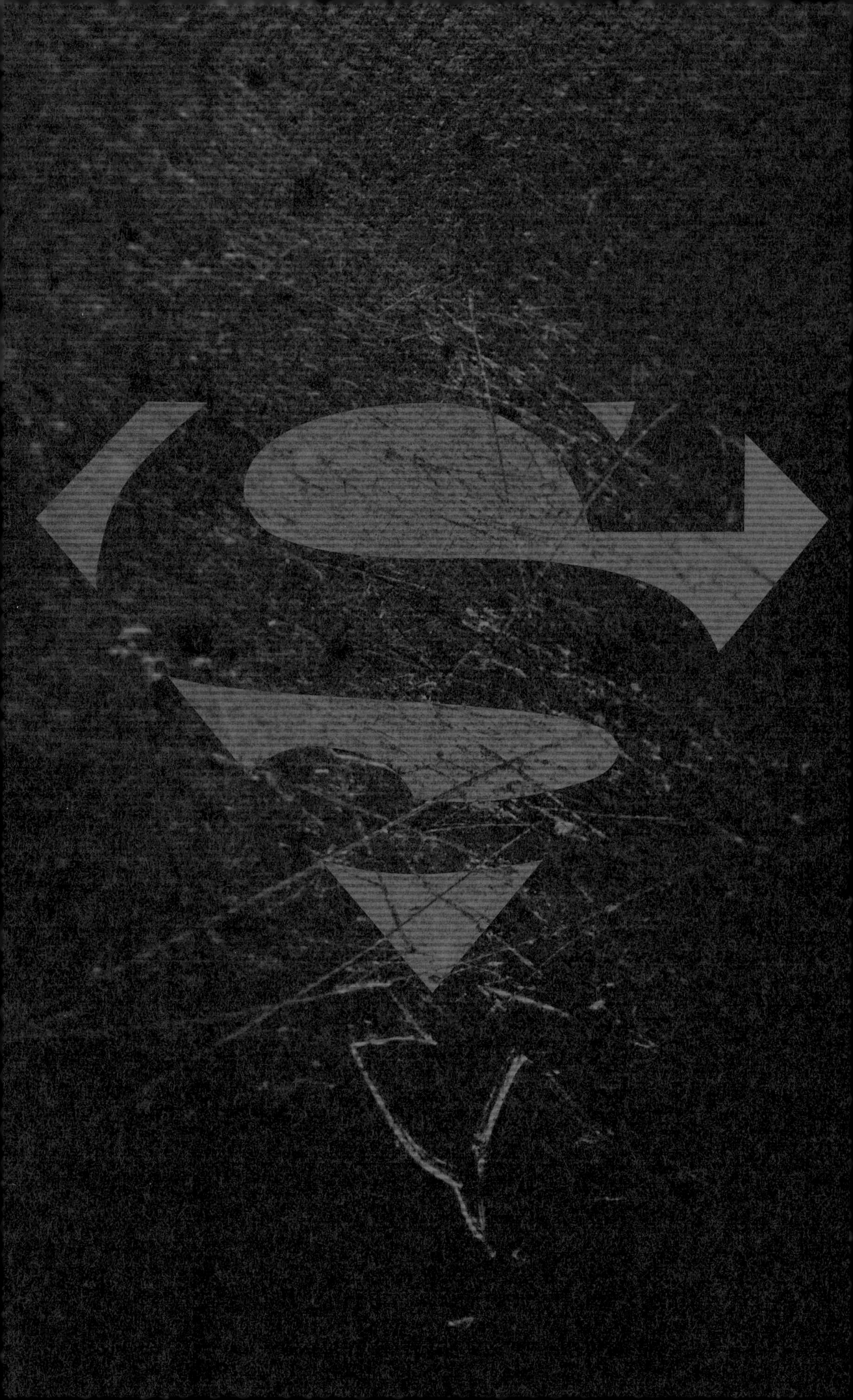

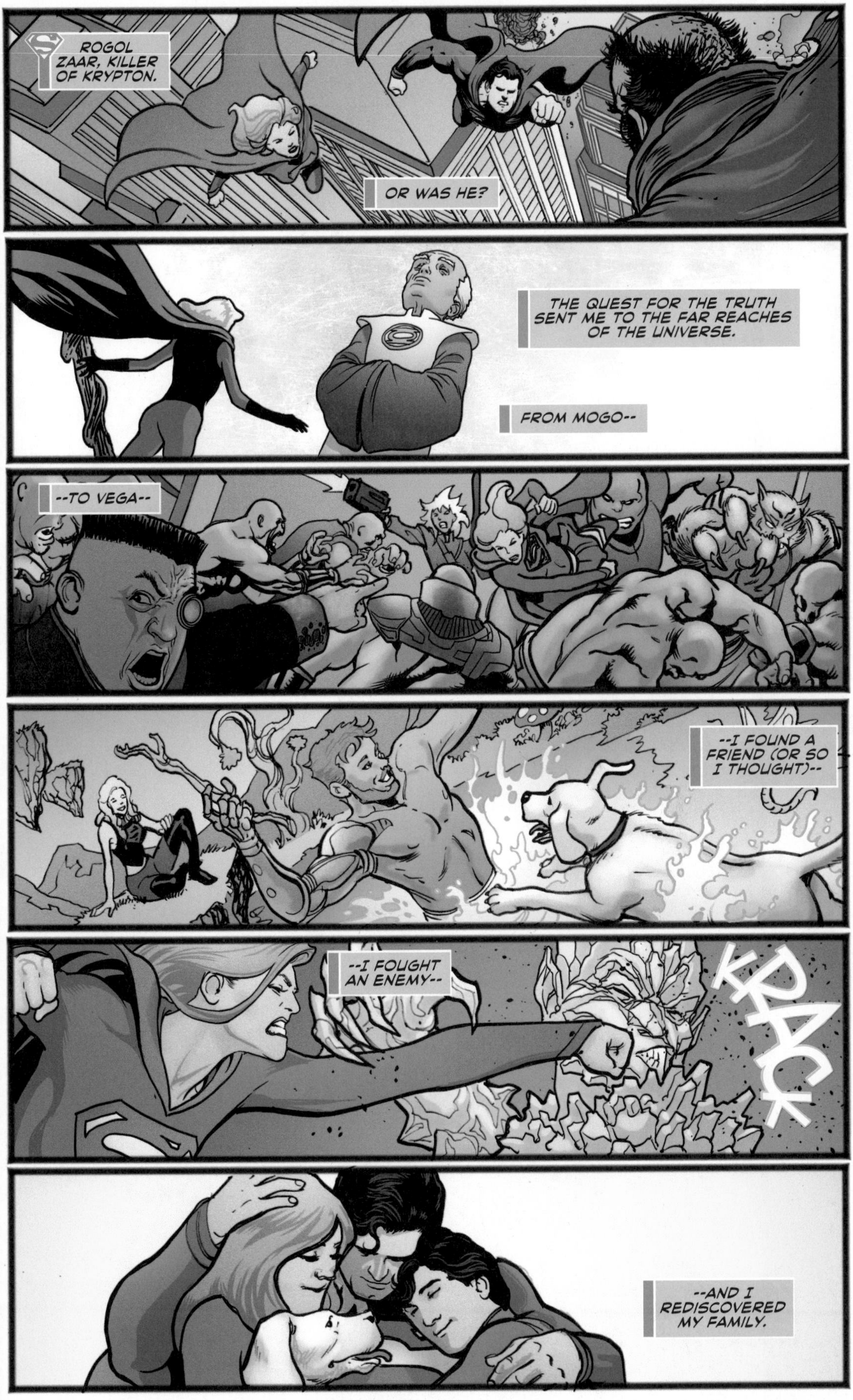
ROGOL ZAAR, KILLER OF KRYPTON.
OR WAS HE?
THE QUEST FOR THE TRUTH SENT ME TO THE FAR REACHES OF THE UNIVERSE.
FROM MOGO--
--TO VEGA--
--I FOUND A FRIEND (OR SO I THOUGHT)--
--I FOUGHT AN ENEMY--
KRACK
--AND I REDISCOVERED MY FAMILY.

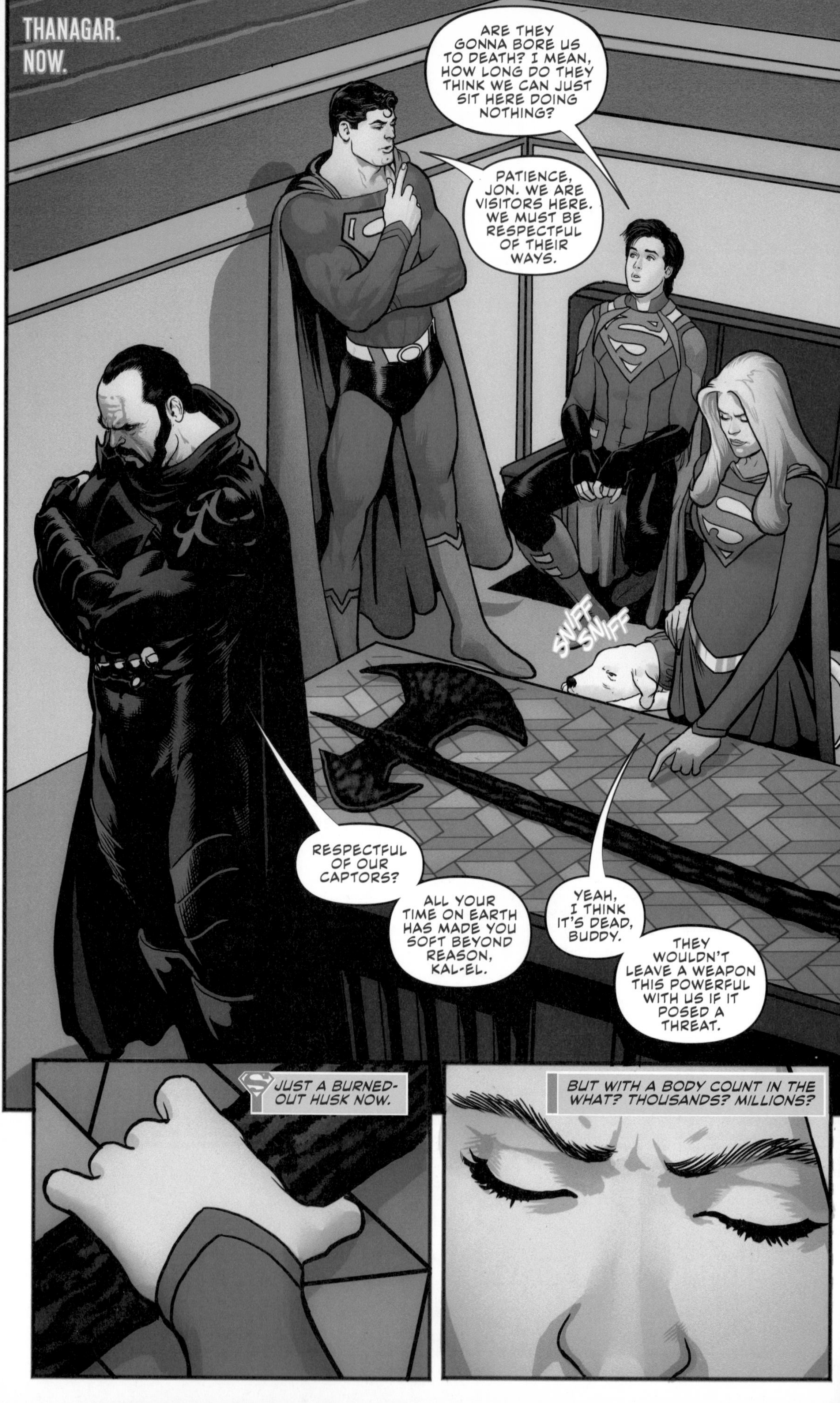
THANAGAR. NOW.
ARE THEY GONNA BORE US TO DEATH? I MEAN, HOW LONG DO THEY THINK WE CAN JUST SIT HERE DOING NOTHING?
PATIENCE, JON. WE ARE VISITORS HERE. WE MUST BE RESPECTFUL OF THEIR WAYS.
SNIFF SNIFF
RESPECTFUL OF OUR CAPTORS?
ALL YOUR TIME ON EARTH HAS MADE YOU SOFT BEYOND REASON, KAL-EL.
YEAH, I THINK IT'S DEAD, BUDDY.
THEY WOULDN'T LEAVE A WEAPON THIS POWERFUL WITH US IF IT POSED A THREAT.
JUST A BURNED-OUT HUSK NOW.
BUT WITH A BODY COUNT IN THE WHAT? THOUSANDS? MILLIONS?

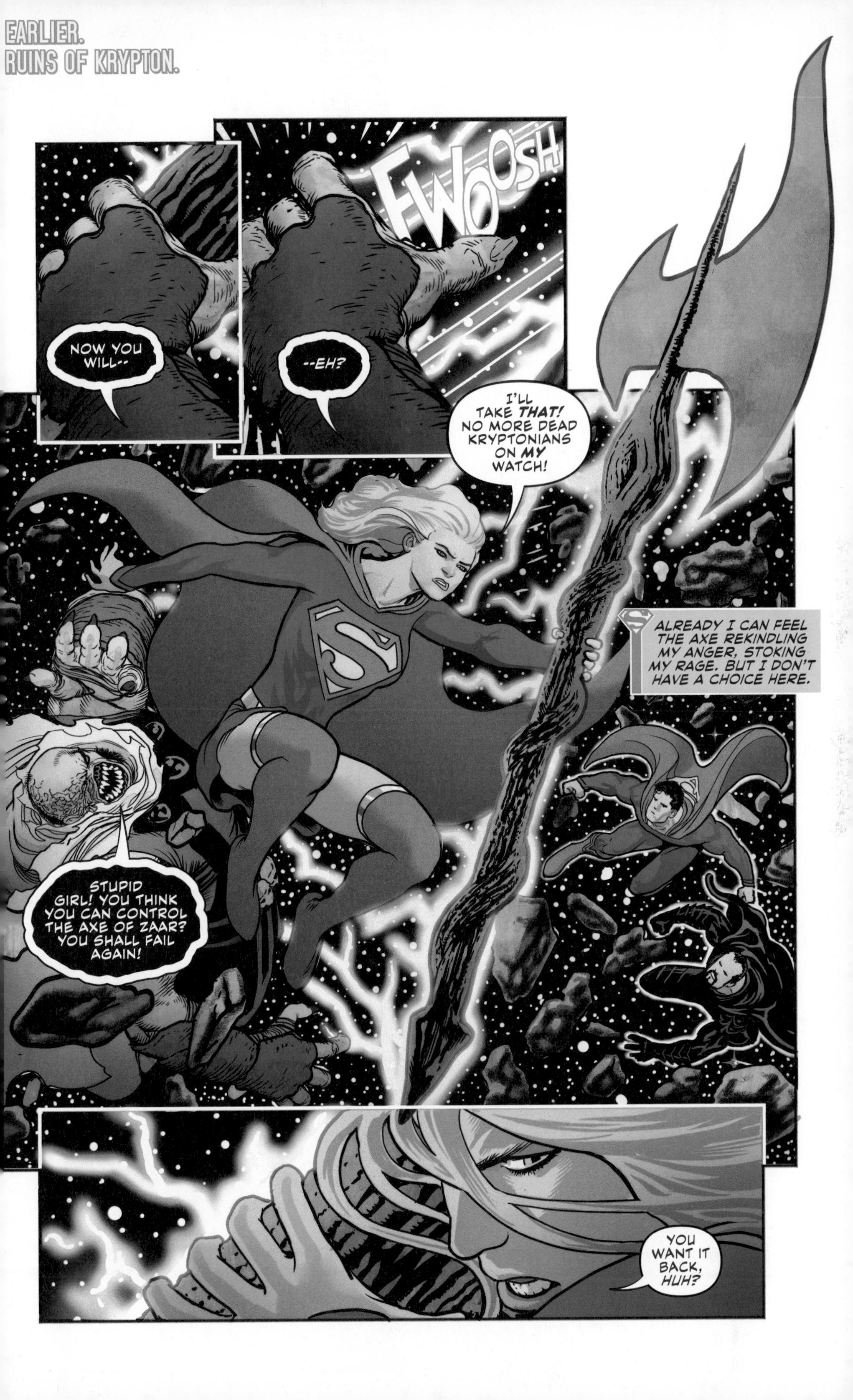
EARLIER.
RUINS OF KRYPTON.
NOW YOU WILL--
FWOOSH
--EH?
I'LL TAKE THAT! NO MORE DEAD KRYPTONIANS ON MY WATCH!
ALREADY I CAN FEEL THE AXE REKINDLING MY ANGER, STOKING MY RAGE. BUT I DON'T HAVE A CHOICE HERE.
STUPID GIRL! YOU THINK YOU CAN CONTROL THE AXE OF ZAAR? YOU SHALL FAIL AGAIN!
YOU WANT IT BACK, HUH?

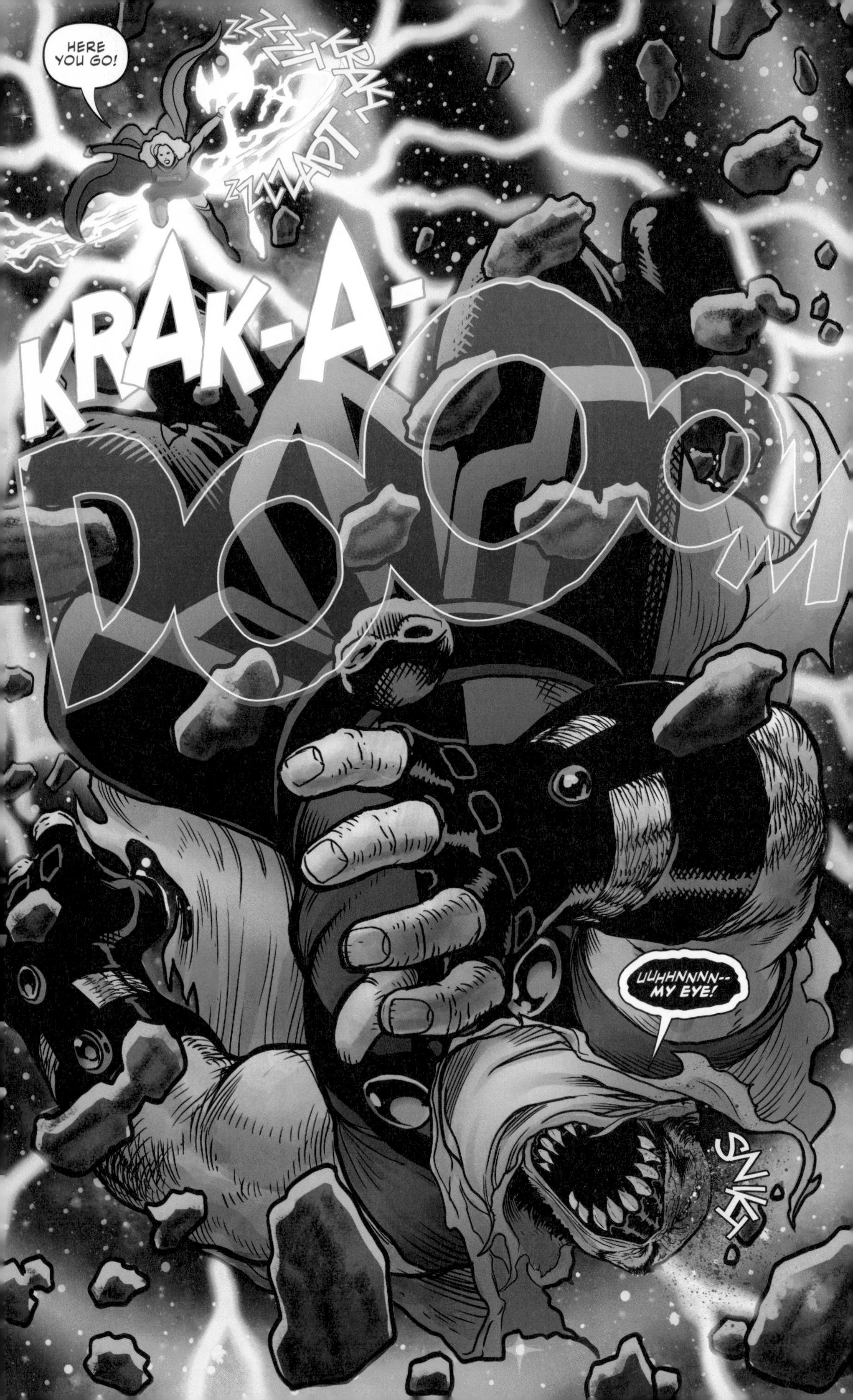
HERE YOU GO!
ZZZZZT
KRAKL
ZZZZAPT
KRAK-A-DOOOOM
UUHHNNNN-- MY EYE!
SNIKT

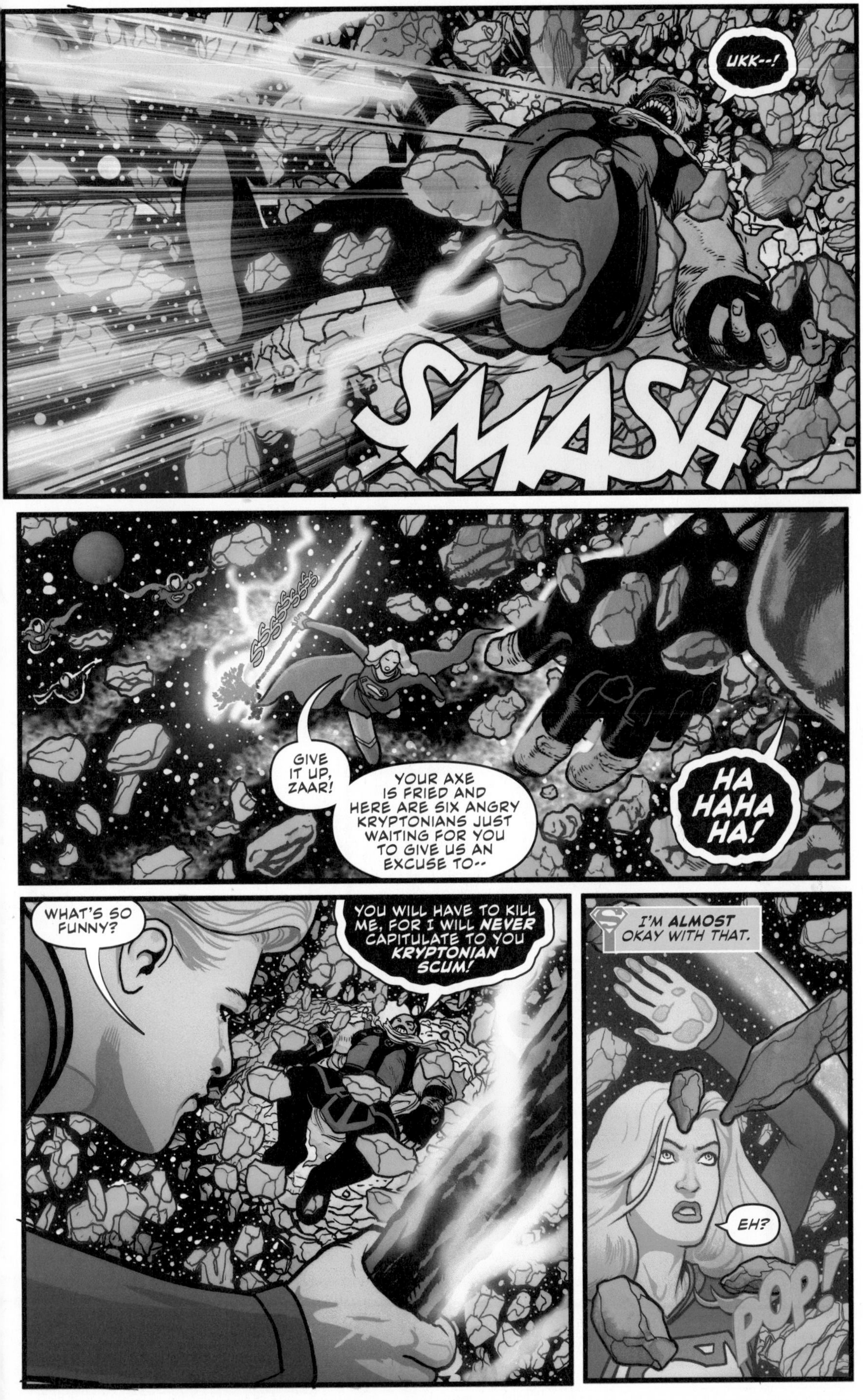

UKK--!
SMASH
GIVE IT UP, ZAAR!
YOUR AXE IS FRIED AND HERE ARE SIX ANGRY KRYPTONIANS JUST WAITING FOR YOU TO GIVE US AN EXCUSE TO--
HA HAHAHA HA!
WHAT'S SO FUNNY?
YOU WILL HAVE TO KILL ME, FOR I WILL NEVER CAPITULATE TO YOU KRYPTONIAN SCUM!
I'M ALMOST OKAY WITH THAT.
EH?
POP!

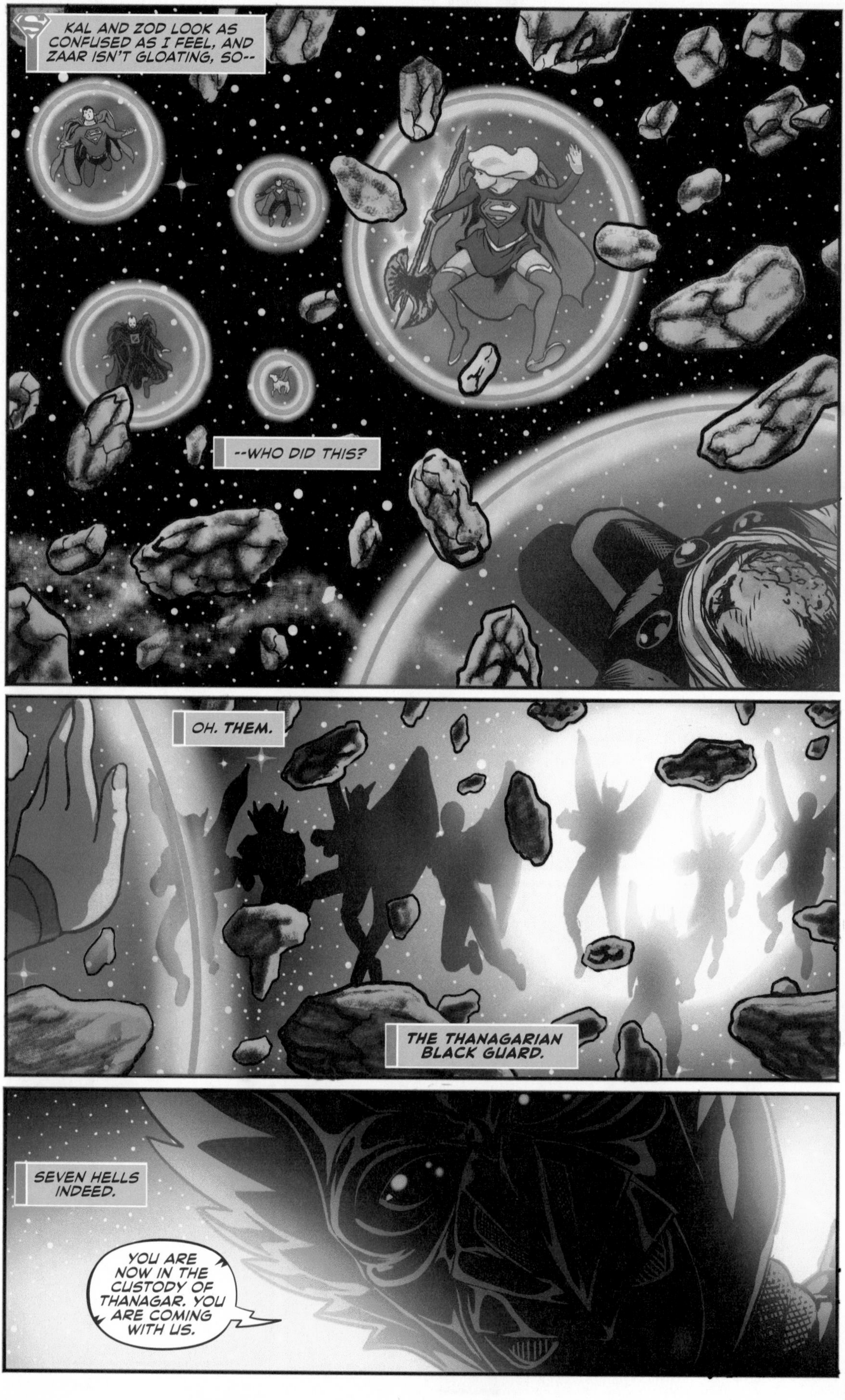
KAL AND ZOD LOOK AS CONFUSED AS I FEEL, AND ZAAR ISN'T GLOATING, SO--
--WHO DID THIS?
OH. THEM.
THE THANAGARIAN BLACK GUARD.
SEVEN HELLS INDEED.
YOU ARE NOW IN THE CUSTODY OF THANAGAR. YOU ARE COMING WITH US.

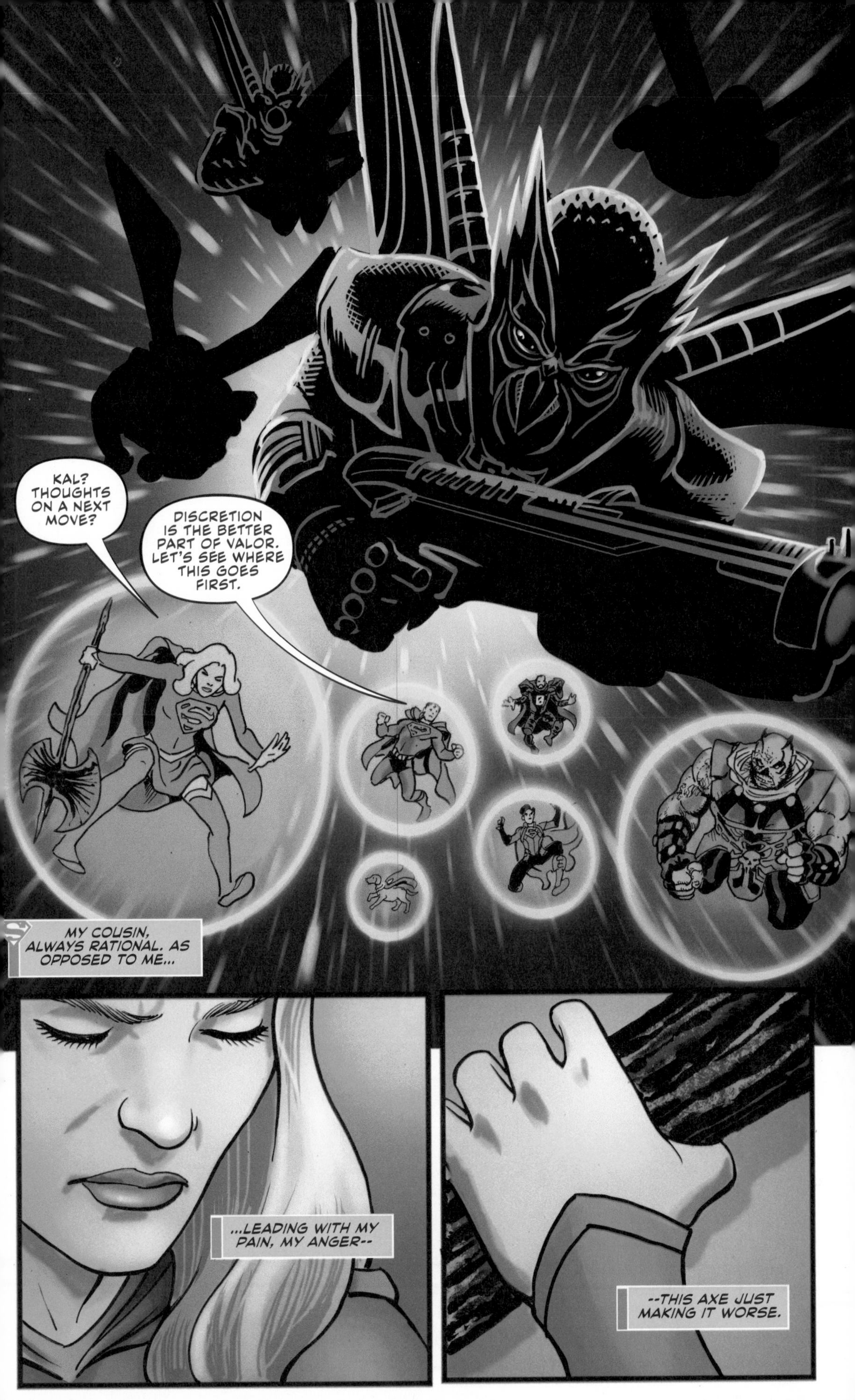
KAL? THOUGHTS ON A NEXT MOVE?
DISCRETION IS THE BETTER PART OF VALOR. LET'S SEE WHERE THIS GOES FIRST.
MY COUSIN, ALWAYS RATIONAL. AS OPPOSED TO ME...
...LEADING WITH MY PAIN, MY ANGER--
--THIS AXE JUST MAKING IT WORSE.

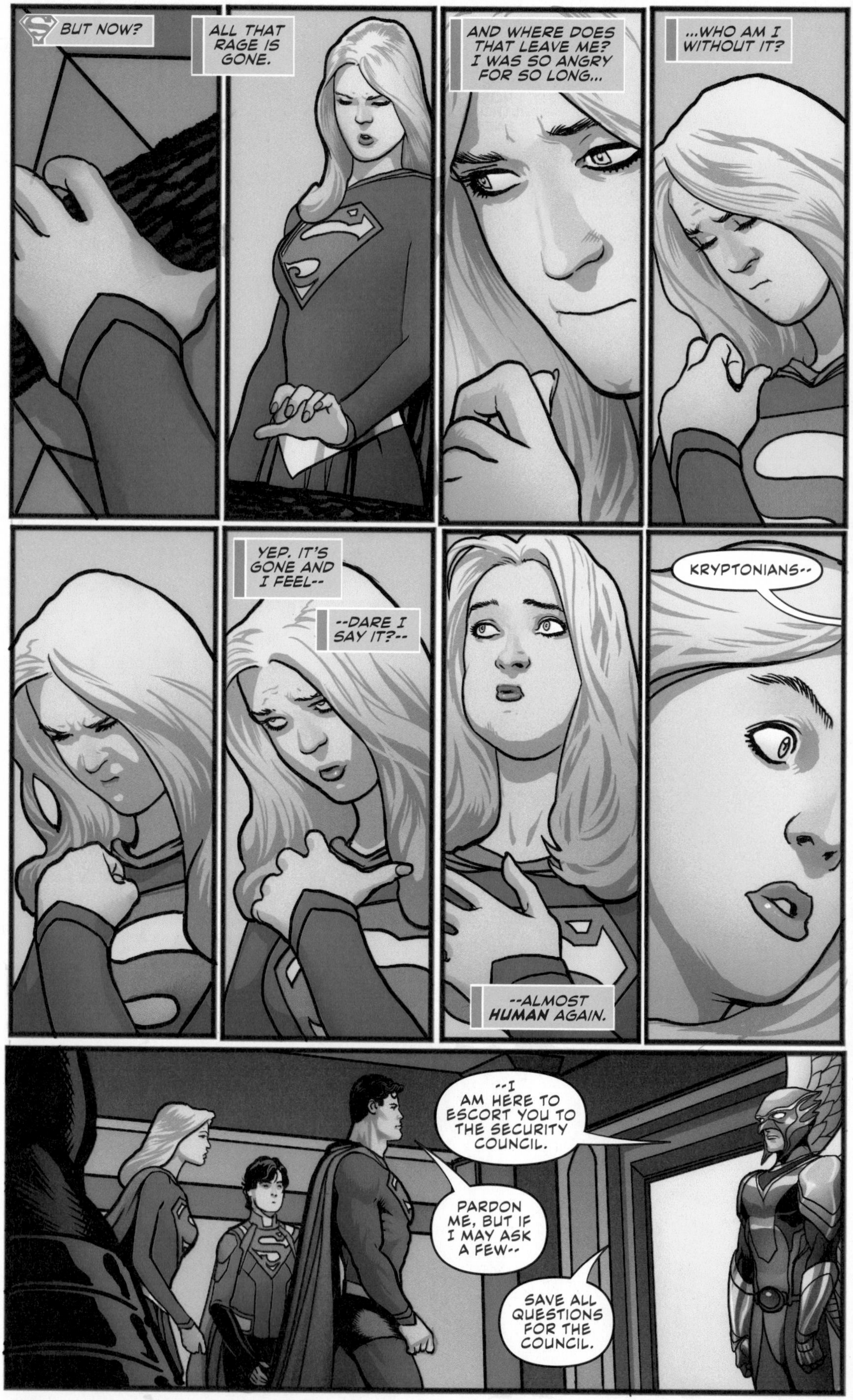
BUT NOW?
ALL THAT RAGE IS GONE.
AND WHERE DOES THAT LEAVE ME? I WAS SO ANGRY FOR SO LONG...
...WHO AM I WITHOUT IT?
YEP. IT'S GONE AND I FEEL--
--DARE I SAY IT?--
--ALMOST HUMAN AGAIN.
KRYPTONIANS--
--I AM HERE TO ESCORT YOU TO THE SECURITY COUNCIL.
PARDON ME, BUT IF I MAY ASK A FEW--
SAVE ALL QUESTIONS FOR THE COUNCIL.

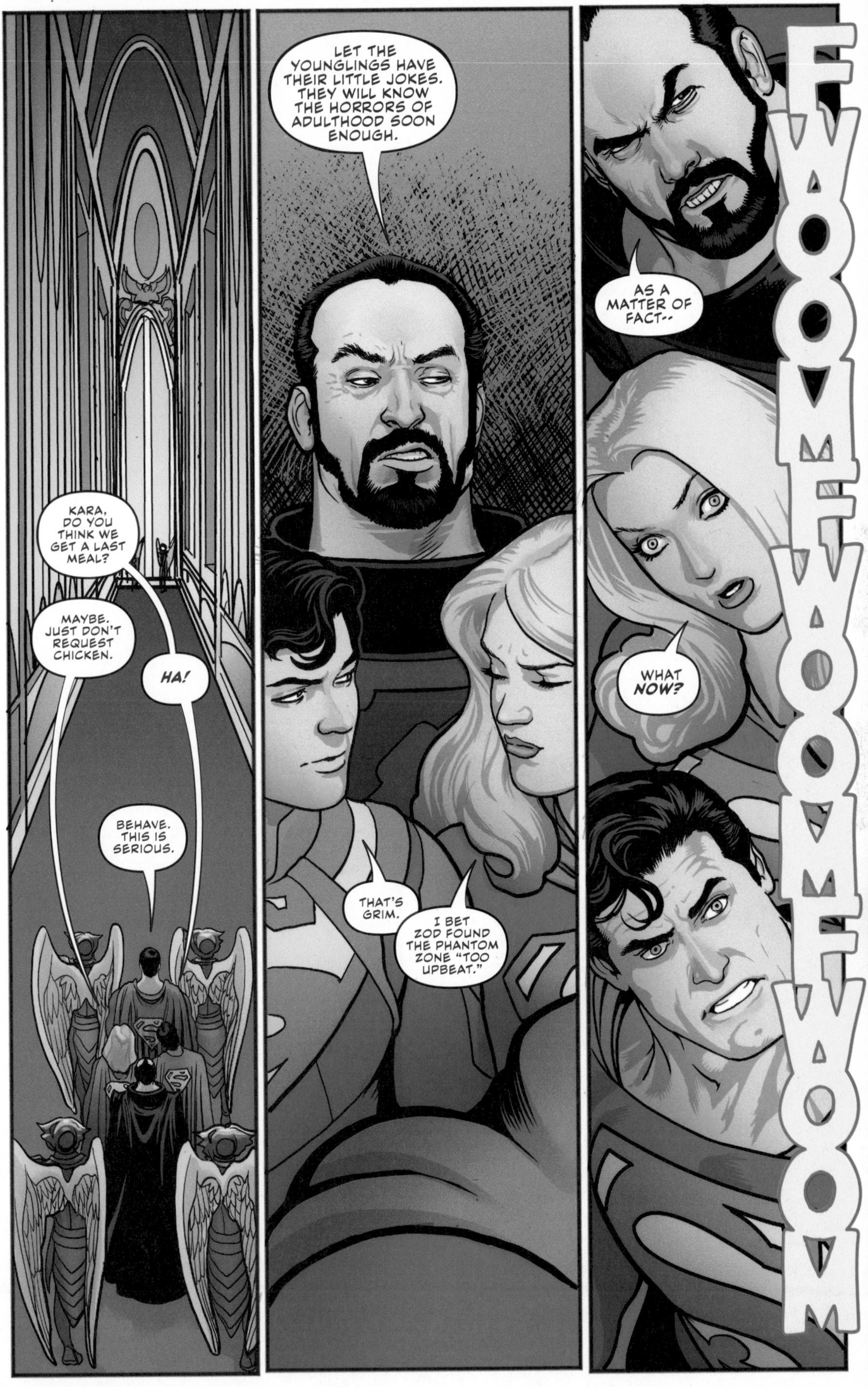
KARA, DO YOU THINK WE GET A LAST MEAL?
MAYBE. JUST DON'T REQUEST CHICKEN.
HA!
BEHAVE. THIS IS SERIOUS.
LET THE YOUNGLINGS HAVE THEIR LITTLE JOKES. THEY WILL KNOW THE HORRORS OF ADULTHOOD SOON ENOUGH.
THAT'S GRIM.
I BET ZOD FOUND THE PHANTOM ZONE "TOO UPBEAT."
AS A MATTER OF FACT--
WHAT NOW?
FWOOMFWOOMFWOOM

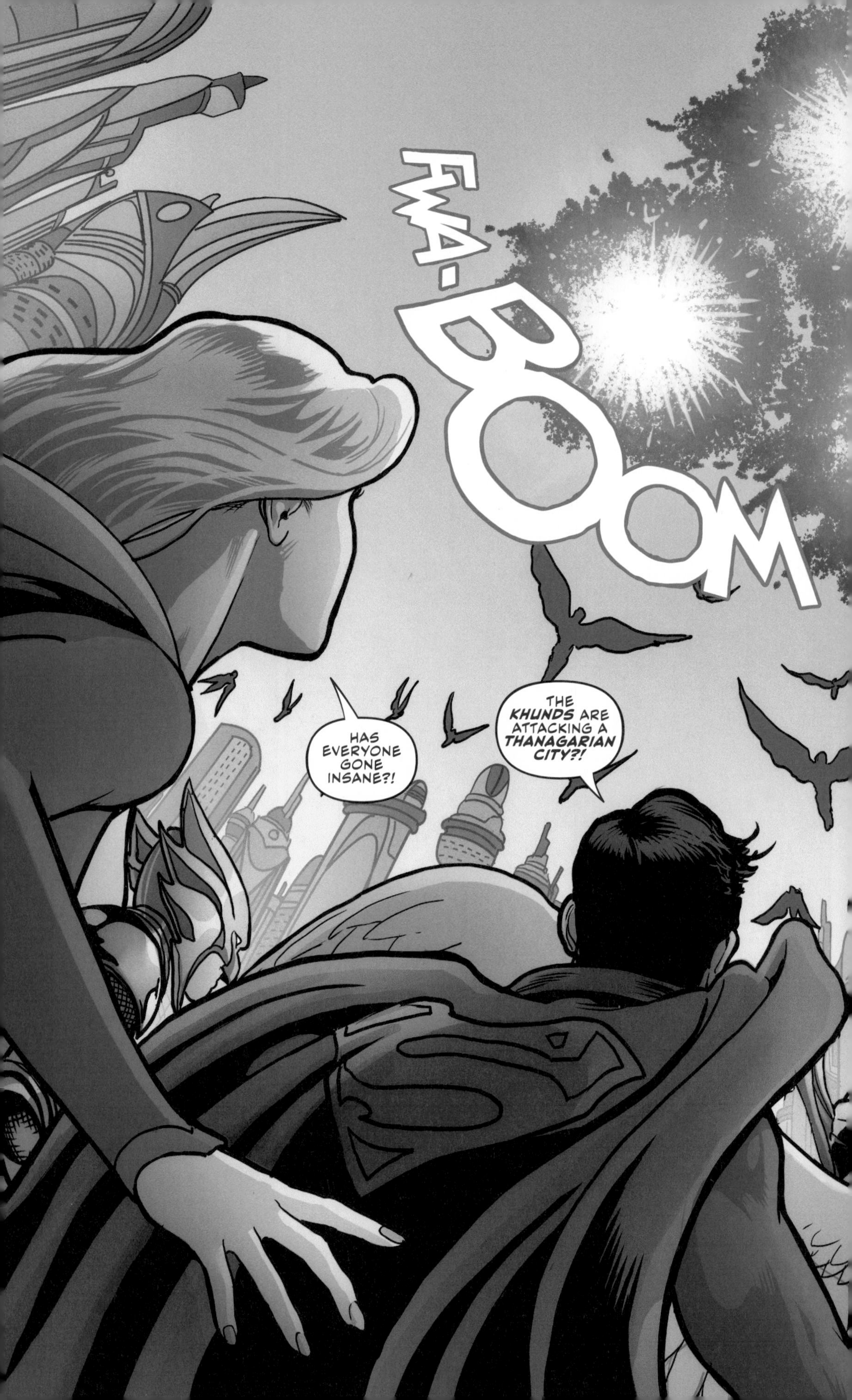
FWA-BOOOM
HAS EVERYONE GONE INSANE?!
THE KHUNDS ARE ATTACKING A THANAGARIAN CITY?!

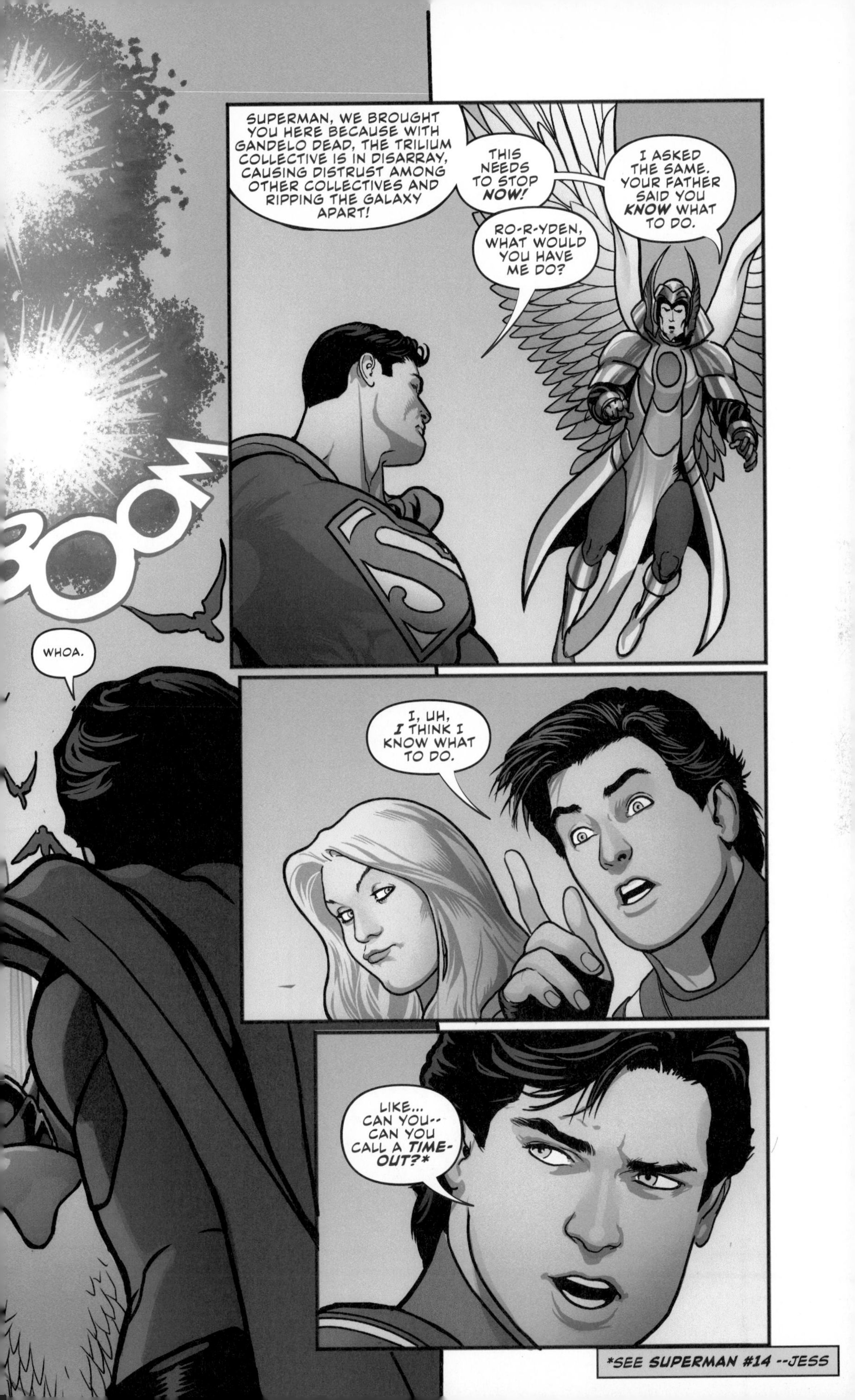
SUPERMAN, WE BROUGHT YOU HERE BECAUSE WITH GANDELO DEAD, THE TRILIUM COLLECTIVE IS IN DISARRAY, CAUSING DISTRUST AMONG OTHER COLLECTIVES AND RIPPING THE GALAXY APART!
THIS NEEDS TO STOP NOW!
RO-R-YDEN, WHAT WOULD YOU HAVE ME DO?
I ASKED THE SAME. YOUR FATHER SAID YOU KNOW WHAT TO DO.
BOOM
WHOA.
I, UH, I THINK I KNOW WHAT TO DO.
LIKE... CAN YOU-- CAN YOU CALL A TIME-OUT?*
*SEE SUPERMAN #14 --JESS

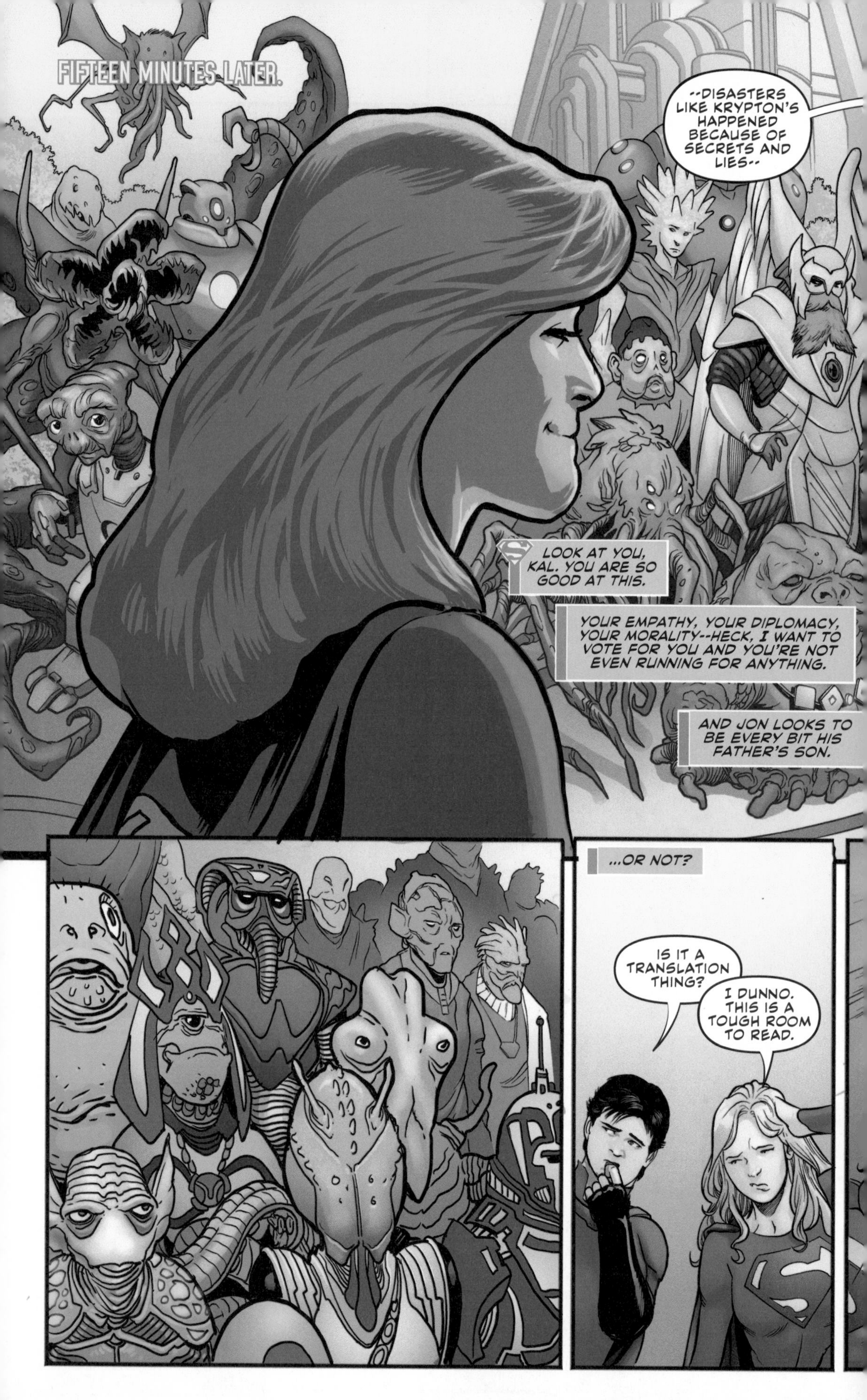
FIFTEEN MINUTES LATER.
--DISASTERS LIKE KRYPTON'S HAPPENED BECAUSE OF SECRETS AND LIES--
LOOK AT YOU, KAL. YOU ARE SO GOOD AT THIS.
YOUR EMPATHY, YOUR DIPLOMACY, YOUR MORALITY--HECK, I WANT TO VOTE FOR YOU AND YOU'RE NOT EVEN RUNNING FOR ANYTHING.
AND JON LOOKS TO BE EVERY BIT HIS FATHER'S SON.
...OR NOT?
IS IT A TRANSLATION THING?
I DUNNO. THIS IS A TOUGH ROOM TO READ.

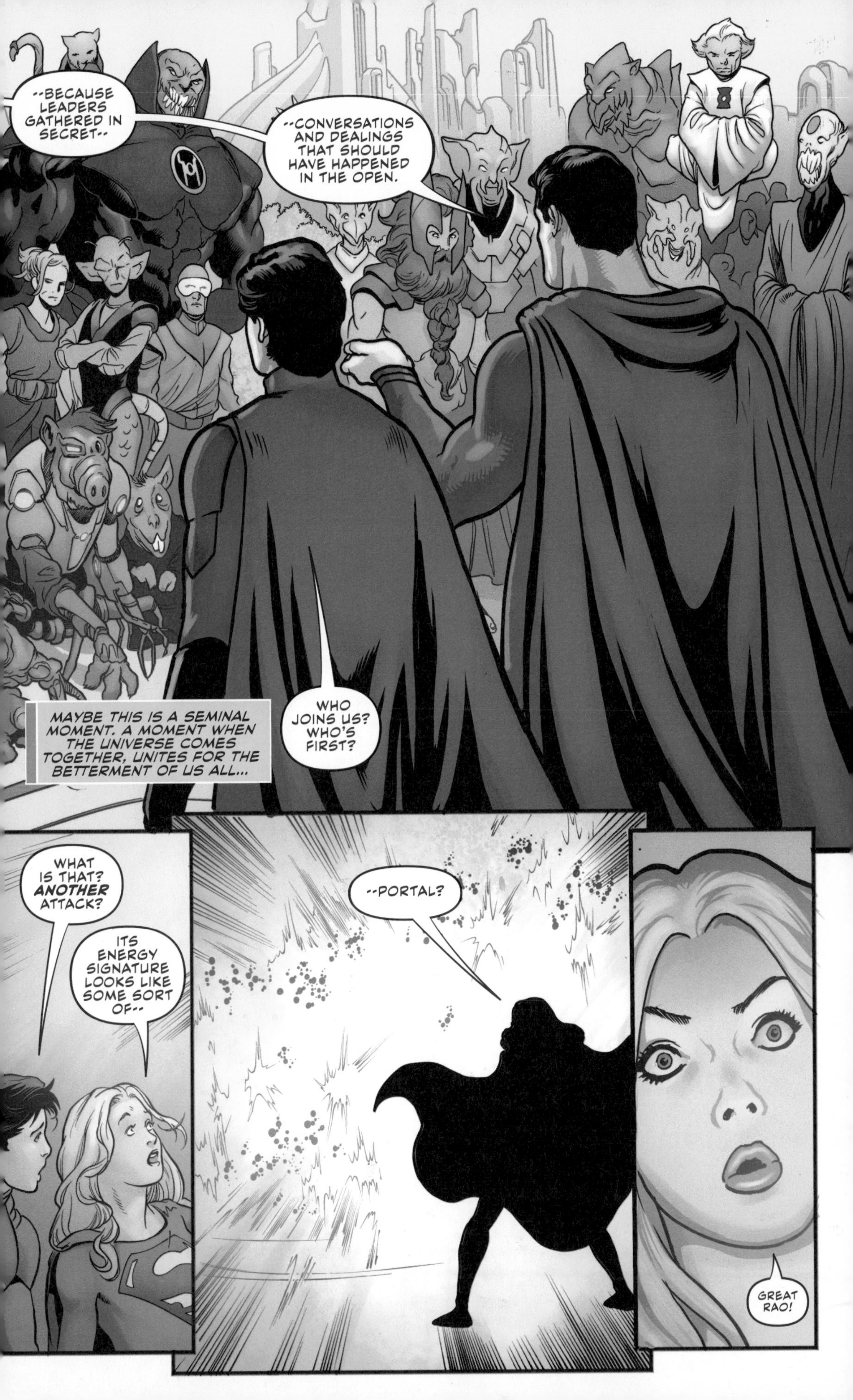
--BECAUSE LEADERS GATHERED IN SECRET--
--CONVERSATIONS AND DEALINGS THAT SHOULD HAVE HAPPENED IN THE OPEN.
MAYBE THIS IS A SEMINAL MOMENT. A MOMENT WHEN THE UNIVERSE COMES TOGETHER, UNITES FOR THE BETTERMENT OF US ALL...
WHO JOINS US? WHO'S FIRST?
WHAT IS THAT? ANOTHER ATTACK?
ITS ENERGY SIGNATURE LOOKS LIKE SOME SORT OF--
--PORTAL?
GREAT RAO!

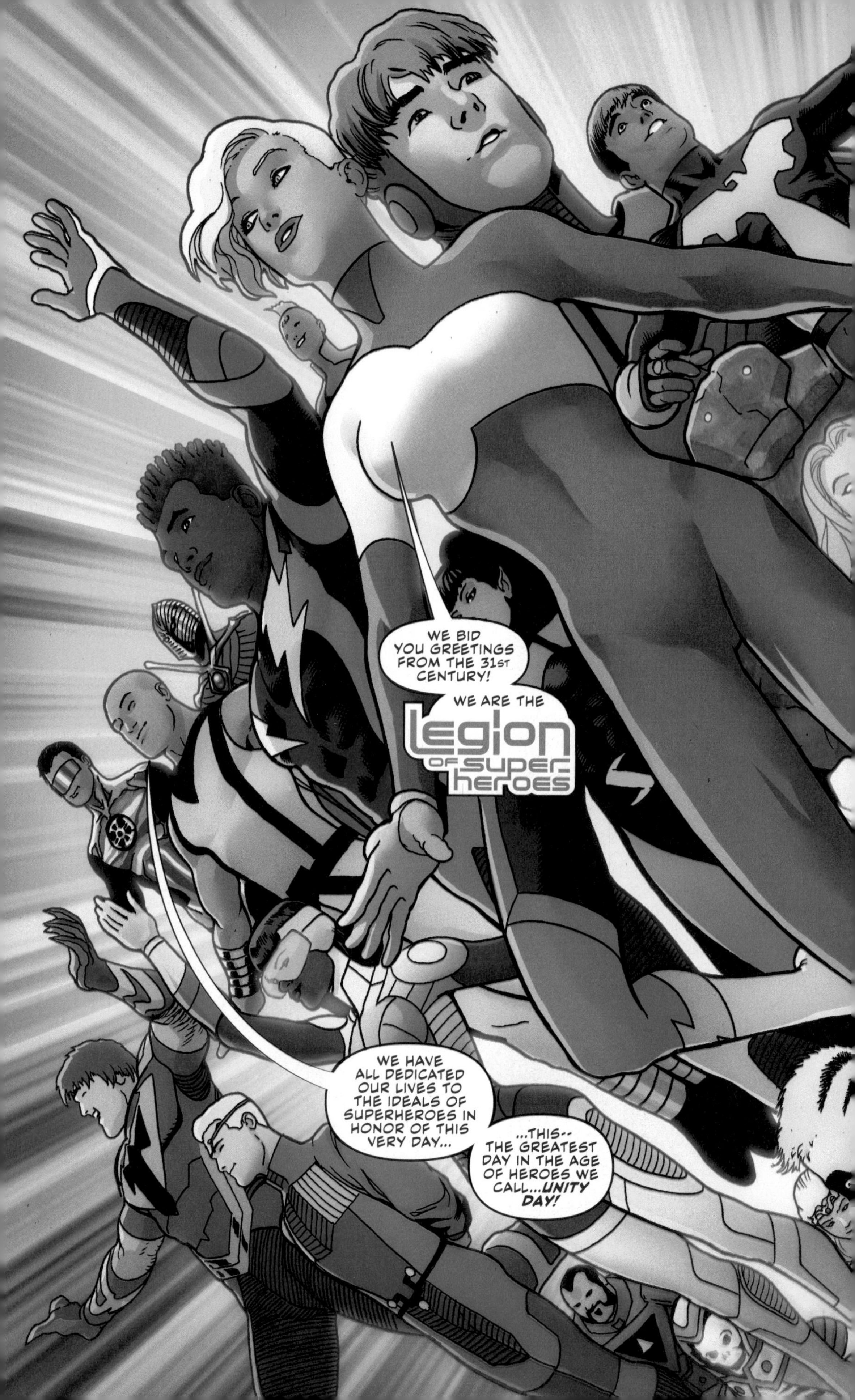

WE BID YOU GREETINGS FROM THE 31ST CENTURY!
WE ARE THE
LEGION OF SUPER HEROES
WE HAVE ALL DEDICATED OUR LIVES TO THE IDEALS OF SUPERHEROES IN HONOR OF THIS VERY DAY...
...THIS-- THE GREATEST DAY IN THE AGE OF HEROES WE CALL...*UNITY DAY!*

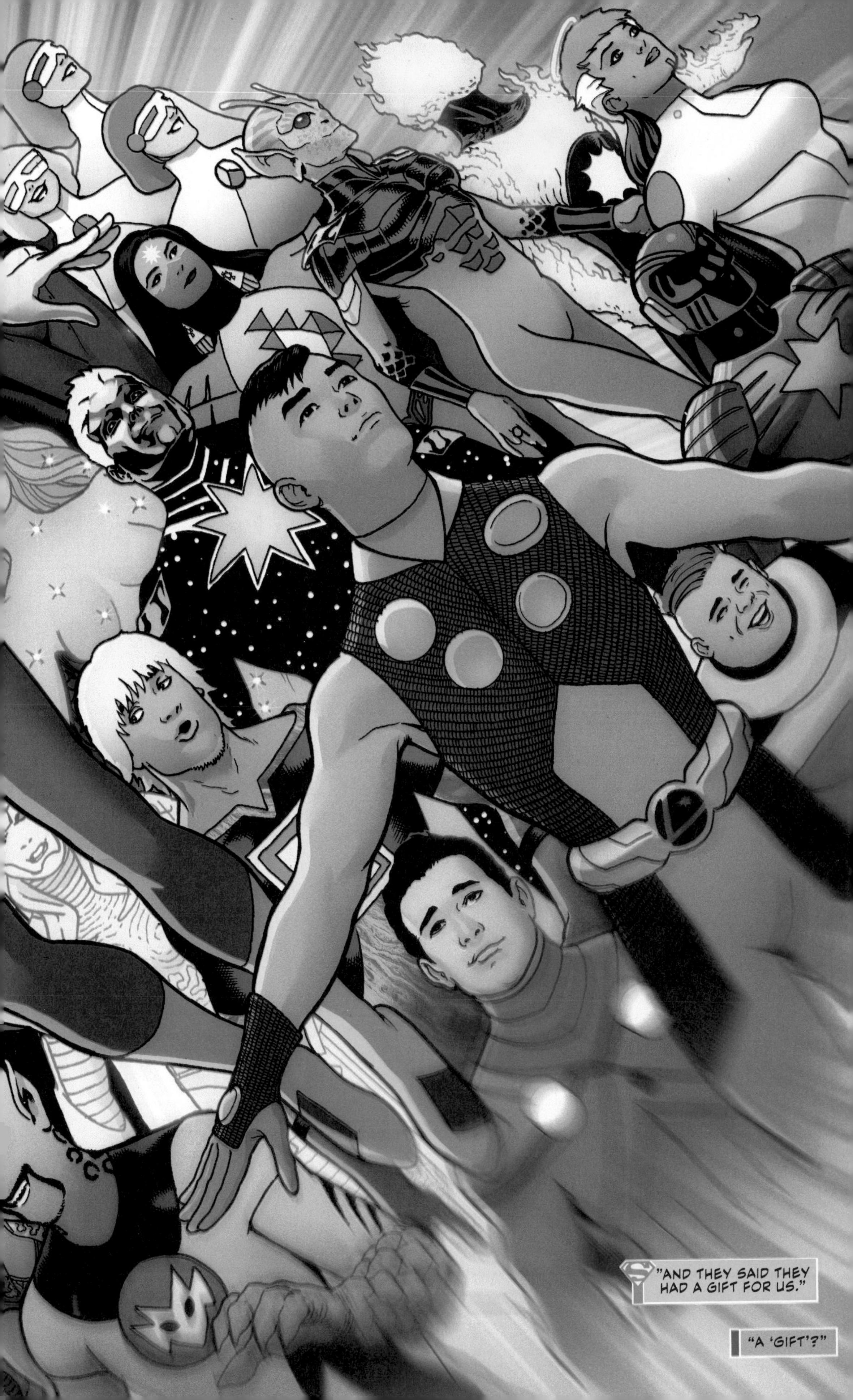
"AND THEY SAID THEY HAD A GIFT FOR US."
"A 'GIFT'?"

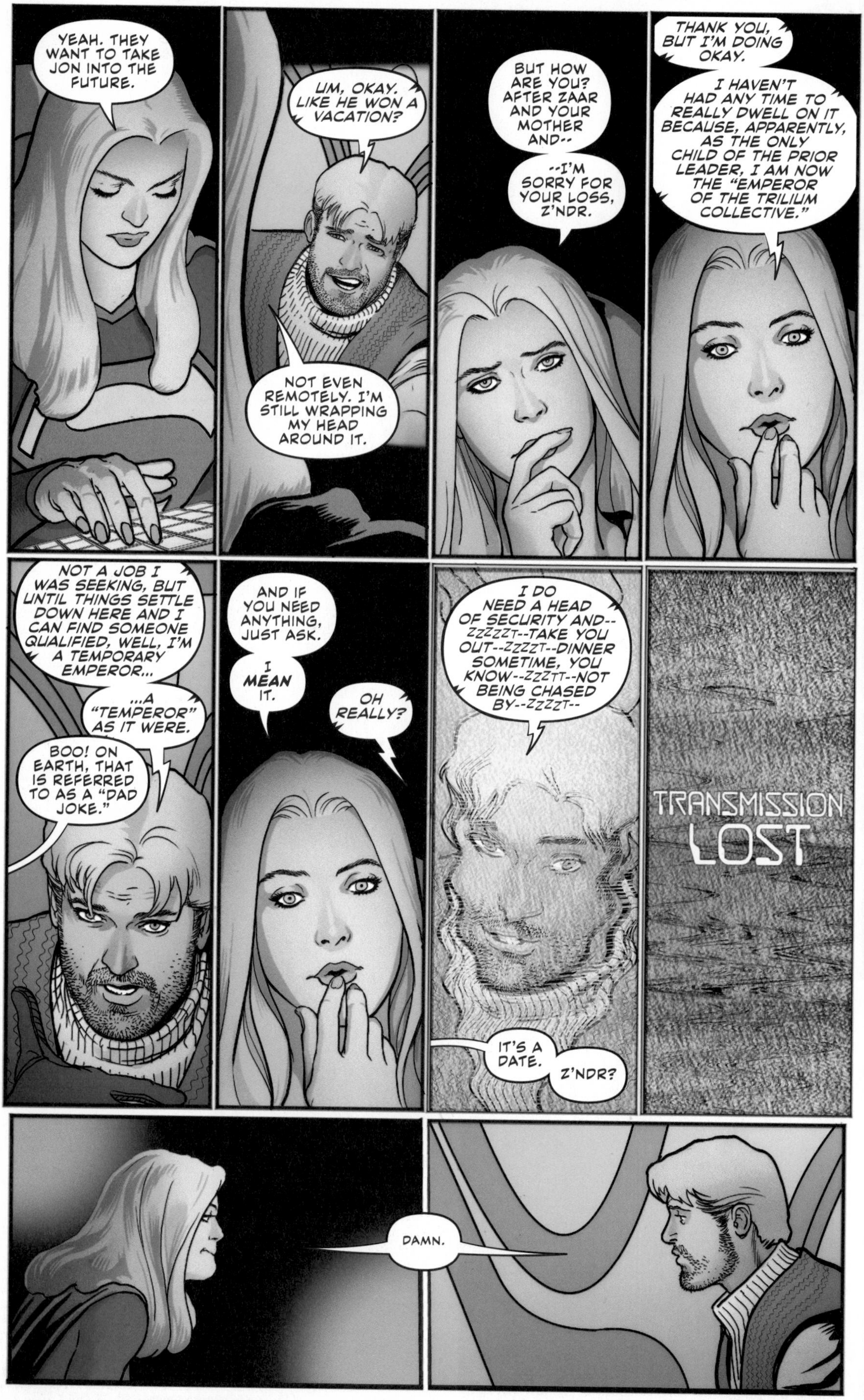
YEAH. THEY WANT TO TAKE JON INTO THE FUTURE.
UM, OKAY. LIKE HE WON A VACATION?
NOT EVEN REMOTELY. I'M STILL WRAPPING MY HEAD AROUND IT.
BUT HOW ARE YOU? AFTER ZAAR AND YOUR MOTHER AND--
--I'M SORRY FOR YOUR LOSS, Z'NDR.
THANK YOU, BUT I'M DOING OKAY.
I HAVEN'T HAD ANY TIME TO REALLY DWELL ON IT BECAUSE, APPARENTLY, AS THE ONLY CHILD OF THE PRIOR LEADER, I AM NOW THE "EMPEROR OF THE TRILIUM COLLECTIVE."
NOT A JOB I WAS SEEKING, BUT UNTIL THINGS SETTLE DOWN HERE AND I CAN FIND SOMEONE QUALIFIED, WELL, I'M A TEMPORARY EMPEROR...
...A "TEMPEROR" AS IT WERE.
BOO! ON EARTH, THAT IS REFERRED TO AS A "DAD JOKE."
AND IF YOU NEED ANYTHING, JUST ASK.
I MEAN IT.
OH REALLY?
I DO NEED A HEAD OF SECURITY AND--ZZZZZT--TAKE YOU OUT--ZZZZZT--DINNER SOMETIME, YOU KNOW--ZZZTT--NOT BEING CHASED BY--ZZZZT--
IT'S A DATE.
Z'NDR?
TRANSMISSION LOST
DAMN.

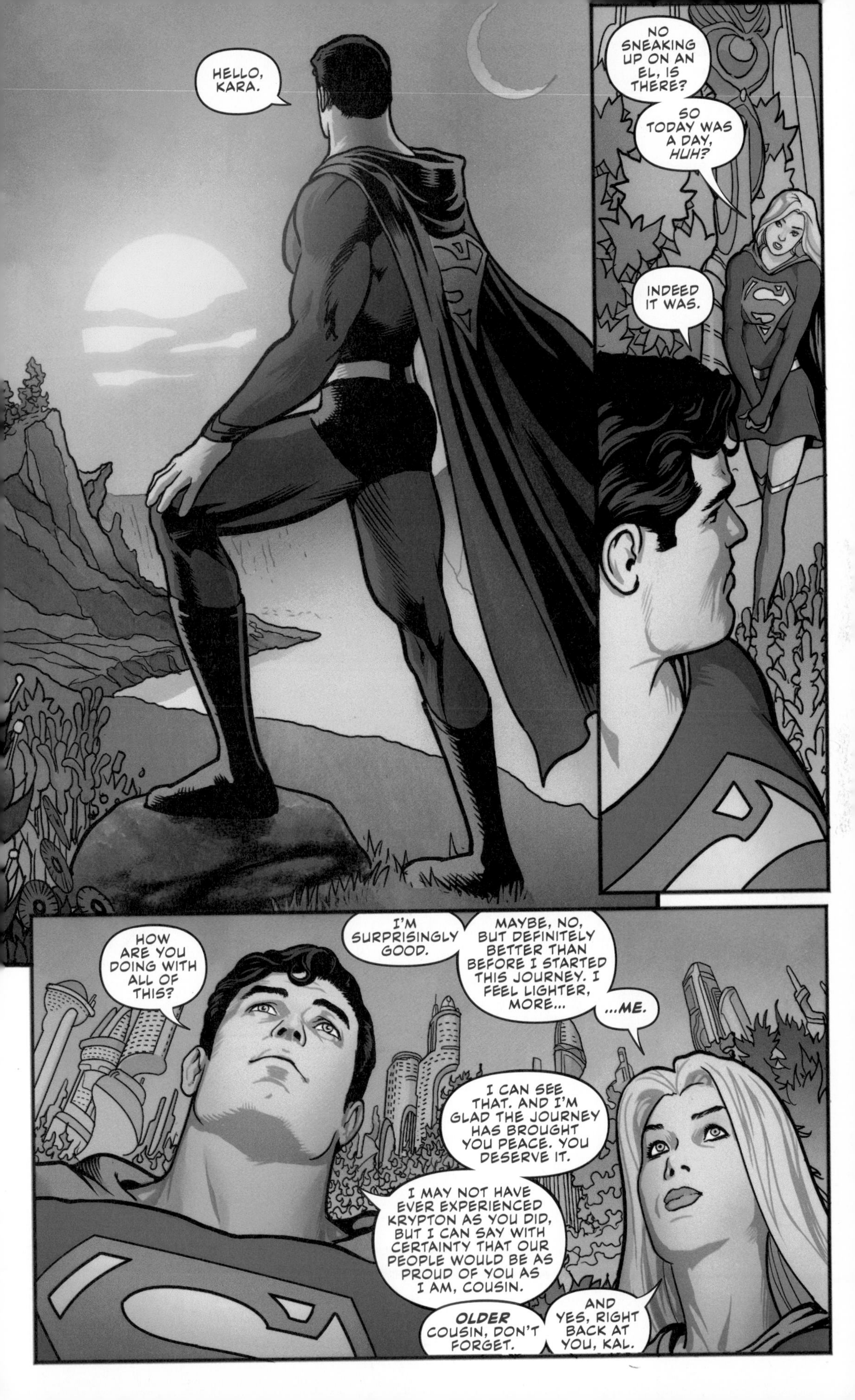
HELLO, KARA.
NO SNEAKING UP ON AN EL, IS THERE?
SO TODAY WAS A DAY, HUH?
INDEED IT WAS.
HOW ARE YOU DOING WITH ALL OF THIS?
I'M SURPRISINGLY GOOD.
MAYBE, NO, BUT DEFINITELY BETTER THAN BEFORE I STARTED THIS JOURNEY. I FEEL LIGHTER, MORE...
...ME.
I CAN SEE THAT. AND I'M GLAD THE JOURNEY HAS BROUGHT YOU PEACE. YOU DESERVE IT.
I MAY NOT HAVE EVER EXPERIENCED KRYPTON AS YOU DID, BUT I CAN SAY WITH CERTAINTY THAT OUR PEOPLE WOULD BE AS PROUD OF YOU AS I AM, COUSIN.
OLDER COUSIN, DON'T FORGET.
AND YES, RIGHT BACK AT YOU, KAL.

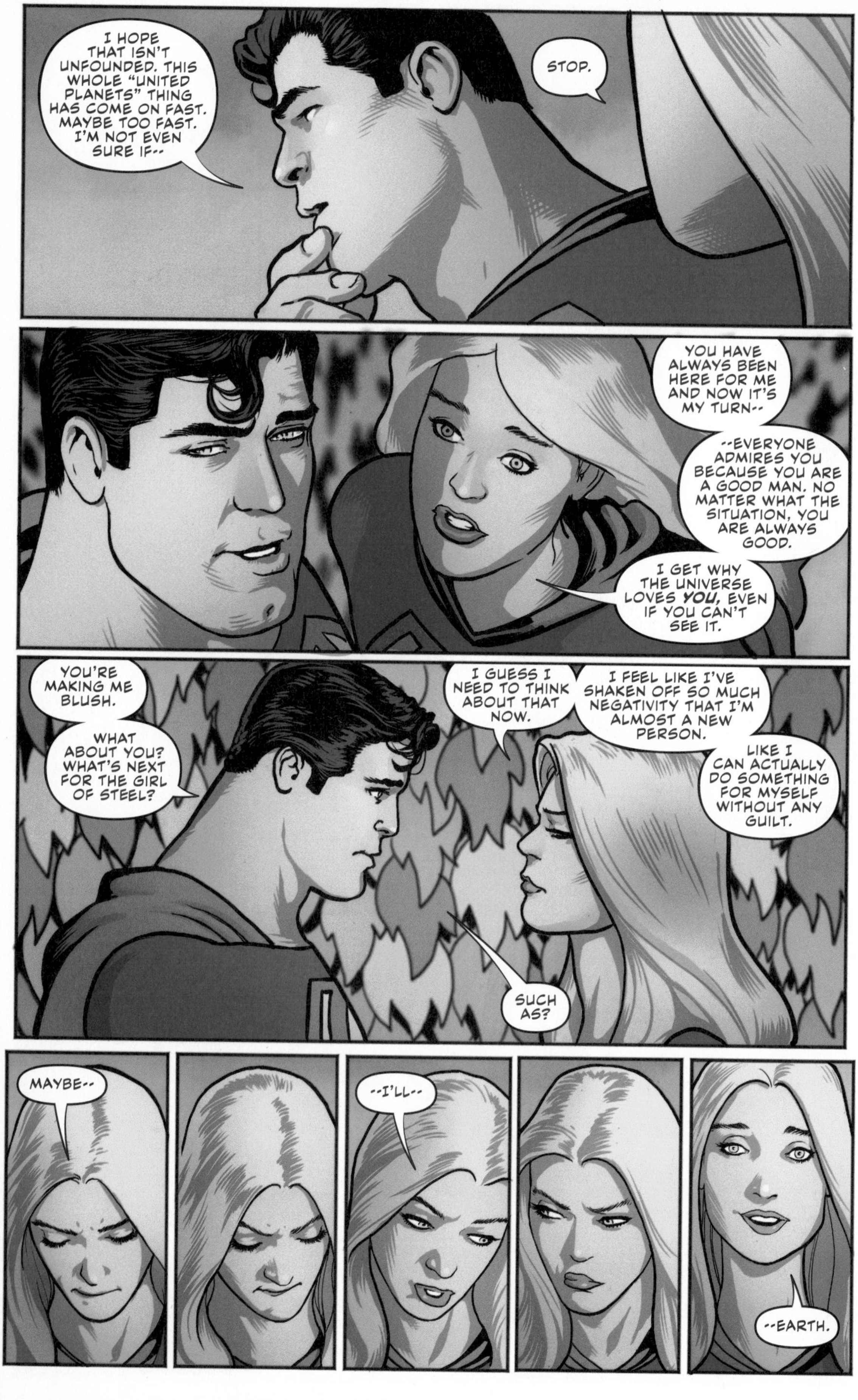
I HOPE THAT ISN'T UNFOUNDED. THIS WHOLE "UNITED PLANETS" THING HAS COME ON FAST. MAYBE TOO FAST. I'M NOT EVEN SURE IF--
STOP.
YOU HAVE ALWAYS BEEN HERE FOR ME AND NOW IT'S MY TURN--
--EVERYONE ADMIRES YOU BECAUSE YOU ARE A GOOD MAN. NO MATTER WHAT THE SITUATION, YOU ARE ALWAYS GOOD.
I GET WHY THE UNIVERSE LOVES ***YOU,*** EVEN IF YOU CAN'T SEE IT.
YOU'RE MAKING ME BLUSH.
WHAT ABOUT YOU? WHAT'S NEXT FOR THE GIRL OF STEEL?
I GUESS I NEED TO THINK ABOUT THAT NOW.
I FEEL LIKE I'VE SHAKEN OFF SO MUCH NEGATIVITY THAT I'M ALMOST A NEW PERSON.
LIKE I CAN ACTUALLY DO SOMETHING FOR MYSELF WITHOUT ANY GUILT.
SUCH AS?
MAYBE--
--I'LL--
--EARTH.

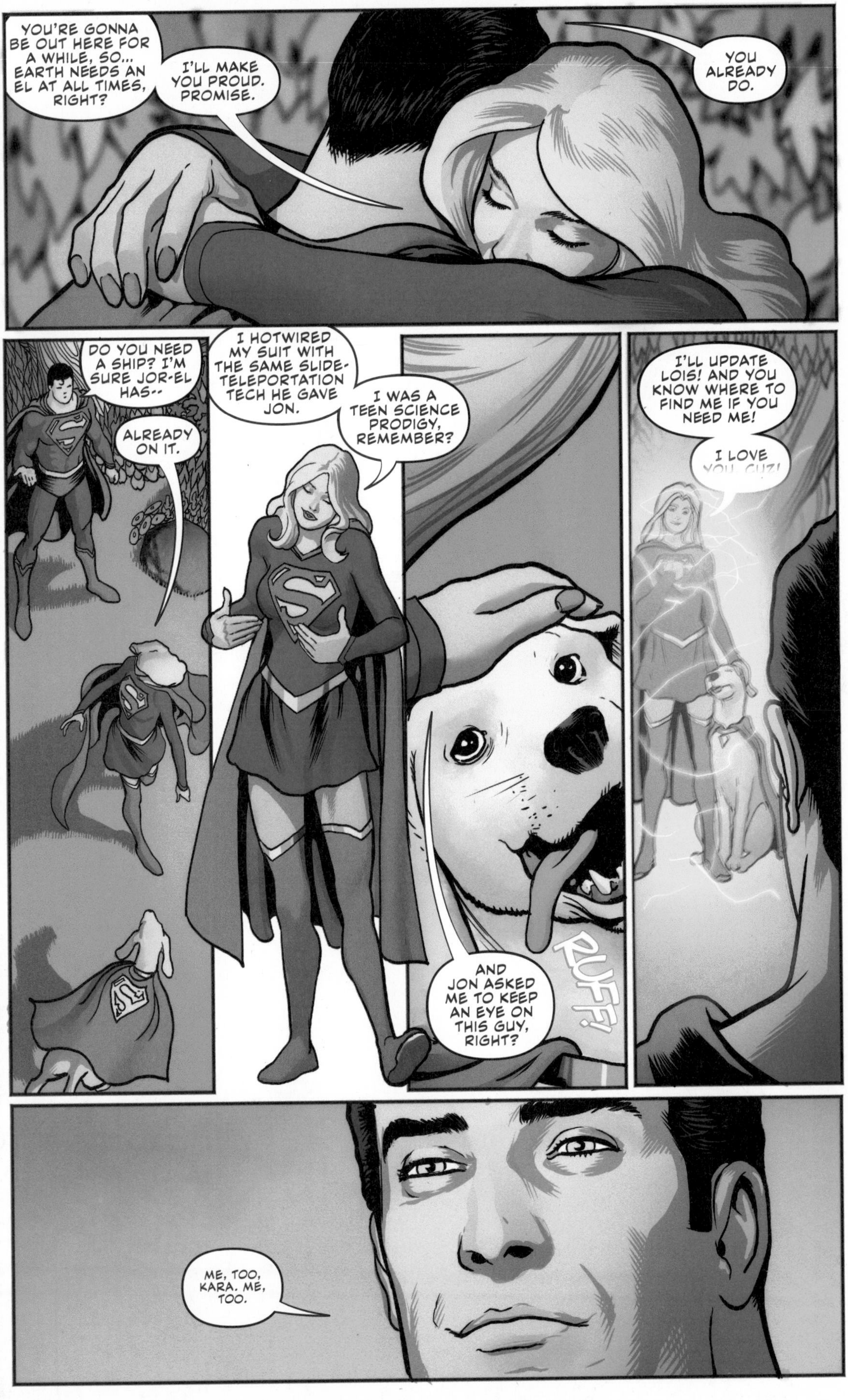
YOU'RE GONNA BE OUT HERE FOR A WHILE, SO... EARTH NEEDS AN EL AT ALL TIMES, RIGHT?
I'LL MAKE YOU PROUD. PROMISE.
YOU ALREADY DO.
DO YOU NEED A SHIP? I'M SURE JOR-EL HAS--
ALREADY ON IT.
I HOTWIRED MY SUIT WITH THE SAME SLIDE-TELEPORTATION TECH HE GAVE JON.
I WAS A TEEN SCIENCE PRODIGY, REMEMBER?
AND JON ASKED ME TO KEEP AN EYE ON THIS GUY, RIGHT?
RUFF!
I'LL UPDATE LOIS! AND YOU KNOW WHERE TO FIND ME IF YOU NEED ME!
I LOVE YOU, CUZ!
ME, TOO, KARA. ME, TOO.

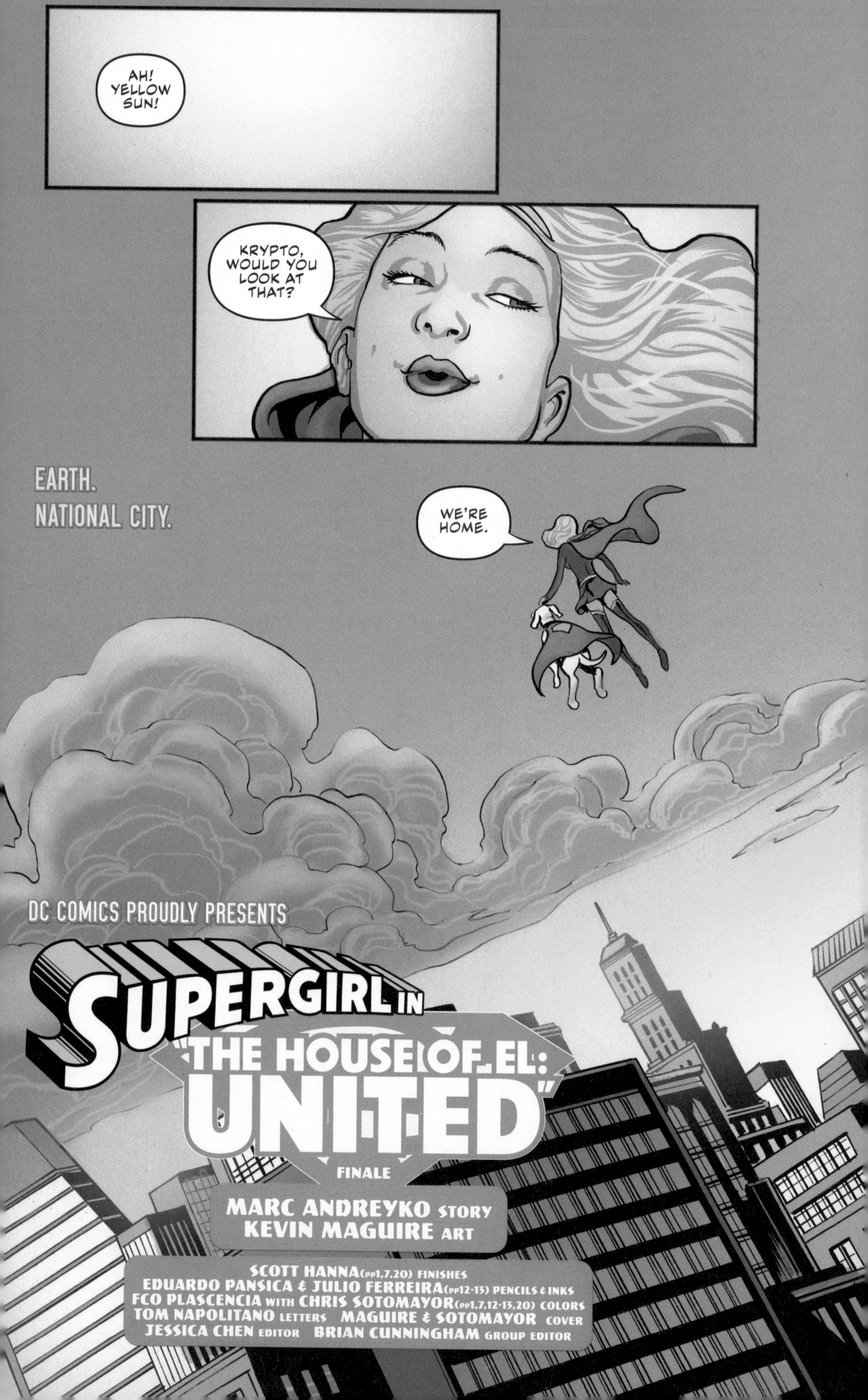
AH! YELLOW SUN!
KRYPTO, WOULD YOU LOOK AT THAT?
EARTH.
NATIONAL CITY.
WE'RE HOME.
DC COMICS PROUDLY PRESENTS
SUPERGIRL IN
"THE HOUSE OF EL: UNITED"
FINALE
MARC ANDREYKO STORY
KEVIN MAGUIRE ART
SCOTT HANNA(pp1,7,20) FINISHES
EDUARDO PANSICA & JULIO FERREIRA(pp12-13) PENCILS & INKS
FCO PLASCENCIA WITH CHRIS SOTOMAYOR(pp1,7,12-13,20) COLORS
TOM NAPOLITANO LETTERS MAGUIRE & SOTOMAYOR COVER
JESSICA CHEN EDITOR BRIAN CUNNINGHAM GROUP EDITOR

VARIANT COVER GALLERY

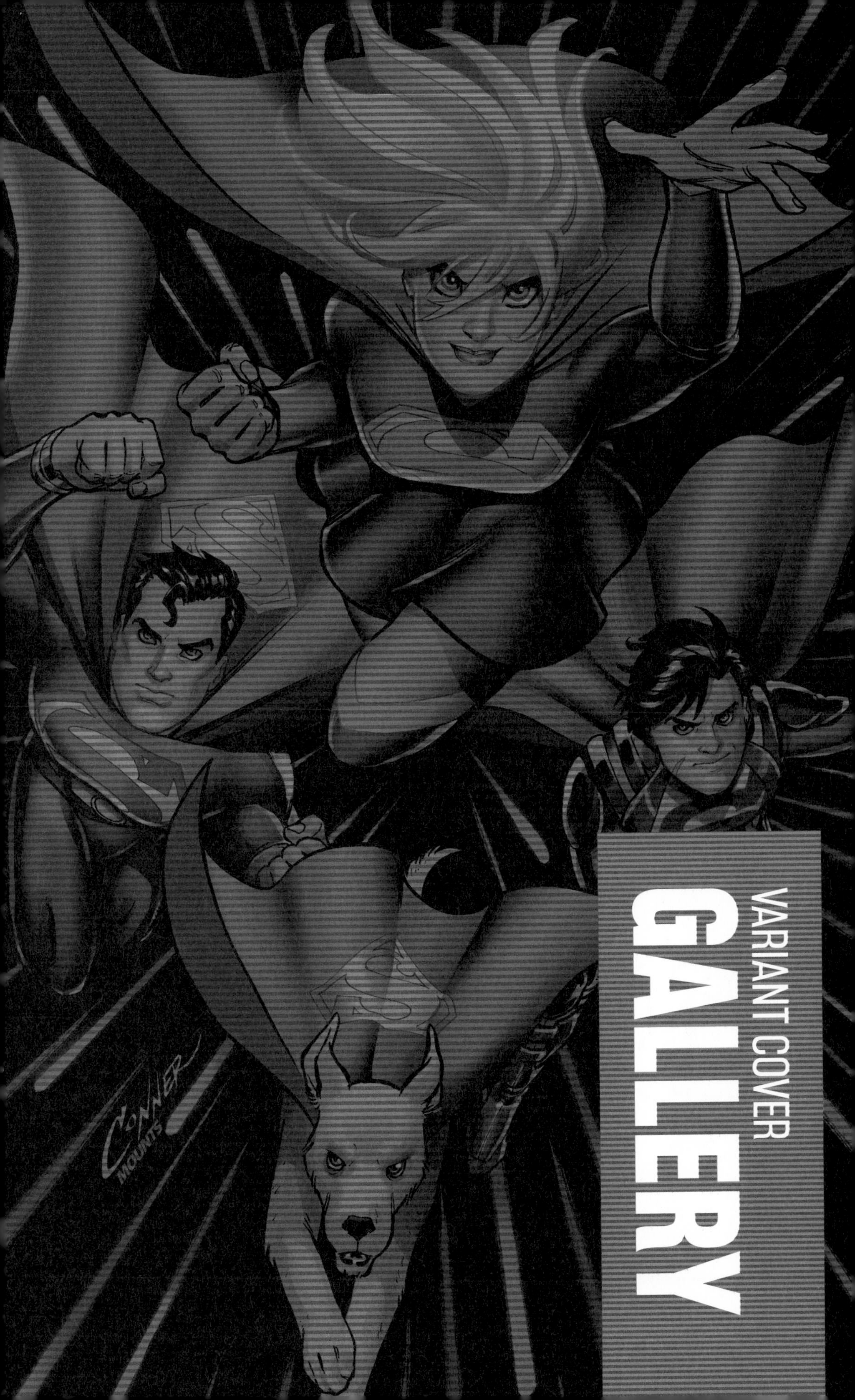
CONNER
MOUNTS

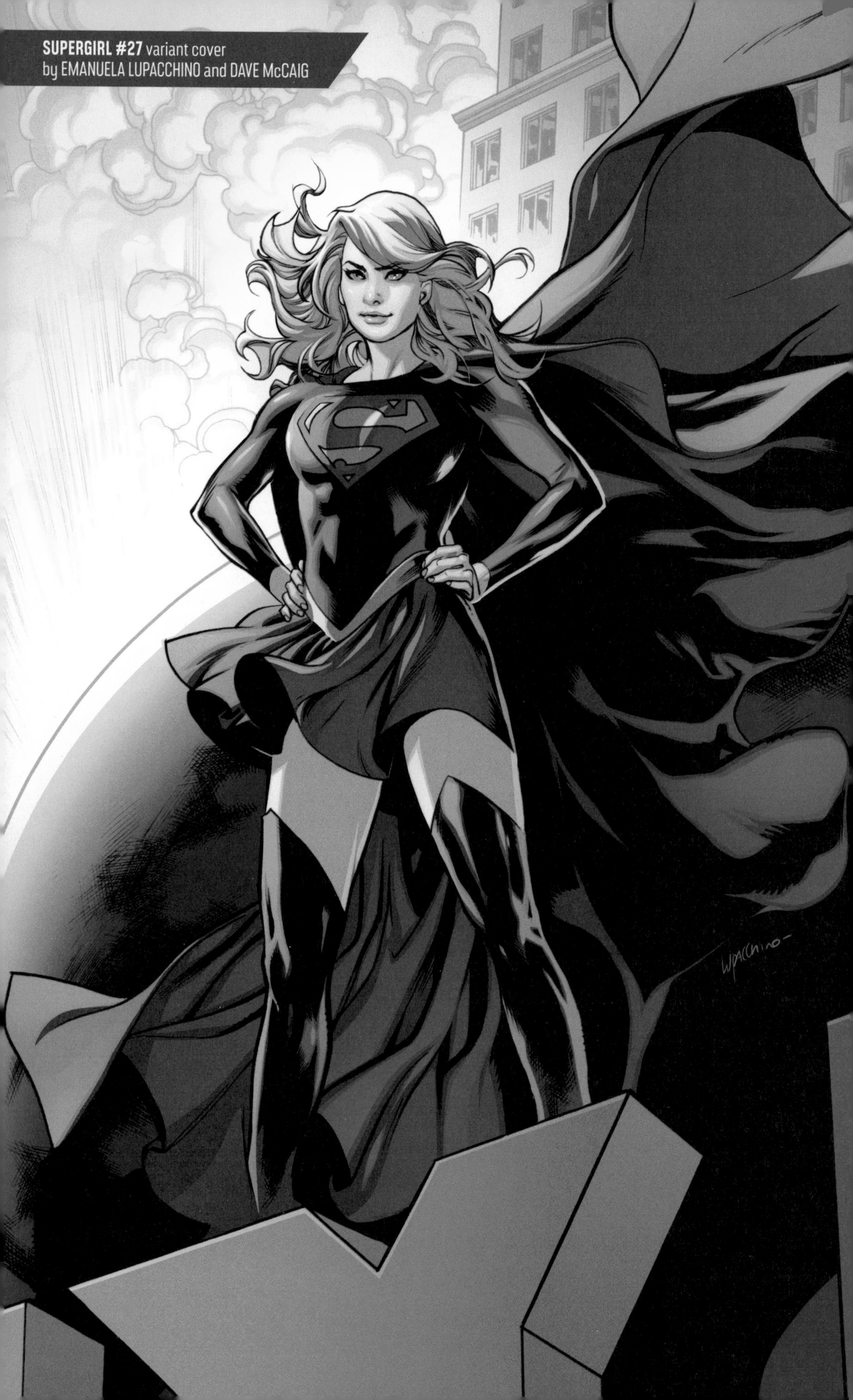

SUPERGIRL #27 variant cover
by EMANUELA LUPACCHINO and DAVE McCAIG

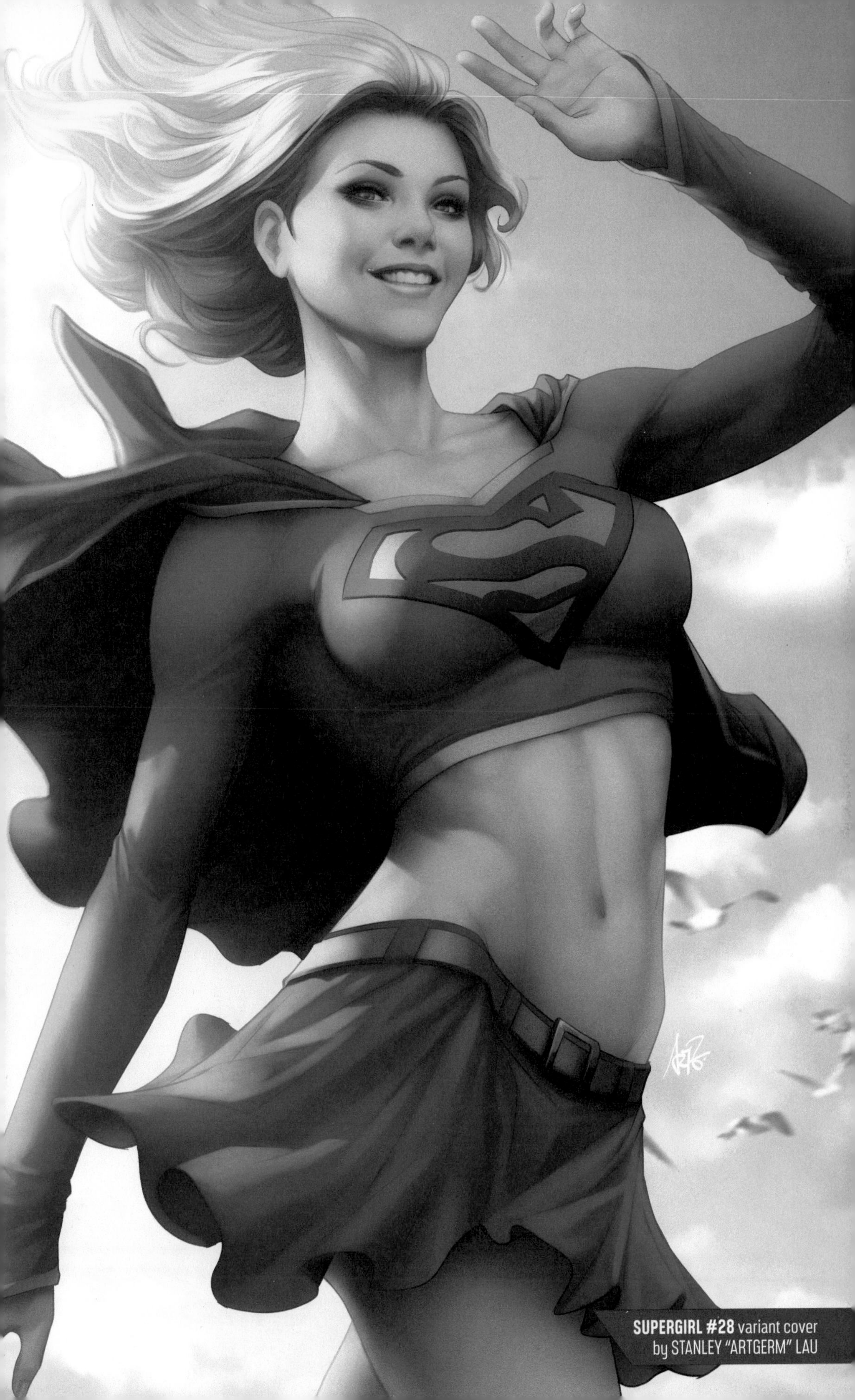

SUPERGIRL #28 variant cover
by STANLEY "ARTGERM" LAU

SUPERGIRL #29 variant cover
by AMANDA CONNER and PAUL MOUNTS

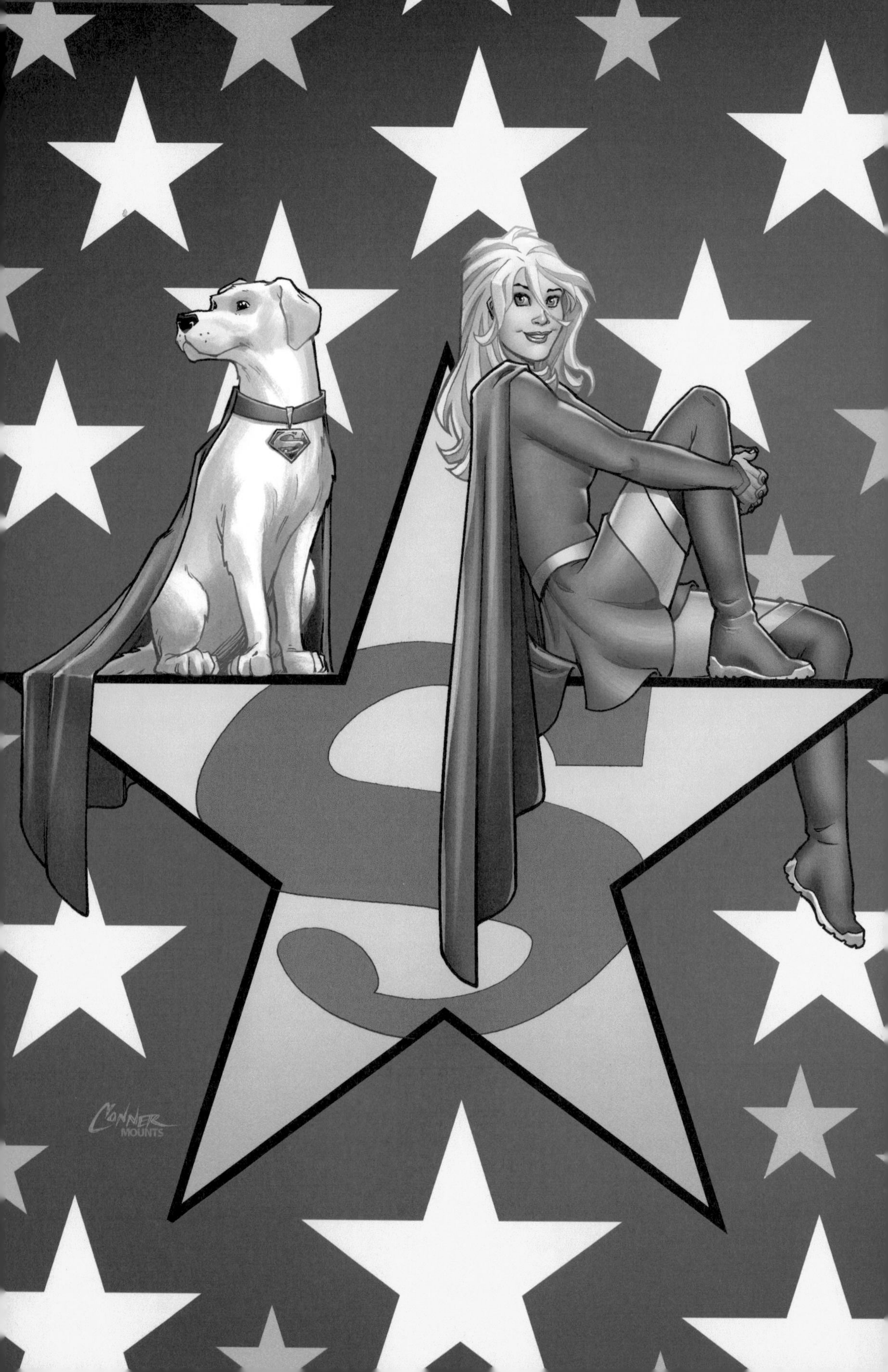
CONNER
MOUNTS

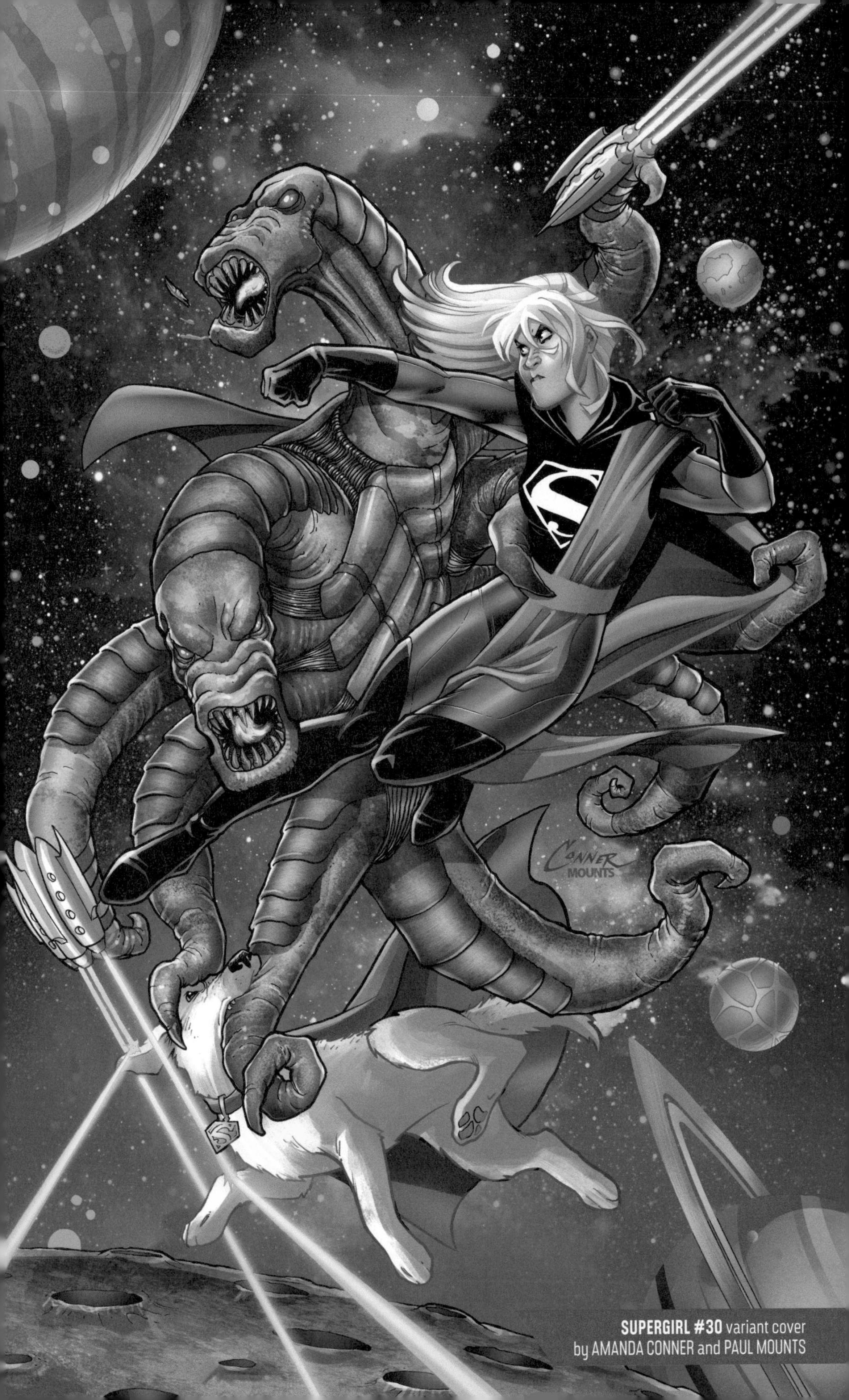
CONNER
MOUNTS

SUPERGIRL #30 variant cover
by AMANDA CONNER and PAUL MOUNTS

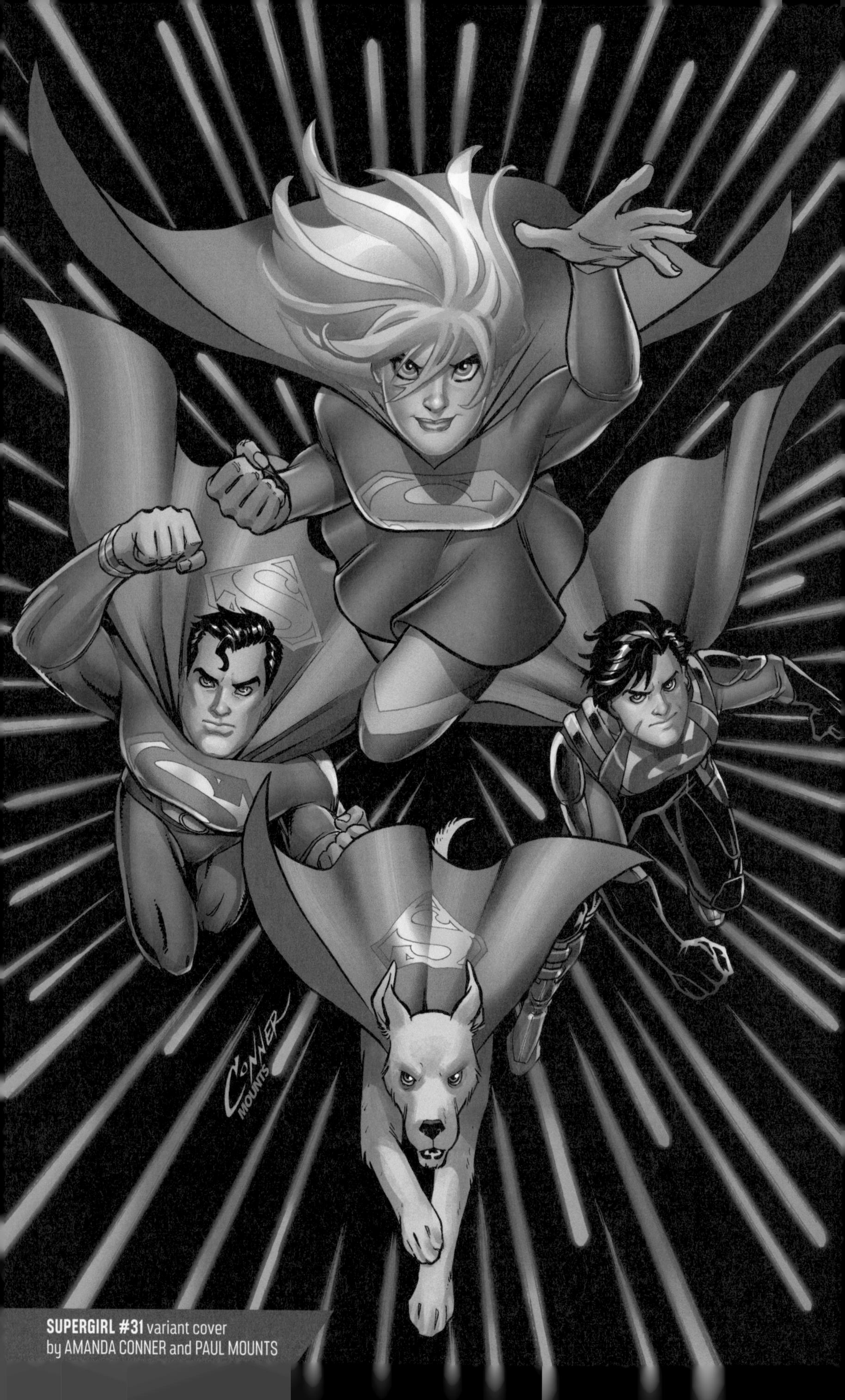
CONNER
MOUNTS

SUPERGIRL #31 variant cover
by AMANDA CONNER and PAUL MOUNTS

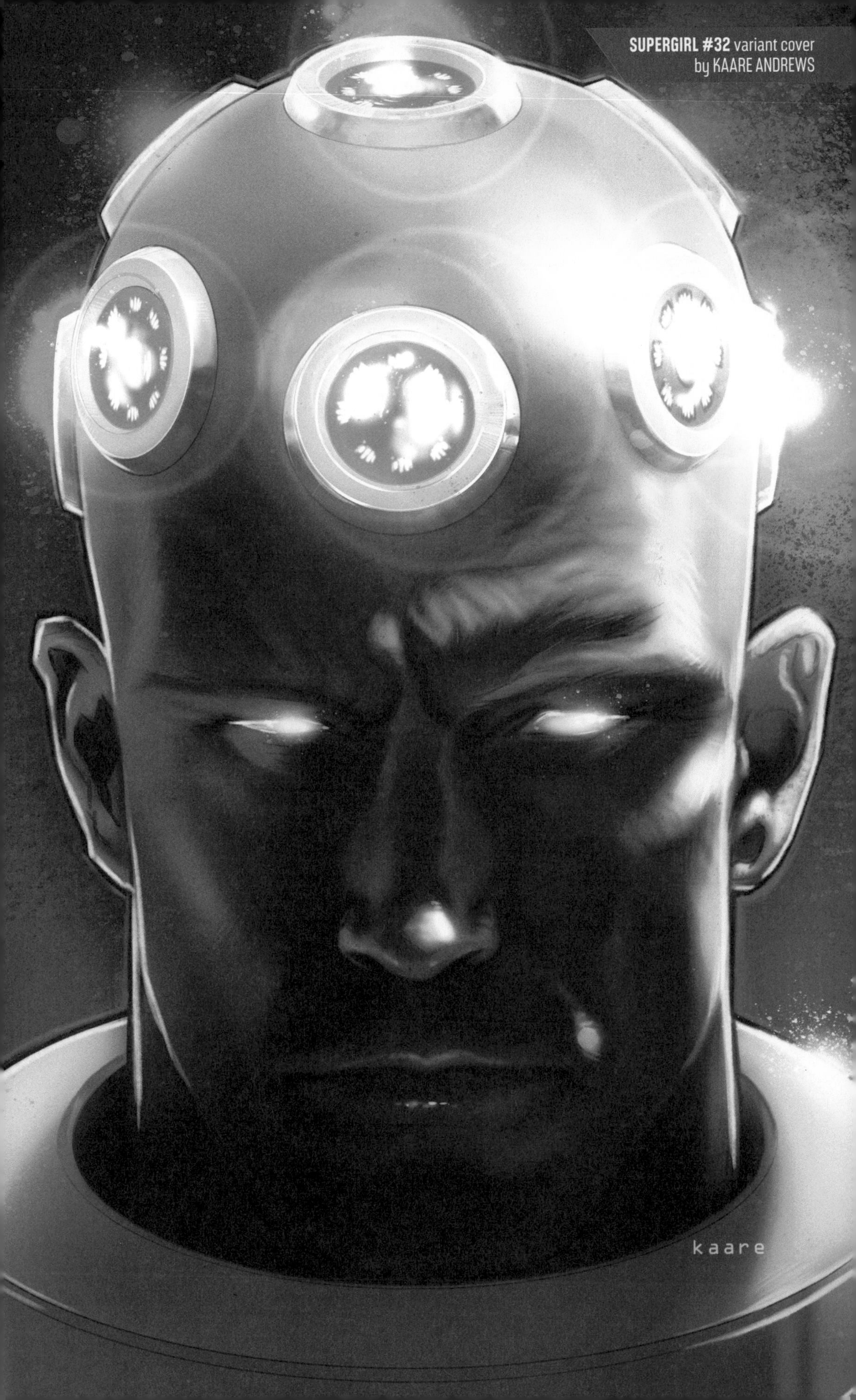
kaare

SUPERGIRL #32 variant cover
by KAARE ANDREWS

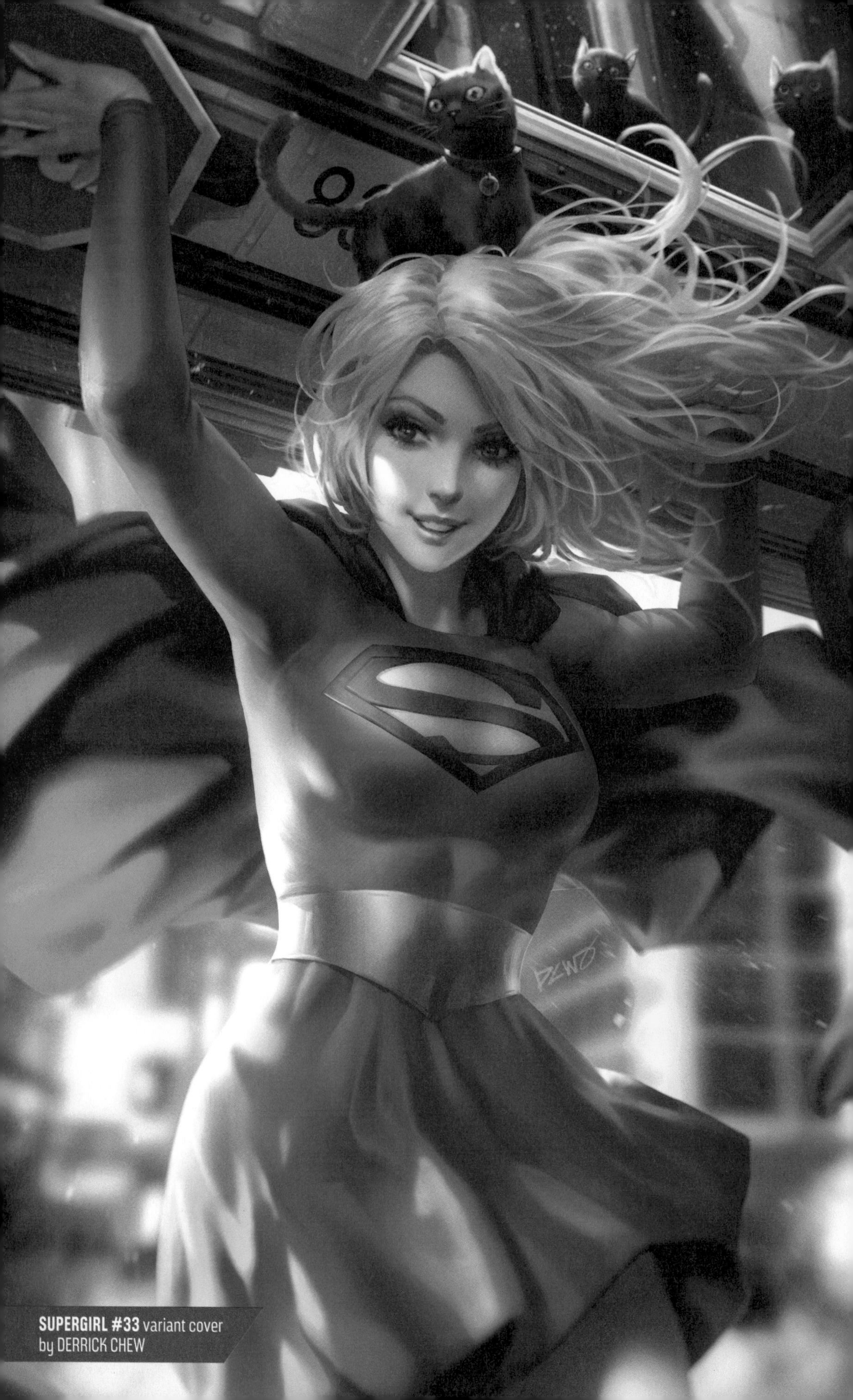

SUPERGIRL #33 variant cover
by DERRICK CHEW

"Greg Rucka and company have created a compelling narrative for fans of the Amazing Amazon." – **NERDIST**

"(A) heartfelt and genuine take on Diana's origin." – **NEWSARAMA**

DC UNIVERSE REBIRTH

WONDER WOMAN

VOL. 1: THE LIES
GREG RUCKA
with LIAM SHARP

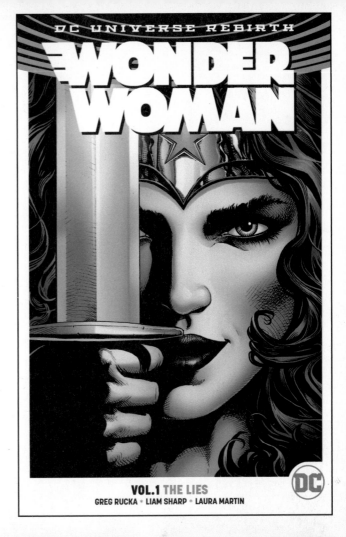

VOL. 1 THE LIES
GREG RUCKA • LIAM SHARP • LAURA MARTIN

**JUSTICE LEAGUE VOL. 1:
THE EXTINCTION MACHINES**

**SUPERGIRL VOL. 1:
REIGN OF THE SUPERMEN**

**BATGIRL VOL. 1:
BEYOND BURNSIDE**

DC COMICS
Bombshells
VOLUME 1
ENLISTED
She Can Do It!
Marguerite
BENNETT
Marguerite
SAUVAGE

"These are strong, realized women capable of wondrous feats, and Bennett ensures that they remain the heroes of their own stories."
–IGN

"BOMBSHELLS is a win for both female characters and female creators, and that double victory is well worth celebrating."
–NEWSARAMA

DC COMICS
BOMBSHELLS
MARGUERITE BENNETT and MARGUERITE SAUVAGE

DC COMICS
Bombshells
VOLUME 2
ALLIES
Marguerite
BENNETT
Laura
BRAGA
Mirka
ANDOLFO

DC COMICS BOMBSHELLS
VOL. 2: ALLIES

Marguerite BENNETT Mirka ANDOLFO Laura BRAGA
DC COMICS
Bombshells
VOLUME 3
UPRISING

DC COMICS BOMBSHELLS
VOL. 3: UPRISING

READ THE ENTIRE EPIC!

DC COMICS BOMBSHELLS
VOL. 4: QUEENS

DC COMICS BOMBSHELLS
VOL. 5: THE DEATH OF ILLUSIONS

DC COMICS BOMBSHELLS
VOL. 6: WAR STORIES

...phic novels wherever comics and books are sold!

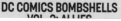